Mutiny, Mayhem, Mythology

Mutiny, Mayhem, Mythology

Bounty's Enigmatic Voyage

Alan Frost

SYDNEY UNIVERSITY PRESS

First published by Sydney University Press
© Alan Frost 2018
© Sydney University Press 2018

Reproduction and communication for other purposes
Except as permitted under the Act, no part of this edition may be reproduced, stored in a retrieval system, or communicated in any form or by any means without prior written permission. All requests for reproduction or communication should be made to Sydney University Press at the address below:

Sydney University Press
Fisher Library F03
University of Sydney NSW 2006
AUSTRALIA
sup.info@sydney.edu.au
sydney.edu.au/sup

 A catalogue record for this book is available from the National Library of Australia.

ISBN 9781743325872 paperback
ISBN 9781743325889 epub
ISBN 9781743322116 mobi
ISBN 9781743325940 pdf

Cover image: Dodd, Robert, 1748–1815, *The Mutineers turning Lieut. Bligh and part of the officers and crew adrift from His Majesty's Ship the Bounty.* London: B.B. Evans, 2 October 1790. Reproduced courtesy of the Dixson Library, State Library of New South Wales, DL Pf 137.

Cover design and maps by Miguel Yamin.

For Michelle,
who somehow emerged
from the unfathomable depths
of our departed time.

Contents

List of Figures	ix
List of Plates	xi
List of Tables	xiii
Preface	xv
Introduction: The Troubled History of *Bounty*'s Story	1

Part I History's Shrouds and Silences

1	A Serious Affair to Be Starved: The Resentment of Sailors When Not Properly Fed	57
2	A Soul in Agony: Fletcher Christian's Torment	95
3	Somewhere Between Sea and Sky: The Enigma of Fletcher Christian's Death	127

Part II The Making of *Bounty*'s Story

4	Discovering Nature: The Rise of British Scientific Exploration, 1660–1800	185
5	Information and Entertainment, Image and Archetype: The Cardinal Points of the Exploration Narrative	225
6	Men Who Strove with Gods: James Cook, William Bligh, Fletcher Christian	253
	Conclusion: The Enduring Intrigue of *Bounty*'s Voyage	293
	Acknowledgements	299
	References	301
	Index	317

List of Figures

Figure 1 The voyage of the *Bounty* to Tahiti, 1787–8.	xxii
Figure 2 Wordsworth's Lake District.	94
Figure 3 The conjectured routes of the *Bounty* in 1789, after the mutiny.	128
Figure 4 The Pitcairn settlement in the 1790s.	162
Figure 5 Mary Christian's headstone on Norfolk Island.	169

List of Plates

Plate 1 *The Bread Fruit of Otahytey* by George Tobin, from Tobin's sketches on the HMS *Providence*, 1791–93.

Plate 2 William Wordsworth, aged twenty-eight, by William Shuter, 1798.

Plate 3 Fletcher Christian's signature.

Plate 4 William Hodges, *The Resolution and Adventure among Icebergs*.

Plate 5 George III posthumously awarded James Cook with a coat of arms in September 1785, six years after Cook's death.

Plate 6 The frontispiece of Thomas Bankes's *System of Geography* (1787) shows Cook ascending to glory.

Plate 7 The author's daughters, Melissa and Clea, beneath a breadfruit tree, Tahiti, 1976.

List of Tables

Table 1 The ages of the alleged mutineers.   29

Table 2 Standard weekly ration for a seaman in the 1780s.   71

Table 3 'Proportion of each species of provisions', as set out by the Victualling Board.   73

Preface

Anyone watching HM Armed Vessel *Bounty* sail out from Spithead (Portsmouth) under the command of Lieutenant William Bligh on a wintery day in December 1787 could have had no expectation that the voyage would take on a momentous significance. True, its purpose, to bring a cargo of breadfruit and other food plants from the islands of the central Pacific Ocean and the East Indies to the West India islands, was unusual. Still, this was by no means the first large-scale transfer of plants between hemispheres that Europeans had undertaken; and in itself *Bounty*'s voyage simply could not have had the global impact of Christopher Columbus's voyages to the Americas; Bartholomeu Dias's and Vasco da Gama's to the Cape of Good Hope and India; Ferdinand Magellan's circumnavigation; and James Cook's three very lengthy voyages of survey, charting and collecting. No one could ever have expected to write, or be justified in writing, of *Bounty*'s voyage as Abbé Raynal wrote of the pioneering ones to America and India:

> No event[s] [have] been so interesting to mankind in general, and to the inhabitants of Europe in particular, as the discovery of the New World, and the passage to India by the Cape of Good Hope ... [They have given] rise to a revolution in the commerce, and in the power of nations; and in the manners, industry, and government of the whole world.[1]

And yet.

---

1   Raynal 1776, vol. 1, p. [1].

What with the arduousness of its passage outwards to Tahiti, the idyllic (for the Europeans) stay on the island, the mutiny by Fletcher Christian and part of the crew in April 1789, and the colony established on isolated Pitcairn Island by nine of the mutineers and their Polynesian companions, *Bounty*'s voyage has become the stuff of legend to a degree that the earlier, much more geographically, economically and politically significant voyages have not. It is estimated that more than 3000 books and articles (running to millions upon millions of words) about *Bounty*'s voyage and its various aftermaths have been published. It has been the subject of novels, poems and plays, feature films and documentaries.

However, legend is not necessarily conducive to good history; and as I show in the Introduction, despite all the attention paid to *Bounty*'s voyage and its attendant circumstances, there has been little fundamental increase in our historical understanding of these things in the past 225 years. Indeed, much of the history of the voyage has been seriously flawed.

There are a number of reasons for this. One is that writers have often failed to read the documentary sources with sufficient care and wariness, but rather have taken statements at face value. This has been especially true where William Bligh's various accounts are concerned. When these accounts do not contain outright falsifications, they are often either 'economical with the truth' or blind to any details detrimental to the upright character that Bligh strove to project to the Admiralty, his patron Sir Joseph Banks, the public, and self-righteously to himself.

A second is that, surprisingly, writers have shown inadequate understandings of conditions of naval service towards the end of the eighteenth century, and of sailors' expectations and their tenacity in clinging to what they conceived to be their 'rights', in particular where the allocation of food was concerned.

A third is that, generation after generation, commentators have perpetuated earlier views, sometimes even simply repeating what previous writers have said. Depending on whether they have been for or against Bligh, the uncritical acceptance of such writers has meant that a pair of binary images has dominated analysis: either Good Bligh/Bad Christian or Bad Bligh/Good Christian. Even diligent writers with sound scholarly methodologies have found it difficult to avoid this trap, which has had the effect of crimping analysis. An associated problem has been the reliance on clichés, entailing long-discredited psychology.

Preface

It is in the nature of things that historical explanations should vary according to the predilections of writers and the preoccupations of their age. For example, in the first half of the twentieth century, in the contexts of rampant capitalism and the Great Depression, Charles Beard's economically focused histories of the making of the United States constitution and of the nation more generally held sway. In the second half of the century, when attention had turned to the extensive seventeenth- and eighteenth-century considerations in Britain and Enlightenment Europe of the nature of individual and political freedoms and of the rights and responsibilities of states and citizens, Bernard Bailyn's intellectual and demographic studies came to prominence.

So it has been with the history of *Bounty*'s voyage. In 1936, Owen Rutter titled his account *The True Story of the Mutiny in the Bounty*. The title of the English edition of Alexander McKee's 1961 version was *The Truth about the Mutiny on the Bounty*. Bengt Danielsson wanted to call his 1962 publication *The True and Complete Story of All That Happened on Board the Bounty on Her Voyage to the South Seas 1787–1789 with an Account of What Happened after the Mutiny to the Protagonists in the Drama*. Caroline Alexander subtitled her 2003 account *The True Story of the Mutiny on the Bounty*.

Danielsson's publisher did not allow him to use his preferred title. This was a wise decision, and not only because it was impossibly clumsy. It would have been good if the other authors had also eschewed their claims to truth. For none of their tellings of *Bounty*'s story is either complete or, within its limits, of unblemished truthfulness. Each is flawed in a number of ways, but especially by a too-ready acceptance of Bligh's versions of events.

In his writings, Bligh was an inveterate suppressor of adverse circumstance and a prevaricator, endeavours in which he was abetted by his editors. Nonetheless, it may be that he believed some of his self-serving assertions, for, as historian Rolf Du Rietz has remarked, in moments of crisis he was prone 'to believe what he wanted to believe, thus forming those deceptions and illusions apparently forming such an indispensible support for his self-confidence'. Either anticipating challenges to his veracity or responding to them, Bligh repeatedly asserted that he had told the truth. He wrote to Banks from Batavia:

> I can however Sir promise to you that my honor and character is
> without a blemish, & I shall appear as soon as I possibly can before
> the Admiralty that my conduct may [be] enquired into, and where
> I shall convince the World I stand as an officer despising mercy &
> forgiveness if my conduct is at all blameable.

Later, he told Banks, 'Captain Bligh declares every thing in his *Narrative* to be sacred truths, & defies the utmost Malice to pervert them.'[2]

However, what was 'sacred truth' for William Bligh was manifestly not so, but rather a melange of despicable distortions and lies, for John Fryer and James Morrison, for Fletcher Christian and William Purcell, and for the rest of *Bounty*'s crew. In stating this, I am not adopting the postmodernist stance that recognises only indeterminacy. Even given the inevitable variations in perception exhibited by the major participants in the events of the voyage, the mutiny and the Pitcairn aftermath, I think it is possible to offer a sounder history than we have previously had.

There are four things above all others that we must do to have this. The first is to abandon the long fixation on the binary sets of images of Good Bligh/Bad Christian and Bad Bligh/Good Christian. Harry Maude's sixty-years-old comment remains applicable to much of what has been written on the subject since: 'the protagonists of Bligh and Christian are still engaged in apportioning the blame; an exercise which one feels at times tells us more about the personality of the writer than [about] the characters and motives of the two opponents'.[3]

In order to get beyond this impasse, we need to assess the events of the voyage with a better understanding of the realities of late-eighteenth-century naval life. Then, we need to undertake a rigorous re-examination of the primary sources, not accepting their accounts at face value but rather questioning and comparing them one with another, to see if some sort of consensus emerges.

Finally, we need to face openly the awkward difficulty – awkward from the point of view of presenting it – that there is much in the history of *Bounty*'s voyage that we now cannot either know or be sure about. It is much

---

2   Du Rietz [2003] 2009, pp. 24–5; Bligh to Banks, 13 October 1789, Bligh 1989, p. 30; Bligh to Banks [December 1792], Bligh Miscellaneous, p. 19.
3   Maude 1968, p. 4.

better to acknowledge the gaps and silences of the past than to seek to fill them with supposition, dubious theory, discredited psychologising and false consciousness, all of which obscure more than they enlighten.

∗ ∗ ∗

In Part I (Chapters 1–3) of this book, I do not offer yet another account of the physical progress of *Bounty*'s voyage. Rather, I consider three aspects that, despite all that has been written, have not yet received proper attention. The first of these is how Bligh's practices as purser violated the crew's customary expectations and thereby created an atmosphere in which mutinous thoughts might fester. The second concerns the difficulties of knowing nearly as much as we need to in order to understand what moved Fletcher Christian to rebel against his commander. Here, given the paucity of records about Christian's life, I invoke the example of William Wordsworth's to suggest the likely nature of Christian's childhood. This is not so far-fetched as it may initially seem. Both were born in Cumbria in the middle decades of the eighteenth century; both lost their fathers when they were young; both received a good education; and both then attempted to make a way in the wider world – with the consequence that the one failed miserably and the other succeeded. In contemplating this conundrum, we may perhaps gain some insight into Fletcher Christian's motivations. The third is how anachronisms, conflicts and uncertainties in the source materials make it impossible to know precisely what happened on Pitcairn Island in the first ten years of the mutineers' settlement; and in particular, whether Fletcher Christian did indeed die on this isolated island, or rather returned to England. Together, these chapters present reassessments and new arguments, and thus advance our understanding of important, but little understood, aspects of the voyage.

However, if close textual analysis and rigorous argument can help us to a better understanding of some of the obscure circumstances of *Bounty*'s voyage and its aftermaths, in themselves they can do little to explain the public's enduring interest in the voyage and its principal protagonists. To understand this interest better, we need to see that there is another level of discourse present in the central records of the voyage, as indeed there is in other narratives of sea and land explorations of the time.

In Part II, I am concerned to show how, while it remained grounded in scientific observation and was presented to the public in a plain style, the exploration narrative in its fully developed form encapsulated modes of discourse that were decidedly unscientific; and how this feature has distorted our understandings of the history they purport to convey. To put it bluntly, many of the exploration narratives published in the last decades of the eighteenth century were as much literary creations as they were scientific records. In the case of William Bligh's *A Voyage to the South Sea* (1792), this was much more of the first characterisation than the second; and this has had the very unfortunate consequence of giving us a false sense of *Bounty*'s voyage for more than 200 years.

I start by sketching the stages by which the principles of the dawning Scientific Revolution were applied to exploration (Chapter 4). When it first began to take form in the middle of the seventeenth century, the exploration narrative was intended to be written in a plain, unadorned style, so as to be a straightforward record of times and courses, latitudes and longitudes, coastlines, lands and their geographical features, their produce and peoples. This chapter is not a detailed examination of the daily work of naturalists at sea or on land, such as Iain McCalman offers in *Darwin's Armada* (2009) and Glyn Williams in *Naturalists at Sea* (2013). Rather, I intend it to provide a context for an examination of how, in the course of the eighteenth century, the character of the exploration narrative was transformed.

We may see beginnings of this transformation in William Dampier's *A New Voyage round the World* (1697), and in Richard Walter and Benjamin Robins's account of George Anson's circumnavigation, *A Voyage round the World* (1748). John Hawkesworth developed it fully in his account of James Cook's first voyage, which formed part of his amalgamation of the journals of John Byron, Samuel Wallis, Philip Carteret, James Cook and Joseph Banks, *An Account of the Voyages ... for Making Discoveries in the Southern Hemisphere* (1773).

In Chapter 5, I indicate the kind of changes that John Hawkesworth made to original records he worked from. His narrative became a model for later ones, including those of Cook's second and third voyages (1777, 1784). I then examine four other narratives in detail: William Bartram, *Travels through North & South Carolina, Georgia,*

Preface

East & West Florida (c. 1791); Samuel Hearne, *A Journey from Prince of Wales's Fort in Hudson's Bay, to the Northern Ocean* (1795); James Bruce, *Travels to Discover the Source of the Nile* (1790); and Mungo Park, *Travels in the Interior Districts of Africa* (1799). I show that, in common with Dampier's and Hawkesworth's, each of these narratives exhibits the motif of the hero who braves adversity and leaves the familiar world for a strange, unknown one, who faces the threat of personal dissolution, and who either dies tragically or returns home. That is, I show that the figure whom Joseph Campbell called 'the hero with a thousand faces' and the narrative structure that Mircea Eliade termed 'the myth of the eternal return' inform the exploration narrative in the last decades of the eighteenth century.

The incorporation of both these tropes into the exploration narrative reflected publishers' and editors' (and in some cases also the explorer's) judgement about what would interest the public. In Chapter 6, I analyse their presence in the published narratives of Cook's second and third voyages, and of *Bounty*'s voyage. The geographical circumstances of James Cook's second voyage meant that he and Canon Douglas, his editor, found it comparatively easy to represent him as a mythic voyager, while keeping closely to his original manuscript. However, Douglas did embellish the records significantly when he again portrayed Cook as such in the account of his third voyage.

What with pervasive rearrangements of details, distortions and omissions, Bligh's *A Voyage to the South Sea* was a much more consciously 'constructed' work again, with the aim of elevating Bligh to the status of naval hero. And, as I show, the various piecemeal representations of Fletcher Christian, together with the silences that attend his life, are also intended to lead us to see Christian in this light. In the published narratives of Cook's, Bligh's and Christian's ventures, history has been transmuted into myth.

We need to make four advances, then, if we are to enlarge our understandings of what happened on the voyage and at Pitcairn Island, and of the public's enduring interest in the whole story of *Bounty*'s voyage.

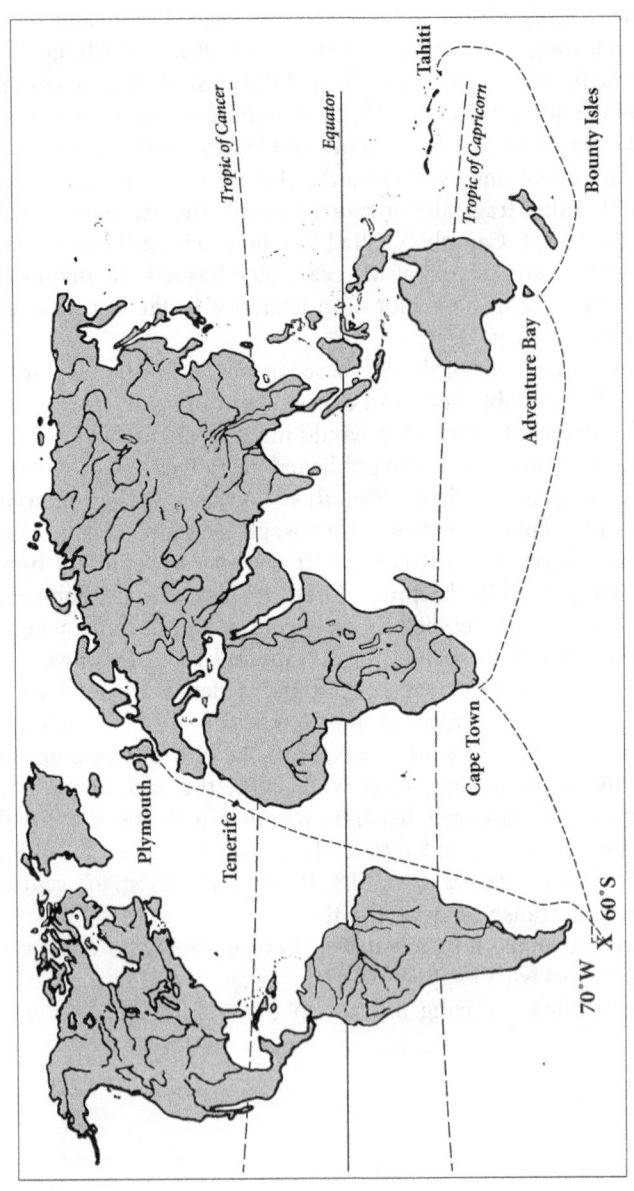

Figure 1 The voyage of the *Bounty* to Tahiti, 1787–8.

Introduction: The Troubled History of *Bounty*'s Story

In itself, *Bounty* was not a noteworthy ship. Built as a merchantman, it was small, being some 91 feet long and 24 feet 4 inches at its widest (around 28 x 7 metres), of some 215 tons (195 tonnes) burden,[1] with a designated crew of forty-five. (In the event, it carried forty-four when it sailed, for one of those entered on its books was a 'Widow's Man', whose pay went to the support of destitute wives of dead seamen.) It was therefore not large enough to be commanded by a senior officer or to have a separate purser. The Admiralty combined these roles in the person of a lieutenant, William Bligh.

The remainder of the *Bounty*'s complement was comprised as follows. There were six midshipmen training to be officers. There were men appointed by Navy Board warrant for their particular skills – master, boatswain, gunner, carpenter, surgeon, butcher, armourer, cooper, cook, sailmaker, quartermaster, master-at-arms, together with their various mates and assistants, a clerk and a servant. There were thirteen able-bodied seamen (ABs). (A number of the midshipmen and petty officers were rated AB for wages.) There were no marines. There were two civilian gardeners.

The ages of four of *Bounty*'s crew are unknown. Of the others, while there are some discrepancies between the various sources, it seems that at the time of sailing four were younger than twenty; twenty-three

---

1 In their survey of 23 May 1787, the Deptford Yard officers gave the burden as 220 tons; see Knight 1936.

were between twenty and twenty-nine; eleven were between thirty and thirty-nine; and two were forty.[2] This age profile reflects the fact that naval service then was predominantly a young man's occupation. We do not know how old the senior gardener David Nelson was. His assistant, William Brown, was twenty-six. Of these forty-six men, only three had previously done anything of particular note. William Peckover had sailed on all three of James Cook's circumnavigations, variously in the capacities of AB, gunner's mate and gunner; and Bligh and Nelson had sailed on the third, Bligh as master of the *Resolution* and Nelson as botanical collector on the *Discovery*.

Initially, then, there was only its purpose that gave *Bounty*'s voyage any particular significance. This was to bring a cargo of fruit plants from tropical islands in the Pacific and Indian oceans to the West India islands. It was unusual naval service to move 1000 plants from one hemisphere to another. As Sir Joseph Banks told the First Lord Commissioner of the Admiralty after Bligh's second breadfruit voyage – aboard HMS *Providence* in 1791–93 (Plate 1) – had succeeded, 'the undertaking was of so original a nature as to make the success of its execution difficult and uncertain'.[3] This somewhat overstates the situation, however. By the 1780s, Europeans had been transferring plants across oceans for hundreds of years. While these shipments had not been made on such a scale or in such a concerted manner as *Bounty*'s, they nonetheless provided precedents for it, and lessons on how it might best be done.

Bearing in mind that a series of unforeseen circumstances soon made the success of the second breadfruit voyage irrelevant to economic developments, it is reasonable to think that *Bounty*'s voyage, had it succeeded, would have left scarcely a furrow in the ocean of history. It was mutiny, and what followed from it, that gave this voyage what has proved to be a visceral significance. In the morning of 28 April 1789, as the ship was sailing through the western Pacific Ocean on its return voyage with a healthy cargo of Tahitian plants, Acting Lieutenant Fletcher Christian rebelled against the commander, Lieutenant William Bligh. Christian and a group of followers seized

---

2   See Table 1 below.
3   Banks to Chatham, 1 September 1793 (draft), Banks Online 54.01.

Introduction: The Troubled History of *Bounty*'s Story

the ship and set Bligh and eighteen men who remained loyal to him adrift in one of the ship's boats, with minimal food supplies and navigational aids and only four cutlasses for weapons.

Against all odds, Bligh and seventeen of his followers (one was killed soon after the mutiny) reached Coupang in Timor after a harrowing 3600-mile (5750-kilometre) passage; and Bligh then arrived back in England in March 1790. After vicissitudes, sixteen of the remaining Bountys (to identify the crew collectively by the name of their ship) left it at Tahiti (where two were subsequently killed), while Christian and eight others (together with a number of Polynesian men and women) sought a haven on Pitcairn Island.

Sailing in HMS *Pandora*, Captain Edward Edwards arrested the fourteen Bountys still at Tahiti in March and April 1791, and closely confined them. Four of them drowned when the *Pandora* sank after striking a reef off the north-east Australian coast.

Edwards delivered the survivors to Portsmouth in June 1792. They were court-martialled in September. Four who had clearly not joined in the mutiny but for whom there had been no room in the launch were acquitted. Six were convicted and sentenced to death. Two, whom, the court recommended for mercy were pardoned. The execution of one was postponed while authorities considered his appeal on a point of law, which resulted in his also being pardoned.

The reasons for the mutiny have been intensely debated for more than 200 years, with writers oscillating between two poles of interpretation. Immediately on his arrival back in England with details of the mutiny and with the story of his miraculous open-boat voyage, William Bligh was feted a hero. The *London Chronicle*, for example, commented, 'The distresses [Lieutenant Bligh] has undergone entitle him to every reward. In navigating his little skiff through so dangerous a sea, his seamanship appears as matchless, as the undertaking seems beyond the verge of probability.' As the politician William Windham told Fanny and James Burney in May: 'But what officers you are! *you men of Captain Cook*; you rise upon us in every trial! This Captain Bligh, – what feats, what wonders he has performed! What difficulties got through! What dangers defied! And with such cool, manly skill!' Soon after, writing as one old Pacific hand to another, James Matra told Sir Joseph Banks, 'The

3

escape of poor Bligh & his companions is a Miracle that has not been equalled these 1700 years.'[4]

Conversely, those who put Bligh and his loyalists to such trials must be treacherous and degenerate wretches. Bligh asserted privately that Fletcher Christian, Peter Heywood and George Stewart, the junior officers whose families he had obliged by taking them on the voyage, and whom (he said) he had constantly favoured during it, had completely betrayed his trust: 'these great Villains joined with the most able Men in the Ship[,] got possession of the Arms and took the *Bounty* from me, with huzza's for Otaheite [Tahiti]'. 'I have been run down by my own Dogs,' he remarked bitterly. Ahead of his doing so himself in his *Narrative* of the mutiny and the open-boat voyage, the *General Evening Post* offered Bligh's additional assessment that:

> with regard to the conduct of the conspirators, the most probable conjecture is, that, being principally young men, they were so greatly fascinated by the Circean blandishments of the Otaheitean women, they took this desperate method of returning to scenes of voluptuousness unknown, perhaps, in any other country.[5]

The actions of the authorities after Bligh's arrival back in London on 14 March 1790 were designed to reinforce these representations. On Wednesday 17 March, Commodore Gardner, one of the Lords Commissioners of the Admiralty, presented the lowly lieutenant to the King, whereupon he 'laid his journal of the voyage to the South Seas before His Majesty'.[6] A comparison of texts shows that this was not a log as such, but rather the 'Original Narrative' that Bligh had prepared as he returned from the East Indies. On 27 March, the Admiralty Secretary informed Banks that 'His Majesty approves of the narrative of Lt Bligh's proceedings, after he was dispossessed of the *Bounty* Armed Vessel[,] being printed and published in the manner you have suggested.' Three

---

4 *London Chronicle*, 16–18 March 1790; D'Arblay 1904–5, vol. 4, p. 378; Matra to Banks, 7 May 1790, BL Add. MS 33979, fo. 29.
5 Bligh to Elizabeth Bligh, 19 August 1789, Bligh 1989, pp. 23–4; *General Evening Post*, 16–18 March 1790.
6 *General Evening Post*, 16–18 March 1790.

Introduction: The Troubled History of *Bounty*'s Story

days later, the *Whitehall Evening Post* announced that 'Capt. Bligh is going to print the Journal of his wonderful escape at sea, in an open boat, for 49 days.' When it appeared in June, it was with the Admiralty's imprimatur – 'By Authority of the Lords Commissioners of the Admiralty, This day was published, Lieut. William Bligh's Narrative'.[7] On 22 October 1790, the mandatory court martial exonerated Bligh of responsibility for the loss of the *Bounty*. On 15 November, he was promoted to Master and Commander, and appointed to the *Falcon*, a 14-gun sloop. Waiving the usual requirement of at least three years' service in this lesser position, on 15 December the Admiralty promoted him to Post Captain, and attached him, for rank only, to the *Medea*, a 6th-rate of 28 guns.

Simultaneously, the authorities acted to reassure a concerned public that the piratical seizure of one of His Majesty's ships on a particular and expensive mission and the abandonment of its commander and those who remained loyal to him were crimes the Admiralty would not tolerate. As 'A Captain in the Navy' stressed, the 'dangerous consequences of such a mutinous disposition as our seamen have shown of late years in men-of-war, Indiamen, and smaller vessels' required a decisive demonstration of the 'determination to punish mutiny in whatever part of the world it may be committed'.[8] The *St James's Chronicle* announced on 31 March that 'by the express command of His Majesty, two new sloops of war ... are to be instantly fitted to go in pursuit of the pirates who have taken possession of the *Bounty*'.[9] The Nootka Sound armament delayed the mounting of this expedition, and when it did sail in early November it consisted only of the *Pandora*, a 24-gun frigate.

By the time William Bligh arrived back in England in August 1793 from the second, and very successful, breadfruit voyage, though, fortune's wheel had turned against him. The testimony that the Bountys who

---

7 ADM Minute, 25 March 1790, NA ADM 3/107; 'Extract from the Logg Book of Lieutenant William Bligh ... at Coupang on the Island of Timor', which the Admiralty sent to the Home Office on 25 March 1790, NA HO 28/7, fos. 119–20; Stephens to Banks, 27 March 1790, Banks Online, 48.03; *Whitehall Evening Post*, 30 March–1 April 1790, 1–3 June 1790.
8 *St James's Chronicle*, 1–3 April 1790.
9 *St James's Chronicle*, 30 March–1 April 1790.

were arrested at Tahiti had given at their court martial in September 1792 had shown him in a very different light to that of an extraordinary officer: as a foul-tempered bully who had grievously oppressed his crew. The details that also came out at the court martial concerning Captain Edwards's inhumane treatment of the mutineers, including his failure to release most of them as the *Pandora* was sinking, might only reinforce the perception that the mutiny on the *Bounty* was the result of unbearable mental pressure caused by the tyrannical exercise of authority. No sooner had the *Providence* docked at Deptford than one of the members of the court martial told Midshipman Matthew Flinders, who had sailed on it, 'Your Capt. will meet a very hard reception – he had Dam'd himself.'[10] And so it proved. The first lord of the Admiralty declined to receive Bligh – as he complained to Banks, 'Captains every day I have been at the Admiralty have had an interview with Lord Chatham. – His Lordship not seeing me is certainly a slight.'[11] The Admiralty also delayed the usual reward of promotion for the successful accomplishment of a difficult voyage for his junior officers.

Then, in 1794, Edward Christian published testimony obtained from members of *Bounty*'s crew that showed his brother in a much better light and therefore, inevitably, Bligh in a much worse one. Edward Christian summed up his extensive evidence with:

> And though public justice and the public safety can allow no vindication of any species of Mutiny, yet reason and humanity will distinguish the sudden unpremeditated act of desperation and phrenzy, from the foul deliberate contempt of every religious duty and honourable sentiment; and will deplore the uncertainty of human prospects, when they reflect that a young man is condemned to perpetual infamy, who, if he had served on board any other ship, or had perhaps been absent from the *Bounty* a single day, or one ill-fated hour, might still have been an honour to his country, and a glory and comfort to his friends.[12]

---

10 Pasley to Flinders, 7 August 1793, NMM, FL 1/01.
11 Bligh to Banks, 30 October 1793, Banks 2008–13, vol. 4, no. 90, p. 160.
12 Christian [1794] 1952, p. 79.

Introduction: The Troubled History of *Bounty*'s Story

Rather than one of treachery driven by lust, then, *Bounty*'s central story was of a 'noble mind o'erthrown', of a life of youthful promise destroyed by excessive tyranny.

In a series of letters to Sir Joseph Banks and in an ineffectual pamphlet, in which he did not address the charges against him directly, Bligh sought to counter the damage done to his reputation by the publication of the minutes of the court martial and Edward Christian's *Appendix*, but to little avail.[13]

✳ ✳ ✳

By the mid-1790s, the opposing pairs of binary images that have ever since been central to the seemingly never-ending retellings of *Bounty*'s story were established. On the one hand, there was the concerned and exceptionally competent commander and the self-indulgent and treacherous deputy. On the other, there was the abusive and tyrannical commander and his good-hearted, popular deputy, who broke under intolerable emotional pressure.

The second pair of images dominated public perception for most of the nineteenth century. This was the consequence of three main factors: Bligh's subsequent behaviour when in positions of command; the continuing influence of the opinions of those who had suffered under him on the *Bounty* and their supporters; and the supposed miracle of Pitcairn Island.

As with the leopard and its spots, William Bligh never changed his prideful character and his bombastic treatment of subordinates. According to Francis Bond, lieutenant on the *Providence*, 'Hardly had the voyage commenced when Cap. Bligh's arbitrary disposition and exasperating language began again to render his ship a most unfortunate one for his officers.'[14] While Bond conceded that ill-health may have been a contributing factor, he ascribed most of Bligh's 'passion' to 'the fury of an ungovernable temper'. His detailed characterisation of a commander 'great ... in his own good opinion' is withering:

---

13   Bligh Miscellaneous and Bligh [1794] 1952.
14   F.H. Bond, summary of his father's notes, in Bond 1961, p. 32.

> The very high opinion he has of himself makes him hold every one of our profession with contempt, perhaps envy. Nay, the Navy is but a sphere for fops and lubbers to swarm in, without one gem to vie in brilliancy with himself. I don't mean to depreciate his extensive knowledge as a seaman and nautical astronomer, but condemn that want of modesty, in self-estimation ... He has treated me (nay, all on board) with the insolence and arrogance of a Jacobs [meaning Jacobite? Jacobin?] ... He expects me to be acquainted with every transaction on board, notwithstanding he himself will give the necessary orders to the Warrant Officers before I can put [them] into execution. Every dogma of power and consequence has been taken from the Lieutenants, to establish, as he thinks, his own reputation ... Among many circumstances of envy and jealousy, he used to deride my keeping a private journal, and would often ironically say he supposed I meant to publish. My messmates have remarked he never spoke of my possessing one virtue.

Decades later, George Tobin, another junior officer on the voyage, echoed this characterisation: 'I am sure ... that in the *Providence* there was no settled System of Tyranny exercised by him likely to produce dissatisfaction. It was in those violent Tornados of temper when he lost himself.'[15]

So it was ever afterwards to be with William Bligh. When in command of the *Monarch* after the Battle of Copenhagen in April 1801, 'his manners and disposition were not pleasant, and his appointment ... gave very general disgust to the Officers'.[16] In 1805, when in command of the *Warrior*, he was brought to a court martial when Lieutenant Frazier complained that he had:

---

15   Bond to Thomas Bond [c. December 1792], in Bond [1953] 1796, pp. 69–71; Tobin to Bond, 15 December 1817, in Bond [1949] 1976, p. 33. (Bond wrote 'Jacobs', so the expansion to 'Jacobite', a follower of the Stuarts, or 'Jacobin', the name of one of the parties of the French Revolution whose members became notorious for violent repression, is conjectural.)
16   W.S. Millard, Extract from his journal of the voyage of the *Monarch*, SLNSW, Mitchell MS ab 60/15.

Introduction: The Troubled History of *Bounty*'s Story

> publicly on the quarter deck ... grossly insult[ed] me and ill treat[ed] me ... by calling me a rascal, scoundrel and shaking his fist in my face and that at various times ... he behaved himself towards me and other commissioned, warrant and petty officers ... in a tyrannical and oppressive and unofficerlike behaviour.

After a plethora of testimony that he had abused various members of his crew with such characterisations as 'rascal', 'rascal and villain', 'rascal and scoundrel', 'damned impertinent fellow', 'disgrace to the service', 'lubber', 'infamous scoundrel', 'dastardly villain', 'old thief', 'Jesuit' and 'damn long pelt of a bitch', and manhandled some of them, Bligh was forced into the humiliating concession that he was not:

> a tame & indifferent observer of the manner in which Officers placed under my orders conducted themselves in the performance of their several duties; a signal or any communication from a commanding officer have ever been to me an indication for exertion & alacrity to carry into effect the purport thereof & peradventure I may occasionally have appeared to some of those officers as unnecessarily anxious for its execution by exhibiting any action or gesture peculiar to myself as such.

He asked his judges to attribute 'the warmth of temper, which I may at intervals have discovered, to my zeal for that service in which I had been employed without an imaginary blemish on my character for upwards of thirty five years'. They did and didn't, deciding that he should be 'reprimanded and to be admonished to be in future more correct in his language'.[17]

No sooner had it been given, though, than this lesson was lost on Bligh. During the voyage out to Sydney in 1806 to become governor of New South Wales, he quarrelled bitterly with Joseph Short, the captain of the warship escorting the convoy. Short had intended to settle in the colony, but once at Sydney Bligh forced him back to England to face a court martial. Short's wife and one of their children died on the return voyage. The court martial acquitted him, and recommended that he be

---

17 Quoted in Kennedy 1989, pp. 274–8.

compensated for his losses, which included those from the forced sale of the farming equipment he had taken out.

Thereafter, Bligh continued to behave in his usual fashion, quickly falling out with most of the leading colonists. He reportedly told John Macarthur, who had recently returned from England with prized merino sheep and the promise of land on which to breed up a flock:

> What have I to do with your sheep, Sir? What have I to do with your cattle? Are you to have such flocks of sheep and such herds of cattle as no man ever heard of before? No, Sir, I have heard of your concerns, Sir, you have got 5,000 acres of land, Sir, in the finest situation in the country, but by God you shan't keep it.

When Macarthur protested that the land had been granted to him by the secretary of state and the Privy Council, Bligh evidently raged, 'Damn the Privy Council, and damn the Secretary of State, too; he commands at home, I command here.'[18]

The officer commanding the New South Wales Corps also complained bitterly about Bligh's 'indecorous and … oppressive conduct':

> First, his interfering in the interior management of the Corps by selecting and ordering both officers and men on various duties without my knowledge; his abusing and confining the soldiers without the smallest provocation, and without ever consulting me as their commanding officer; and again, his casting the most undeserved and opprobrious censure on the Corps at different times in company at Government House.[19]

In January 1808, Macarthur and the officers of the New South Wales Corps deposed Bligh as governor.

✳ ✳ ✳

---

18 Onslow [1914] 1973, p.137–8.
19 Johnston to Gordon, 8 October 1807, *HRNSW*, vol. 6, p. 652.

Bligh died in 1817. While most of the additional complaints against him were not generally known during his lifetime, the people who thereafter put *Bounty*'s story before the public were familiar with them. Peter Heywood (midshipman) and James Morrison (boatswain's mate) were the two men who were convicted of mutiny and then pardoned. In 1825, Heywood, who by this time had Morrison's journal in his possession, contributed most of the information for his own entry in John Marshall's *Royal Naval Biography* series. Inevitably, the image of Bligh there conveyed was highly unfavourable. 'It would be folly to look for any statement [from Bligh] having a tendency to implicate his own conduct,' the authors asserted; and pointed to the 'unjust and harsh proceedings' which had given rise to the mutiny.[20]

In 1831, in his obituary for Heywood in the *United Services Journal*, W.H. Smyth went a good deal further, saying that Bligh's 'lure of Otahiti' explanation for the mutiny was a 'mere matter of moonshine'; and that 'apologies for cruelty not only injure the service, but also cast a slur upon it, by an appearance of countenancing atrocity'. While conceding that mutiny was always inexcusable, he argued that it arose 'but from one of these two sources, excessive folly, or excessive tyranny; therefore as it is admitted that Bligh was no idiot, the inference is obvious'. The evidence given at the court martial had exposed the falsity of many of Bligh's assertions in his *Narrative*. Moreover, 'every act of his public life after this event, from his successive command of the *Director*, the *Glatton*, and the *Warrior*, to his disgraceful expulsion from New South Wales, was stamped with an insolence, an inhumanity, and coarseness, which fully developed his character'.[21]

Sir John Barrow, the Second (effectively, permanent) Secretary of the Admiralty (1804-6, 1807-48), brought the image of Bligh as an abusive tyrant to its nadir in *The Mutiny of the Bounty* (1831). While he conceded that Bligh was an excellent navigator and had performed bravely in battle, the perception that 'his temper was irritable in the extreme' underpinned his view of his character. Accepting the truth of the accounts of Bligh's tirades given by the Bountys who testified at the court martial and by James Morrison in his journal (to which he also

---

20   Marshall 1825, pp. 747-8.
21   Smyth 1831, p. 469.

had access), Barrow said 'it is difficult to believe that an officer in His Majesty's service could condescend to make use of such language to the meanest of the crew, much less to gentlemen'. He summed up:

> unable longer to bear the abusive and insulting language, [Christian] had meditated his own escape from the ship the day before [the mutiny], choosing to trust himself to fate, rather than submit to the constant upbraiding to which he had been subject; but the unfortunate business of the cocoa-nuts drove him to the commission of the rash and felonious act, which ended, as such criminal acts usually do, in his own destruction, and that of a great number of others, many of whom were wholly innocent.

Later in the century, Lady Diana Belcher, Heywood's stepdaughter, re-presented these images in *The Mutineers of the Bounty and their Descendants in Pitcairn and Norfolk Islands*. Drawing on what her stepfather had told her, and quoting extensively from Morrison's journal, she characterised Bligh as 'being of an irritable and passionate disposition', and 'of a most suspicious turn of mind'. The language with which he habitually addressed the officers and men was exceptionally 'harsh and offensive'. In accusing Christian of stealing his coconuts, he 'made the most unwarrantable accusations of falsehood and theft; serious imputations on the character of a gentleman; and especially galling and humiliating to an officer who stood next in command of the vessel'. As he brooded over the wrongs Bligh had done him, a 'terrible conflict [raged] in the breast of Fletcher Christian', and he was 'goaded as it were to madness'. For months past, he had borne such 'indignities' with 'patience and forbearance', but now 'it seemed as if endurance had passed its utmost limits. The tyranny to which Christian had been subjected appeared more insupportable on considering how difficult, how almost impossible, it would be for him, as a junior officer, to bring his oppressor to a court-martial with any hope of success'. In his confused state, Christian could see only 'one mode of escape'.[22]

※ ※ ※

---

22   Barrow [1831] 1989, pp. 81–93; Belcher 1870, pp. 14, 31–3.

Introduction: The Troubled History of *Bounty*'s Story

From early in the nineteenth century, these binary images of Bligh the bombastic tyrant and Christian the good young man too much put-upon were joined by a sub-set that showed how good might come of evil. For the discovery of the tiny settlement on Pitcairn Island seemingly brought to light not only a history of bloody murder but also one of how, belatedly informed by God's grace, the old mutineer John Adams had led his tiny flock of islander women and mixed-race children into a life of admirable piety. The American sealer Mayhew Folger wrote of his very brief visit in February 1808: 'I think [the Pitcairners] a very humane & hospitable people, and whatever may have been the Errors or Crimes of [Adams] the Mutineer in times Back he is at present in my opinion a worthy man', and his flock 'a truly good people'.[23]

The visit of Sir Thomas Staines and Philip Pipon, captains of the HMS *Briton* and *Tagus*, to the island in September 1814 led them to similar conclusions. Staines described the 'venerable old Man, named John Adams', who:

> is the only surviving Englishman of those who last quitted Otaheite in her [the *Bounty*], & whose exemplary conduct & fatherly care of the whole of the little Colony could not but command admiration. The pious manner in which all those born on the Island have been reared, the correct sense of Religion which has been instilled into their young minds by this old man, has given him the pre-eminence over the whole of them, to whom they look up as the Father of the whole & one family.[24]

Pipon went a good deal further in his praise:

> Those born in the Island are extremely fine young Men, very athletic, with the finest forms, & countenances indicating much benevolence & goodness. The young women are still more to be admired, wonderfully strong, most pleasing countenances, & a degree of modesty & bashfulness that would do honour to the

---

23 Entries, 6 and 7 February 1808, Folger (PN 4).
24 Staines, p. [2] (PN 8).

most virtuous nation ... When therefore you consider there are many fine young Men & certainly very handsome women here, it is natural to expect hereafter there will be a progeny of beautiful people upon the Island. There is no debauchery here, no immoral conduct, & Adams informd me, there is not one instance of any young Woman having proved unchaste: the men appear equally moral & well behaved, & from every information there has not appeared any inclination to seduction on the part of the young men.[25]

In 1817, Amasa Delano, who had discussed the mutiny and the settlement at length with Folger, and who was familiar with Barrow's largely verbatim inclusions of the British captains' reports in the *Quarterly Review*, brought this trope to full fruition. After describing the Pitcairners' simple life, their abundant foods, their hospitality and (as a consequence of Adams's instruction) their 'purest morals' and remarkable 'obedience to the laws of continence', he wrote that when Folger left them:

> their unaffected and amiable manners, and their earnest prayers for his welfare, made a deep impression upon his mind, and are still cherished in his memory. He wished to decline taking all that was brought him in the overflow of friendship, but [Adams] told him it would hurt the feelings of the donors, and the gifts could well be spared from the island. He made as suitable a return of presents as his ship afforded, and left this most interesting community with the keenest sensations of regret. It reminded him of Paradise, as he said, more than any effort of poetry or of the imagination.[26]

Later visitors to the island continued to embellish this image. Captain Beechey, who called there in December 1825, observed:

---

25 Pipon, p. [4] (PN 9).
26 Delano 1817, pp. 142–4 (PN 7).

Introduction: The Troubled History of *Bounty*'s Story

> [Adams] had an arduous task to perform. Besides the children to be educated, the Otaheitan women were to be converted; and as the example of the parents had a powerful influence over their children, he resolved to make them his first care. Here also his labours succeeded; the Otaheitans were naturally of a tractable disposition, and gave him less trouble than he anticipated: the children also acquired such a thirst after scriptural knowledge, that Adams in a short time had little else to do than to answer their inquiries and put them in the right way. As they grew up, they acquired fixed habits of morality and piety; their colony improved; intermarriages occurred: and they now form a happy and well-regulated society, the merit of which in a great degree belongs to Adams, and tends to redeem the former errors of his life.[27]

This lesson of how, against all expectation, Heaven might be wrought from Hell was one to appeal to a society greatly concerned with spreading Christianity over the world. Lady Belcher repeated it in 1870:

> By the mercy of God, and by the aid of his Bible and Prayer-Book, which he had so earnestly studied, John Adams succeeded in establishing such a community as has been the dream of poets, and the aspiration of philosophers! and the result of his humble endeavours was shown by the exercise 'of all that is lovely and of good report' in the isolated Pitcairn colony, far away in the vast Pacific Ocean.

At the end of the century, the native Pitcairner Rosalind Young added more enhancements. True, she did counsel that, just as Satan had led Adam and Eve astray, so too were there vice and sin among the islanders, but she explained that, nonetheless, much of the 'beautiful simplicity' that had marked the lives of those under John Adams had endured. She provided a lyrical description of the lush vegetation and fruits of the 'Gem of the Pacific', and a fetching story of how the 'simple-hearted islanders' had 'most hospitably entertained' the *Blossom*'s

---

27 Beechey (2), vol. 1, p. 95 (PN 13).

officers during their December 1825 visit, when the young women had also made 'wreaths of sweet-smelling flowers' to decorate the officers' caps every day.[28]

This trope continued strongly in the twentieth century. In 1936, Owen Rutter, whose exceptional editorial work on important primary sources should have led him to be much more wary of trusting to old images, extolled the Pitcairners' virtues:

> Thus they live, isolated and remote, leading healthy, simple lives: fishing, cultivating their gardens, and making their souvenirs, but apparently content, on … 'a very good little spot in the Pacific', and still honouring the memory of that remarkable man who, mutineer though he may have been, must have his peculiar place in the roll of Empire as the builder of as strange a colony as the world has ever known.[29]

Fifty years later, Glynn Christian, Fletcher Christian's great-great-great-great grandson, waxed even more lyrical. 'Pitcairn's way of life,' he wrote, had shown him 'that the message of basic Christianity can work, that brotherly love and kindness are more sustaining than the rewards offered by industrialized societies.' Lacking newspapers, television and radio service, the Pitcairners live 'the life of small settlements throughout Europe and America during the mid to late nineteenth century'. 'The Golden Rule – Do unto others as you would that they should do unto you – is indeed golden here.' Moreover, 'to live in Adamstown is to bathe in a perpetual glow of friendship and trust, with no thought of locked doors or theft, no worries about dark streets or social levels, no fear of loneliness or of wounding gossip'. All of this led him to conclude that 'men and women are born inherently good and continue that way, a far more triumphant dogma than that of original sin'.[30]

It was not until the turn of the twenty-first century, when it became clear that the sexual molestation of minors had been pervasive in the

---

28   Belcher 1870, p. 188; Young 1894, pp. 44–53, 62–3, 252–3 (PN 24).
29   Rutter 1936a, p. 181.
30   Christian 1982, pp. 244–5.

Pitcairn settlement for generations, that the world came to understand how much the Serpent had long ago insinuated himself into this particular Garden.

※ ※ ※

In the first half of the twentieth century, some writers continued to promote the narrative of the Bounty Bastard and his amiable and honourable young deputy driven frantic by his bullying.[31] However, this period was also marked by an exponential increase in primary sources, as family papers emerged and more diligent searching brought more official or semi-official records to light; and as publication made both classes more readily available.

With the advantages of a much richer documentary record and also now being able to draw on modern psychological insights, a number of writers offered more nuanced accounts of the voyage, of the principal protagonists, and of the causes of the mutiny. George Mackaness had access to the extensive sets of papers that came by purchase and donation from the Bligh family to the State Library of New South Wales. In his voluminous biography (1931; second edition 1951), he conceded that Bligh 'was a man of passionate temper, prone to outbursts of violence, and addicted at times to the most intemperate language'. The captain was also not blameless in other respects, for example in his purser's activities, which were 'a tarnish on his shield'. Nonetheless, it was mostly because he 'worshipped efficiency' that he was overly demanding of his officers, who repeatedly let him down: 'their inefficiency and continual neglect of duty often sorely tried the temper of their captain'. The fourteen seamen who joined in the mutiny were rough, intractable characters whom he had been forced to punish and who had succumbed to Tahiti's allures. Mackaness also praised Bligh for his 'unceasing vigilance on behalf of the comfort and health of his men'.[32]

As well as publishing editions of Bligh's log and other records of the voyage in the 1930s, Owen Rutter wrote an account of *Bounty*'s voyage

---

31 E.g. Sir Cyprian Bridge's 1915 introduction to Barrow's account: Barrow 1989, p. ix.
32 Mackaness 1951, pp. 112–6, 131–3.

and a biography of Bligh. Relying on crude psychology, he argued that Bligh's and Christian's behaviour was the result of 'a clash of two irreconcilable temperaments; the clash of Bligh the Cornishman and Christian the man of Cumberland with Manx blood in his veins'. In general, though, he too greatly favoured Bligh's cause over Christian's. He summed up:

> Bligh's conduct to his crew was not the cause of the mutiny; nor his final quarrel with Christian over the coconuts. But had it not been for that quarrel, or had Christian been man enough to accept his captain's unspoken apology and sup with him that night, he might never have thought of deserting the ship.

If Bligh had any responsibility for the mutiny, said Rutter, it was 'not for his punishments or abuse, but rather for his error of judgment in keeping the *Bounty* so long at Tahiti and giving his men too much freedom ashore'. 'The true and direct cause of the mutiny were those whispered words of Stewart's: "The people are ripe for anything!" But for them Christian would never have been stung to action; once the idea was in his mind he had no difficulty in finding men to follow him.'[33]

In *What Happened on the Bounty* (1963), Bengt Danielsson presented Bligh as a person who, though given from time to time to unfortunate outbursts of temper and abusive language, was meticulous in his attention to his naval duties, solicitous of the welfare of his crew and resolute in the face of difficulties, with his actions being marked by 'energy', 'drive' and 'enterprize'. He summed up:

> There is no evidence whatever to support the general conception of [Bligh] as an inhuman monster. In fact, he was anything but this, and might even be described by the standards of his day as a mild and benevolent captain. The facts, as any unbiased person can clearly see, speak for themselves.

---

33   Rutter 1936a, pp. 84–5; Rutter 1936b, pp. 126–7.

Introduction: The Troubled History of *Bounty*'s Story

On the other hand, *Bounty*'s junior officers were repeatedly 'guilty of dereliction of duty and cowardice'; and many of the crew were 'incompetent and unreliable'.[34] Given all this, the mutiny was certainly not William Bligh's fault!

In *Who Caused the Mutiny on the Bounty?* (1965), Marge Darby also came out on Bligh's side, laying the blame for the mutiny partly on Bligh's repeated quarrels with his recalcitrant junior officers, partly on the men's strong desire for Tahitian women, and partly on incipient class struggle.

In 1972, downplaying the significance of his being 'a man of uncouth ways, foul language and evil temper', Richard Hough also acknowledged Bligh's brilliance as a navigator and praised his concern for his crew. Conversely, Christian was a 'weak, moody, temperamental and sentimental young man', and 'no leader' – 'Where Bligh had moments of magnificence as a leader, Christian had none.' The mutiny arose from Bligh's loss of authority over his officers and a more general breakdown of discipline, and from a 'sort of madness' that overwhelmed the ship's company after they left Tahiti, with Bligh and Christian being the most grievously afflicted.[35]

In 1978, Gavin Kennedy found Christian much more responsible than Bligh for what happened. Bligh 'was a man of immense personal courage and determination'; and 'if we are asked whether [he] was a tyrant we must also look at the actions of the mutineers when they were free of him ... The bloody sequel and murderous actions of the mutineers, Christian included, must weigh heavy in the balance of right and wrong in this controversy.' While he conceded that the 'scornful impatience' with which Bligh came to treat his officers may have made Christian perform badly, and that Bligh's particular criticisms of him may even have driven him to madness, to blame Bligh for his disturbance is 'unjust'. Rather, he argued, 'the mutiny is best explained by the coincidence of the collapse in the authority of the commander and an emotional storm in an immature and possibly mentally unstable young man'. Moreover, 'that so many [men] went with Bligh, and others

---

[34] Danielsson 1963, pp. 49, 64, 131, 156, 202.
[35] Hough 1972, pp. 34, 131, 304.

wanted to, speaks volumes for the so-called tyrant and little for Christian the "liberator".[36]

Taken together, and also with Mackaness's revised edition of his biography (1951), these works constituted a strong effort to rescue Bligh from the opprobrium of the previous century, which had more recently been bolstered by the film portrayals of him by Charles Laughton (1935) and Trevor Howard (1962). However, this effort had only limited success. Each of the works had significant flaws. Darby made many errors of fact and interpretation. Hough turned speculation into assertion. Kennedy neglected important primary sources, and misinterpreted some that he did attend to. Then again, suspicion of Bligh and of those who would argue his cause remained strong – as the (Sydney) *Bulletin* titled a severe critic's review of Danielsson's book, 'Bligh Whitewashed Again'.[37]

In the same period, other writers revived the images of Bligh and Christian that had dominated nineteenth-century storytelling. In 1961, Alexander McKee portrayed Bligh as possessing 'a fierce professional pride' and being concerned about the welfare of his crew; but also as boastful, avaricious, much given to posturing and flogging, and guilty of recording selectively:

> [Bligh] talked with his hands. He was light-tongued, too, volleying abuse to let off steam, and making threats which he never meant to carry out. He had a fierce professional pride in himself and the naval service, but quite failed to see how damaging his conduct could be to the pride of others. Where the welfare of his crew and their efficiency were one and the same thing, he was thoughtful and far-sighted. Yet he habitually was unable to prevent himself from striking at the roots of discipline in his own ship by foully abusing the competence of his officers in the hearing of the men, and of shaking his fists threateningly in their faces, as if he was about to hit them.[38]

---

36 Kennedy 1978, pp. xi, 98–9.
37 For a detailed analysis, see Du Rietz 1965 and 2009; M.H. Ellis, 'The Mutiny on the *Bounty*: Bligh Whitewashed Again', *Bulletin*, 16 February 1963.
38 McKee 1962, pp. 14–15.

Introduction: The Troubled History of *Bounty*'s Story

In 1982, Glynn Christian published an account of his quest to give a fuller character to Fletcher Christian and to know the reality of his forebear's life on Pitcairn Island. Two quotations sum up his view of the causes of the mutiny succinctly: 'The available evidence [proves] overwhelmingly the traditional harsh view of Bligh, except that he was never as physically cruel as films [have] made him out to be'; and that Bligh's bullying and abusive treatment forced Christian into 'an abnormal state of mind' – literally, caused him to become insane.[39]

So the pendulum of historical gaze continued to swing backwards and forwards. In 1989, Kennedy published a significantly revised study, *Captain Bligh: The Man and His Mutinies*, in which he took account of more primary sources and extended his analysis of Bligh's later tribulations. However, he did not much alter his views of Bligh, Christian and the *Bounty* mutiny: 'The causes of the mutiny were as simple and as complicated as the fact that these two men clashed, and one broke.' On the other hand, Roy Schreiber considered that Bligh 'was a complex mixture of vile and admirable qualities, and it was impossible to predict which ones would predominate at a particular moment in his life.'[40]

In 1992, Greg Dening published *Mr Bligh's Bad Language*. For reasons given in the next section, Dening was not particularly interested in ascribing individual blame for the mutiny. However, embedded in his analysis are essential portraits of the main protagonists. Bligh was someone whose position as commander gave him power, but he deployed it unwisely when he confused public and private interests, so that he was unable to maintain a necessary authority. Christian's seaman's skills gave him authority where the crew were concerned, but he lacked power, being dependent on Bligh for the little that he had. Christian's 'moodiness and over-reactive response to tensions that Bligh caused in him' made him vulnerable, creating circumstances he could not control.[41]

In her 2003 study, Caroline Alexander conceded that Bligh was 'passionate' and 'irascible', but she nonetheless evinced broad sympathy

---

[39] Christian 1999, pp. 185, 189.
[40] Kennedy 1989, p. [ix]; Schreiber 1991, p. 3.
[41] Dening 1992, pp. 80–1, 310.

for him, presenting him as possessed of a 'fundamental humanity'. Christian, on the other hand, was mentally unstable and suffered a breakdown when Bligh accused him of stealing the coconuts.[42]

In 2010, Rob Mundle published another version of Bligh's story. While he mentioned some of the troubles during *Bounty*'s voyage, he did not really analyse the causes of the mutiny, nor did he pay much attention to Bligh's shortcomings. His general view of his subject is well summed up in his dedication: 'To those individuals who, like Bligh, have stood proud through adversity, slander and ridicule and gone on to achieve great things.'[43]

Then, in 2011, presenting a paradox she did not resolve, Anne Salmond characterised Bligh as capable of being 'magnificent in the care of his men', but argued that his 'incessant accusations' of neglect of duty and incompetence gave rise to his poor relations with his officers. Once the homeward voyage commenced, she considered, Christian and others found circumstances 'intolerable':

> Crammed below decks and cooped up with a commander whom they no longer respected, it was a torment to recall the joys of island life – the freedom to dance and feast on shore; their kind-hearted, generous *taio* [bonded friends]; the delicious puddings, pork, fish and fresh fruit; and the warm, scented nights with their island lovers.

So Salmond revived the explanation for the mutiny that Bligh himself offered in its immediate aftermath, that of *le mirage tahitien* [the misleading allure of Tahiti]; but now, in a new twist, she also included him in it: 'Likewise, Bligh was suffering from a sense of loss, after the ease and affection that had surrounded him on the island; and as his temper frayed, the relationship between him and his officers became increasingly tense and bitter.' Bligh's tirades at the Tongan island of Nomuka about the wooding and water party's performance and off Tofua (also in Tonga) about the missing coconuts produced a human irruption in Fletcher Christian as intense as the volcanic one the crew

---

42 Alexander 2003, pp. 129, 137–8, 329.
43 Mundle 2010, p. [v].

watched the night before the mutiny. In the most recent retelling of the story, Diana Preston attends to Bligh's frequent rages and abusive language, and his inability to understand the effect that these had on those about him.[44]

In a determined attempt to introduce more rigour and accuracy into the telling of Bligh's and *Bounty*'s stories, in a series of publications beginning in the 1960s and continuing up to the present, the formidably learned Swedish bibliographer and historian Rolf Du Rietz has pointed out simple errors, neglect of important primary sources, and conceptual and methodological failings. He has drawn particular attention, first to Bligh's abusive and humiliating treatment as the major factor that triggered Christian's rebellion; and then to Bligh's need to construct an explanation of the mutiny and the loss of the ship favourable to himself, which he did by resorting to distortions, omissions and lies. Sadly, though, often other writers have not paid sufficient attention to Du Rietz's views.[45]

※ ※ ※

As the French saying goes, *plus ça change, plus c'est la même chose* – the more things change, the more they stay the same. To put it bluntly, our historical understanding of *Bounty*'s strange story remains at a real impasse, with the binary pairs of images that emerged in the 1790s still dominating and distorting its telling.

This is not to say that there have been no worthwhile advances in our knowledge of certain aspects of *Bounty*'s voyage and of the personalities of the chief protagonists in more recent times; however, they have been incremental ones. In his interesting encyclopedia *Mutiny and Romance in the South Seas* (1989), Sven Wahlroos has brought his insights as a professional psychologist to bear on the business. He thinks that 'Bligh was not the cruel monster he has often been portrayed as, nor was he the kind and considerate and righteous man of honour that recent efforts to whitewash him have claimed he was.' Rather:

---

44   Salmond 2011, pp. 127, 196, 205–11; Preston 2017, passim.
45   Du Rietz 1965, 1979, 1981, 2007, 2009.

Bligh's character was an interesting mixture of highly admirable qualities and pernicious flaws. Certainly he was a man of great courage. He was also one of the finest navigators in maritime history and a superb cartographer. He was a man of boundless energy, had a strong sense of duty, and was totally dedicated to his profession. He was diligent and conscientious in the extreme ...

But Bligh had a disastrous flaw in his character. Although in most respects he showed evidence of superior foresight, he had no understanding of the impact his frequent emotional outbursts and insulting accusations had on other people. He could call someone, even an officer, an 'infernal scoundrel' or a 'contemptible thief' or an 'incompetent mongrel' or a 'cowardly rascal' in front of the whole ship's company, yet a short while later behave as if nothing had happened.

Especially, Bligh 'could not conceive of any imperfections in himself: he felt he had absolutely nothing to do with the misfortunes that befell him during his life'.[46]

On the other hand, Wahlroos thinks that Fletcher Christian may have suffered from a 'borderline personality disorder'. Quoting from the American Psychiatric Association's *Diagnostic and Statistical Manual of Mental Disorders* (third edition, 1987), he indicated that in this condition:

inter-personal relations are often intense and unstable with marked shifts of attitude over time. Frequently there is impulsive and unpredictable behaviour that is potentially physically self-damaging ... The borderline person will often go from idealizing a person to devaluing him.

Further, Bligh's humiliating tirade over the coconuts likely brought on in Christian a 'brief reactive psychosis', which those with borderline personality disorder are prone to:

---

46 Wahlroos 1989, pp. 19, 30, 226.

The essential feature is the sudden onset of a psychotic disorder of at least a few hours' but no more than two weeks' duration, with eventual return to pre-morbid level of functioning. The psychotic symptoms appear immediately following a recognizable psychosocial stressor that would evoke significant symptoms of distress in almost anyone ... Invariably there is emotional turmoil ... Suicidal or aggressive behaviour may be present.[47]

As the result of having discovered Charles Christian's autobiography among the family's ancestral papers, Glynn Christian has provided a handful of new details about Fletcher's life before the *Bounty* voyage. He has reiterated H.S. Montgomerie's earlier suggestion of hyperhidrosis as the cause of Fletcher Christian's excessive perspiration; and also endorsed Wahlroos's view that his forebear had suffered 'a brief psychotic disorder with marked stressors' (as the condition is now known).[48] And, drawing on her extensive knowledge of Polynesian culture, Anne Salmond has richly increased our understanding of the interactions between the Bountys and the Tahitians.

However, Greg Dening's *The Bounty: An Ethnographic History* and *Mr Bligh's Bad Language* has been undoubtedly the most innovative of more recent studies, introducing important new perspectives on what happened during the voyage and how it happened. Let me now concentrate on the second, longer work. Dening's central concerns were to offer an 'anthropology' of life on the ship, to explicate the theatre and ritual that filled its various spaces and to identify the discourses according to which men lived their lives while on board. He started from a highly sophisticated conception of what constitutes discourses and where they are played out – in the semioticians Peter Stallybrass and Allon White's formulation:

Patterns of discourse are regulated through the forms of corporate assembly in which they are produced. Alehouse, coffeehouse, church, law-court, library, drawing-room of country mansion: each place of assembly is a different site of intercourse requiring different manners

---

47 Wahlroos 1989, pp. 30–31, 61.
48 Christian 1982, pp. 45–6 and 1999, pp. 306–13; Montgomerie 1937, p. 31.

and morals. Discourse space is never completely independent of social space and the formation of new kinds of speech can be traced through the emergence of new public sites of discourse and the transformation of old ones.

Dening then suggested:

Add a ship to this list of places of discourse. Add the space created by the collective sense of being 'navy'. Add tonality, silence, looks and glances, winks and nudges, and a sense of corporate reaction to our understanding of the ways in which language and discourse are expressed. The Wooden World of sailors was classified in a complex system of signs whose mastery gave seamen their identity and set them apart.[49]

In this perspective, Bligh's hot temper and vituperative tirades ruptured normal shipboard spheres of influence and disrupted hierarchies of power, thereby creating a fertile breeding ground for mutiny. Bligh's language, he suggests, 'was bad, not so much because it was intemperate or abusive, but because it was ambiguous, because men could not read in it a right relationship to his authority'.[50]

This explanation has considerable force, but I think we need to qualify it in two important ways. First, Bligh's language was more intemperate and abusive than Dening allowed. After their return to England, the Bountys complained that in his fits of anger he had called them 'scoundrels, damned rascals, hounds, hell-hounds, beasts and infamous wretches'; that he had assured them that he would 'trim' them (i.e. put them in order, with the overtone of 'do away' with them); and that he would make them 'eat grass like cows'.[51] It would be hardly surprising if some men were to turn surly after eighteen months of such abuse. But which men? I think Dening's hypothesis much better explains the officers' failure to support Bligh than it does the seamen's joining with Christian in mutiny.

---

49 Dening 1992, pp. 379. Stallybrass and White 1986, p. 80.
50 Dening 1992, p. 61.
51 Christian [1794] 1952, p. 63.

Introduction: The Troubled History of *Bounty*'s Story

* * *

When we consider the telling of *Bounty*'s story over more than 200 years, it is difficult to avoid the conclusions that most writers have wandered in a maze from which they have been unable to find a straight way out; and that, for all the millions of words that have been written about the voyage and its aftermaths, we continue to see some of the most important aspects as through a glass darkly.

There have been a number of reasons for these impasses. Some authors have been more storytellers than historians, while the primary professional expertise of others has not been in history, so that they have not properly understood the complexities of the circumstances they have sought to describe. These inadequacies have resulted in a range of flaws, which include elementary factual errors and conceptual and methodological lapses.

Here is a very brief sample of factual errors. It is not true that John Adams was 'lying peacefully asleep in his hammock' when the mutiny began – Bligh and others identified him as one of the core group of mutineers. Nor is it true that the old rogue told only one version of his story – he offered at least a dozen versions to visitors to Pitcairn. It is not so that there is 'absolutely no evidence' that Bligh sought to benefit himself financially 'by giving his crew short rations' – the evidence is clear that he did. Bligh *did* advance Christian money at the Cape of Good Hope. It is not true that the expedition became troubled only at Tahiti and, more particularly, on the return passage – there was abundant trouble on the outward voyage. Bligh *did not* indicate that Midshipman George Stewart was 'dark-skinned' in his List of Mutineers. *Bounty*'s voyage was *not* the first attempt 'to exploit the discoveries made by the numerous English-sponsored voyages to the Pacific' – a number of fur-trading ventures to the north-west American coast and the colonisation of New South Wales preceded it. The suggestion of Polynesian migration to New South Wales was James Burney's, not Bligh's.[52]

---

52 (In order) Alexander 2003, p. 364; McKee 1962, p. 78; Danielsson 1963, p. 37; Darby 1965, p. 69; Montgomerie 1937, p. 21, Darby 1965, p. 80, Alexander 2003, p. 127; Salmond 2011, p. 215; Hough 1979, p. 63; Darby 1965, p. 57, Hough 1979, p. 112.

Now, we all can make such mistakes, but even simple ones can have significant interpretative consequences. Here is one example. In general, Alexander McKee's account is better than most. He was alert to Bligh's prevarications and omissions, and to his determination to show the world that he was blameless for what happened. But then, in discussing the mutiny, McKee said:

> The indecision of [Stewart and Heywood], and also that of some even of the actual mutineers, is hard to understand if they are thought of as mature men, capable of weighing the consequences of their acts. But, in fact, they were all youngsters; for some of them, it was the first time they had ever been to sea. [At the time of the mutiny,] Heywood was seventeen, Stewart twenty-three; most of the able seamen were aged about twenty. It was a collection of kids, led by a young man acting on impulse; hence the muddled nature of the affair. That it succeeded, was a measure of Bligh's incompetence as a manager of men.[53]

As we do not know the exact birth dates of most of *Bounty*'s crew, it is difficult to be precise about their ages at the time of the mutiny (28 April 1789). Let me therefore give the ages of those whom Bligh listed as mutineers, as stated in the ship's muster and paybooks when they signed on between August and November 1787, and in Bligh's description of them immediately after the event (Table 1).[54]

There are some obvious discrepancies in this table. Christian was in fact twenty-three years and seven months at the time of the mutiny. Ellison's true age at signing on seems to have been fifteen. Burkett could not have aged only one year between 1787 and 1789, nor Hilbrant. Williams could not have gone from being twenty-six to twenty-five; Martin could not have stayed at thirty, nor Skinner at twenty-two. Muspratt could not have aged three years, nor Thompson.

Nonetheless, let us look at the lists as they stand. Of those identified (rightly or wrongly) as mutineers, only Peter Heywood and Tom Ellison

---

53   McKee 1962, pp. 126–7.
54   1) Inclusion in Bonner Smith 1936; 2) Bligh, [List of Mutineers], Bligh 1987, pp. 213–18.

Introduction: The Troubled History of *Bounty*'s Story

Midshipmen (1), (2)	**Seamen (1), (2)**
	Alexander Smith [i.e., John Adams] 20, 22
Fletcher Christian, 21 [22], 24	Thomas Burkett, 25, 26 Michael Byrne, –, 28 Charles Churchill, 28, 30 Joseph Coleman, 36, 40
	Thomas Ellison, 19 [15], 17
Peter Heywood, 15, 17	Henry Hilbrant, 24, 25
	Isaac Martin, 30, 30
George Stewart, 21, 23	William McCoy, –, 25 Thomas McIntosh, –, 28 John Mills, 39, 40
Edward Young, 21, 22	John Millward, 21, 22 James Morrison 28
	William Muspratt, 27, 30 Charles Norman, –, 26
Gardener	Matthew Quintal, –, 21
William Brown –, 27	Richard Skinner, 22, 22
	John Sumner, 22, 24
	Mathew Thompson, 37, 40
	John Williams, 26, 25

Table 1 The ages of the alleged mutineers, as stated in (1) the ship's muster and (2) Bligh's description of them immediately after the event. Ages given in square brackets indicate known corrections.

can accurately be described as 'youngsters'. Nor is it true that 'most of the seamen were aged about 20'. It would seem that at the start of the voyage only two (Ellison and perhaps Quintal) were under twenty; that five (Adams, McCoy, Millward, Quintal, Skinner) were twenty to twenty-three; and that the rest were twenty-four and upwards. When we remember (as I pointed out earlier) that the navy was a young man's occupation, these seamen are likely to have together possessed a wealth of experience. Unfortunately, we simply don't know enough about the previous histories of most of them to be able to establish this beyond doubt. However, take the example of Fletcher Christian. At the age of twenty-two to twenty-four years, he was on at least his fourth sea-service aboard the *Bounty*, with that on the *Eurydice*, first at Portsmouth, then to India and back, having occupied some twenty-six months.

McKee's earlier, countervailing, characterisation of the seamen who mutinied is in fact the more apt one. Pointing out that they included nine of the ten men whom Bligh had flogged (and he might also have added that seven had received treatment for venereal infection), he described them as the 'armed, hardened, and determined core of the revolt'.[55] It is obvious that the preference for one view rather than the other makes a real difference to interpretation. If the mutineers were a collection of young, inexperienced men, then Bligh's tyranny and mismanagement caused them to rebel; if, on the other hand, they were mostly a bunch of toughs, then Bligh was indeed (as he said) run down by his own dogs and betrayed by those he had cared for. Which view better accords with *Bounty*'s history?

✳ ✳ ✳

Many of the factual errors and the faulty conclusions drawn from them might be corrected fairly easily. However, the conceptual and methodological failings in the telling of *Bounty*'s history are less tractable.

As Rolf Du Rietz has repeatedly pointed out, it was Christian who mutinied against Bligh, with some junior and warrant officers and a group of seamen joining him:

> Mutiny, by definition, means rebellion against established authority, and as the commander himself was the only person on board who was superior to Christian in rank, it follows that Bligh was the one, and the only one, against whom Christian's mutiny could be directed. The two principal protagonists, or indeed antagonists, of the drama are thus identified beyond any

---

55 McKee 1962, p. 94.

reasonable doubt, quite regardless of the motives of Christian's action, or the motives of his supporters.

As it is very doubtful that there would have been a mutiny without Christian's agency, rather than 'Who or what caused the mutiny?', the relevant questions to ask are 'What caused Christian to mutiny?' and 'What led the officers and seamen to follow him?' And here, as Du Rietz has also pointed out, what George Stewart or anyone else said to Christian did not *cause* him to act as he did.[56] Neither was the absence of a detachment of marines a *cause* of the mutiny, as Bligh claimed. (And in any case, what is there to say that marines might not also have supported Christian rather than Bligh?) These might seem straightforward points, but many writers have done their level best to avoid recognising them.

There is a more pernicious flaw, however – one that has resulted in a fundamental falsification of *Bounty*'s history for these past 228 years. This is a far too easy acceptance of the accuracy of what Bligh wrote about the voyage and the mutiny.

Ever since his narratives were published (1790, 1792), some critics have questioned Bligh's impartiality and accuracy. In 1794, Edward Christian raised these issues with Banks; and in his *Appendix to the Minutes* (1794), while not excusing his brother's mutiny, he asserted that 'every friend to truth and strict justice must feel his attention awakened to the true causes and circumstances, which have hitherto been concealed or misrepresented'. In 1831, W.H. Smyth indicated that Bligh's *Narrative* was 'proved to be false in many material bearings, by evidence before a Court-Martial'; and Barrow said that 'the accusation ... of Bligh having falsified his *Narrative* is a very heavy charge and, it is to be feared, is not wholly without foundation'.[57] This last is a charitable assessment, for the fact is that William Bligh, first, and then his editors, ruthlessly 'adjusted' the generic account so as to absolve him of blame.

---

56   Du Rietz 2007, p. 196, and 1965, p. 14.
57   For a reflection of the contents of Christian's letters, see Bligh's letters to Banks, [December 1790], Bligh Miscellaneous, pp. 19–26; Christian [1794] 1952, p. 61; Smyth 1831, p. 469; Barrow [1831] 1989, p. 81.

The imperatives of *Bounty*'s voyage made this manipulation essential, for its failure was a catastrophe for just about all concerned. The Admiralty lost a good ship. The Pitt administration lost a large investment in the cargo of plants. Sir Joseph Banks's prestige and his influence with the government were threatened. William Bligh lost his first Royal Navy command, and the prospect of a handsome reward. The Bountys lost their careers and their possessions. Numbers of them also lost their lives, as did dozens of islanders. The British public was uncomfortably reminded of the tenuous nature of social cohesion.

The one thing above all others that might restore the normal order of things for Bligh, the authorities and the public would be the demonstration that this mutiny was an irruption of chaos as unpredictable as it was unwarranted. If it could be clearly shown that Bligh had been a compassionate commander with the welfare of his crew always in mind; that the voyage had gone smoothly until the mutiny; and that Christian and his followers were ungrateful men set on pursuing their own selfish and lustful ends, who had given no prior indication of their evil intentions, then the genie of chaos might be forced back into the bottle.

From the moment he began to write about the mutiny, Bligh started this process of establishing what he termed these 'sacred truths', and thereby absolving himself of any responsibility for events.[58] Over and over, he represented himself as the good commander betrayed by evil men whose friend he had been. He wrote to his wife, Betsy, from Coupang on 19 August 1789, for example, that he had left the Friendly Islands (Tonga) at the end of April with 'my expectations raised to the highest pitch, of the great success I was likely to meet with – The Ship in the most perfect order and every soul well'; and that 'the Secrisy of this Mutiny is beyond all conception so that I cannot discover that any who are with me had the least knowledge of it'.

From Batavia, he told his former employer Duncan Campbell and Banks the same things. He repeated these claims in his first narrative of events and his log, both of which he worked on during the passage home from Batavia; then in the published *Narrative of the Mutiny, on Board His Majesty's Ship Bounty*; and again in the *Voyage to the South*

---

58   Bligh to Banks, [undated], Bligh Miscellaneous, p. 19.

Sea. Also, at Batavia, the survivors were required jointly to swear an affidavit giving details of the mutiny and stating that Bligh had not been responsible for the loss of the ship.[59] As we shall see, however, the truth is that Bligh had anything but a harmonious relationship with his officers and seamen during the voyage, which was marked from the outset by his verbal abuse and duplicity and their resentment and dissension.

We are hampered in our quest to understand the full extent of Bligh's misrepresentations and lies because at crucial points his recording was neither complete nor contemporaneous. While his account of the open-boat passage is as near a daily record as sailing conditions permitted, what we have for *Bounty*'s voyage to and from Tahiti are two versions of a log, parts of which Bligh wrote up subsequently. Here, it is very significant that almost the whole section dealing with the stay at Tahiti, from 26 October 1788 to 4 April 1789, is missing from the Mitchell Library copy, which seems to antedate the Admiralty one. However, the index to this section that Bligh compiled refers to some circumstances that are also not included in the later copy. For example, there are the entries 'Mr Hallett's Contumacy' and 'Mr Hallett's behaviour', which might refer to the midshipman's refusal to enter deep water because he could not swim or to additional incidents – i.e. Bligh might have suppressed several criticisms of John Hallett. Given this, who can now say just how much evidence of his junior officers' performance (faulty or otherwise) and of the crew's general discontent he chose not to record?[60]

Nonetheless, from records kept by others and from some of Bligh's later private comments, we can identify many incidents that he did not mention in either version of his log. On the outward voyage, these include disputes over missing cheeses, substitution of pumpkin for bread, and a failure to ascertain that the contents of the meat casks

---

59   Bligh to Elizabeth Bligh, 19 August, to Campbell, 12 October, to Banks, 13 October 1789, Bligh 1989, pp. 23–4, 29, 31, 33; Bligh 1790, p. 20; entry, 28 April 1789, Bligh Log 2, vol. 2, pp. 122–3; Bligh 1790, pp. 9–10; Bligh 1792, pp. 162–4; Bligh [1794] 1952, pp. 6–8.
60   Bligh Index, with references to pp. 180 and 206 of the missing section of Bligh Log 1.

weighted correctly. At Tahiti, there were the troubles involving Hallett and the midshipman Thomas Hayward; a list of names of supposed deserters/mutineers found in Charles Churchill's chest after he deserted the ship with two others on 5 January 1789; and Bligh's finding fault with Christian. On the return voyage, there was the criticism of Christian's handling of the ship; and the incident of the missing coconuts. Then there were the disputes with Fryer on the Barrier Reef islands. Clearly, Bligh decided that to include details of these events would be inimical to his maintaining the necessary depictions of himself as a good and caring commander and of the voyage as trouble-free until the moment of mutiny.

In preparing *A Voyage to the South Sea* for publication, Bligh and his editors James Burney and Sir Joseph Banks were also very concerned to maintain these depictions – as Banks told Bligh: 'we shall Abridge considerably what you wrote in order as far as we are able to Satisfy the Public & place you in such a Point of view as they Shall approve'.[61] To do so, the editors continued the process of suppression and misrepresentation that Bligh had begun. As Bligh had not expunged details of all potentially unfavourable incidents from the fair copy of his log, the editors chose to downplay the seriousness of some and to ignore others entirely. They omitted all details of Bligh's frequent and comprehensive rages against his officers for their incompetence and wilful neglect of duty, such as those for 5 January 1789, following the desertion of the three seamen and for 17 January 1789, when he learnt that the master and boatswain had evidently failed to air the spare sails properly.[62] For Burney and Banks to have mentioned these incidents would have made apparent the fiction of a trouble-free voyage.

Similarly, these editors reduced the incidence of punishment during the voyage. They did include the flogging of Matthew Quintal (twenty-four lashes on 3 March 1788 for 'insolence and mutinous behaviour'), and of Isaac Martin on 30 January 1789 (nineteen lashes for 'striking an Indian').[63] However, they did not mention Bligh's

---

61 Banks to Bligh, 21 July 1791, Banks 2008–13, vol. 3, no. 178, p. 242.
62 Entries, 5 and 17 January 1789, Bligh Log 2, vol. 2, pp. 12, 18.
63 Bligh 1792, pp. 26–7, 120.

Introduction: The Troubled History of *Bounty*'s Story

ordering John Williams '6 lashes for neglect of duty in heaving the lead' on 25 May 1788; the twelve lashes he gave to William Muspratt on 27 December for 'neglect of duty'; and the twelve lashes he gave to Robert Lamb, the butcher, on 29 December for 'suffering his Cleaver to be Stolen'. Neither did they mention his stopping John Mills's and William Brown's grog for refusing to dance on 19 October.[64]

Then there is the way in which the editors altered Bligh's account of the desertion of Charles Churchill, William Muspratt and John Millward. With the help of Tahitian friends, this trio fled to another island on 5 January 1789, taking with them arms and ammunition. After chiefs had located them, Bligh captured them on 23 January. The next day, he gave Churchill twelve lashes and Muspratt and Millward each twenty-four, and put them in irons. On 4 February, he repeated these floggings, then released the men back to duty. There is no mention of these punishments in the *Voyage*, nor that Bligh 'disrated' Thomas Hayward, the midshipman who had been in charge of the watch when the trio absconded, and 'turned him before the Mast' (i.e., punished him by making him do duty as a common seaman).[65]

Similarly, Burney and Banks downplayed the troubles Bligh had with some of the men during the open-boat voyage to Timor. Presumably on the assumption that it demonstrated Bligh's admirable concern for the general welfare of his men, they did include his statement that he gave Robert Lamb 'a good beating' for stealing away to consume the birds he caught himself, rather than sharing them with his ravenous companions.[66] They also included a truncated account of how Bligh challenged William Purcell to a duel with cutlasses, after they had quarrelled over oysters and Purcell had said that he 'was as good a man' as Bligh. Fryer said that when Purcell refused to fight his commander (which would have entailed an offence punishable by death), Bligh swaggered 'with [a] cutlass over the carpenter's head'.

---

64 Entries, 25 May, 19 October, 27 and 29 December 1788, Bligh Log 2, vol. 1, pp. 222, 360, vol. 2, pp. 7–8.
65 Entries, 5–24 January and 4 February 1789, Bligh Log 2, vol. 2, pp. 11–23, 30. Cf. Bligh 1792, pp. 113–4, 118–20.
66 Entry, 2 June 1789, Bligh Log 2, vol. 2, p. 199; Bligh 1792, pp. 215–6.

Burney and Banks also omitted from this particular story the detail that when Fryer tried to arrest him, Bligh threatened to kill him first.[67]

Even when these editors did include details of such incidents, they repeatedly diminished their significance. We learn in the *Voyage* that by the time Bligh caught up with the deserters, they had become tired of their fugitive life and wished to return to the ship, so as 'to avoid the disgrace of being seized and brought back'. This is practically the opposite of what Bligh wrote in the log, which was:

> How far true this might be I could not judge with certainty, but I beleive that they were so much harassed by the Natives that they were attempting to get to Morea or some of the other Islands without any intention to return to me if the bad weather had not forced them into the Harbour, and even here perhaps I should not have got them, if their Ammunition had not got Spoiled by the Wet.[68]

In the *Voyage*, we also read that when Bligh challenged him on Sunday Island, Purcell 'immediately made concessions'; and the editors have Bligh comment, 'I did not allow this to interfere further with the harmony of the boat's crew, and every thing soon became quiet.'[69] In the log, though, Bligh recorded that the tumult with Purcell and Fryer 'lasted about a quarter of an hour'; and he qualified his concern for his men with: 'I did not suffer this to interfere with the harmony of the well disposed who it is my duty to make known.' He named ten men. That is, Bligh considered the other seven inveterate troublemakers; and he gave a strong indication of how fraught circumstances had become when he said that he challenged Purcell to the duel as 'I did not just now see where this was to end, I therefore determined to strike a final blow at it, and either to preserve my Command or die in the attempt.' He added that thereafter he 'determined never [not] to have [a cutlass] ... under

---

67 Bligh 1792, pp. 209–10; Fryer 1934, pp. 71–3;
68 Bligh 1792, p. 119; Entry, 23 January 1789, Bligh Log 2, vol. 2, p. 22.
69 Bligh 1792, p. 210.

my seat, or out of my Reach'.[70] This is the very opposite of everything soon becoming 'quiet' and 'harmonious' again.

And if all this is not enough evidence of the disjuncture between the real story and its public representation, there is this. At Coupang, Bligh obtained a small vessel, which he named the *Resource*, to get him and his men to Batavia. By the time they reached Surabaya, on the north-east coast of Java, relations between him and his remaining crew were again at flashpoint. Having gone on shore to organise supplies of fresh food, Bligh returned on board to find Elphinstone and Hallett indisposed below. According to Bligh, when he asked Fryer whether they were ill or drunk, the master replied, 'Am I a Doctor?' When Bligh demanded, 'What do you mean by this insolence?', Fryer replied, 'It is no insolence. You not only use me Ill, but every Man in the vessel and every Man will say the same.'

Upon this, Bligh 'seized a Bayonet and instantly put the Master and Carpenter below'. He then had the town's commandant question 'my Mutinous Fellows', to learn that one or other of them had told Dutch soldiers and sailors that 'I should be hanged or blown from the Mouth of a Cannon as soon as I got home.' Next, Bligh requested the governor to conduct a formal enquiry, and to continue Fryer's and Purcell's arrests, not only to Batavia but also to England, where he intended to have them tried for 'having acted tumultuously on board His Brittanick Majesty's Schooner *Resource*'.

When questioned, Fryer told the governor and commandant that Bligh had falsified financial accounts at Coupang; and he and Purcell said that it had been Bligh's stinting of the food ration that had led to the mutiny. Somehow, this second mutiny was resolved when Fryer wrote another letter of abject apology (presumably dictated by Bligh). Tellingly, though, when Bligh took the pair ashore to be examined, he did so accompanied by others, 'for I no longer found my Honour or Person safe among these people'. And when they proceeded on to Batavia, Bligh would not have the mutinous pair in the *Resource*, insisting that they travel in accompanying prows.[71]

---

70 Entry, 31 May 1789, Bligh Log 2, vol. 2, p. 192.
71 For the details following, see 'Particular Transactions at Sourabya', 15–17 September 1789, Bligh 1937, pp. 64–71.

Although Bligh recorded the details of this tumult in his original record, he did not mention them in the narrative he wrote during his passage from Batavia to Cape Town. Rather, he offered only the two mundane statements, 'on the 13th [September] I arrived at Sourabya Latd 7°10'S 1°52'W', and 'on the 17th September sailed from Sourabya'. He merely repeated these statements in the published *Narrative*.[72] Nothing about it appears in the *Voyage*, where Burney and Banks contented themselves with paraphrasing Bligh's description of how pleasant and fertile the environs of Surabaya were; and with mentioning how the Java horses were small but 'handsome and strong', and how the mountains behind were 'infested with a breed of fierce tygers, which makes travelling inland very dangerous'.[73] (Here, I am assuming that Bligh preserved the details of the doings at Surabaya in the copy of this section of his log that went to Burney. Even if he did not, though, the point concerning deliberate suppression remains.)

The longstanding charge that Bligh, and after him his editors, resorted to distortion, omission and lies in order to present a narrative of events that would exonerate him from all blame is entirely justified. As Du Rietz summed up, 'Nearly every detail in [Bligh's] version seems to be designed with the purpose of convincing the authorities, patrons, and friends in England that William Bligh was not to blame, and that he was the innocent victim of totally undeserved misfortune.'[74]

✳ ✳ ✳

Unfortunately, many modern writers have gone to great lengths to avoid confronting the inconvenient truth that Bligh's versions of *Bounty*'s story are riddled with suppression and misrepresentation. Danielsson and Darby, for example, accepted without question that Bligh's accounts are accurate. Kennedy prefaced his 1978 study with the wise caveat:

---

72 Bligh 1790, p. 158; Bligh 1790, p. 87.
73 Bligh 1792, pp. 249–50. Cf. 'Particular Transactions at Sourabya', 15–17 September 1789, Bligh 1937, pp. 70–1.
74 Du Rietz 2009, passim, and pp. 23–24.

books and documents on Bligh are crowded with misrepresentation and outright falsehood, and to get through to the essential person it is necessary to comment on the literature that purports to represent his life. The motives of the writers must be looked at and nothing accepted uncritically.

Nonetheless, when it came to Bligh's accounts, Kennedy accepted their veracity, announcing that he had based his story of *Bounty*'s voyage up to the point of the mutiny on Bligh's 'daily' log, because:

> The ship's Log was a legal document, and the legal presumption was that it was an accurate reflection of what went on during a voyage. Captains were obliged to keep a Log and record all events; punishments, the weather, any sailing orders such as changes in the sails, and any work the crew was ordered to carry out. It was a faithful record of everything, momentous and trivial, and with the Captain's remarks written alongside provided the Admiralty with a legal picture of what had happened.[75]

So, *ipso facto*, a legal document tells the truth! This is nonsense. Legal documents may sometimes set forth a matter accurately, but frequently they are designed to obfuscate rather than illuminate, often where fraud, property disputes and failed relationships are concerned, all of which were present on *Bounty*'s voyage.

Some writers have offered convoluted – indeed, preposterous – explanations in their efforts to avoid the obvious conclusions. Mackaness observed:

> Bligh had been accused both of deliberately falsifying his published account and also, by suppressing certain incriminating passages, of presenting his own case in the best possible light ... We are compelled to conclude that while he is certainly not guilty of deliberately falsifying his narrative, he *is* guilty of suppressing important passages.

---

75 Kennedy 1978, pp. xi, 30–31.

Evidently, suppression is no indication of wishing to avoid the truth getting out – that is, of dishonesty! Mackaness concedes that Bligh never published his account of the 'Particular Transactions at Sourabya' in his log of the voyage in the *Resource* – he 'kept entirely silent about the affair'; but because he 'committed to paper the whole of the unpleasant details [with] Pepysian frankness', this means that his record must be true.[76]

Kennedy repeated this fundamental error when he asserted that because Bligh included a narrative of events at Surabaya in one copy of his log and that in it he made 'no effort to gloss over [his opponents'] charges against him', his is 'an authentic account of what they said'. Possibly. But did Bligh give the full story? And why did he omit this narrative in the copy of the log he gave to the Admiralty? Again, then, in Kennedy's view Bligh's recording details of the conflict at Surabaya makes his record true, but omitting later mention of it is not a sign of duplicity, but rather that he was acting 'in his own best interest'; but then, Kennedy termed Edward Christian 'hypocritical' for attempting to present his brother in a favourable light.[77] Why the double standard?

Concerning the events at Surabaya, Alexander said, 'Bligh's unsqueamish report of the range of complaints against him would tend to indicate that these were not issues in which he feared public scrutiny.' This really raises the question of how there might have been any scrutiny when Bligh concealed the details? And she says more generally of the charge that Bligh 'deliberately omitt[ed] certain events' from *A Voyage to the South Sea*, 'the fact that he had so casually turned this project over to a colleague can only indicate that for William Bligh the events on the *Bounty* had been, quite literally, an open book'.[78] The evidence that I have just presented shows rather that Bligh was comfortable with Burney and Banks preparing the work for publication because he knew that they would continue the process of omission and misrepresentation that he had begun.

* * *

---

76   Mackaness 1951, pp. 133, 164
77   Kennedy 1978, pp. 234–5, and 1989, pp. 173, 177.
78   Alexander 2003, pp. 158, 179.

Nowhere has this naive reliance on Bligh's narratives had a more detrimental effect on the telling of *Bounty*'s story than in the portrayal of the commander's unfortunate subordinate officers. Of the major commentators in the past eighty-odd years, there has been only one who has not readily accepted the accuracy of Bligh's accounts of his quarrels with and the validity of his criticisms of that much put-upon pair, John Fryer (master) and William Purcell (carpenter). Mackaness found Fryer to have been 'perverse and cantankerous', 'as obnoxious as Purcell', 'troublesome' and guilty of 'culpable neglect'; while Purcell was 'one of the most troublesome men on board', repeatedly guilty of 'mutinous and insolent behaviour'. Rutter said 'almost every page [of Fryer's account of the voyage] smoulders with a sulky resentment, and … it becomes plainer and plainer how Fryer hated Bligh: hated him with all the intensity of the weak man's ineffectual hatred of the strong'.[79]

Montgomerie agreed that Bligh and Fryer came to hate each other, but he also thought Fryer incompetent and, to boot, 'a dreaming, conceited, sentimental, and unpractical person, not in the least likely to commend himself to such an uncompromising realist as Bligh'; and that 'on controversial matters [Fryer's narrative] is only to be accepted with great caution, if at all'.[80] (An aside: I wonder how Montgomerie would have felt if his commanding officer had read the Articles of War to force him to do something against his conscience; or told him that when they were back in England he would have him dismissed from the service 'in five minutes'; or threatened to run him through, or else to 'break every bone in [his] skin'?[81] But of course to contemplate this, one would need to accept Fryer's narrative as truthful.)

In Danielsson's view, Fryer was 'irresolute', and given to making 'a fool of himself', while Purcell was an 'incorrigible trouble-maker', 'hot-tempered and sharp-tongued'. Hough thought Fryer was a 'difficult, quarrelsome man', one who was 'sloppy and indolent', and that 'but for his slackness there could never have been a mutiny', while Purcell was also a 'troublemaker'. Kennedy considered it quite likely that Fryer

---

79 Mackaness 1951, pp. 109, 110, 132; Rutter, Introduction, Bligh 1934, p. 18.
80 Montgomerie 1937, pp. 19, 295.
81 Memoranda, 8 July and 16 September 1789, Fryer 1934, pp. 79, 81.

was 'one of [the world's] most consistent liars'. He also found Purcell 'obstructive' in his behaviour and guilty of refusing to do duty. Dening found Fryer 'weak', 'cantankerous and easily wounded', while Purcell was 'the most troublesome man on the *Bounty*' (though he did concede that he was also 'much maligned'). To Alexander, Fryer was weak and untrustworthy, 'tight-lipped and self-righteous' and given to dwelling on 'petty personal slights and oversights'.[82] Mundle saw Fryer as 'belligerent and troublesome' and Purcell as 'recalcitrant', and that together they tried to 'create disorder'.[83] Only Rolf Du Rietz has clearly understood how awry have been the representations of these warrant officers, though even he has not tied Bligh's distortions to the way in which his demands required them to compromise themselves in fulfilling their duties.[84]

※ ※ ※

While Fryer and Purcell were the officers who most aroused Bligh's ire, at one time or another he damned many of the others for their failings: Fletcher Christian; the midshipmen John Hallett, Thomas Hayward, Peter Heywood and George Stewart; the boatswain William Cole; the butcher Robert Lamb. Bligh's complaints about the officers were comprehensive:

> Such neglectfull and worthless petty Officers I beleive never was in a Ship as are in this. No Orders for a few hours together are Obeyed by them, and their conduct in general is so bad, that no confidence or trust can be reposed in them, in short they have drove me to every thing but Corporal punishment and that must follow if they do not improve.[85]

---

82 Danielsson 1963, pp. 45, 46, 66, 81; Hough 1972, pp. 16, 19, 212; Kennedy 1978, pp. 42–4, 120; Dening 1992, pp. 81, 83–4 98; Alexander, pp. 159–60, 174–5.
83 Mundle 2010, pp. 99, 111, 187.
84 Du Rietz 1981, esp. p. 8.
85 Entry, 5 January 1789, Bligh Log 2, vol. 2, p. 12

Introduction: The Troubled History of *Bounty*'s Story

True to form, the majority of writers have taken Bligh at his word. Montgomerie observed, 'He could look for little assistance from his officers whom he had to supervise minutely in every way lest their carelessness and incompetence should destroy the whole undertaking.' Dening said much the same thing, remarking that though Bligh himself had been largely responsible for choosing his officers:

> one day he would come to curse their incompetence, to berate their lack of commitment, to despair at their irresponsibility. He always had the sour sense that they had somehow been put upon him. And they, to judge from their extravagant ineptitude, had a sense that they were owed, more than that they were owing.[86]

There are strange aspects here, though. Before *Bounty*'s voyage, Fletcher Christian sailed in the *Eurydice* out to Madras in the capacity of midshipman, where the captain promoted him to acting lieutenant when he was nineteen and a half years old – a move that must reflect approval of his demeanour and abilities. After *Bounty*'s voyage, Fryer had a long career as ship's master and received strong praise for his work, including that from Captain Foley that he was 'a very good navigator, a very sober man, well informed in his profession and of great exertion'.[87]

How to explain the discrepancy between these circumstances and Bligh's bitter criticisms? Rutter's way was to stick with Bligh, though with the rather subverting qualification that 'he had a sinister knack, often noticeable in schoolmasters and other persons in authority, of drawing out the worst from another's character rather than the best'. McKee followed Rutter, saying that Bligh's personality seemed 'to bring out the worst in the men he commanded. And his uncontrolled rages had no effect whatever, but rather the reverse of what was intended, producing sullen hostility instead of a smartening of discipline'. Kennedy's was similar. Speculating that after *Bounty* sailed from Tahiti, Christian became distressed by the loss of the island's easy life and of his lover Mauatua, distress compounded by the thought that she would

---

86 Montgomerie 1937, p. 25; Dening 1992, p. 21.
87 Fryer Naval Service 2, p. 2.

soon take another and by Bligh's loss of confidence in him, Kennedy wrote:

> There must have been a contrast between the West Indian voyages where Bligh and Christian had liked and trusted each other, and the new scornful impatience which Bligh was showing all his officers as his command structure fell apart. These stresses may have made [Christian] inefficient, and Bligh's tetchiness may have increased his mental torment.[88]

Do competent people suddenly become incompetent? Yes, sometimes, when subjected to extreme stress or grief, or when the anxieties of old age overwhelm them. But there is another way we might approach this problem, which is to ask whether Bligh's assessments of his officers' failings were objective, and therefore trustworthy. What if these assessments were examples of his irrational raging, designed (whether consciously or not) to shift responsibility for any impending failure of the voyage to his officers? Fryer later told his daughters that Bligh was 'as Tyrannical in his temper in the boat as in the Ship, and that his Chief thought was his own comfort' – which I take to be an oblique reference to the claim made by Fryer in his narrative that during the passage to Timor Purcell and others had often seen Bligh give himself greater amounts of food than those he served to the rest of the party.[89]

Let us look at three examples: two involving Fryer's and Christian's management of the *Bounty*, the third Fryer and Cole's care of the sails. At the onset of the wet season, with its powerful storms and torrential rains, Bligh decided to move *Bounty* from Matavai Bay, on the north coast of Tahiti, to the much more secure To'aroa Harbour, in the district of Pare to the south. After Fryer had examined the anchorage on 24 December 1788, finding '16 to 17 fathoms of Water with a good bottom all the Way', the next day Bligh sent Christian ahead in the launch with the shore party's equipment and spare spars, with instructions to meet the ship at the entrance to the harbour and lead it to safety. As they

---

88   Rutter, Introduction, Bligh 1934, p. 18; McKee 1962, p. 67; Kennedy 1978, pp. 97–8.
89   Fryer Naval Service 1; Fryer 1934, p. 78.

approached the rendezvous, Bligh placed a man in the chains and Fryer on the foreyard to respectively sound and scout the passage ahead. However, at the entrance the ship went to windward of the launch, thus becalming it, so that the *Bounty* passed into the harbour ahead of its intended guide. It then grounded lightly on a small platform reef that Fryer had not seen on the previous day, when the sky and sea had been dark with rain. Using anchors, they succeeded in freeing the ship without its suffering significant damage.[90]

Bligh professed himself 'astonished' at this untoward event, and implicitly blames it on Fryer's and Christian's ineptitude. However, it was probably a simple misadventure. Morrison's account is much more mundane:

> standing in, [the ship] run on a coral rock which had escaped the Masters sight; the sea Breeze being set in gave us some trouble before we got her off[,] which however we did before night, & moord with one Bower & and the Kedge, till Morning; when we moord with Both bowers.[91]

When we remember that in Cook's passage up the Queensland coast inside the Great Barrier Reef, 'without ever once having a Leadsman out of the Chains, with sometimes one two and three boats a head to direct us',[92] and moreover sailing gently on a 'clear moonlight night', the *Endeavour* still grounded on a platform reef, we may consider that navigation in a clumsy ship in tropical, reef-strewn seas was inevitably a hazardous business. When difficulties arose, they were not necessarily due to incompetence.

The second incident relates to Christian's handling of *Bounty* on 21 April 1789, when they were nearing the Tongan Islands on the return voyage. In his log, Bligh noted, 'Very Squally and dark gloomy Wr with constant Rain', and that the night was 'Windy and Weather very unsettled'. However, he made no criticism of Christian. Neither

---

90 Entries, 24 and 25 December 1788, Bligh Log 2, vol. 1, p. 427, vol. 2, p. 5.
91 Morrison 1935, p. 30.
92 Entry, 11 June 1770, and to Walker, 13 September 1771, Cook 1955–67, vol. 1, pp. 343–4, 508.

did Morrison mention a clash. The sailmaker Lawrence Lebogue later sketched the incident: 'The Captain came on deck one night and found fault with Christian, because in a squall he had not taken care of the sails.' Fryer was enigmatic, saying, 'Mr Bligh and Mr Christian had some words, when Mr Christian told Mr Bligh – Sir your abuse is so bad that I cannot do my duty with any Pleasure, I have been [in] hell for weeks with you[.] Several other disagreeable words past which had been frequently the case in the course of the voyage.'[93] Given the absence of detail, how are we to judge whether Christian performed incompetently?

The third incident concerns Fryer and Cole's care of the spare sails. Bligh recorded for 17 January 1789, about halfway through their stay at Tahiti:

> This Morning the Sail Room being cleared to take the Sails on shore to Air, the New Fore Topsail and Fore sail, Main Topmt Stay sail & Main Staysail were found very much Mildewed and rotten in many places.
>
> If I had any Officers to supercede the Master and Boatswain, or was capable of doing without them, considering them as common Seamen, they should no longer occupy their respective Stations. Scarce any neglect of duty can equal the criminality of this, for it appears that altho the Sails have been taken out twice since I have been in the Island, which I thought fully sufficient and I had trusted to their reports, Yet these New Sails never were brought out, [n]or is it certain whether they have been out since we left England, yet notwithstanding as often as the Sails were taken to air by my Orders they were reported to me to be in good Order. To remedy the deffects I attended and saw the Sails put into the Sea and hung on shore to day to be ready for repairing.[94]

As someone who has lived in tropical Queensland, where the monsoon and cyclone season usually extends from about mid-

---

93 Entry, 21 April 1789, Bligh Log 2, vol. 2, p. 108; Lebogue, Affidavit, Bligh [1794] 1952, p. 25; Fryer 1934, p. 53.
94 Entry, 17 January 1789, Bligh Log 2, vol. 2, p. 18.

Introduction: The Troubled History of *Bounty*'s Story

November until the end of March, I can say that it would be unsurprising if the spare sails had mildewed while *Bounty* was at Tahiti, again without this necessarily being evidence of incompetence; but to pursue this further would be only to speculate. On the other hand, we may legitimately wonder whether Bligh exaggerated their poor condition. Morrison reports that early in May 1789, as *Bounty* was sailing for Tubuai after the mutiny, a 'heavy squall ... split the Fore topsail'. He adds, 'this was the first accident of the kind we experienced during the voyage, and was Chiefly owing to the sails being much worn, however it was soon replaced'.[95] As *Bounty*'s voyage continued for another eight months, we may wonder how decrepit the spare foretopsail actually was.

The more important question here is what corroborating evidence do we have that Christian, Fryer and Cole were as culpable as Bligh said? The short answer is none. Yet writer after writer has simply accepted the veracity of Bligh's strictures – for example, Mackaness:

> We have noted also the righteous indignation of the commander when he discovered that, through the neglect of the master and the boatswain, the new sails had become mildewed and rotten. Sails, the only means of progress or escape possessed by the ship, were allowed, through culpable neglect, to rot and mildew by those in whose charge they had been placed.[96]

As I make the issue of the sources' reliability central to my analysis in the first three chapters, let me give only one example of where we do have more than one person's version of events here, and of where those versions are contradictory. After negotiating a passage through the Great Barrier Reef in the open boat, Bligh made a series of short stays at small islands so that his emaciated and exhausted men might find food and rest. They were at one of the Bird cays on 2 June 1789, where they spent the night ashore in order to 'give the People rest by a good fire'. In his notebook of the passage to Timor, this is Bligh's only reference to a fire. In the *Voyage*, however, he tells the story of how,

---

95 Morrison 1935, pp. 47–8.
96 Mackaness 1951, p. 132.

through disobedience of orders, selfishness and stupidity, one of the party started a fire that put them all at great risk:

> Towards evening, I cautioned every one against making too large a fire, or suffering it after dark to blaze up. Mr Samuel and Mr Peckover had the superintendence of this business, which I was strolling about the beach to observe if I thought it could be seen from the main. I was just satisfied that it could not, when on a sudden the island appeared all in a blaze, that might have been discerned at a much more considerable distance. I ran to learn the cause, and found that it was occasioned by the imprudence and obstinacy of one of the party, who, in my absence, had insisted on having a fire to himself; in making which the flames caught the neighbouring grass and rapidly spread. This misconduct might have produced very serious consequences, by discovering our situation to the natives [i.e. on the mainland]; for, if they had attacked us, we had neither arms nor strength to oppose an enemy. Thus the relief which I expected from a little sleep was totally lost, and I anxiously waited for the flowing of the tide, that we might proceed to sea.

He added that he later sent some men to catch turtle, but these had no success: 'This did not surprise me, as it was not be expected that turtle would come near us, after the noise which had been made at the beginning of the evening in extinguishing the fire.'[97]

John Fryer was the person who started the fire. He was outraged by Bligh's depiction of him as a selfish pyromaniac, and wrote a rejoinder after Bligh's *Voyage* had been published. He said that he fell asleep in the late afternoon:

> After I awaked I went in search of some dry wood as the People told me that was lying by the fire they could find none that would burn. I made the Butcher Robert Lamb and Thos Hall the cook go with me we take one of the small Axes & cut down an old tree that was dry & rotten – when I came back it was almost dark. I

---

97 Entry, 2 June 1789, Bligh 1987, p. 135; Bligh 1792, pp. 214–16.

took a small peice of Fire out and said that I will make a fire in that other thicket not with any intention of making a large Blaze – but that I might lay warm. Mr Bligh says that he was down on the beach, looking out and had left Directions with Mr Peckover and his clerk about the fire – I dont recollect that either of them was on the spot — neither did I know that Mr Bligh had left any Directions – I am sorry to say that this is like some other mean tricks that Captain Bligh have commited; the fire had not been lighted long before a spark flew out and communicated to some dry Grass that was near and it Blazed away very fast – when Captain Bligh was very much alarmd fearing the Natives should come and cut him to pieces – but I soon extinguish the Fire by pulling up the dry grass before it – Captain Bligh says the reason of not catching Turtle was in consequence of the Noise that was made. I do not recollect any Body making a noise but Himself.[98]

So we have two quite conflicting accounts of this incident. Bligh says that he left Samuel and Peckover to supervise. Fryer says that neither 'was on the spot'. Bligh says that he 'cautioned every one against making too large a fire, or suffering it after dark to blaze up'. Fryer says that he was unaware of any such direction. Bligh characterises Fryer's action as imprudent, obstinate and selfish. Fryer indicates that he was helping colleagues to obtain fuel for the comforting fire that Bligh had said they might have. He implies that he chose to make one among some bushes so as to conceal it, and that its spread was accidental. Bligh says that the island was 'all in a blaze'. Fryer says that he soon got the fire under control. Bligh presents himself as the concerned commander who is again made anxious by the action of a reprobate crew member. Fryer also indicates that he was concerned for his party's welfare, and says that Bligh's account is another instance of his deceit. Bligh says the commotion attending the fire frightened the turtles away. Fryer says that Bligh was the only one who yelled.

There is no other account of this incident. Given this, and given how much they are at variance, it is difficult to see on what evidential or logical basis we should prefer the one over the other. Perhaps, though,

---

98   Fryer 1934, pp. 72–3.

there is a way to differentiate. Bligh wrote to further his trope of the concerned commander doing his utmost in the face of adverse circumstances, dangers, and recalcitrant and disloyal subordinates. Fryer wrote privately in offended response to what Bligh said in his published narrative. Which circumstance is more likely to involve honesty? But why have almost all writers so readily accepted that the business was as Bligh described it, no matter how potentially prejudicial his account is to Fryer's reputation? As Du Rietz observed:

> Fryer disliked and criticized Bligh, and recorded unfavourable things about him, and therefore his narrative could not be accepted. The fact that the fairness of Bligh's attitude to Fryer was completely unsupported by any evidence, whereas the fairness of Fryer's attitude to Bligh was supported by quite an overwhelming amount of evidence, was blithely overlooked or silently suppressed.[99]

Two more things. Why did Bligh make no mention of the bushfire in his notebook? Is it possible that his published account is a gross exaggeration? And if the party were so emaciated and exhausted as a number of sources (including Bligh's) indicate – David Nelson, for example, could not walk without assistance – how was it that Bligh was able to *run* to the camp, unless he had been feeding himself more?

This naive acceptance of Bligh's narrative demonstrates the essential truth of George Santayana's adage that 'those who cannot remember the past are condemned to repeat it'; or, to adapt it to the present purpose, those writers who have not undertaken a rigorous analysis of the sources so as to be able to recognise the mistakes in earlier accounts will only repeat those mistakes.

✳ ✳ ✳

Some other factors have also marred the writing of *Bounty*'s history. One is the pretension to be able to discern truth from fiction intuitively, or according to some private knowledge not available to others. Glynn

---

99   Du Rietz 1981, p. 8.

Introduction: The Troubled History of *Bounty*'s Story

Christian recognised the problematic nature of the versions of John Adams's story recorded by visitors to Pitcairn, with their contradictory twists and turns. But then, by which criteria did he determine that the last version the old mutineer gave to the world was the 'most reliable'? Only because it best conformed to the story he had already decided to tell?

And then what is the basis of the idea that Christian was working close to his home on the day he was killed, because the birth of his third child was imminent and, indeed, did occur on this very day. Robert Nicolson made this claim in 1965. In the first edition of *Fragile Paradise* (1982), Glynn Christian said that Isabella (Mauatua) 'was due to have another baby at the end of September [1793]', and that Te'ehuteatuaonoa [Jenny], one of the Tahitian women, said that 'Fletcher was working close to home that day, for his wife was about to give birth to their third child. In the second edition (1999), he emphasised that Jenny had said this 'specifically'.[100]

There is a real problem in accepting this claim, for where is the evidence to support it? I have read and reread the published accounts of the interviews with Jenny. In neither the first one (published 1819) nor in either version of the second one (1826, 1829) is this statement ascribed to Jenny. Did Glynn Christian have another source available to him? He doesn't say so, only that 'the easiest place to read what [Jenny] said is in the *United Services Journal* [1829]'. Is this then rather a family tradition? And here, it should also be noted that there is no unimpeachable written or material source to tell us precisely on which late September 1793 day these events supposedly occurred, for, as I shall show, the 'facts' given in the *Pitcairn Island Register* are as problematic as those in Bligh's narratives. And then, on what basis did Anne Salmond decide that the 'further details' of what happened on Pitcairn Island that Glynn Christian gave 'from local island traditions' were authentic and therefore provided valuable insights?[101]

We should be very wary of the accuracy of 'family tradition', which is much more likely to misrepresent the past than to state it accurately. Take my own case. My mother always said that I and my identical

---

100 Nicolson 1965, p. 42; Christian 1982, pp. 198, 241; Christian 1999, p. 402.
101 Christian 1982, pp. 198, 200; Salmond 2011, p. 508.

twin brother were born three months prematurely; that I weighed a mere 30 ounces (850 grams) at birth; that the nurses painted a blue stripe on my brother's foot to distinguish us; and that he died two days after birth. For decades, I simply accepted the accuracy of these details, and repeated them – after all, surely my mother, who was immediately involved in the circumstances of our birth, would know what she was talking about? Then I obtained the Cairns Base Hospital's records, which stated that my and my brother's term of foetal development was at least eight months, which also calls into question my mother's memory of my birth weight. In addition, the records stated that my brother died twelve and three-quarter hours after birth. From another source, I learnt that my brother's head had been so distorted by the forceps used to deliver him that there could be no confusion about which baby was which. If such disparities can arise in the course of one generation's telling of a story, then how much more unreliable must that story become when repeated through seven generations?

Then there have been the speculations for which there is little or no historical warrant. For example, Darby postulated that Fletcher Christian had a 'dual personality' and suffered from 'paranoid delusions', which caused him to develop a love–hate relationship with Bligh, which had a homosexual aspect.[102]

Hough carried the homosexual hypothesis further, reasoning that since this practice was not unknown in Royal Navy ships, it must also have been present on *Bounty*, and therefore best explains the mutiny. His view is that Christian 'loved' Bligh during the voyage out – a feeling that Bligh reciprocated – but that when put in charge of the shore camp at Tahiti, Christian eagerly reverted to heterosexual life, causing Bligh to develop a prolonged jealous rage. On the passage west to Tofua, this rage led to Bligh's intensifying his abuse of officers and seamen to such an extent that 'a sort of madness ... overwhelm[ed] the ship', and the disaffected mutinied. There is no good evidence to support this homosexual hypothesis; and, as Kennedy pointed out, if Bligh and Christian had been lovers, it is impossible that this should not have been known and remarked on by others: 'in all the streams of invective

---

102 Darby 1965, pp. 77–83, 109.

that emerged from the men on board, none of them accused Bligh of homosexuality (which surely would have finished him)'.[103]

Both Darby and Hough also suggested that Edward Young had played a hidden role in inciting the mutiny, by insinuating subversive ideas into Christian's head and those of other mutineers. Hough: 'It needed a Ned Young – the *Bounty*'s Iago – to put steel into Christian's resolve, and to bring about the most celebrated mutiny of all time.' That Young should have had a significant hand in events is not impossible. Alexander has drawn attention to a mid-nineteenth-century report that seems to be based on something Midshipman Robert Tinkler said, that the seamen paid attention to Christian and Young 'because they were genteelly connected'. However, it is by no means clear how directly this story derived from Tinkler, or how much the mid-nineteenth-century writer George Borrow adapted it to suit his purpose thirty-five or so years later. Given these uncertainties, the only real evidence we have for Young's possibly having been a puppetmaster relates to his activities on Pitcairn Island rather than on *Bounty*'s voyage.[104]

Then again, Darby postulated that the democratic ideals of the French Revolution were a factor in the mutiny:

> [It] took place in 1789, the year of the outbreak of the French Revolution, and the class struggle was about to erupt with great violence all over Europe. The conflict between the privileged and under-privileged must therefore be counted as a factor in the affair.

There are some severe difficulties in the way of our accepting this idea. There is no evidence that *Bounty*'s seamen's thinking was imbued with the dangerous and seditious notions of the French Revolution. How could it have been, unless these men were preternaturally endowed with knowledge of the future – an anticipation doubly difficult for those who were illiterate? The French Revolution did not occur until

---

103 Hough 1972, pp. 53, 75–6, 131, 296–300; Kennedy 1978, p. 100, and 1989, pp. ix–x.
104 Darby 1965, pp. 66–8, 116–8; Hough 1972, pp. 162, 305; Alexander 2003, p. 388, Borrow, vol. 2, pp. 294–6.

nineteenth months after *Bounty* sailed for the Pacific Ocean; and naturally no word of it reached Tahiti while the crew sojourned there. It seems that new political notions did play some part in the sailors' great mutinies at Spithead and the Nore in 1797, but to view the Bountys' collective consciousness in this light is to falsify history.[105]

※ ※ ※

As I said earlier, our understanding of the many of the circumstances of *Bounty*'s voyage and of its various outcomes has certainly increased in the past 200 years and more.

Various factors have contributed to this. In the 1920s and 1930s, naval historians such as Rupert Gould, David Bonner Smith and C. Knight established the technical details of the ship and added information about its crew. More extensive research in archives and the acquisition by libraries of private papers massively expanded the documentary base available to historians; and skillful editing and publishing of these texts, together with facsimile reproduction and now digitisation have made these sources much more readily available. In this, the labours of Owen Rutter and Neil Chambers in Britain and Paul Brunton and his colleagues at the State Library of New South Wales have been particularly noteworthy. Biographical studies have provided a better sense of Bligh's character. Some scholars have developed new insights by bringing perspectives from other disciplines – e.g. Greg Dening (ethnography) and Anne Salmond (anthropology).

Nonetheless, many of the tellings of the story of *Bounty*'s voyage have continued to be marred by incomplete knowledge of the circumstances of naval service in the second half of the eighteenth century; inadequate critical analysis of the sources; the repetition, often over decades, of clichés; and the ignoring of calls, most notably by Rolf Du Rietz, for greater rigour in research and analysis. It is my hope that this study will prepare the way for more enquiring and sounder accounts.

---

105 Darby 1965, p. 41

Part I
History's Shrouds and Silences

1

A Serious Affair to Be Starved: The Resentment of Sailors When Not Properly Fed

The mutiny on HM Armed Transport *Bounty* occurred between about 5.30 am and 8 am on 28 April 1789, when the ship was in the western Pacific Ocean, some 30 miles (50 kilometres) to the south-west of Tofua, one of the Tongan islands. This is how William Bligh described the startling turn of events:

> Just before Sun rise Mr Christian, Mate, Charles Churchill, Ships Corporal, John Mills, Gunners Mate, and Thomas Burkett, Seaman, came into my Cabbin while I was a Sleep and seizing me tyed my hands with a Cord behind my back and threatned me with instant death if I spoke or make the least noise. I however called so loud as to alarm every one, but the Officers found themselves secured by Centinels at their Doors. There were four Men in my Cabbin and three outside, viz. Alexander Smith [i.e. John Adams],[1] John Sumner and Matthew Quintal. Mr Christian had a Cutlass in his hand, the others had Musquets and Bayonets. I was forced on Deck in my Shirt, suffering great pain from the Violence with which they had tied my hands. I demanded a reason for such a violent Act, but I received no Answer but threats of instant death if I did not hold my tongue. Mr Hayward & Hallett were in Mr Christians Watch, but had no Idea that any thing was doing untill they were all armed.

---

1   John Adams, which is how I shall henceforth identify him, was his true name. See Scott 1982.

The Arms were all Secured so that no one could get near them for Centinels. Mr Elphinstone, the Mate, was secured to his Birth. Mr Nelson Botanist, Mr Peckover Gunner Mr Ledward Surgeon & the Master [i.e. John Fryer] were confined to their Cabbins, as also Mr John Samuel (Clerk), but who from finesse got leave to come upon Deck. The Fore Hatchway was guarded by Centinels, the Boatswain and Carpenter were however allowed to come on Deck where they saw me Standing abaft the Mizen Mast with my hands tied behind my back, under a guard with Christian at their Head. The Boatswain was now ordered to hoist the Boat out, with a threat if he did not do it instantly to take care of himself.[2]

There was much confusion in this tumult, and many changes of plan. It was first the mutineers' intention to set only Bligh, Samuel and the midshipmen Thomas Hayward and John Hallett adrift; but then, as more and more of the crew refused to join in the mutiny and indicated that they wished to go with Bligh, Christian agreed that the loyalist party should have the sound launch, some navigational instruments, a meagre supply of food and drink, and four cutlasses. In the end, eighteen men went into the boat with Bligh.

Bligh listed twenty-five men as comprising the mutineers:

Fletcher Christian, master's mate and acting lieutenant
Peter Heywood, midshipman
George Stewart, midshipman
Edward Young, midshipman
Charles Churchill, corporal
John Mills, gunner's mate
James Morrison, boatswain's mate
Joseph Coleman, armourer
Charles Norman, carpenter's mate
Thomas McIntosh, carpenter's crew
Thomas Burkett, AB
Matthew Quintal, AB
John Sumner, AB

---

2   Entry, 28 April 1789, Bligh Log 2, vol. 2, pp. 118–19.

1 A Serious Affair to Be Starved

John Millward, AB
William McCoy, AB
Henry Hilbrant, AB
William Muspratt, AB
Alexander Smith, AB
John Williams, AB
Thomas Ellison, AB
Isaac Martin, AB
Richard Skinner, AB
Mathew Thompson, AB
Michael Byrne, AB
William Brown, botanist's assistant

However, not all of these men participated in the mutiny. At least four would have gone in the boat with Bligh if there had been room and the rebels had let them. After Bligh wrote on their behalf, Coleman, Norman, McIntosh and the half-blind fiddler Byrne were acquitted at the subsequent court martial. Heywood and Morrison were convicted. One naval officer who witnessed the proceedings said that he was 'equally struck with horror and astonishment at hearing them being included in the sentence of condemnation, as was every one in the Court. Indeed, so very slender were the evidences in favour of the prosecution, that they really did not amount to crimination.'[3] A sufficient number of the members of the court martial evidently shared this view, for they recommended the pair to the King's 'mercy'. They were subsequently pardoned. At most, then, the 'Pirates under arms' numbered nineteen (though even two or three of this group were probably not enthusiasts).

※ ※ ※

From the moment it happened, people have wondered about the *Bounty* mutiny. However, as I showed in the Introduction, there has been little fundamental advance in historical understanding of the

---

3   [An Officer on the Brunswick], undated but after 29 October and before 21 November 1792, *Gentleman's Magazine*, vol. 62, part 2 (December 1792), p. 1097.

causes of the mutiny and the motives of those who participated in it in the past 228 years.

To begin with, many writers have not been sufficiently discerning about modes of mutiny in the eighteenth-century Royal Navy, which were as varied as the colours of the rainbow. Mutiny might be as simple a thing as a sailor refusing to doff his cap to an officer; or a sailor arguing with an officer; or the disobeying of an order – e.g. a drunkard's refusing to hand over the key to his chest where he is storing his liquor. Or, an angry sailor might strike an officer. Or, friends might muster in support of seamen who have been confined for misbehaviour. Or a subordinate officer might refuse to obey an order given by his superior. Or mutiny might involve mass resistance to the command of an unpopular officer.

Nicholas Rodger, a leading historian of the Royal Navy, has pointed out that it was rare for mass mutinies to occur at sea. Mostly, these occurred when a ship was in port, and the most common cause was money – that is, when crews whose ships had just returned to port refused to put to sea again until they had been paid. Most often, he says, 'mutiny provided a formal system of public protest to bring grievances to the notice of authority. It was a sort of safety-valve, harmless, indeed useful, so long as it was not abused.'[4]

Surprising as it may seem to us now, authorities were often willing to excuse or downplay the significance of mutinous behaviour in the interest of having a good working ship. For example, in April 1763, having just returned to port, the crew of the *Antelope* refused to put out again, saying 'they had a right to be paid off as well as other ships, that they had served the King faithfully for many years in the war, now in peace they could better themselves'. The commander-in-chief at Portsmouth decided not to order the ship to sea, knowing that if he did, 'matters would be carried to extremities, which I could not avoid when no persuasion would prevail with them'. He added, 'I don't find that one is more to blame than another; the whole speaks, or we could have silenced a few.'[5]

---

4   Rodger 1986, pp. 243–4.
5   Cited in Rodger 1986, p. 240.

Nonetheless, there were commonly understood limits as to when and to what degree mutiny might be tolerated. In essence, these were that mutiny should address grievances involving violations of accustomed service conditions (such as being paid); that while there might be shouting and threats, there should be no personal violence; and that there should not be mutiny at sea or in battle, when it might put a ship and its entire company at risk. Especially, there must not be mutiny that would affect the capacity of the Royal Navy to defend the nation.[6]

When mutiny exceeded these unwritten boundaries, the authorities' retribution was usually severe. In 1748, for example, off Cape Coast Castle in West Africa, Lieutenant Couchman seized the *Chesterfield* when the captain and other officers were ashore. The crew soon regained control of the ship; Couchman was sentenced to death and shot. In September 1797, when the *Hermione* was on wartime service in the West Indies, its crew rose against its brutal captain, Hugh Pigot, killing him and ten others. They then sailed the ship into a Spanish port. Over the next ten years, authorities pursued the mutineers with great determination, recapturing some thirty-three and hanging twenty-four. This is one example of what recent studies by Rodger, Jonathan Neale, Ann Coats and Philip MacDougall and others have established – that in response to wartime needs in the last decades of the eighteenth century, the Royal Navy enforced discipline and punished transgressions more rigorously than it previously had.

Nonetheless, though it occurred in April 1789, the *Bounty* mutiny is best seen in terms of earlier circumstances; but we should also be aware that there were a number of instances of mutiny on the voyage, rather than one. There was, of course, the rebellion of a junior officer against his superior. However, as I examine Fletcher Christian's character and actions in the next chapter, I do not consider these things here.

There was also a series of refusals by warrant officers to obey the commander's orders, and while these have been much commented on, they have not been properly examined. They should be, for they give the lie to Bligh's repeated claim that the voyage was trouble-free until they left Tahiti, a claim that has been too easily repeated. These individual mutinies involved *Bounty*'s carpenter, William Purcell, and its master, John Fryer. In so far as it is now possible to understand the circumstances, it seems

---

6   See Rodger 1986, p. 238.

that these warrant officers' recalcitrance arose from Bligh's demanding that they perform tasks and accept responsibilities that were not part of their established duties, or that involved compromising their integrity.

The first incident occurred in August 1788 at Adventure Bay in Van Diemen's Land, while the ship was en route to Tahiti, when Bligh clashed with Purcell and then drew Fryer into the conflict. According to the navy's *Regulations and Instructions*, a carpenter was 'to take upon himself the Care and Preservation of the Ship's Hull, Masts, Yards, Bulkheads and Cabins, etc and to receive into his Charge the Sea-Stores committed to him by Indenture from the surveyor of the Navy'. While at sea, he was:

> to visit daily all the Parts of the Ship, and see if the Ports are well secured, and Decks and Sides be well caulked, and whether any Thing gives Way; and if the Pumps are in good Order; and from Time to Time to inspect into the Condition of the Masts and Yards, and to make a Report of every Thing.

He was to be 'very frugal' in expending his stores, and to report 'all that are any way wasted, embezzled or misapplied', and to guard against their damage or loss. At sea, a carpenter reported, and was answerable, only to the captain. At the conclusion of the voyage, he was required 'to deliver just Accounts thereof to the Surveyor of the Navy, audited and vouched by the Captain and Master, with an Account of all Stores that he hath been supplied with'.[7]

As Rodger explains, having undergone years of intensive training 'in a complex and demanding job', a ship's carpenter was 'a highly skilled man in an essential craft', who had 'no rival among the non-seamen aboard'. He was not one of the 'seamen petty officers' – e.g. quartermasters and quartermaster's mates, boatswain's mates – who were expected to share in the seamen's work.[8] But this is what Bligh demanded when he ordered Purcell to join the wooding party while they were at Adventure Bay. When he later demanded that Purcell be court-martialled, Bligh said that when he reprimanded him for cutting

---

7 Royal Navy 1787, pp. 113–14.
8 Rodger 1986, pp. 23–26.

the timber into pieces too long to be conveniently stowed, the carpenter replied 'with great contumacy and disrespect[,] "I suppose you are come on shore on purpose to find fault" and uttered other impertinent expressions'.

This doesn't seem to be the whole story, however. In his log, Bligh said that 'on my expressing my disapprobation of his Conduct with respect to orders he had received from me concerning the Mode of working with the Wooding Party, [Purcell] behaved "a most insolent and reprehensible manner"'. This suggests that Bligh's criticism comprehended more than the length of the logs that Purcell was cutting. However this was, Bligh ordered him back on board, 'there to assist in the general duty of the ship'.[9]

Three days later, Bligh ordered Fryer to see that all the officers not otherwise employed join in the preparations for sailing. When Fryer directed Purcell to help load full water casks into the hold, he refused. When Bligh came back on board, Fryer reported this, but Purcell then also refused Bligh's order, saying that 'he would do any thing in his line, but as to that duty he could not comply with it'.

Bligh told Purcell that he would not be fed until he agreed to obey orders, 'and promised faithfully a severe Punishment to any Man that dared to Assist him'. Purcell changed his mind. Bligh said that he would have liked to have 'closely confined' him until he could have him court-martialled. Given the nature of the voyage, this could not have happened for a very long time; and in the interval Bligh could not do without Purcell's services:

> It was for the good of the Voyage that I should not make him or any Man a prisoner. The few I have even in the good State of health I keep them, are but barely sufficient to carry on the duty of the Ship, it could then answer no good purpose to lose the use of a healthy Strong Young Man in my situation.

He therefore contented himself with taking sworn statements concerning Purcell's behaviour.[10]

---

9   Entry, 23 August 1788, Bligh Log 2, vol. 1, p. 295; Bligh to Stephens, 7 October 1790, NA, ADM 1/5328.
10 Entry, 26 August 1788, Bligh Log 2, vol. 1, p. 299.

As having all hands work together was clearly conducive to the voyage's succeeding, we may well have some sympathy for Bligh here; however, a more empathetic commander might have achieved this desirable end by cajoling rather than compelling. In ordering Purcell to join in the work of the common seamen, he was both distracting the carpenter from his mandatory daily duties and publicly humiliating him. In requiring Fryer to order Purcell to assist in loading the water, he was also asking the master to do something that was not 'in his line' – that is, it was not part of a master's duty to supervise a carpenter.[11]

Bligh evidently overreached himself further at Adventure Bay, for, according to Morrison, as well as confining Purcell briefly, he 'found fault with the innatention of the rest [of the officers], to their duty, which produced continual disputes[,] evry one endeavouring to thwart the others in their duty'. Morrison adds that the 'seeds of eternal discord between Lieutenant Bligh and his Officers' were sown at Adventure Bay and that on the next leg of the voyage:

> Mr Bligh and His Mess mates the Master & Surgeon fell out, and seperated, each taking his part of the stock, & retiring to live in their own Cabbins, after which they had several disputes & seldom spoke but on duty; and even *then* with much apperant reserve.[12]

Just before they reached Tahiti, there was another mutinous incident, this time involving John Fryer. One of a master's duties was to countersign the ship's books regularly. In doing so, he was to be 'very careful not to sign any Accounts, Books, Lists, or Tickets, before he has thoroughly informed himself of the Truth of every Particular contained in the same'.[13] On 9 October, Bligh asked Fryer to sign the boatswain's and carpenter's expense books and his purser's books for August and September. Fryer said he would not do so unless Bligh first signed a certificate stating that he 'had done nothing amiss during his time on board'. Bligh replied that he could not approve of Fryer's doing his duty

---

11   Memorandum, 8 July 1789, Fryer 1934, p. 79.
12   Morrison 1935, p. 27.
13   Royal Navy 1787, p. 97.

'conditionally', whereupon Fryer again refused to sign the books. Bligh then assembled the whole crew and, after reading the 'Articles of War, with other particular parts of the Instructions', said to Fryer, 'Now Sir Sign them Books.' Fryer did so, but with the ominous qualification: 'I sign in obedience to your Orders, but this may be Cancelled hereafter.'[14]

Morrison observes darkly that Fryer said this 'for reasons best known to himself';[15] but actually, the master's reasons are not hard to find. Given the poor relationship that had developed between the pair, it is likely that Fryer wished to have some 'insurance' against any future charges by Bligh of neglect of duty and disobedience of orders, such as Purcell was then facing. In any case, by this stage of the voyage Bligh's malpractices as purser and in other roles were plain for all to see. In ordering Fryer to sign unverified or false accounts, Bligh was requiring him to breach his duty as master – that is, Bligh was putting Fryer in an impossible position.

Nor was this evidently the only instance of Bligh's falsifying documents. In his shorter account, Morrison says that during the voyage the officers had 'been base enough to sign false *Survey-Books* and papers to the prejudice of His Majesty & Government'; and that at the Cape of Good Hope Muspratt and Hayward had signed documents testifying that Bligh had bought items at the prevailing rate as though they were 'respectable Merchants of that place'. And Fryer evidently gathered evidence that Bligh made 'extravagant charges to Government' for items he had bought at Coupang.[16]

Bligh and Purcell clashed again at Tahiti. In early December, Bligh ordered the carpenter to shape a grindstone for one of the chiefs to use to keep his prized metal tools sharp. Purcell refused, saying (according to Bligh), 'I will not cut the stone, for it will spoil my Chissel, and tho there is Law to take away my cloaths, there is none to take away my Tools.' When Bligh repeated this order, Purcell refused to obey it a second time, 'in an insolent manner, and with a threatening aspect'. Purcell's resentment is hardly surprising. Bligh's was another illegitimate order, for it was not a carpenter's duty to cut stone, nor was it reasonable to require him to ruin

---

14 Entry, 9 October 1788, Bligh Log 2, vol. 1, p. 349; Morrison 1935, p. 27.
15 Morrison 1935, p. 27.
16 Morrison Memorandum, p. 39; Bligh, 'Particular Transactions at Sourabya', 15–17 September 1789, Bligh 1937, p. 68.

his tools, which were his private possessions. As at Adventure Bay, Bligh ordered Purcell to his cabin, but released him the next day.[17] Bligh also gave Fryer further cause for resentment by confiscating his pigs.

Conflict between the commander and the master and carpenter continued in the East Indies. Bligh was again dissatisfied with Purcell's work – or, more likely, his recalcitrance – and again he also castigated Fryer. As they prepared the *Resource*, the small vessel that Bligh purchased at Coupang to take his party to Batavia, Bligh 'directed' Fryer 'to attend and see that the carpenter did not loiter away his time, and to report to me, if, when I was absent, he saw anything doing he thought was contrary to my directions, when I received for answer that he was no carpenter and did not understand that he had a right to attend to it'. Fryer asked Bligh to put his order in writing.[18]

This conflict continued for some days. On 9 July, as Fryer relates it,

> About 9 oclock am Mr Bligh came out of his room and ask[ed] questions of the Gentlemen and people about the Carpenters work [on] the Vessel, he then ask[ed] me w[h]ere the Carpenter left off. I said Sir I inform'd your last nigh[t]. He ask[ed] me if I had been down this morning – I told him no – I was onwell Sir. What is your complaint he said – I told him the pricky heat was much out on me and that the Doctor told me to take care, and not catch cold – he said is that all your complaint – take [fisick?].
>
> I told him the Doctor was the only man to prescribe on that matter – he said Sir its my order that you see that the Carpenter at Work every morning by Daybreak – and keep him at work – I said Sir I am not a judge of Carpenters work neither do I think it my Duty to attend the Carpenter – He said it is your Duty Sir and you shall do it – and sir you are very Impertinent to tell me you are not a judge of Carpenter work and was you in any place where I could try you I would confine you Emmideately.[19]

---

17 Bligh to Stephens, 7 October 1790, NA, ADM 1/5328.
18 Entry, 6 July 1789, Addenda, Bligh 1937, p. 80.
19 Fryer, Memorandum, 8 July 1789, Fryer 1934, p. 79.

1 A Serious Affair to Be Starved

During the passage to Batavia, there was further conflict between Bligh and Fryer and Purcell. As they prepared to sail from Surabaya, Bligh organised for provisions to be brought to the ship, some in the commandant's boat in which he came out, and some in a second boat crewed mostly by the midshipmen Thomas Hayward and John Hallett and the warrant officers William Peckover, William Purcell, William Elphinstone and William Cole. These preferred to keep drinking on shore, so that they were tardy in following Bligh, who had to order them to do so.

When Bligh reached the *Resource* he thought one of his bottles was missing. Fryer relates:

> He said the first thing [that] was to be done was to find that Bottle – search was made and it was found in his Cabin where his Clark had put it – he then order'd me to weigh Anchor which I emmideally gave orders for so doing – and call'd Mr Elphinstone – Master's Mate – who was below in the teer to come up – I called him several times[.] He said he was unwell – Lieut Bligh came in a great Passion and ask[ed] the reason why Mr Elphinstone was not on Deck. I told [him] he was below in the teer and said he was not well – he ask[ed] what was the matter with him. I told him I did not know whether he was sick or drunk, he said you dont know whether he is sick or drunk – no sir I said – he said God damn you sir why don't you know – I told him the Doctor was the person that should know best, whether he was sick or not'.

Bligh then became bombastic and abused Fryer. Fryer continues: 'I then told him he used me very ill – not me only, but every Body'. Upon this, stirring up others, Purcell joined in the criticism. 'Yes by God we are used damned ill, nor have we any right to be used so'. Bligh recorded: 'the Carpenter now became Spokesman and with a daring and Villainous look uttered the above expressions who with the Masters Sneers and provocation in supporting their cause by saying I had used him ill and every body on Board, made an open tumult'. Bligh then ordered Fryer and Purcell to go below.[20] Fryer said that he 'Emmedially

---

20 Fryer, Memorandum, 16 September 1789, Fryer 1934, p. 81; Bligh, 'Particular transactions at Sourabya', Bligh 1937, p. 65.

obey'd his order and went below – when he call'd me all the Ill names he could think of and got a Bayonet and swore if I offer'd to look up that [he] would run me through.'[21]

Then, Bligh learned that while on shore Purcell had spoken loosely that he, Bligh, would 'be hanged or blown from the mouth of a cannon' when they got home. Incensed, he requested the Dutch governor and commandant to hold a formal enquiry into his conduct and the complaints against him, and sent witnesses and Fryer and Purcell, whom he considered to be the chief instigators of the tumult, ashore as 'prisoners' to be questioned, so as to create a record for a court-martial once they reached England again.[22]

By the time the *Bounty* was on the return voyage, Bligh had so alienated his officers that, with the notable (and how ironic) exception of Fryer, they were unwilling to stand up for him in the mutiny. As Morrison observed:

> The behaviour of the Officers on this Occasion was dastardly beyond description[,] none of them ever making the least attempt to rescue the ship ... Their passive obedience to Mr Christians orders even surprised himself and he said immediately after the boat was gone that something more than fear had posessd them to suffer themselves to be sent away in such a manner without offering to make resistance.[23]

Fryer was right to highlight Bligh's tirades, but, as we shall see, the captain's 'bad language' was not the only reason that the officers had turned surly.

※ ※ ※

Edward Young (midshipman), Charles Churchill (master-at-arms, or corporal), John Mills (gunner's mate) and William Brown (gardener) joined in the mutiny. As there are no first- or second-hand accounts of

---

21 Fryer, Memorandum, 16 September 1789, Fryer 1934, p. 81.
22 Bligh, 'Particular transactions at Sourabya', Bligh 1937, p. 65.
23 Morrison 1935, pp. 43–4.

1 A Serious Affair to Be Starved

their motives, it is futile to speculate about these, more than to say that Bligh's explanation – the lure of Tahiti – is likely to have been a factor. There is also some suggestion that they may have found common cause with the sailors resentful at Bligh's actions.

Bligh termed the thirteen ABs who rebelled as 'the most able Men on board the Ship'.[24] What was it that led these men to turn themselves into pirates? One factor was camaraderie. It is clear that, prior to the mutiny, they had bonded in ways in which others in the ship had not. These were the skilled hands, the 'topmen' or 'yardmen', who worked among the spars and sails high above the deck. There, they could talk to each other without those below hearing. At Tahiti, some or most (all?) of them had spent time at the shore camp of which Christian was in command. All but one of them were tattooed, mostly on their buttocks with Tahitian motifs, which signified they were adults who might marry. And 'marry' they enthusiastically did, learning some Tahitian in the process. A number also carried a star on their chest. Anne Salmond has made the interesting suggestion that this was an imitation of the insignia of the Order of the Garter, and in this case indicated membership of a closed circle, the 'Knights of Otaheite'. In any case, it was no coincidence that in the tumult of the morning of 28 April 1789, these men told Bligh and others to *mamoo* (*mamu*: silence/shut up!).[25]

But if shared experience and deliberate bonding indicate why these sailors rather than others of *Bounty*'s crew should have constituted the core of the mutineers, it does not explain their group action. On the face of things, it is not easy to fit the rebellion into the pre-1780s matrix. The crew had not been unjustly denied their pay. Just before they sailed, they had received the customary two months' advance to enable them to purchase items for the voyage. Despite the popular image of him as a stern taskmaster, as best conveyed by the Hollywood fables, Bligh was not a 'Tartar' devoted to the cat. Dening has established that he flogged less often and gave fewer lashes than any other British captain who ventured the Pacific Ocean in the second half of the eighteenth

---

24 Entry, 28 April 1789, Bligh Log 2, vol. 2, p. 120.
25 Salmond 2011, pp. 178, 233; Belcher, Remarks, December 1825, PN 16, p. [9]; Dening 1992, p. 58.

century.[26] Nor does class solidarity seem to have been an overt factor, for the crew had not risen at Tahiti when Bligh confined and punished the three who had stolen arms and deserted.

Even Bligh's favoured explanation lacks force. No doubt, some of the seamen were quite pleased at the prospect of regaining Tahiti's easeful life; but on the other hand, apart from Churchill, Muspratt and Millward's temporary desertion, which no doubt indicates a preference for Tahitian living, neither in Bligh's journals and letters nor in other sources is there any suggestion that approximately half the crew were reluctant to begin the homeward voyage. Dening's 'bad language' explanation is also inefficacious. Inured as they were to the everyday coarseness and brutalities of naval life, the seamen were unlikely to have been much 'hurt' by the cranky bastard's outbursts.

We need an explanation of a different order to understand why the majority of the seamen rose against Bligh, one more closely attuned to the circumstances of naval service in general and those of the *Bounty*'s voyage in particular. Disgruntlement over Bligh's practices as purser provides this explanation.

✳✳✳

Early in the eighteenth century, the Victualling Board determined a standard weekly ration for a seaman. Table 2 lists the standard ration in 1787.[27]

Given that salting and drying were the only effective means of preserving food at this time, and roasting, boiling and baking the only modes of preparing it for sailors to eat, this ration had an inevitable sameness. However, it provided a hot meal daily, with meat four times a week, together with bread, cheese and beer. So long as these items remained 'sweet', they had a combined daily energy value of something like 5000 calories, 'far in excess of the 3350 k cals required by the average 65 kg man employed on heavy labour'.[28] The seaman's diet,

---

26 Entry, 24–28 November 1788, Bligh Log 2, vol. 1, p. 13; Dening 1992, pp. 62–3.
27 Royal Navy 1787, p. 61; 'His Majesty's Allowance to a Seaman for Every Day in the Week', NA, ADM 30/44; Rodger 1986, p. 83; Macdonald 2006, p. 10.
28 See Macdonald 2006, pp. 177–8; and Watt 1989, p. 144.

1 A Serious Affair to Be Starved

	Bread	Beer	Beef	Pork	Pease	Oatmeal	Butter	Cheese	Vinegar
Sunday	1 lb	1 gallon	-	1 lb	½ pint	-	-	-	-
Monday	1 lb	1 gallon	-	-	-	1 pint	2 ozs	4 ozs	-
Tuesday	1 lb	1 gallon	2 lbs	-	-	-	-	-	-
Wednesday	1 lb	1 gallon	-	-	½ pint	1 pint	2 ozs	4 ozs	-
Thursday	1 lb	1 gallon	-	1 lb	½ pint	-	-	-	-
Friday	1 lb	1 gallon	-	-	½ pint	1 pint	2 ozs	4 ozs	-
Saturday	1 lb	1 gallon	2 lbs	-	-	-	-	-	-
Allowance per week	7 lbs	7 gallons	4 lbs	2 lbs	2 pints	3 pints	6 ozs	12 ozs	½ pint

Table 2 Standard weekly ration for a seaman in the 1780s.

then, constituted a more-than-adequate intake in terms of quantity. Indeed, as a number of naval historians have pointed out, sailors ate significantly better than the bulk of the British labouring population and the poor.[29]

There are some peculiarities to notice here, however. It was customary for officers and men to provide some food themselves, and while they consumed this rather than the official ration they built up a reserve of the latter. As Nicholas Rodger explains:

> every officer and man was allowed the standard ration, but he was not obliged to eat it, and he was entitled to credit for whatever he did not consume ... Those who had provided themselves with private stocks would take part or none of the purser's victuals until their own provisions ran out and they had to revert to the naval ration.[30]

Also, it was not feasible for many ships to carry sufficient preserved foods for voyages longer than about twelve to eighteen months. The Admiralty's expectation was that the captains and pursers of ships on long voyages would replace home supplies at foreign ports of call,

---

29 E.g., Rodger 1986, pp. 85–6; Lloyd [1968] 1970, pp. 231–2.
30 Rodger 1986, pp. 89–90.

such as Jamaica, Rio de Janeiro, Cape Town and Batavia. If supplies of food ran low because that in the casks perished or because progress was unexpectedly retarded, commanders of squadrons or captains of individual vessels had permission to reduce rations. If they did so, 'the Men [were to] be punctually paid for the same' – i.e. to be paid the value of the food they had not received. What 'punctual' meant is not entirely clear. Since a purser kept his books month to month, it may have meant at the beginning of each new month, or perhaps at three-monthly intervals. The purpose of this requirement was to give the seamen the means to purchase their own food.[31] Of course, money might be of no use to hungry sailors if they were far from ports where it was accepted, as was often the case on voyages of Pacific exploration.

And then, replacement supplies of some items might not be available when far from home – e.g. Asian ports did not usually offer flour and beer. To meet this latter contingency, the Victualling Board had a fixed schedule of equivalents, viz Table 3.[32] Depending on what supplies were locally available, a purser might also need to issue substitutes in proportions not included in this table.

Eighteenth-century seamen were conservative and instinctively resisted changes to their established diet – as Rodger says, they did not like 'the foreign substitutes for their regular diet, which sometimes had to be served on overseas stations, such as chick peas, or flour or yams in lieu of bread'.[33] Even when the alternatives were clearly in the interest of their health, the men might resist them. When the *Dolphin* reached the Strait of Magellan in December 1767, for example, Samuel Wallis gave wine to the sick in place of the usual grog, and ordered that the entire company be served 'Ground Wheat for Breakfast, with a large Quantity of Wild Cellery cut down amongst it, and four pound of portable Soop'. George Robinson, the ship's master, commented, 'This made an Excelent Good Meall, but several of the Seamen Complain that they did not think it fitt to Eate.'[34]

---

31 Royal Navy 1787, p. 61, Article II. I am grateful to Professor Rodger for advice on these points. See also Macdonald 2006, p. 94.
32 'Proportion of each Species of Provisions', NA, ADM 30/44.
33 Rodger 1986, p. 86.
34 Robertson 1948, p 38.

1 A Serious Affair to Be Starved

Provision		Equal to	
Wine	1 pint	Beer	1 gallon
Arrack, rum or brandy	½ pint	Beer	1 gallon
Flour Suet	3 lbs ½ lb	Beef	1 piece (4 lbs)
Rice	4 lb	Oatmeal	1 gallon
Oil	1 pint	Butter	1 lb
Raisins	4 lbs	Beef	1 piece (4 lbs)
Suet	2 lbs	Beef	1 piece (4 lbs)
Flour Suet Raisins	(3 lbs) ¼ lb ½ lb	Beef	1 piece (4 lbs)
Pease	2 pints	Oatmeal	3 pints
Cheshire cheese	2 lbs	Suffolk cheese	3 lbs
Stockfish	4 lbs	Oatmeal	1 gallon
Wheat	1 gallon	Oatmeal	1 gallon
Sugar	1 lb	Oil	1 pint
Potatoes or yams	2 lbs	Bread	1 lb
Calavances (chickpeas)	2 pints	Oatmeal Pease	3 pints 2 pints
Sugar Cocoa	1 ½ lbs ½ lb	Butter	1 lb
Pearl barley	1 lb	Oatmeal	1 pint

Table 3 'Proportion of each species of provisions', as set out by the Victualling Board. Where a provision was unavailable, it could be substituted by the items listed in the corresponding column. (NA, ADM 30/44)

Such was the situation on each of Cook's three voyages. On the first, he gave two men twelve lashes each at Madeira 'for refusing to take their allowance of fresh Beef'. (This is a rather puzzling refusal; however, it may be that the men suspected it was rather horse or goat meat.) Then followed the famous problem of getting the seamen to eat sauerkraut, which Cook solved by having the officers consume it in front of them. He reflected, 'such are the Tempers and disposissions of Seamen in general that whatever you give them out of the Common way, altho it be ever so much for their good yet it will not go down with them and you will hear nothing but murmurings gainest the man that first invented it'.[35]

On the second voyage, when at Dusky Sound in the south island of New Zealand, Cook gave the crews some 'spruce beer' he had brewed. He considered this a 'very wholsom Beer and [made] up for the want of Vegetables', but Charles Clerke recorded that there were some seamen who 'dislik'd it vastly – prefer'd water to it'.[36] Given that the water in the casks often stank when a ship was well into its voyage, this comment is eloquent of the seamen's opposition to the makeshift beer.

In April 1778, when at Nootka Sound, the crew of the *Resolution* at first resolved not to drink the 'spruce beer' Cook brewed.[37] Then, in December 1778, when the ships were among the Hawaiian Islands, they also rejected the 'sugar cane beer' that Cook had had brewed, and which he and the officers were drinking. 'When the Cask came to be broached,' he recorded, 'not one of my Mutinous crew would even so much as taste it.' 'I beleive no one will doubt but it must be very wholsom,' he continued, 'though my turbulent crew alleged it was injurious to their healths.'[38]

The seamen conveyed their refusal by letter when they also complained about being on short rations while in sight of islands blessed with food.[39] Cook berated them for their 'very mutinous Proceeding', telling them:

---

35   Entries, 16 September 1768 and 13 April 1769, Cook 1955–67, vol. 1, pp. 7, 74.
36   Entry, 2 April 1773, Cook 1955–67, vol. 2, p. 114; Clerke, entry, 5 April 1773, Cook 1955–67, vol. 3, p. 479.
37   Entry, 7 December 1778, Cook 1955–67, vol. 3, p. 479.
38   Entries, 6 and 7 December 1778, Cook 1955–67, vol. 3, pp. 478–9.
39   Watts, entry, 10 December 1778, Cook 1955–67, vol. 3, p. 480.

that it was the first time He had heard any thing relative to the shortness of the Allowance, that he thought they had had the same Quantity usually serv'd them at the other Islands, that if they had not enough, they should have more & that had He known it sooner, it should have been rectified. He likewise understood[,] he said[,] they would not drink the Decoction of Sugar Cane imagining it prejudicial to their Healths, he told them it was something extraordinary they should suppose the Decoction unwholesome when they could steal the Sugar Cane & eat it raw without Scruple[.] He continued to tell them that if they did not chuse to drink the Decoction he could not help it, they would be the Sufferers as they should have Grog every other day provided they drank the Sugar Cane, but if not the Brandy Cask should be struck down into the Hold & they might content themselves with Water.[40]

When the crew persisted in their refusal on 11 December, Cook withdrew the grog ration. On 12 December, he flogged the cooper for emptying a cask of the sugar cane beer that had gone sour. On each voyage, Cook explained these 'mutinous turbulent' refusals of rations by pointing to the men's innate conservatism: 'Every innovation whatever tho ever so much to their advantage is sure to meet with the highest disapprobation from Seamen, Portable Soup and Sour Krout were at first both condemned by them as stuff not fit for human beings to eat.'[41]

***

Nonetheless, seamen might accept substitutes for items in the established ration in the interest of having home supplies eked out, or of continuing to be fed, so long as they knew that: 1) this was necessary; 2) they were being given correct equivalents; and 3) if on short rations, they were being properly credited for the proportion of the standard ration they were not receiving.

---

40 Watts, entries, 10–12 December 1778, Cook 1955–67, vol. 3, pp. 479–80.
41 Cook and Watts, entries, 6–12 December 1778, Cook 1955–67, vol. 3, pp. 478–80.

It was here that the purser played a crucial role. Appointed by warrant by the Navy Board, he was the officer responsible for dispensing the ship's provisions and clothing ('slops'). He did not pay for these directly, but their value was charged against his account, to be reconciled at the end of a voyage. He was required to pay for 'necessaries' for the ship (such things as wood and coal, oil, candles, hammocks and beds), and then wait until the voyage was over to be reimbursed, once his accounts had been 'passed' by the Victualling Board. He was also able to purchase additional items in foreign ports, but again had to keep strict records, including evidence that he had bought at prevailing market prices. If it happened that these were above the prices in the Board's schedules, he was not paid the difference. He was required to keep precise records of what he gave out daily to each officer and man, and, at times of reduced rations, what he did not, so that proper credit might be recorded. If this credit was called for before the ship reached a home port, then the purser paid it out of his own pocket.

The purser received a small wage. (In 1790, this was £2 per lunar month for a 6th-rate ship.) In addition, he was paid a commission on what he served out (e.g. 2d per lb of cheese); and he was entitled to serve items at 14 oz rather than 16 oz to 1 lb, to account for wastage and seepage. It was also usual for him to buy stocks of some items – e.g. tobacco – for private sale to the men during the voyage.

The purser's lot was not an easy one. Before sailing, he had to pay for items he personally provided; and then, if the navy rations ran low during the voyage, for replacements. This he usually did by drawing 'bills of exchange' on merchants or friends at home. This meant that it might then take months or even years for the Victualling Board to clear his accounts and reimburse him. He therefore usually needed large amounts of credit for long periods from his private backers, who might unexpectedly call in their debts. Bankruptcy was an ever-lurking threat in a purser's life.

Then there was the suspicion with which the purser was often viewed by his shipmates. Considering themselves already deprived by the 'purser's pound', seamen were ever alert to any further infringement of their entitlements. Officers, too, were on the lookout for sharp practices. There were a number of ways in which the purser might cheat: by invoicing the Victualling Board for more fresh provisions than he actually served when

1 A Serious Affair to Be Starved

in port; by using false weights and measures; or by not serving proper equivalents for items in the official ration. The navy did institute controls to prevent fraud or short-changing. The captain or commander, who was 'responsible for the whole Conduct and good Government of the Ship', was charged with overseeing the purser's activities; and the master, purser and the other warrant officers were required to ascertain that items served out were in the quantities stipulated.[42]

In order to 'judge whether the Flesh, served to His Majesty's Ships, holds out in just Weight', the required procedure was:

> Every Twenty-eight Pieces of Beef, cut for Four Pound Pieces, taken out of the Cask as they rise, and the Salt shaken off, are to weigh One Hundred Pounds Averdupois and every Fifty-six Pieces of Pork, cut for Two Pound Pieces, and taken out and shaken in a like Manner, are to weigh One Hundred and Four Pounds; and therefore if, according to this Standard, upon the weighing a whole Cask of Beef or Pork, in the Presence of two or more of the Warrant Officers of the Ship, there shall be found a deficiency of Weight, the Captain may order the Purser to issue to the Seamen so much more Beef or Pork as shall make up the Deficiency.[43]

A purser's need to act with integrity and at the same time keep the seamen happy was highlighted in the court martial of James Allen, the purser of the *Diana*, at Portsmouth in September 1780. Allen was charged by a lieutenant who suspected him of using 'false steelyards' to serve out quarters of beef – that is, that his scales were showing more weight than he was in fact serving.

On being charged, Allen asked that his scales and weights be sealed. At his trial, he defended himself vigorously, stating:

> The Offence[,] Gentlemen[,] I stand charged with is of a most serious Nature and reflects the Deepest Dishonour and Disgrace that a Man of principle can feel – That of Defrauding and cheating a Valuable Body of Men of their fair Allowance of provisions and Necessaries.

---

42   Royal Navy 1787, pp. 43, 97, 116.
43   Royal Navy 1787, pp. 62–3.

> It is much easier to attack than to defend a Character[.] And yet – I trust – Mine stands and ever will Superior to any Attack of Fraud – especially upon a sailor. It has ever been my Wish and endeavour to preserve the Character of an Honest Man.

Not only had he not cheated in his daily practices, Allen said, he had regularly 'supplied [the seamen] with Articles when at Short Allowance at my own private Expense', including during the ship's patrol in the Bay of Biscay the previous winter, when he told his steward 'to lett the Men have as much Oatmeal as they pleased, to make their water Gruel, as they were complaining of their short Allowance'. On 'Kings Birth days and other rejoicing Days', with the captain's agreement, he had given 'the men a Can of Grog apiece, letting them have a Pint on that Day, and the other Pint the next', so as to avoid its 'hurting' them.

Allen produced references from previous captains praising his exemplary performance of his duties. The *Diana*'s master testified that Allen had scrupulously followed the captain's order that 'a Mate, a Quarter-master, and a Fore Castle Man should attend the Cutting up of the Meat[,] that there might be no Complaint'. His assistant supported his assertion that Allen had at his own expense regularly given out more food than required. The crew supported him too, with one sailor telling the court:

> The *Diana* is the 7th Ship, I have served His Majesty in, and I was never better Victualled in my Life, and I never heard any Man make the least Complaint whatever. I have heard Mr Allen frequently give strict Directions to his Steward in this Manner – 'By no means lett us have any Complaints – be sure and give full weight and Measure. I would rather give a whole Allowance than have any Complaint'.

The Victualling Board tested Allen's equipment and found it to be accurate. He was acquitted.[44]

※ ※ ※

---

44   Court-Martial of James Allen, 2–4 September 1780, NA, ADM 1/5316.

1 A Serious Affair to Be Starved

As I said, the *Bounty* mutiny occurred in the early morning of 28 April 1789, when the ship was about 30 miles (50 kilometres) south-west of Tofua Island.

While there was tumult aplenty, the mutineers had agreed beforehand that there should be no murder, and there wasn't. In this, they kept to one of the unwritten rules of mutiny. Otherwise, however, there were some very strange aspects to this particular insurrection. With the exception of John Fryer, none of the officers attempted to stop it. What makes this the more curious is that the active mutineers, who totalled nineteen at best, were always in a minority.

Then, while they gave Bligh and those who went with him very little food and only four cutlasses for arms, the mutineers did give them a sound rather than a rotten boat; and Christian gave Bligh his own sextant. That is, the mutineers gave those whom they were casting adrift the means to survive – as it proved, the means to reach a European outpost and thus to return home and report the mutiny. This return made an expedition to arrest the mutineers inevitable. Given these circumstances, the mutineers' generosity was odd.

And then there was this. When he informed Peter Heywood that Christian 'had taken the ship from the Captain, whom he had confined upon deck', Mathew Thompson added that they would now 'have more provisions and better usage than before'. As the mutineers were leading the bound William Bligh from his cabin to the quarterdeck, Fryer asked what they intended to do with him. John Sumner answered: 'Damn his eyes, put him into the boat, and let the bugger see if he can live upon three-quarters of a pound of yams per day.' On deck, Bligh remarked to Edward Young, 'This is a serious affair, Mr Young,' to which Young replied, 'Yes, it is a serious affair to be starved, I hope this day to get a belly full.'[45]

There had been trouble about food the previous day. After accusing Fletcher Christian and others of stealing his coconuts, Bligh had said, 'I suppose you'll Steal my Yams next'; and he told John Samuel to 'Stop these Villains Grog, and Give them but Half a Pound of Yams tomorrow, and if they steal then, I'll reduce them

---

45   Marshall 1825, p. 774; *Bounty Court-Martial (Minutes)*, p. 7; Christian [1794] 1952, p. 64.

to a quarter'.⁴⁶ So we may see how ¾ lb or ½ lb of yams became an issue. Yet there is a distinct puzzle here, for while there is much in the story of the mutiny that we now cannot know well, we can be sure that at this moment *Bounty*'s men were not going hungry.

The ship had left Tahiti on 4 April, only twenty-four days previously. While at this 'Paradise of the World' (as Bligh himself termed it), the whole crew had eaten lavishly of 'the best of Meat and finest Fruits in the World'. In his log in the weeks leading up to their departure, Bligh referred repeatedly to there being an abundance of provisions; and when he sailed, in addition to the 1000 breadfruit plants and dozens of other fruit trees and tubers, the deck was crowded with hogs, goats, breadfruit, coconuts and plantains. He replenished this store as the ship passed other islands while sailing west. On 28 April 1789, 'starving' the Bountys manifestly were not.⁴⁷

Why, then, when they mutinied did some of the officers and seamen represent themselves as starving? In order to answer this question, it is necessary for us to understand that, from the first, the voyage was distinctly different from how Bligh repeatedly portrayed it, to himself and to the world. Bligh recorded in his log that he left Tenerife in January 1788 'with a Chearful & happy Ships Company all in good health and Spirits'.⁴⁸ He wrote from the East Indies that he had left Nomuka 'with a Ship in most perfect Order and all my Plants in a most flourishing condition[,] All my Men and Officers in good health[,] and in short every thing to flatter and insure my most sanguine expectations and Success'.⁴⁹ And this was the explanation he later published, saying that up to 27 April 1789 'the voyage had advanced in a course of uninterrupted prosperity, and had been attended with many circumstances equally pleasing and satisfactory'.⁵⁰ In fact, however, the *Bounty*'s voyage was troubled from the start – really, even before it started; and the trouble centred on food – or, rather, on Bligh's manipulation of the

---

46 Morrison 1935, p. 41.
47 Enclosure in Bligh to Banks, 13 October 1789, Bligh 1989, p. 35; entry, 5 April 1789, Bligh Log 2, vol. 2, p. 70.
48 Entry, 10 January 1788, Bligh Log 2, vol. 1, p. 45.
49 Enclosure in Bligh to Banks, 13 October 1789, Bligh 1989, p. 33. Cf. Bligh to Elizabeth Bligh, 19 August 1789, Bligh 1989, p. 23.
50 Bligh 1792, p. 153.

1 A Serious Affair to Be Starved

rations, partly for disciplinary purposes but more particularly for his own financial benefit.

Bligh was in a position to control the food ration because he was both commander and purser of the *Bounty*, and his clerk John Samuel was also his purser's steward. It was standard navy practice for the roles of commander and purser to be combined on small ships with small crews. James Cook, for example, had played both roles on his three circumnavigations. However, it was an arrangement that was fraught with potential difficulties. On a large ship, if officers and crew suspected the purser of malpractice, they could complain to the captain. On *Bounty*, whom was there to complain to about the machinations of purser William Bligh?

The troubles concerning food became overt immediately after the *Bounty* left Tenerife. As Morrison describes it:

> The Weather still Continuing fine a few days after, the Cheese was got up to Air, when on opening the Casks two Cheeses were Missed by Mr Bligh[,] who declared that they were stolen, the Cooper declared that the Cask had been opend before, while the Ship was in the River [Thames] by Mr Samuel's order and the Cheeses sent to Mr Bligh's house – Mr Bligh without making any further inquiry into the Matter, ordered the Allowance of Cheese to be stoppd from Officers and Men till the deficiency should be made good, and told the Cooper He would give him a dam'd good flogging If He said any More about it.
>
> These orders were strictly obey'd by Mr Samuel, who was both Clerk and Steward; and on the next Banyan day butter only was Issued, this the seamen refused, alledging that their acceptance of the Butter without Cheese would be tacitly acknowledging the supposed theft, and Jno. Williams declared that He had carried the Cheeses to Mr Blighs house with a Cask of Vinager & some other things which went up in the Boat from Long Reach[.] As they persisted in their denial of the Butter, it was kept also for two Banyan days and no more notice taken.[51]

---

51 Morrison 1935, pp. 18–19. A 'banyan' day was one without meat.

That is, Bligh chose to make up the deficit by withholding cheese for the time in which the missing pieces would have been consumed. This was punishment for a theft the men had not committed. When they stood on their honour and said they would not have butter without its usual accompaniment, Bligh added to the injustice by withholding the butter also.

The next incident followed hard on this one. Knowing that the voyage might well be prolonged because he was attempting to round Cape Horn so late in the season, Bligh reduced the allowance of bread to two-thirds – i.e. ⅔ lb daily.[52] This was standard practice on a long voyage, and Morrison says that it was 'cheerfully received'. But in another move to preserve the bread supply, Bligh had purchased pumpkins at Tenerife to serve in lieu. According to the established exchange, Bligh should have given each man 2 lb pumpkin for 1 lb bread, or, with rations reduced, 1⅓ lb for ⅔ lb. However, 'the People being desirous to know at what rate the exchange was to be, enquired of Mr Samuel who informd them that they were to have one pound of Pumpion in lieu of [⅔ lb] of bread'.[53] That is, Bligh offered a third of a pound less than the required equivalent.

The crew's refusal to accept this inadequate exchange called forth another tirade. Coming on deck in a 'violent passion', Bligh summoned all hands and told them, 'You dam'd Infernal scoundrels, I'll make you eat Grass or any thing you can catch before I have done with you.' He ordered Samuel 'to Call the first Man of every Mess and let him see Who would dare to refuse it, or any thing else that He should order to be Served'.[54]

Morrison adds that following Bligh's outburst 'evry one took the pumpion as Calld, Officers not excepted, who tho it was in their eyes an imposition said nothing against it'. He also says that, since the men had obtained 'a Good Stock of Potatoes' at Spithead before sailing, they did not feel the 'reduction of their Bread' as 'severely' as the officers.[55] This conveys two more salient points. The seamen had acted consciously

---

52 Entry, 11 January 1788, Bligh Log 2, vol. 1, p. 47; Morrison 1935, p. 18.
53 Morrison 1935, p. 19. Morrison wrote 'two pounds', but in view of the official ration being 1 lb bread per day, this seems a mistake.
54 Morrison 1935, p. 19.
55 Morrison 1935, p. 19.

1 A Serious Affair to Be Starved

to build up credit for that portion of the official ration they did not consume; if Bligh were not to allow this, they would have further cause for grievance. On the other hand, not having acted with such foresight, the officers were the more vulnerable to Bligh's reduction of the ration. The fact that by this time the pumpkins were rotting in the tropical heat presumably did not help the situation.

Bligh again violated required practice in the distribution of the meat. As commander, he was to oversee the weighing of the contents of casks as they were opened, to ensure that they contained true weight, a task which in practice was usually delegated to the ship's master and mates. As purser, Bligh was supposed not to 'make any undue Use of the Provisions or Stores under his Charge' – e.g. by taking the best pieces for himself or by selling items privately. In the event of the captain's reducing rations, he was 'not to supply any Officer at Whole Allowance, whilst the rest of the Company are at short; but all are to be equal in Point of Victualling'.[56]

Neither as commander nor purser did Bligh follow these requirements. Rather, Morrison says, when 'the Beef and Pork [appeared] very light, and there had never yet been any Weighd when Opend, it was supposed that the Casks ran short of their Weight, for which reason the people applyd to the Master, and beggd that he would examine the business and procure them redress'. When Fryer reported the crew's concern, Bligh ordered all hands on deck, and told them that everything was being done according to his direction, and that he would 'flog the first Man severely who should dare attempt to make any Complaint in future and dismissd them with severe threats'.[57]

When a cask was opened thereafter, Morrison says, the officers saw 'all the prime pieces taken out, for the Cabbin table, while they were forced to take their Chance in common with the Men of what remain'd[,] without the satisfaction of knowing whether they had their Weight or Not; being forced to take it as Markd'. He adds that the men decided to postpone further complaint until the end of the voyage, when they would seek 'redress', but that the officers 'were not so easy satisfied and made frequent Murmurings among themselves about the smallness of their Allowance

---

56 Royal Navy 1787, pp. 61, 122.
57 Morrison 1935, pp. 19–20.

and Could not reconcile themselves to such unfair Proceedings'.[58] The more Bligh manipulated the food ration, the more he gave the officers and men common cause for complaint. The situation of the officers not knowing that the pieces of meat weighed true, Morrison says, 'while it served to increase their distress and to draw forth heavy Curses on the Author of it[,] in private [it] helpd to Make the Men reconciled to their part, seeing that it [i.e. Bligh's malpractice] was not level'd at them alone but that all shared a like fate'.[59]

Nor did Bligh's manipulations end there. In his shorter account of the voyage, Morrison says that when the butter and cheese were exhausted, Bligh served oil in their stead, but at the rate of ½ pint instead of the required 1 pint to 1 lb; that he served only 1 oz sugar, instead of 4 oz, in place of 4 oz cheese; and that he also served the officers' peas and oatmeal 'in sparing quantities'.[60]

As they struggled to round the Horn, Bligh ordered wheat and barley to be served hot to the men for breakfast, a gesture that after the mutiny he raised as evidence of his concern for their welfare. However, Morrison says that 'the Quantity of wheat was one Gallon for 46 men, and Barley 2 lbs for the like Number', and that 'this scanty Allowance caused frequent Broils and disputes at the Coppers where it was divided, in one of which Churchill had his hand scalded and at another time Thos Hall the Cook, had two of his Ribs broke, and at last it became necessary that one of the Masters Mates should superintend the Division of it'.[61]

※ ※ ※

The trouble over food steadily intensified at Tahiti. Immediately on arrival, Bligh appointed the gunner William Peckover, who had learnt something of the Tahitians' language and culture during his previous voyages, to 'manage our Traffic with the Natives'. A brisk official trade developed, with the Europeans immediately obtaining 'great abundance

---

58 Morrison 1935, p. 20.
59 Morrison 1935, p. 20.
60 Morrison Memorandum, p. 13.
61 Christian [1794] 1952, pp. 67–8; Morrison Memorandum, pp. 15–17.

of Hogs, Cocoa Nutts, Breadfruit, Plantains, and Apples, some Red Peppers or Capsicoms, and Oil which is expressed from the Cocoa-nut'.

The next day, they had 'great abundance of Cocoa Nutts and Breadfruit, besides Plantains and a few Yams'. Given this, Bligh ceased serving any of the official rations except grog – 'My people at no allowance'.[62] Trade continued like this in the next weeks and months, with Bligh writing in February 1789, 'This day I received great supplies of Breadfruit and other articles of provisions'; 'Sufficient Supplies of Hogs, Breadfruit and Cocoa Nutts'; 'We have Supplies as much as we are in need of'. As he said, 'no Men ever lived in such abundance as we do at present'.[63]

Bligh's assertion would have been the more convincing if the Bountys had in fact been getting the foods that he listed; but as so often with Bligh's story of the voyage, the reality was decidedly different. Some of the pigs the Europeans obtained weighed as much as 200 lb, and Bligh set about salting their meat for later use. From one point of view, he was only being prudent, for a large new supply of meat was a valuable resource for a ship on such an extended voyage – as he put it, he was ensuring that he had 'a sufficiency of provisions in case of scarcity hereafter'.[64] From another point of view, however, Bligh was up to his usual pursery tricks.

For one thing, although he had pork in abundance, Bligh did not serve it; rather, he had the cook make a broth from the bones, adding to this what greens were available. He represented this as an instance of his virtuous care for his crew. However, Morrison tells us that he was allowing each man 2 lb of pork bones and 'such parts as were not fit for salting' per day; and that 'it became a favour for a man to get a Pound extra of His own hog'.[65] We may suppose that Bligh's motive in this seizure of food and parsimonious dispensing of it was to make more money, and not only from preserving more of the official ration. On his return to England, he claimed reimbursement for what he 'expended'

---

62 Entries, 28 and 29 October 1788, Bligh Log 2, vol. 1, pp. 373–4.
63 Entries, 29 October and 14, 16 and 21 February 1789, Bligh Log 2, vol. 1, p. 374, vol. 2, pp. 37, 39, 41.
64 Entry, 29 October 1788, Bligh Log 2, vol. 1, p. 374.
65 Entry, 4 November 1789, Bligh Log 2, vol. 1, p. 385; Morrison 1935, pp. 28–9.

on Tahitian pigs, for many of which he had paid nothing. He must have been disappointed with the Victualling Board's response, that this was 'a speculation common in the Pursery line and not at the Charge and risk of the Government'.[66]

For another thing, he expropriated food that was rightfully the men's. While at Tahiti, the Bountys were able to obtain private supplies either by trading directly themselves or by becoming *taio* of Tahitian men. One of the obligations of this bonded friendship was that each person should share freely of his resources with the other. What the Europeans had to offer were clothes, metal items (such as axes, knives, nails and buttons), and perhaps red cloth or feathers. What the Tahitians had to offer were women, artefacts and food. Tahitian men were soon bringing pigs and fruits to their new friends. These should have been the seamen's private property, but Bligh decreed otherwise. Morrison tells us that he took to seizing all the pigs 'that came to the ship[,] big & small[,] Dead or alive, taking them as his property, and serving them as the ship's allowance at one pound pr Man pr Day'. When Fryer protested at Bligh's seizing his pigs, Bligh responded, 'He Mr Bligh would convince him that evry thing was *his*, as soon as it was on board, and that He would take nine tenths of any mans property and let him see who dared say any thing to the contrary.'[67]

Despite Bligh's machinations, the Bountys certainly did not go hungry at Tahiti. When Bligh started seizing the pigs they sent to their friends, the Tahitian men smuggled others on board while he was absent. Discovering this, Bligh ordered the officer in charge of each watch to keep a record of 'the Hogs or Pigs with the Weight of each that came into the Ship'. The Tahitians accordingly took to hiding pieces of pork in the baskets of breadfruit and coconuts that they brought. In this way, Morrison says, the men continued to enjoy Tahiti's bounty, for there was 'always sufficient to enable them to live well'.[68] Nonetheless, Bligh's giving them pork broth made from bones and making it more difficult for them to obtain meat were other things to rankle with the seamen.

---

66 Quoted in Rutter 1936b, p. 119.
67 Morrison 1935, p. 29.
68 Morrison 1935, pp. 28–9.

1 A Serious Affair to Be Starved

The Tahitians kept supplying their *taio* with food as the *Bounty* prepared to sail. These supplies and those that Bligh purchased meant that the ship was 'loaded with Cocoa Nutts, Plantains, Breadfruit and Hogs and goats'. Also on board were taro (*Colocasia esculenta*), a tuber that grows 10 to 12 inches (25 to 30 centimetres) long, and yams (*Dioscorea alata*), the brown variety of which can grow 6 or even 8 feet (around 2 to 2.5 metres) long. The day before their departure, Bligh observed that the *Bounty* was carrying 'as much fruit as I could Stow, 25 Hogs and 17 Goats'. He added a little to this store at nearby Huahine, buying 'about 150 lbs' of yams, and some plantains and coconuts.[69]

As they sailed west, Bligh served 1 lb of fresh pork daily, which was the right amount. However, once more wishing to husband the bread supply, he reduced the ration to ⅔ lb daily. But he did not serve out the ship's bread; rather, he again substituted other items. On 6 and 7 April, he served breadfruit and coconut. From 8 to 14 April, he served plantain. On 15 April, he served plantain and taro; plantain only on 16 April; plantain and taro on 17 April; and plantain only on 18 April, when he wrote, 'this is the last of our Plantains'. From 19 to 22 April, he served taro. He did not record in his log what he served from 23 to 25 April.[70]

While Bligh did not specify the amounts of fruit and vegetables he served at this time, the equivalent should have again been about 1⅓ lb. Morrison says that he served six plantains per person. Depending on their size, these may or may not have weighed 1⅓ lb. Bligh later said that he served 1½ lb of vegetables, which would have been a little more than required. Morrison, however, says that it was rather 1 lb, which would have been significantly less.[71] Given that 1 lb was the amount of pumpkin that Bligh had served while in the Atlantic Ocean, Morrison's figure is more likely to be the accurate one.

From 24 to 26 April, Bligh and the crew traded at Nomuka, one of the Tongan islands. Pigs were in short supply and, perhaps because the Europeans expressed a strong preference for yams, the islanders

---

69 Entries, 2, 4 and 6 April 1789, Bligh Log 2, vol. 2, pp. 68–9, 84.
70 Entries, 4–26 April, Bligh Log 2, vol. 2, pp. 82–117.
71 Morrison 1935, p. 36; Bligh, 'Particular Transactions at Sourabya', 15–17 September 1789, Bligh 1937, p. 68.

brought only small quantities of breadfruit, coconuts and plantains for barter. On the other hand, the tubers were 'in great abundance[,] some of which weighed above 45 lbs and were in general proportionally large'. So as to keep prices stable, Bligh again appointed Peckover to oversee trade; however, he gave him permission to act on behalf of the men also.[72]

Then, when wooding and watering had been completed, Bligh announced that anybody might trade for two hours.[73] Since they knew this was likely to be the last island at which metal would be in demand, the men went to it with a will, offering iron goods in exchange for 'Matts, Spears & many Curiositys and a quantity of Yams for Private Store with Cocoa Nuts etc'. Morrison says, 'what with Yams and Clubs in all quarters the ship was [so] fairly lumberd that there was scarcely room to stir in any part'. Bligh said they sailed with 'great supplies of the finest Yams'.[74]

Having now an abundance, Bligh served 2 lb of yams with the pork on 26 and 27 April.[75] The men must have thought that things had turned for the better. But then followed the infamous episode of the coconuts. Coming on deck in the afternoon of 27 April (land time), Bligh thought that some of his purser's stock was missing. When no one owned up immediately to taking them, Bligh summoned all the crew and ordered all the coconuts on board to be brought up. He questioned the officers closely, first about whether they had seen anyone taking his coconuts, and then, when they said they had not, about how many they had each obtained.

Christian admitted to having drunk from one coconut in the early morning watch but said that he hoped Bligh didn't consider him 'so mean as to be Guilty of Stealing yours'. This admission called forth another fearsome tirade from Bligh: 'Yes you dam'd Hound I do – You must have stolen them from me or you could give a better account of them'. He then told 'the people to look after [i.e. to keep a sharp eye on] the officers, and the officers to look after the people, for there never

---

72 Entries, 24–26 April 1789, Bligh Log 2, vol. 2, pp. 113–17.
73 Morrison 1935, p. 39; Fryer 1934, p. 55.
74 Morrison 1935, p. 39; entry, 26 April 1789, Bligh Log 2, vol. 2, p. 117.
75 Entries, 26 and 27 April 1789, Bligh Log 2, vol. 2, p. 117.

were such a set of damned thieving rascals under any man's command in the world before'.[76] And he told the officers further, 'God dam you, you Scoundrels, you are all thieves alike, and combine with the men to rob me. I suppose you'll Steal my Yams next, but I'll sweat you for it, you rascals, I'll make half of you Jump overboard before you get through Endeavour Streights.'[77]

Bligh ordered that all the coconuts be confiscated; and, as we've seen, he instructed Samuel to 'Stop these Villains Grog, and Give them but Half a Pound of Yams tomorrow, and if they steal then, I'll reduce them to a quarter.' Morrison says that the officers 'got together and were heard to murmur much at such treatment, and it was talked among the Men that the Yams would be the next seized, as Lieutenant Bligh knew that they had purchased large quantitys of them and [they] set about secreting as many as they Could'.[78]

Once again, then, at a time when there was plenty of food on board, Bligh reduced the public ration and threatened to confiscate private stores – actions that would have given him a greater return at the end of the voyage. The mutiny occurred the next morning. In that tumult, he lost many valuable items. As he reported to Banks, 'Mr Samuel my Clerk secured to me a Quadrant & Compass, some Cloaths, my Journals, and a few material Ships Papers, but all my Valuable Instruments with a time peice of Three hundred and fifty Guineas Value, a Valuable collection of Books, Maps and Drawings, with all my remarks and observations for Fifteen years past, were kept from me.' He also made sure to obtain his purser's ledgers, not only with legitimate reimbursement in mind. 'I have saved my pursing Books,' he assured his wife from Timor, 'so that all my profits hitherto will take place and all will be well.'[79]

✶ ✶ ✶

---

76 Morrison 1935, p. 41; Christian [1794] 1952, p. 64.
77 Morrison 1935, p. 41.
78 Morrison 1935, p. 41.
79 Enclosure with Bligh to Banks, 13 October 1789, and Bligh to Elizabeth Bligh, 19 August 1789, Bligh 1989, pp. 33, 25.

There are a number of ways to conceptualise this pattern of tensions and 'murmurings' over food. As I said earlier, I do think Bligh's illegitimate orders and tirades go a good way to explaining the officers' lack of willingness to come to his aid in the mutiny. Bligh had repeatedly impugned their personal honour, criticised them for lack of attention to duty, and humiliated them in public. He had also stolen their private stores of food. Thereby, he had eroded their respect for his authority and made even simple friendship between him and them impossible. By the end of April 1789, the officers were in no mood to stand up for their impossible commander.

Rather than by Bligh's 'bad language', however, I think the *Bounty*'s seamen were moved to rebellion by Bligh's manipulation of their rations. In a famous article, the social historian E.P. Thompson established that, in eighteenth-century Britain, while food riots in times of dearth might be triggered by malpractices among dealers and soaring prices, these grievances arose within a popular consensus about what were legitimate and illegitimate practices in marketing, milling, baking and selling. He also pointed out that this consensus was grounded in a traditional view of social norms and obligations, and of the proper economic roles of the various parties within the community and their responsibilities to each other, which when taken together can be seen as constituting a 'moral economy'. More than actual deprivation, it was perceived violations of these shared assumptions that commonly led the labourers and poor into direct action.[80]

I think that the *Bounty* mutiny offers a striking example of the workings of such a 'moral economy'. In late April 1789, the *Bounty* people were most certainly not starving. However, Bligh's practices as purser had given the seamen great offence in three ways. First, he had violated navy regulations and their customary expectations. Eighteenth-century sailors would not have harboured any illusions that there might not be cuts, sometimes severe, in rations during a long and difficult voyage. What they would have expected, however, was that their commander would make these cuts through necessity, to ensure common survival; and that when they occurred, all on board would receive reduced amounts. What they would *not* have expected was that their rations would be stinted

---

80 See Thompson 1971.

1 A Serious Affair to Be Starved

at times when their ship was carrying abundant supplies, or that their commander would look after himself first.

Second, Bligh had comprehensively confused public and private domains. As he himself conceded, much of the food on board the *Bounty* as it sailed from Tahiti was private, either bartered for by the men or given freely to them.[81] In confiscating foods and making them part of the ship's general issue, Bligh was illegitimately transforming private items into public ones. His reason for doing so was, quite simply, that he wanted to make money. The seamen knew from the beginning of the voyage that their commander was intent on filling his own pockets at their expense. They both resented his attempts to do so and held him in contempt for his manifest self-interest.

Bligh offended the crew further when he punished them for their resistance to his malpractices. They hadn't stolen the cheeses, but he withheld their cheese and butter. They didn't refuse to eat the pumpkins, even though these were spoiling; they did ask, however, to be served the proper equivalent. Bligh withheld their food again. At Tahiti and on the voyage back, he seized their private stores, refused to compensate them and told them he was once more reducing the ration. If court-martialled for his pursery practices, William Bligh would certainly have been found guilty of malfeasance; yet he repeatedly shifted the responsibility of his actions to his crew.

William Bligh was a thief who tried to distract attention from his dishonesty by blustering and bullying. Bounty after Bounty pointed to his malfeasance as a central factor in the mutiny. In the tumult of mutiny on 28 April 1789, John Sumner complained not about having been flogged for 'neglect of duty' sixteen days before but about the lack of food: 'Damn his eyes, put him into the boat, and let the bugger see if he can live upon three-quarters of a pound of yams per day.' As Bligh begged for 'arms, ammunition, and more provisions', John Millward, whom he had flogged and put in irons at Tahiti in February for desertion, jeered, 'Go and see if you can live upon a quarter of a pound of yams per day.'[82]

---

81 Entry, 31 March 1789, Bligh Log 2, vol. 2, p. 66.
82 *Bounty Court-Martial (Minutes)*, pp. 7, 42.

As they sailed west for Torres Strait, the people in the boat inevitably discussed the mutiny. When Bligh remarked how he had served the company 'fine messes of wheat', midshipman John Hallet commented, 'If it had not been for your fine messes, and fine doings, we should have had the ship for our resource instead of the boat.'[83] When they reached the Barrier Reef islands, the mild-mannered David Nelson remarked bitterly, 'Yes[,] damn his blood[,] it is his Oeconomy [i.e. management of the rations] that brought us here'; and when Bligh told William Purcell, 'if I had not been with you, you would have all aperished', Purcell replied ironically, 'yes Sir, ... if it had not been for you we should not have been here'.[84]

In the East Indies, Fryer complained to Dutch authorities that Bligh had given '[the] Ships Company short allowance of Yams and therefore [they] had taken away the Ship'. Purcell also said, 'the cause of the Ship being taken was owing to [Bligh's] stopping provisions'.[85] Many of the returned Bountys told Edward Christian concerning Bligh's response to the supposedly stolen coconuts, 'the ship's company were before greatly discontented at their short allowance of provisions, and their discontent was increased from the consideration that they had plenty of provisions on board, and that the Captain was his own purser'.[86]

Decades later, old John Adams repeated this explanation, telling Captain Beechey and his officers that what 'made the majority of the Crew yield so easily to the persuasions of Christian was, that the Captain stinted them in their allowance'. He had begun to do so, Adams asserted, while the ship was in the Atlantic Ocean, when he had shortened the amount of pumpkin served in lieu of bread; and, while at Tahiti:

> no Ships Provisions of any kind was served out, and the Men were obliged to their own resources to get a meal, except that when Hogs were received on board, after the meat was cut from the bones, they were served out to the Crew. If a Man was detected in bringing a Yam or any thing else [into] the Ship for his own use it was taken from him, and he was punished.

---

83 Christian [1794] 1952, pp. 67–8.
84 Fryer 1934, pp. 70–1.
85 Bligh, 'Particular Occurrences at Sourabya', 15–17 September 1789, Bligh 1937, p. 68.
86 Christian [1794] 1952, p. 64.

1 A Serious Affair to Be Starved

Adams repeated this explanation to the French explorer J.A. Moerenhout shortly before his death, saying that, at Tahiti, Bligh 'did everything possible to annoy us, including reducing the fresh provisions which were so readily available'.[87]

The explanation that Bligh's 'stinting' of the food ration disposed the seamen to support Christian in the mutiny lacks the glamour of that of a sadistic captain or of an alluring tropical island. Nonetheless, it is the true one. We should believe it.

---

[87] PN 12, p. [8]; PN 14, p. 80; and PN 17, vol. 2, p. 286.

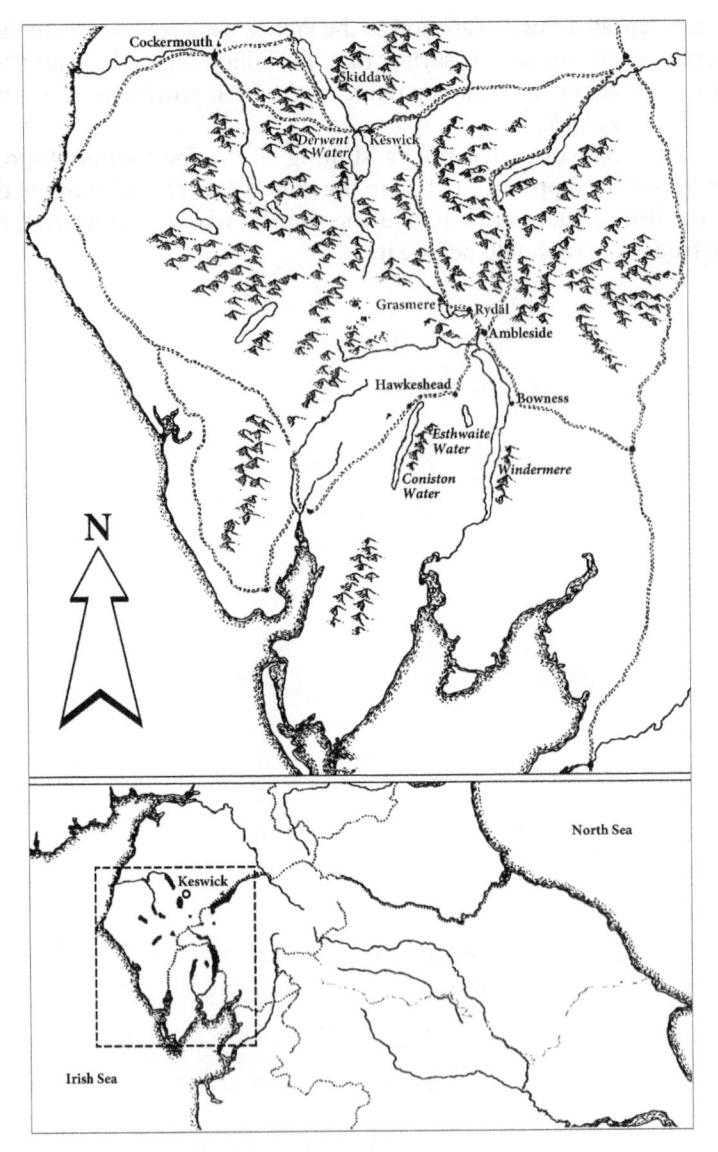

Figure 2 Wordsworth's Lake District. (Based on that in Juliet Baker, *Wordsworth: A Life*, p. xi.)

2
A Soul in Agony: Fletcher Christian's Torment

William Bligh professed bewilderment at the loss of *Bounty*. He wrote to the Admiralty from Batavia:

> To assign the cause of such a revolution, we can only imagine from the huzzas of the Mutineers, that they have promised themselves greater pleasure and advantages at Otaheite than they were likely to meet with in their Native Country. To this Land of Guile they are certainly returned – a Land where they need not labour, and where the allurements of dissipation are more than equal to any thing that can be conceived.[1]

And he repeated this explanation frequently, in his log, in other letters and in his published narratives.

Bligh was mistaken on a number of counts. He was wrong about what had motivated the men to rise against him and the officers not to support him. As we have seen in the previous chapter, by his manipulations of the food ration he had created bitter resentment in the men, a resentment shared by the officers whom he had humiliated repeatedly. He also mistook attendant circumstances for the central cause. Without the lead of a respected officer, it is most unlikely that a group of seamen would have rebelled against their commander. Much more likely, they would have simply continued the voyage, albeit deeply

---

[1] Bligh to Stephens, 15 October 1789, Bligh 1934, p. 36.

disgruntled and probably determined to complain to the Admiralty when it was over.

So we are left still with this question: what caused Fletcher Christian to rebel against his commander William Bligh, when at the start of the voyage the pair had been on friendly terms? In the quest for an answer, we must look first into Christian's psyche. To do so, I must take you to a wild country, and tell you the stories of two boys, who then went out into the world. As we know so little about Christian, I shall suggest the likely nature of his childhood and adult experiences by reference to those of William Wordsworth. Then, I shall investigate the destructive relationship that developed between Christian and Bligh during the voyage.

∗ ∗ ∗

The Lake District is that region in the north-west corner of England famous for its natural beauty. In the early 1950s in Far North Queensland, to have a 'Lakeland' set of coloured pencils was to be envied by the other schoolchildren who did not. With colours at once more delicate and more vibrant than the coarse Australian alternatives, these pencils produced more attractive drawings. This almost-lost detail is another link between my past and the history I am concerned with here. In my adult life, I have travelled repeatedly to the Lake District, to watch its deer in the woods and meadows at dawn, to meander about its lakes and climb its fells, to walk among its daffodils in spring, to see the tints of its trees and bracken, and hear the lilt and gurgle of its rills in autumn.

In the 1760s, the county of Cumbria, in which the Lake District lies, did possess some towns with civil amenities: Kendal, Ambleside, Keswick, Cockermouth, Penrith and the ports of Workington and Whitehaven in the west. Guarding the northern marchlands was Carlisle, the site of an old Roman camp and then a medieval fortress town. Among the villages were Grasmere, Bowness-on-Windermere and Hawkshead. Away from these settlements, however, Cumbria was a half-savage country where woodsmen, miners, watermen, wagoners, farm labourers, dry-stone wallers and shepherds and their families lived arduous lives, working from dawn to dusk in summer, grateful for their solid stone-built cottages in the severe winters. In the 1770s,

2 A Soul in Agony: Fletcher Christian's Torment

Cumbria began to acquire its aura as a place for rewarding pedestrian tours, to which William Hutchinson's *An Excursion to the Lakes* (1774) contributed. For its workers, poor and outlaws, however, it remained a hard country.

Fletcher Christian was born in 1764, while William Wordsworth was born in 1770. The families lived not far from each other, with the Christians residing at Moorland Close, and the Wordsworths in the nearby town of Cockermouth. As we know a great deal about the early life of the one, and very little about that of the other, I shall outline William Wordsworth's first.

Wordsworth was born in Cockermouth. He was one of five children, the others being Richard (b. 1768), Dorothy (b. 1771), John (b. 1772) and Christopher (b. 1774). Their father, John, was steward (estate manager) for Sir James Lowther, created Earl of Lonsdale in 1794. Their mother, Ann, was a member of the numerous Cookson family. She died in 1778, whereupon Dorothy was sent to live with her aunt Elizabeth Threlkeld in Halifax. When their father died in 1783, the family was further dispersed. In the times between school terms, the boys went to stay with one relative or another. William and Dorothy did not see each other for nine years.

The family's situation was made much more difficult by Lord Lonsdale's refusal to repay the large sums that John Wordsworth had expended on his behalf. These circumstances made the Wordsworth siblings forever after deeply conscious of the desolation of homelessness, and the value of community, friendship and sustaining family love. Dorothy wrote in 1787, after she and her brothers had spent the summer in the Cookson household, where they endured arguments and humiliations from guardians and servants alike, 'I absolutely dislike my Uncle Kit who never speaks a pleasant word to one, and behaves to my Brother William in a particularly ungenerous manner.' 'We always finish our conversations which generally take a melancholy turn,' she said bitterly, 'with wishing we had a father and a home.'[2]

In 1795, William and Dorothy Wordsworth were at last able to establish a home, first at Racedown in Dorset, then at Alfoxden in Somerset. From

---

2   Dorothy Wordsworth to Jane Pollard, late July and 6–7 August 1787, Wordsworth 1967, pp. 1–5, 7–8.

mid-September 1798 to late April 1799, they lived in Germany. Towards the end of December 1799, they returned to the Lake District, where they settled at Grasmere. In 1804, William married Mary Hutchinson. When three adults and the advent of children made the small cottage impossibly crowded, the Wordsworth family moved, first to Allen Bank on the opposite side of the village, and then to nearby Rydal Mount.

From an early age, William Wordsworth felt that he was someone set apart, and that it was his destiny to be a poet. And indeed it was. Together with Samuel Taylor Coleridge and others, he pursued new modes of apprehending and conveying reality, now known as Romanticism. For sixty years, he produced a vast body of poetry, some of it so accomplished (for example, the 1805 version of *ThePrelude*) as to justify our considering him to be the greatest English poet after Shakespeare.

'The child is father of the man', Wordsworth wrote gnomically in one of his poems. What he meant was that our childhood experiences determine our adult psyche. Partly because of the thousands of letters that members of the Wordsworth family wrote to each other and to friends, partly because of the nature of Wordsworth's avocation, and partly because of the devotion of his sister and his wife, who copied and preserved the multitudinous drafts of his poems, we know about most of William Wordsworth's life in great detail.

As a young boy, Wordsworth was given to uncontrollable tantrums. 'I was of a stiff, moody, and violent temper,' he later said; 'so much so that I remember going once into the attics of my grandfather's house at Penrith, upon some indignity having been put upon me, with an intention of destroying myself with one of the foils which I knew was kept there. I took the foil in hand, but my heart failed.'[3]

For a time, William attended Cockermouth Free Grammar School. Together with Richard (and later John and Christopher) he continued his education at Hawkshead Grammar School from 1779, where his landlady Ann Tyson tamed him by allowing him to do almost anything he wished. At all hours of the night and day, he would roam the woods and the verges, row on the Esthwaite Water and Coniston, climb nearby hills, fish, trap woodcocks, steal raven's eggs from nests high in the crags and skate on frozen ponds, all the time absorbing the colours and scents of

---

[3] 'Autobiographical Memoranda (November 1847)', Wordsworth 1974, vol. 3, p. 372.

2 A Soul in Agony: Fletcher Christian's Torment

earth, water and sky. During these rambles, he would lose consciousness of the separation between his self and his environment. 'I was often unable to think of external things as having external existence,' he later remembered. 'I communed with all that I saw as something not apart from but inherent in my own immaterial nature. Many times while going to school have I grasped at a wall or tree to recall myself from this abyss of idealism to the reality.'[4] Equally important for his future poetic development, he also paid careful attention to the people about him, whatever their social status.

At Hawkshead, Wordsworth studied Latin and Greek; mathematics and science; English literature and composition; and French. He read history and geography books from the school library and, encouraged by two of his teachers – William Taylor and Thomas Bowman, who were enthusiasts – he read widely in contemporary English poetry, developing the habit of reciting passages as he rambled. Edward Christian, Fletcher's older brother, was another of his teachers; but we do not know what, if any, influence he had on the boy's imaginative development. About 1783–84, Wordsworth himself began to write verse – 'My ears began to open to the charm / Of words in tuneful order, found them sweet / For *their own sakes* – a passion and a power / And phrases pleased me, chosen for delight, / For pomp, or love.'[5] For a dozen years, however, his poetry was conventional, as he imitated the forms and styles of those writers he had read at school.

The church was a common calling for men in Wordsworth's extended family, and his guardians intended that he should follow it. He commenced at Cambridge University in 1787. But he grew increasingly dissatisfied there. In the summer of 1790, he and his friend Robert Jones took themselves off on a three-month tour of France, northern Italy, Switzerland and Germany. They used river transport where available, but otherwise they walked, for two of the three thousand miles they covered.

Wordsworth returned to Cambridge to finish his degree, which he did in January 1791. He left, though, without a fellowship or a profession, so that he remained dependent on his family for money. He then spent four months in London. At first, he was attracted by the bustle and variety

---

4   Wordsworth 1993, p. 61.
5   Wordsworth, *Prelude* [1805] 1979, Book V, ll. 577–81.

of the great city. He toured its architectural monuments, listened to its prominent politicians in parliament and to its public speakers, became acquainted with some of its intellectuals and writers, and attended its theatres. He constantly experienced its extraordinary street life, with its mixture of merchants, workmen, thieves and prostitutes, its sailors from all the continents except Australia, its performers, acrobats and exotic animals. However, he came to see that he was wasting his time and talents, and he went to Wales to spend more time with Robert Jones. At one point, the pair climbed Mount Snowdon at night, so as to witness the sunrise from its heights.

At the end of November 1791, attracted by the promise of a new, fairer society held out by the French Revolution – 'Bliss was it in that dawn to be alive, / But to be young was very heaven!'[6] – Wordsworth travelled to France again. He sojourned in Paris for a time, where there was a circle of English expatriates and radicals, including James Watt, the son of the developer of the steam engine, and the lawyer James Losh. Then, wishing to learn the language better, he settled in the ancient royal city of Orléans. Presumably, Wordsworth hoped that fluency in French would bring him employment as a tutor or companion to a nobleman's son; in the event, his move to Orléans quickly led him into a passionate affair with Annette Vallon, a well-educated woman six years older than he. The couple had a daughter, Caroline, on 15 December 1792. But with public events having turned exceedingly violent and its having become dangerous for foreigners to be in France, with no money to support a family and – given his unmarried status and Annette's religion – no hope of persuading his guardians to provide any, he returned to England, evidently without seeing his daughter.

There are serious gaps in our knowledge of Wordsworth's life between 1793 and 1796, with few letters from these years and with his later unusual reticence about what he did then. It is clear that, disapproving of his behaviour, his guardians closed their doors to him. Presumably partly in the hope of making some money, he did publish two slim volumes of poetry, *An Evening Walk* and *Descriptive Sketches*, at the end of January 1793. However, these were conventional and undistinguished; and even Dorothy told him so. These works were not reviewed well, and did not sell.

---

6 Wordsworth, *Prelude* [1805] 1979, Book X, ll. 692–3.

2 A Soul in Agony: Fletcher Christian's Torment

At first, Wordsworth stayed with his brother Richard, now a lawyer in London. We know that he undertook some more pedestrian tours. He travelled to Wales again, where he saw Robert Jones and viewed the ruins of Tintern Abbey. There are also some hints that he may have returned clandestinely to France to see Annette and Caroline. But what the silences of these years mostly relate to, it seems, is an extended crisis of confidence, with Wordsworth becoming seriously depressed and suffering what we would loosely term a mental breakdown. We cannot be certain about the causes – or, perhaps better, the occasions – of it. His separation from his French wife and child must have been one factor, and his poverty another. But there may well have been others. He was probably discouraged that, despite London and some provincial centres having become hotbeds of radical sentiment, the English people did not rise against centuries of class exclusion and social oppression; and that with the outbreak of war with France in February 1793, the British government pursued measures to stifle dissent. And he had not yet found his poetic métier.

During the height of this crisis, it seems that Wordsworth relapsed into his childhood practice of losing himself in nature. Apart from rest, what seems to have released him from his despair was the kindness of friends and his sister's love, his rich friendship with another young poet, Samuel Taylor Coleridge, and his finding his true poetic voice. It is a remarkable thing about William Wordsworth that, repeatedly, somehow sensing his latent destiny, young acquaintances went out of their way to help him. In 1794, Raisley Calvert, dying from tuberculosis, left him a legacy of £900 a year – as William told his brother, 'to set me above want and to enable me to pursue my literary views or any other views with greater success or with a consciousness that if these should fail me I would have something at last to turn to'.[7] In July 1795, much to their father's annoyance when he found out, John and Azariah Pinney, the sons of a rich Bristol merchant and West India planter, offered William and Dorothy Racedown Lodge in Dorset rent-free, where at long last the two were able to enjoy the domesticity they had so yearned for. Coleridge first met Wordsworth

---

7   Wordsworth to Richard Wordsworth, 10 October [1794], Wordsworth 1967, p. 131.

in August or September 1795. He too sensed Wordsworth's potential, and was very generous in encouraging it.

In 1797, William and Dorothy moved to Alfoxden House in Somerset, to be nearer to Coleridge, who was then living with his family at Nether Stowey. The three became inseparable, visiting each other and rambling together, all the while discussing politics, philosophy and poetry intensely. From this collaboration came *Lyrical Ballads* (1798), which ushered in the new poetic age. Coleridge contributed the magical 'Rime of the Ancient Mariner' to the collection. Wordsworth's major offering was 'Lines written a few miles above Tintern Abbey, on revisiting the Banks of the Wye during a Tour, July 13, 1798'.

In this poem, Wordsworth first evokes the scene before him in language of great simplicity yet effect:

> The day is come when I again repose
> Here, under this dark sycamore, and view
> These plots of cottage-ground, these orchard-tufts,
> Which, at this season, with their unripe fruits,
> Among the woods and copses lose themselves,
> Nor, with their green and simple hue, disturb
> The wild green landscape. Once again I see
> These hedge-rows, hardly hedge-rows, little lines
> Of sportive wood run wild; these pastoral farms
> Green to the very door; and wreathes of smoke
> Sent up in silence, from among the trees. (ll. 9–19)

He then reflects on his mental turmoil during his visit five years previously, when he was 'more like a man / Flying from something that he dreads, than one / Who sought the thing he loved' (ll. 71–3). What is different on this second visit is that he is now able to articulate his vision, with its keynotes of 'emotion recollected in tranquillity' and the power of those moments of communication with the universal being that result mainly from immersion in the natural world:

> Though absent long,
> These forms of beauty have not been to me,

2 A Soul in Agony: Fletcher Christian's Torment

> As is a landscape to a blind man's eye:
> But oft, in lonely rooms, and mid the din
> Of towns and cities, I have owed to them,
> In hours of weariness, sensations sweet,
> Felt in the blood, and felt along the heart,
> And passing even into my purer mind
> With tranquil restoration ... (ll. 23–31)

In the second edition of *Lyrical Ballads* (1800), Wordsworth added his famous essay on his poetics, in which (inter alia) he stated that his purpose was:

> to make the incidents of common life interesting by tracing in them, truly though not ostentatiously, the primary laws of our nature: chiefly as far as regards the manner in which we associate ideas in a state of excitement. Low and rustic life was generally chosen because in that situation the essential passions of the heart find a better soil in which they can attain their maturity, are less under restraint, and speak a plainer and more emphatic language.[8]

It is the poems of *Lyrical Ballads*, then, that present the first clear evidence of Wordsworth's having now attained the vision that marks his greatest poetry and – equally as important – having found the voice to convey it.

Towards the end of 1798, William and Dorothy Wordsworth and Samuel Coleridge travelled to Germany, to learn the language and to become better acquainted with German philosophy and literature. There, in one of the severest winters of the century, William became depressed once more. In an effort to overcome his renewed despair and to regain his creativity, he undertook an extended examination of the factors that had shaped his imagination, beginning with his earliest childhood experiences. The result was his long autobiographical work, *The Prelude: Or, Growth of the Poet's Mind* (to give its modern title), in which his central insight is:

---

8   Wordsworth and Coleridge, *Lyrical Ballads* [1798] 1991, pp. 244–5.

> There are in our existence spots of time,
> Which with distinct pre-eminence retain
> A renovating virtue, whence, depressed
> By false opinion and contentious thought,
> Or aught of heavier or more deadly weight
> In trivial occupations and the round
> Of ordinary intercourse, our minds
> Are nourished and invisibly repaired.[9]

In its thirteen-book form of 1805, *The Prelude* is one of the most extraordinary poems in English, or indeed in any European language. Previously, others had written epic poems on a variety of grand subjects, for example: war (Homer, *Iliad*); a mythic hero's adventures (Homer, *Odyssey*); the emergence of civilisation (Virgil, *Aeneid*); the Christian creation story (Dante, *La Divina Commedia*); the Christian notion of the Fall (Milton, *Paradise Lost*); a nation's imperial endeavour (Camões, *Os Lusíadas*). William Wordsworth, however, made an epic of his self, of the development of his poetic imagination. It was an audacious undertaking, one then without parallel, and a towering achievement.

There are many portraits of William Wordsworth at different stages of his life. The lightly coloured pencil one by Henry Edridge, done in 1806, shows a rather sharp-faced man of early middle age, with a prominent nose and receding hair, and an intense gaze – a person who is confident about his imaginative power and the now well-established course in life it has given him (Plate 2).

✷ ✷ ✷

Fletcher Christian was born at Moorland Close, a farm situated on a rise a few miles to the south-west of Cockermouth, in September 1764. He was one of six children who survived into adulthood. (Ewan lived for three years, Jacob lived for one, and the twins Frances and Ann died soon after birth.) Charles Christian, his father, was the scion of an immensely rich family that had provided Deemsters (rulers) of the Isle of Man since

---

9   Wordsworth, *Prelude* [1805] 1979, Book 11, ll. 208–15

2 A Soul in Agony: Fletcher Christian's Torment

medieval times. Charles was raised in Ewanrigg, a vast pile of forty-two bedrooms, which was the family's seat in Cumbria, and practised law in Cockermouth. Fletcher's mother was Ann Dixon, the daughter of Mary Fletcher, whose family had been established in Cumbria for centuries. With its medieval buildings having been enclosed by walls as protection from marauding Scots in olden times, Moorland Close was the Fletcher family's farm. At the beginning of the eighteenth century, the family built a new dwelling outside the walls, with an orchard and garden. While its wealth did not compare with that of the Christians, the Fletcher family was nonetheless well-off.

However, this situation did not remain. The prosperity of Fletcher Christian's branch of the family had begun to diminish before the sudden death of his father in 1768, and it declined precipitately thereafter. By the late 1770s, Ann Christian was struggling to meet the financial demands of her sons as they sought to make their way in life. She was declared bankrupt early in 1780, and the farm was sold to a wealthy relative.

Whereas we know so much about William Wordsworth's childhood, we know so little about Fletcher Christian's. Was he a contented child or a recalcitrant one? We do not know. Did he ramble over the moors and along the waterways near the farm? We do not know. We know – or at least the story has it – that he rode a horse into Cockermouth when he attended the Free Grammar School. Did he become acquainted with William Wordsworth there? Probably not. Fletcher was six years older; and by the time William was enrolled, Fletcher may have followed the path of his brothers and attended St Bees School near Whitehaven. Again, though, there is no firm evidence that he did so.

At school, Fletcher Christian would have studied at least classics, mathematics and English composition. Which of these fields interested him most? We do not know. Did he, like Wordsworth, develop other interests? We do not know. His brother Edward said that he 'stayed at school longer than young men generally do who enter into the navy, and being allowed by all to possess extraordinary abilities, is an excellent scholar'.[10] But excellent at what? There are no records to tell us. Edward's remark suggests that Fletcher may have been destined for a profession but was forced to go to

---

10   Christian [1794] 1952, p. 76.

sea when the family's fortunes collapsed. But when precisely did he leave school? Again, we do not know.

Nor do we know when Fletcher Christian first entered the Royal Navy. We do know that he joined the *Eurydice*, a 24-gun frigate, on 25 April 1783, as a midshipman, as it was preparing to sail out to India. He was promoted to acting lieutenant and leader of a watch in Madras on 24 May 1784. It is curious to think that Arthur Phillip, who would sail to the Pacific Ocean in the same year as Christian, was captain of one of the ships of the East India squadron at this time; however, there is no evidence that the two ever met. The *Eurydice* returned to England in July 1785, when its crew were paid off.

Fletcher Christian then went on two commercial voyages to the West Indies in the *Britannia*, a ship owned by Duncan Campbell, the overseer of the convict hulks on the Thames, who had extensive interests in the islands. Its commander was William Bligh. Given that Bligh's wife, Elizabeth, was from the Isle of Man, there may have been some prior acquaintance between Bligh and Christian; but, again, there is no evidence of it. At Christian's first approach, Bligh evidently said that the list of officers was full, for Christian to reply, 'wages were no object, he only wished to learn his profession, and if Captain Bligh would permit him to mess with the gentlemen, he would readily enter his ship as a Foremast-man, until there was a vacancy amongst the officers'.[11]

The first voyage took place at the turn of 1787. On the second, which occurred in the spring and summer of that year, Christian had an officer's appointment. Precisely what this was is unclear. His brother later said that he sailed as second mate; however, Edward Lamb, who served as first mate, said that Christian was rather appointed gunner.[12]

Bligh and Christian evidently became friends on the first voyage, and it seems that Bligh subsequently invited the younger man to his house in Lambeth. This friendship continued on the second voyage, with Lamb later writing to Bligh:

---

11   Christian [1794] 1952, p. 77.
12   Christian [1794] 1952, p. 78; Lamb to Bligh, 28 October 1794, Bligh [1794] 1952, p. 30.

2 A Soul in Agony: Fletcher Christian's Torment

> when we got to sea, and I saw your partiality for the young man, I gave him every advice and information in my power, though he went about every point of duty with a degree of indifference, that to me was truly unpleasant; but you were blind to his faults, and had him to dine and sup every other day in the cabin, and treated him like a brother in giving him every information.[13]

(We should treat some of this testimony warily, for Lamb offered it after the mutiny, and clearly sought to support Bligh by denigrating Christian.)

Christian signed on for the *Bounty* expedition as master's mate. On 11 January 1788, not yet three weeks into the voyage, Bligh put him in charge of one of the three watches; and then, on 2 March, 'for the Good of the Service', promoted him over the other midshipmen to the position of acting lieutenant.[14] There is other evidence of strong continuing friendship. John Smith, Bligh's servant, later said that Bligh and Christian dined together every two or three days, and that 'Christian always had leave to have grog out of Captain Bligh's case whenever he wanted it'.[15] After the mutiny, Bligh remarked bitterly that he had promised Christian that he would be promoted at the end of the voyage, and that he had rendered him some service 'every day'.[16]

What sort of a person was Fletcher Christian? Someone who spent seven years at school with him said, 'a more amiable youth I have never met with: he was mild, generous, and sincere'. Edward Christian praised his brother fulsomely: 'no young man was ever more ambitious of all that is esteemed right and honourable among men, or more anxious to acquire distinction and advancement by his good conduct in his profession'.[17] According to the testimony that Edward Christian obtained, many of the Bountys held Fletcher in high regard, saying, among other things: 'He was a gentleman,

---

13   Lamb to Bligh, 28 October 1794, Bligh [1794] 1952, p. 30.
14   Entries, 11 January and 2 March 1788, Bligh Log 2, vol. 1, pp. 47, 101.
15   Smith, Affidavit, 1 August 1794, Bligh [1794] 1952, p. 22.
16   Bligh to Elizabeth Bligh, 19 August 1789, Bligh 1989, p. 23.
17   Isaac Wilkinson, quoted in Wilkinson 1953, p. 191; Christian [1794] 1952, p. 76.

and a brave man; and every officer and seaman on board the ship would have gone through fire and water to have served him'; 'He was adorned with every virtue, and beloved by all'; 'He was as good and as generous a man as ever lived'.[18] John Adams, who followed him to Pitcairn Island, said that he was 'universally esteemed & beloved by the Officers and Ship's Company, by his very kind and conciliatory behaviour'.[19] Bligh naturally damned Christian as an ungrateful wretch; and, as we have seen, one or two who sailed with him found fault with him for inattention to duty.

In one of the very few self-appraising comments we have, Fletcher Christian himself evidently remarked after the *Eurydice* had returned from India:

> it was very easy to make one's self beloved and respected on board a ship; one had only to be always ready to obey one's superior officers, and to be kind to the common men, unless there was occasion for severity, and if you are severe when there is a just occasion, they will not like you the worse for it.

This may not be unreliable self-praise. His brother Charles recorded that he later spoke with the surgeon and one of the officers of the *Eurydice*, who said that Fletcher 'was strict, yet as it were, played while he wrought with the Men – he made a Toil a pleasure and ruled over them in a superior, pleasant Manner to any young Officer they had seen'.[20] This is a portrait of a sensible person. However, Lamb also said that he was 'one of the most foolish young men I ever knew in relation to [women]'.[21] In this welter of claim and counter-claim, with all the entrenched interests involved, it is very difficult to locate the truth. Perhaps, as is so often the case with complex personalities, there is no single truth about Fletcher Christian.

There is reason to think, however, that Christian was unusual in his day, in that he was able comfortably to span the principal division of a

---

18 Christian [1794] 1952, p. 76.
19 PN 12, p. [8].
20 Christian [1794] 1952, p. 77; Charles Christian, quoted in Christian 1999, p. 87.
21 Lamb to Bligh, 28 October 1794, Bligh [1794] 1952, p. 30.

2 A Soul in Agony: Fletcher Christian's Torment

Royal Navy ship: that between officers and seamen. On the *Bounty*, he was on good terms with the young midshipmen Peter Heywood and George Stewart, and not discernibly on bad terms with most of the warrant officers (for example, Fryer and Cole). He was evidently athletic, with one story having it that he was able to leap from one empty barrel to another. He was skilful at ship's work and not reluctant to pitch in, and the seamen respected him for both attributes. In showing off a muscular arm to his brother when they met briefly as *Bounty* was on the verge of sailing, he said, 'This has been acquired by hard labour. I delight to set the Men an Example, I not only can do every part of a common Sailor's Duty, but am upon a par with a principal part of the Officers.'[22] The eighteenth-century navy was a good deal more egalitarian than the larger society of which it was a part; perhaps if we knew more about Christian, we should not find this attribute strange. Perhaps, as it had with Wordsworth, his Cumbrian upbringing had led to his interest in people not being determined only by their social status. But again, we do not know enough to decide.

What did Fletcher Christian look like? Here, we have only one strong indication. After the mutiny, Bligh drew up a descriptive list of the rebels for the Admiralty, which he also gave to the Dutch governor at Batavia and sent to Lord Cornwallis in Calcutta and to Governor Phillip in New South Wales. He said that Christian was:

Aged – 24 Years
5 feet 9 in High Dark Swarthy Complexion
Complexion – Dark & very swarthy
Hair – Blackish or very dark brown
Make – Strong
Marks – Star tatowed on the left breast and tatowed on the backside. His knees stands a little out, and [he] may be called a little bow legged. He is subject to violent perspiration & particularly in His hands so that he soils anything he handles.

Given the importance of bringing the ringleader of the mutiny to justice, this is presumably an accurate description.[23]

---

22 Quoted in Christian 1999, p. 87.
23 Bligh 1987, pp. 213, 331.

And yet. What really do we know about Fletcher Christian? There are very few details of his early life. There are no letters between him and his family or his friends. And then, who were his friends; and if he had some, why are there so very few reminiscences about him? There is no portrait of him. There is no will. Especially, there is no explanation from him of why he acted as he did. Tenebrous silence has all but obscured the personality and psyche of he who led what has become the most famous mutiny in all the history of the sea.

※ ※ ※

So far as we can tell from the surviving records, *Bounty*'s voyage seems to have begun well enough for Fletcher Christian, as he enjoyed both Bligh's company and his confidence.

The deterioration in their relationship evidently began at Cape Town. There, Bligh advanced Christian money, receiving from him a bill of exchange drawn on his brother Edward, redeemable for a larger amount. Bligh was out to profit from it, but there seems to have been another ramification of this murky transaction. Adams told Beechey that, thereafter, in moments of anger, Bligh would remind Christian of his obligation:

> The original quarrel between Capt. Bligh and Christian occurred at the Cape of Good Hope, and which was kept up until the mutiny occurred in a greater or less degree[.] Capt. Bligh, it is said, having obliged Mr C. in some manner, was continually making him feel the obligation he was under to him[.] All these aggravations combined was the occasion of the behaviour of Mr Christian.[24]

Precisely when the resentment and humiliation that festered in Christian's psyche first burst into the open is unclear. There is no overt indication that this happened before *Bounty* reached Tahiti. There, however, Christian and Bligh's relationship began to fray

---

24 Bligh, Comment on Edward Christian's third letter (of 17 December [1793]), Bligh Miscellaneous, p. 21; PN 12, p. [8].

2 A Soul in Agony: Fletcher Christian's Torment

publicly. Immediately on arrival, Bligh established a shore party, whose tasks were to be a point of contact with the islanders, and to assist and protect the gardeners as they gathered and nurtured plants for transportation. It is one of the mysteries of the *Bounty* story that we do not know the full membership of this party. We do know that it comprised seven officers and seamen, as well as the two gardeners, David Nelson and William Brown. Christian was in charge. The midshipman Peter Heywood was part of it. So too was the gunner William Peckover, whom Bligh appointed to oversee trade, and four seamen, whose identity we can only conjecture.[25] Presumably, they were four of the principal mutineers, viz. John Adams, Thomas Burkett, Thomas Ellison, Isaac Martin, William McCoy, John Millward, Matthew Quintal, Richard Skinner, John Sumner, Mathew Thompson, John Williams. (It may be that Bligh rotated these men for shore duty.)

If, as Morrison says, Bligh began to find serious fault with his officers at Adventure Bay in Van Diemen's Land, he increased his criticisms at Tahiti. In the night of 30 November 1788, while it was drawn up on shore near the camp, the small boat's rudder was stolen. Bligh blamed the theft on 'the remissness of my Officers & People at the Tent'.[26] On 29 December, he 'punished Robt Lamb butcher with twelve lashes for suffering his Cleaver to be Stolen'. On 5 January 1789, he turned Thomas Hayward before the mast, for having been asleep while in charge of the watch when Churchill, Muspratt and Millward absconded with arms. On 17 January, he found that Fryer, the master, and Cole, the boatswain, had not aired the spare sails regularly, so that they had mildewed and rotted.[27] When precisely he beat midshipman John Hallett, who could not swim, for not venturing into deep water with sufficient alacrity is unclear; as is whether this was the incident that he referred to in his index to the missing Tahiti section of the Mitchell Library log as 'Mr Hallett's Contumacy'.[28]

---

25   Entry, 28 October 1788, Bligh Log 2, vol. 1, p. 373.
26   Entry, 1 December 1788, Bligh Log 2, vol. 1, p. 411.
27   Entries, 29 December 1788, 5 and 17 January 1789, Bligh Log 2, vol. 2, pp. 7–8, 11–12, 18.
28   Bligh Index, referring to p. 180 of the missing section of Bligh Log 1.

As we have seen, Bligh railed and railed against his officers, and even contemplated punishing them corporally.[29] We should note that it was illegal for a commander to so punish a warrant officer. If – as seems likely – Bligh actually threatened them with it, then he gave very grave offence. Had he anyone else to undertake their duties, he added, he would have demoted the master and boatswain to common sailors.

After the three crew members deserted, Bligh searched their belongings, to find in Churchill's chest a list of names, including those of three of the shore party. Bligh did not record the names at this time. Later, he said that they included Christian and Heywood, and that all the men ashore denied any knowledge of the trio's intention to desert. Evidently, they did so convincingly, for Morrison says that Bligh 'was inclined from Circumstances to believe them and said no more to them about it'.[30] It may be that Churchill listed those men who were members of the 'Knights of Otaheite' group, rather than those who had rebellion in mind. We simply cannot know. However, Bligh did something more than question the men and then abandon the matter. In one of those curious lacunae that mark his public record-keeping, he did not mention this incident in his log.

Though it is now impossible to quantify, I do not doubt that there was a decline in discipline among the Bountys while they were at Tahiti. Bligh did not maintain a close supervision of them. In the interests of obtaining the plants and food that he needed, he busied himself in maintaining good relations with the rulers and their wives, entertaining them and being entertained in return, giving and receiving presents, avoiding the pitfalls of their politics, and recording ethnographic details that would help make his projected account of the voyage a good read. Meanwhile, the men lived in the midst of blandishments that most of them found impossible to resist. The minimal amount of ship's work required was not arduous in comparison with what was usual; the task of gathering and potting the plants proceeded without complications; the climate was easeful, despite the warm days and the rain; food was abundant and good; and the women were attractive and complaisant.

---

29 Entries, 5 and 17 January 1789, Bligh Log 2, vol. 2, pp. 12, 18.
30 Bligh to Bond, 26 July 1794, Bond [1953] 1796, p. 57; Morrison 1935, p. 33.

2 A Soul in Agony: Fletcher Christian's Torment

As instances of laxity became more common, Bligh found increasing fault with his officers. Now, too, he evidently became openly critical of Christian, particularly to the Tahitians. According to testimony later given to Edward Christian, Bligh would 'abuse Christian for some pretended fault or other' when entertaining the chiefs at the shore camp. Christian told his friends that he would not have minded, if Bligh had made his criticisms in private. Evidently, Bligh denigrated Christian further by telling the Tahitians that he was only a *towtow* (servant). Given the importance of status in Tahitian culture and Christian's distinguished lineage, this was doubly insulting.[31]

* * *

As if the attempted passage round Cape Horn had not been difficult enough, what was in fact the real challenge of the voyage began when *Bounty* left Tahiti on 5 April 1789. Now, Bligh faced a difficulty of a different order. The ship carried 774 pots, thirty-nine tubs and twenty-four boxes of plants. More than a thousand of these plants were breadfruit, but there were also vee (*vi*), ayah (*'ahi'a*), rattah (*rata*), peeha (*pia*) and 'the fine Maiden Plantain Oraiah' (*vayeeh*). There were also some ettou (*tou*) and matte (*mati*), which when combined produced a 'most beautiful' red dye.[32] Joseph Banks had cautioned the gardeners as they set out that they would need to be constantly vigilant in protecting the embarked plants against the ravages of salt, cold and animals. 'The Whole Success of the Undertaking,' he had told David Nelson, 'depends ultimately upon your diligence and care.' He and his assistant could not hope to succeed unless their 'particular Care and attention' was 'constant and unremitting'. 'One day['s], or even one hour's negligence may at any period be the means of destroying all the Trees and Plants ... and from such a cause the whole of the Undertaking will prove not only useless to the Public, but also to yourself.' They must therefore guard themselves against 'all temptations of Idleness or Liquor'; and they must negotiate prudently with Bligh for the water they would constantly need to wash salt spray off the leaves of the plants. If, on the other hand, they did their work well and reached the

---

31 Christian [1794] 1952, pp. 70–1.
32 Entry, 1 April 1789, Bligh Log 2, vol. 2, pp. 67–8.

West Indies with a large collection of healthy plants, they would receive 'a proportionate reward'.[33]

While it does not appear that Banks gave Bligh such severe warnings in writing, we can be sure that Bligh was in no doubt that his future career depended on his getting a healthy cargo to the West Indies. If he did, he would retain Banks's powerful patronage, be promoted in the navy, and receive a handsome reward from the Jamaica planters: £500, perhaps £1000 – a very significant sum for a junior officer with a young family. Hence, I think, his intense anxiety to assure Banks and the authorities that he lost the *Bounty* through no fault of his own. 'I shall sail in the morning without fail, and use my utmost exertions to appear before their Lordships and answer personally for the loss of His Majesty's ship,' he told the Secretary to the Board of Admiralty from Coupang. 'My honor and character is without a blemish,' he told Banks from Batavia (as we have seen), '& I shall appear as soon as I possibly can before the Admiralty that my conduct may [be] enquired into, and where I shall convince the World I stand as an officer despising mercy & forgiveness if my conduct is at all blameable.'[34]

So, as the *Bounty* sailed west from Tahiti, we may imagine Bligh fussing obsessively over the plants. But then, keeping the plants healthy would be to no avail if the ship were not in a condition to carry them to their destination. Therefore, everything in its working must be just right. The items in the hold must be properly stowed; the running rigging must be in good repair; the spare sails must be serviceable; the rats must be exterminated. And if things did not meet Bligh's demanding expectations, then there was the devil to pay.

Fryer said that it was after leaving Tahiti that Bligh's criticisms of Christian's inattention to duty and management of his watch became more frequent and public. These reached a crescendo in the week before the mutiny. First, as we have seen, he found fault with how Christian handled the sails during the squall in the night of 21 April. Then there was the trouble at Nomuka. Bligh sent watering and wooding parties ashore there on 24 April, one commanded by Christian, the other by Elphinstone. They had muskets, but Bligh ordered them to leave these in the boat. When

---

33   Banks, Instructions to Nelson, 20 August 1787, NA, HO 42/12, fos 173–83.
34   Bligh to Stephens, 18 August 1789, *HRNSW* (1892–1901), vol. 1, part 2, p. 692; to Banks, 13 October 1789, Bligh 1989, p. 30.

2 A Soul in Agony: Fletcher Christian's Torment

they landed, they were surrounded by islanders, who soon realised that the visitors did not intend to shoot at them and therefore became more troublesome in their quest for metal. Soon, they had stolen an axe and an adze. When Christian reported the problems encountered by the landing parties and these losses, Bligh rounded on him, calling him a 'Cowardly rascal' and demanding to know why he was afraid of 'a set of Naked Savages while He had arms': 'G— damn your blood, why did not you fire, – you an officer!' To this, Christian replied, 'The Arms are no use while your orders prevent them from being used.'[35]

The next day, Bligh sent Fryer to assist Christian and the watering party. While Fryer was ashore, the islanders stole his boat's grapnel. When he reported this to Bligh, he said that it was not a great loss, as there was iron on board to make another; to which Bligh responded in a rage, 'By God! Sir, if it is not great to you it is great to me.' He remarked in his log:

> The Men cleared themselves of the Neglect as they could not comply with every part of their duty and keep their Tools in their Hands, and they therefore merit no punishment. As to the Officers I have no resource, [nor] do I ever feel myself safe in the few instances I trust them.[36]

One of the Bountys said later that 'whatever fault was found, Mr Christian was sure to bear the brunt of the Captain's anger'; and Bligh evidently added to the spectacle by 'frequently [shaking] his fist in Christian's face'. It is hardly surprising that Christian should have told Bligh, 'Sir[,] your abuse is so bad that I cannot do my Duty with any Pleasure. I have been [in] hell for weeks with you.'[37]

In one of his tirades, Bligh evidently said that Christian and Stewart were 'as much afraid of Endeavour Straits, as any child is of a rod'.[38] Bligh seems repeatedly to have turned this coming passage into a dire threat as they sailed west. Why he should have done so is rather puzzling. It is true

---

35 Morrison 1935, p. 37; Christian [1794] 1952, p. 63.
36 Fryer 1934, p. 55; Entry, 25 April 1789, Bligh Log 2, vol. 2, p. 116.
37 Christian [1794] 1952, p. 63; Fryer 1934, p. 53.
38 Christian [1794] 1952, p. 63.

that only two European navigators had previously left the Pacific Ocean via Torres Strait: Luís Vaz de Torres in 1606 and James Cook in 1770 – hence Bligh's name for the strait (or, more precisely, for the particular route that Cook had taken in the *Endeavour*). This scarcely known passage was therefore fraught with potential danger. However, rather than indicating Christian's or any other officer's apprehension about the navigation of it, what I think Bligh's comments reflect is his own anxiety. That is, I think we have here a striking example of what psychologists term negative transference, whereby a person is able to recognise an unpleasant, unwanted emotion only by ascribing it to another.

Particularly in view of the *Endeavour*'s near wreck on the platform reef inside the Great Barrier Reef, and given his awareness of the necessity of succeeding with the expedition, Bligh would have been in a state of high agitation as he took *Bounty* towards Torres Strait. Once through it, the voyage would become far easier, as he reached a much better-known ocean, where he would find favourable winds and currents more easily, and therefore be able to count down the leagues to his destination. This is speculation, but it may not be misplaced. It is interesting that in one of their few civil exchanges, in the evening before the mutiny Fryer remarked to Bligh, 'Sir[,] there is a breeze springing up fare and a young moon, which will be lucky for us to come on the coast of New Holland – he said yes Mr Fryer it will be very lucky for us to get on the coast with a good moon.' Also relevant is Bligh's comment in his log, 'I had acted against the power of Chance in case I could not get through Endeavour Straights[,] as well as against any Accident that might befall me in them.'[39]

Then, on 27 April, there was the business of the missing coconuts, when Bligh accused Christian of theft. It seems there was a second clash later this day, when Bligh found further fault with Christian over some supposed inattention to duty. These clashes reduced Christian to tears. He complained bitterly to others, saying, 'flesh and blood cannot bear this treatment'; and that he 'would rather die a thousand deaths, than bear this treatment; I always do my duty as an officer and as a man ought to do, yet I receive this scandalous usage'. When Purcell attempted to calm him down, Christian raised the possibility that Bligh

---

39   Fryer 1934, p. 56; Entry, 28 April 1789, Bligh Log 2, vol. 2, p. 123.

2 A Soul in Agony: Fletcher Christian's Torment

might 'break [i.e. demote] me, turn me before the mast, and perhaps flog me'. He added, 'In going through Endeavour Straits, I am sure the ship will be a hell.' As the loyalists were going into the launch, he told the boatswain, who made a late attempt to reverse the situation, 'I have been in Hell for this Fortnight passd and am determined to bear it no longer, and you know Mr Cole that I have been used like a Dog all the Voyage.'[40] Fletcher Christian found himself in hell well before *Bounty* neared Torres Strait.

Evidently oblivious to the turmoil his abuse was causing, Bligh invited Christian to eat with him that night, for Christian to decline, with the excuse that he was unwell. He was, but his illness was mental rather than physical. Now, he made plans to desert the ship. Obtaining rope and nails from Purcell and Cole, in whom he evidently confided, he tied the cutter's masts to a plank, and hid part of a roast pig and a breadfruit. The *Bounty* was 30 miles (50 kilometres) to the south-west of Tofua, the nearest island, and Christian's proposed raft was rudimentary. He told people after the mutiny that 'he did not expect to reach the shore', but that he hoped he would be picked up by islanders in a seagoing canoe.[41]

Christian then destroyed his papers and gave away his possessions, and he seemingly told Stewart of his plan. Evidently, he hoped to leave the ship before he took charge of the morning watch at 4 am, but there were more men than usual on deck that night, watching a large shark that was swimming close to the ship and an active volcano on Tofua that lit up the sky.

Christian did not go to sleep until after 3 am, and was soon awake again. Precisely what Stewart said to him when he came on deck cannot now be known, for the main reports are contradictory. Morrison gave Stewart's comment as: 'the People are ripe for any thing'. Edward Christian's version, which is pregnant with ambiguity, is: 'When you go, Christian, we are ripe for any thing.' The version that Adams gave Beechey in December 1825 is:

> [Stewart] recommended him, rather than risk his life on so hazardous an expedition, to endeavor to take possession of the ship, which he

---

40 Christian [1794] 1952, pp. 63–5; Morrison 1935, p. 42.
41 Christian [1794] 1952, p. 65.

thought would not be very difficult, as many of the ship's company were not well-disposed towards the commander, and would all be very glad to return to Otaheite, and reside among their friends in that island.

The next day, Adams told the *Blossom*'s junior officers that Stewart said: 'Try the Crew, you know they are not well affected towards the Capt.'[42]

Finding that the midshipmen Hayward and Hallett, who were part of the watch, were not present because they were asleep, Christian set about enlisting a core of warrant officers and seamen in the mutiny, some of whom had been among the shore party at Tahiti: Quintal, Churchill, Thompson, McCoy, Mills, Williams, Burkett, Adams. Heywood's and Stewart's roles, if any, remain uncertain; they were only young officers at the time, and Heywood later denied vigorously that they had taken part in the mutiny.[43] Even more shadowy is the role of Edward Young, the illegitimate son of a West India planter, who may or may not have been an *éminence grise*.

Christian and his party obtained arms. They seized and bound Bligh, and dragged him on deck. As related earlier, their first plan evidently was to cast only Bligh, Hayward, Hallett and Samuel adrift in the sixteen-foot jolly boat; but as more of the Bountys indicated they wished to go with the commander, the loyalist party was given the launch. Evidently, only John Fryer made any significant attempt to reverse the situation. When he did, the mutineers confined him below. Even with all the shouting, imprecations and negotiations, the business was over by 8 am. Eighteen men went with Bligh in the launch, and he got all but one of them to Timor. (John Norton was killed at Tofua four days after the mutiny.)

In the first chapter, I have shown why the seamen joined in the mutiny – because Bligh had angered them with his manipulations of the food ration. But what caused Fletcher Christian to lead the rebellion? There is no easy answer to the question, and perhaps no answer at all. It

---

42 Morrison 1935, p. 44; Christian [1794] 1952, p. 71; PN 13, p. 72. Entry, 5 December 1825, PN 16, p. [8].
43 *Bounty Court-Martial*, pp. 137–61; Heywood to Beechey, 5 April 1830, quoted in Barrow 1989, p. 99.

2 A Soul in Agony: Fletcher Christian's Torment

is apparent that in the weeks immediately prior to the mutiny Christian had become increasingly unstable. After the coconut incident, he told Purcell that if Bligh were to flog him, he would 'take him in my arms and jump overboard with him'. His intention to set off on the makeshift raft was not the plan of a rational mind. One of his friends said that when he came up on deck he was 'much out of order'; 'he looked like a Madman', said another: 'is long hair was luse, is shirt Collair open'.[44] Adams told Beechey that as he organised the mutiny, Christian tied a heavy lead used for sounding round his neck, so as to drown himself if it failed. When Major John Taubman, who had initially recommended that Christian sail with Bligh, asked Bligh privately what had caused Christian to rebel, Bligh replied, 'It was Insanity.'[45]

Charles Christian's explanation for his brother's irrational behaviour was that 'Jealousy and Tyranny had produced Ill Usage to so great an Excess ... and Revenge ensued as an Effervescence from the Opposition of good to bad Qualities.' Edward Christian put it more coherently: 'there is a degree of pressure, beyond which the best formed and principled mind must either break or recoil', and he pointed to a 'sudden unpremeditated act of desperation and phrenzy'.[46]

To an extent, these explanations ring true; however, they do not provide the details we should like. For while we may agree that Bligh's repeated public humiliations were the catalyst for Christian's madness, we need to know much more than we do about his personality. It is here that the dense silence that has settled over his childhood and adolescence becomes relevant. Was Christian, like William Wordsworth, a wild child given to tantrums and depression? How long did he stay at school? When and why did he go to sea? What kind of life did he wish to make for himself? Did he suffer from any mental instability at earlier periods? If so, what were the occasions?

✳ ✳ ✳

---

44 Christian [1794] 1952, p. 64; Morrison 1935, p. 44; Ellison, Defence, 17 September 1792, *Bounty Court-Martial*, p. 175.
45 Christian [1794] 1952, pp. 64, 69; PN 13, p. 72; quoted in Christian 1982, p. 189.
46 Quoted in Christian 1982, p. 189; Christian [1794] 1952, p. 79.

Had I the training, I should develop an analysis of Fletcher Christian's psyche in which the loss of his father at a very young age would be a central consideration. My hypothesis would be that this left an emotional void that Christian thereafter sought to fill by gaining the admiration of older men, particularly those in positions of authority. Hence his need for Bligh's approval, which he sought via personal friendship as well as professional competence. However, Bligh's needs to succeed in his mission and to assert his authority over others by bullying and abuse, which far outweighed any need he may have had for friendship, meant that Christian put himself in a position of being repeatedly humiliated by someone whose approval he craved but could only fleetingly enjoy. So a desperate syndrome developed on *Bounty's* voyage, as Bligh offered Christian approval, only then to withdraw it in bursts of bad temper, then to hold out the prospect again with renewed invitations to dinner and other favours. As Bligh's oscillations between approval and abuse grew more rapid and public, Christian was driven mad with rage and grief, as he was forced to relive the loss of his father.

But I am a historian, not a psychologist. So let me rather relate another history, one that seems to resonate with Christian's story.

In the hope of making money, William Wordsworth spent several months in 1796–7 writing a verse play, *The Borderers*. As the name suggests, this play is set in late medieval times, in the marchlands between southern Scotland and northern England, the country that Christian and Wordsworth knew as children. Wordsworth intended a stirring tale of goodness oppressed by evil, saintliness overwhelmed by greed and revenge. Having travelled to the Holy Land, the old hero Herbert returns home blind, to find himself dispossessed of his title and property. Apart from his religious faith, only his daughter Miranda's selfless love sustains him. The villain Rivers persuades the young hero Mortimer, who is in love with Miranda, that her father has grossly wronged her, and that killing the old man would be an act of rational justice. Unable to do so outright, Mortimer abandons Herbert to a solitary death on the heath, only later to discover that he has been deceived, and that Herbert was innocent.

The Borderers is obviously much indebted to Shakespeare's *King Lear*. However, it also has two powerful contemporary referents. For a time in the 1790s, Wordsworth was attracted to William Godwin's philosophy,

2 A Soul in Agony: Fletcher Christian's Torment

with its emphasis on rational persuasion and moral relativism. But by 1796–7, he had come to believe that Godwin's outlook was flawed, since it ignored fundamental truths of human nature. He therefore made his play a repudiation of Godwinian rationalism, and a study of how false assumptions and perverted judgements can give rise to evil actions, as he showed that Rivers, who disdains conventional morality, was similarly guilty of the atrocious treatment of another person in his youth, and that he sought to convert Mortimer to his way of thinking so as to have a companion in crime and guilt.

In its earliest version, *The Borderers* is an overly complicated drama whose turgid verse lacks impact. With one exception, the revisions that Wordsworth made to it in the spring of 1797 did not markedly improve it. This exception is that now Wordsworth made mutiny central to Rivers's 'great crime'. During a voyage to Syria, Rivers tells Mortimer in a moment of unwonted honesty:

> RIVERS
> I was convinced a foul conspiracy
> Was laid against my honour, that the captain
> Was the prime agent – well – we were becalmed –
> The water of the vessel was exhausted –
> I felt a double fever in my veins.
> My rage suppressed itself – to a deep stillness
> Did my Pride tame my pride – for many days
> Beneath the burning sky on a dead sea
> I brooded o'er my injuries …
> One day at noon we drifted silently
> By a bare rock, narrow and white and bare.
> There was no food, no drink, no grass, no shade,
> No tree nor jutting eminence, nor form
> Inanimate, large as the body of man,
> Nor any living thing whose span of life
> Might stretch beyond the measure of one moon;
> To dig for water we landed there – the captain
> And a small party of which myself was one.
> There I reproach'd him with his treachery.

> His temper was imperious, and he struck me –
> A blow! I would have killed him, but my comrades
> Rush'd in between us. – They all hated him –
> And they insisted – I was stung to madness –
> That we should leave him there, alive – we did so.
> ...
>   'Twas a spot –
> Methinks I see it now – how in the sun
> Its stony surface glittered like a shield:
> It swarmed with shapes of life scarce visible;
> And in that miserable place we left him ...
>   MORTIMER
>   A man by men deserted,
> Not buried in the sand – not dead or dying,
> But standing, walking – Stretching forth his arms:
> In all things like yourselves, but in the agony
> With which he called for mercy – and even so,
> He was forsaken.
>   (Act IV, Scene II, ll. 9–49)

As the literary historians Mary Jacobus and Juliet Barker and others have pointed out, this addition is a version of *Bounty*'s story.[47] The parallels are very strong. Rivers abandons his captain with 'no food, no drink, no grass, no shade': Christian gave Bligh and those who went with him in the open boat only the scantiest of provisions. The Mediterranean rock 'was an island / But by permission of the winds and waves' (ll. 57–8): the *Bounty*'s launch was so overloaded that the waves washed over the stern, so that those in it were required to bail constantly. Rivers's captain 'stretched forth his arms' as he called for mercy: there is Robert Dodd's famous engraving of the pale-faced, white-shirted Bligh imploring those on the ship to throw down extra goods. As they sailed off, Rivers's companions 'scoffed' at the abandoned captain with 'hellish mockery / And laughed so loud ...'

---

47   Jacobus 1976, p. 28; Barker 2000, p. 175.

2 A Soul in Agony: Fletcher Christian's Torment

(ll. 53-4): Christian's companions asked Bligh contemptuously if he could live on three-quarters of a pound of yams a day. Rivers says of his captain, 'He had a daughter ... / She was a lovely maid – she had conjured me / At parting never to forsake her father, / To stand by him in all extremities' (ll. 80-4). Christian had 'danced' Bligh's children on his knees. Rivers laments, 'I had been deceived ... / I had been betrayed' (ll. 68-70). Christian agonised, 'I am in hell.' (In the first version of the play, Wordsworth gave this line to Mortimer.)

Rivers ends his story in an unexpected way. The captain was 'famished', he says, 'and he was innocent'. 'The man had never wronged me.' but crew had approved of his action 'gladly'. Theirs was a plot 'to rid them of a master whom they hated' (ll. 63, 65, 72-3). All this may be no more than a poet's reworking of a story that interested him for its insights into innocence, guilt and motivation. It may be, except ...

Among the 'worthies' whom Edward Christian employed to interview the returned Bountys about the events of the voyage were one of Wordsworth's uncles, Canon Cookson, and his cousin John Wordsworth, the captain of an East Indiaman. Another was James Losh. By 1796, Wordsworth and James Losh knew each other well. Losh's younger brother William had boarded in the same cottage as Wordsworth in Hawkshead in the mid-1780s. Commencing in 1787, Losh had studied law at St John's College, Cambridge, when Wordsworth was also a student there, and Edward Christian a fellow. Caught up like Wordsworth in the excitement of the French Revolution, Losh had gone to Paris in 1792, and there are hints that the pair saw each other there. In the mid-1790s, Losh practised at Lincoln's Inn, where Wordsworth's friend Basil Montagu was also located. Both were members of the intellectual circle that gathered about William Godwin. In 1796-97, suffering from tuberculosis and perhaps also from a nervous breakdown, Losh went to Bath to recover his health. There and at nearby Bristol, Losh saw the brothers-in-law Robert Southey and Samuel Coleridge, at a time when Wordsworth was forging his friendship with Coleridge.

While he lived at Bath, Losh corresponded with Wordsworth, then living at Racedown. Wordsworth spent the last two weeks of March 1797 in Bristol, when he saw Losh repeatedly. It cannot be coincidental that it was during Losh's sojourn at Bath that Wordsworth became interested in Fletcher Christian's story. There are three particular beacons of this interest. The first comes after the publication of the so-called *Letters from Mr Fletcher Christian, Containing a Narrative of the Transactions on Board His Majesty's Ship Bounty*, which appeared in the autumn of 1796. On 23 October, *The Weekly Entertainer* published a short letter from Wordsworth: 'I think it proper to inform you, that I have the best authority for saying that this publication is spurious.'[48] (Three asides: how could Wordsworth be so confident that this publication was not authentic, unless he knew that Christian was *not* its author? How might he know this unless the family or someone close to it had told him so? How might they know this unless they had been able to check with Fletcher?)

The second beacon is Wordsworth's adding the mutiny story to *The Borderers* after he had seen Losh. In a diary entry for April 1798, Losh recorded how he 'explained the real state of Christian's mutiny to Southey and Barry, who both seemed much struck by it.'[49] Unfortunately, he did not similarly record the nature of his conversations with Wordsworth twelve months earlier. Given what I have just outlined, however, it is more than likely that the pair did discuss Bligh and Fletcher Christian. This being so, we may assume that Losh gave Wordsworth details that had not been made public, so that Rivers's explanation of the mutiny in the Mediterranean may convey something of the reality of the *Bounty* one. This is, I know, supposition built on supposition; however, *something* in 1796–97 caused William Wordsworth to become very interested in Fletcher Christian's story. It is reasonable to think that this 'something' was what he learnt from James Losh.

※ ※ ※

As a preface to his drama, Wordsworth wrote a short essay, 'On the Character of Rivers', which I strongly suspect to be an oblique characterisation of Fletcher Christian as well as a repudiation of William Godwin's outlook.[50]

---

48 Wordsworth to the editor, *Weekly Entertainer*, 23 October 1796, Wordsworth 1967, p. 171.
49 Entry, 3 April 1798, Losh.
50 Preface ['On the Character of Rivers'], Wordsworth 1982, pp. 62–8.

2 A Soul in Agony: Fletcher Christian's Torment

Wordsworth begins:

Let us suppose a young Man of great intellectual powers, yet without any solid principles of genuine benevolence. His master passions are pride and the love of distinction. He has deeply imbibed a spirit of enterprize in a tumultuous age. He goes into the world and is betrayed into a great crime.

He then asserts that the basis of the young man's happiness 'immediately deserts him', and that he 'quits the world in disgust, with strong misanthropic feelings'. He becomes obsessed with the nature of virtue and vice, and develops a destructive habit of 'hunt[ing] out whatever is bad in actions usually esteemed virtuous and [in] detect[ing] the good in actions which the universal sense of mankind teaches us to reprobate'.

Wordsworth continues that as he develops this perverse skepticism, the young man's

Natural energy and restlessness impel him again into the world. In this state, pressed by the recollection of his guilt, he seeks relief from two sources, action and meditation. Of actions those are most attractive which best exhibit his own powers, partly from the original pride of his character and still more because the loss of Authority and influence which followed upon his crime was the first circumstance which impressed him with the magnitude of that crime and brought along with it those tormenting sensation by which he is assailed. The recovery of his original importance and the exhibit of his own powers are therefore in his mind almost identified with the extinction of those painful feelings which attend the recollection of his guilt.

Wordsworth then asserts that the young man will develop a 'strong tendency to vice', and continue to commit crimes against humanity, partly because 'he has rebelled against the world and the laws of the world and he regards them as tyrannical masters'. Asking what the young man's motives are, Wordsworth answers:

They are founded chiefly in the very constitution of his character; in his pride which borders even upon madness, in his restless disposition, in his disturbed mind, in his superstition, in irresistible propensities to speculations, in his thoughts and in his feelings, in his general habits and his particular impulses, in his perverted reason justifying his perverted instincts.

He concludes: 'The general moral intended to be impressed by the delineation of such a character is obvious: it is to shew the dangerous use which may be made of reason when a man has committed a great crime.'[51]

As we have seen in the previous chapter and shall see further in the next one, we might aptly apply these characterisations to Christian.

---

51 Preface: ['On the Character of Rivers'], Wordsworth 1982, pp. 62–8.

3

Somewhere Between Sea and Sky: The Enigma of Fletcher Christian's Death

If the absence of documentary sources hinders us in our quest to know more about Fletcher Christian, we are faced with an abundance of materials concerning the mutineers' colony on Pitcairn Island. However, this does not mean that the task of knowing what happened there in the first ten years is any easier than that of understanding Fletcher Christian. It isn't, for the records are confused, contradictory and of dubious reliability. Indeed, it is possible that they conceal a very different outcome to the one that they purport to convey.

After the mutiny, the twenty-five men who remained on the *Bounty* elected Fletcher Christian as its master, and George Stewart as his deputy, these being the two most skilled in navigation. In doing so, they followed the way of the buccaneers. In other gestures towards equality, they made themselves matching jackets out of sails, and divided the spare clothing and Tahitian curiosities equally.[1] Christian ordered most of the plants to be thrown overboard. Even at this early point, there was evidently dissension among those remaining on *Bounty*, with some plotting to seize control of the ship once they were back at Tahiti. Morrison says that Christian took the keys to the arms chest from Coleman and gave them to Churchill, 'who made his bed on the Chest and each of Mr Christian's party were Armd with a Brace of Pistols, Mr Christian himself never going without a Pistol in his pocket'.[2]

---

1   Stewart Journal.
2   Morrison 1935, p. 47.

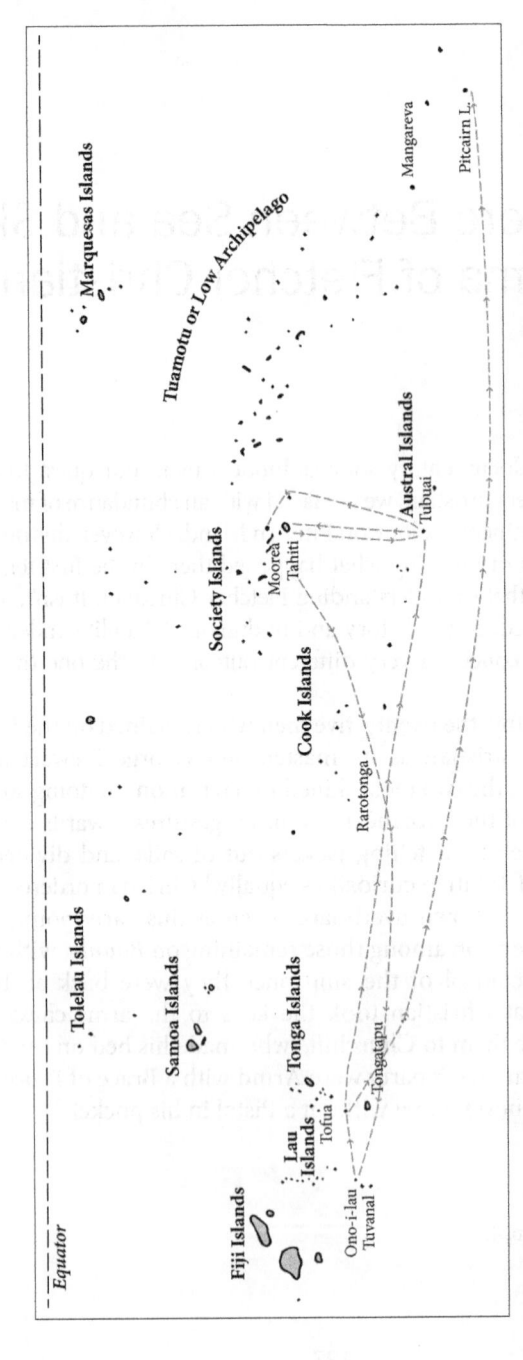

Figure 3 The conjectured routes of the *Bounty* in 1789, after the mutiny. (These routes result from H.E. Maude's detective work. The map is based on that in *Of Islands and Men*, p. 23.)

3 Somewhere Between Sea and Sky

On Christian's advice, the group decided to sail to Tubuai, one of the Austral Islands almost directly south of Tahiti, seen but not landed at by James Cook in 1777, to assess its suitability as a place at which to settle.[3] The passage took four weeks. When they reached Tubuai on 24 May, the islanders did not welcome them. After attacking a boat's crew looking for a good anchorage, they sent a group of 'young and handsom' girls on board to distract the Europeans while more than 700 warriors who came alongside in fifty canoes sought to overrun them. Eleven men and one woman were killed when Christian ordered the Bountys to fire.[4]

After inspecting Tubuai for two days, during which the islanders kept their distance, Christian decided that it was suitable, being stocked with coconut, breadfruit, plantain, yam and taro. However, because it lacked animals, he decided to return to Tahiti, there also to collect women and friends who might mediate between them and the Tubuaians. Dissension among the crew continued, so Christian 'appointed his own Party to keep Constant Guard' on the passage.[5]

The *Bounty* arrived back at Matavai Bay on 6 June. Christian told the islanders a fanciful story about Bligh's having met Cook and the pair having sent him back to obtain resources for a colony. In nine days, he gathered a bull and cow left by Cook, about 460 pigs, fifty goats, and some chickens, dogs and cats.[6] When he sailed on 16 June, there were also nine Tahitian men, ten women and eight or nine boys and girls on board.

The *Bounty* reached Tubuai again on 26 June, and the Europeans immediately became embroiled in rivalries between the island's three principal rulers. While one was welcoming, the others were hostile, and Christian antagonised the senior one by choosing to settle on land controlled by a rival. The Bountys set about building 'Fort George', a large earthen structure, with two sides of 125 feet (38 metres), one of 120 feet (37 metres), and the fourth open to the beach about 300 feet

---

3   In tracing the *Bounty*'s progress after the mutiny, I draw on the admirable detective work of H.E. Maude 1986.
4   Morrison 1935, p. 49.
5   Heywood Journal; Morrison 1935, pp. 50–1.
6   Morrison 1935, p. 52

(about 90 metres) away. The walls were to be 18 feet wide at the base (5 metres), 8–12 feet wide at the top (2–4 metres) and 7 feet high (2 metres), and enclosed by a moat 18 feet wide and 20 feet deep (5 x 6 metres). The Europeans placed 4-pounder cannons at each corner, and swivel guns on the sides. The fact that they thought it necessary to build this structure shows the futility of their hope of living peacefully with the islanders.

Within a couple of weeks of their arrival back at Tubuai, the Bountys were quarrelling with each other again. Christian discovered that Sumner and Quintal had gone on shore without permission. On his asking them to explain, they replied, 'the Ship is moord and we are now our own Masters', whereupon Christian pointed a pistol at the head of one, saying, 'I'll let you know who is Master', and put both of them in irons. When they were brought up from the hold the next day, 'they beg'd Pardon and promised to behave better for the future'. Referring to the same events, the precis of Heywood's journal made by Edward Edwards, captain of the ship sent in pursuit of the mutineers, says:

> Some of the people begun to be mutinous – & on 6th [July] 2 of the Men were put in Irons by a Majority of Votes – & drunkenness fighting & threatening each other's lives was so common that those abaft [i.e. in command] were obliged to Arm themselves with Pistols.

Edwards's precis of Stewart's journal states that on 7 July, 'Articles were drawn up by Christian & Churchill specifying a mutual forgiveness of all past grievances which every Man was obliged to swear to & sign. Matthew Thompson excepted who refused to comply.' Thereafter, two men were allowed to sleep on shore at night, and as many as chose on Sundays.[7]

Relations between the visitors and the islanders soon deteriorated further. The animals that the Europeans turned loose to graze damaged gardens. European parties took food without permission, and one islander who tried to stop them was shot. The islanders stole European goods. John Adams was assaulted. Two islanders were killed when they resisted

---

7   Morrison 1935, p. 55; Heywood Journal; Stewart Journal.

Europeans chasing after women. When Tinarou, the ruler most opposed to the newcomers, refused to barter and return stolen items, Christian seized his 'Gods' and burnt his house down. These conflicts culminated in pitched battles between the Bountys and their Tahitian companions and hundreds of Tubuian men and women, in which dozens of the islanders were killed and many more wounded.[8]

By this time, sexual jealousies had become extreme. Morrison says that many of the Bountys:

> began to Murmur, and Insisted that Mr Christian would head them, and bring the Weomen in to live with them by force and refused to do any more work till evry man had a Wife, and as Mr Christians desire was to perswade rather than force them, He positively refused to have any thing to do with such an absurd demand. Three Days were Spent in debate, and having nothing to employ themselves in, they demanded more Grog[.] This he also refused, when they broke the lock of the Spirit room and took it by force.

After this long, heated discussion, the Bountys voted sixteen to nine to return to Tahiti, 'where they might get Weomen without force'.[9] With some Tubuaians added to the Bountys' Tahitian companions, the ship left on 15 September.

As they sailed, the Bountys sorted slops, trade goods, arms, ammunition and alcohol into equal shares. They were back at Matavai Bay on 21 September, when sixteen left the ship. Some of the islanders went ashore, while others came on board. When Christian sailed again the next morning, it was with eight other Bountys – John Adams, William Brown, William McCoy, Isaac Martin, John Mills, Matthew Quintal, John Williams and Edward Young – and six Polynesian men, twelve women and a child. After four months meandering thousands of miles about the central Pacific Ocean in search of a suitable refuge, Christian brought them to the uninhabited Pitcairn Island, then wrongly locaamted on published charts. Even among this reduced group of mutineers, dissensions evidently continued. In 1834, Frederick Bennett, surgeon on the whaling vessel *Tuscan*, heard that while

---

8   Heywood Journal; Morrison 1935, pp. 58–9.
9   Morrison 1935, pp. 60–1.

Christian was off with a party reconnoitring Pitcairn, 'Mills, the gunner's mate, proposed to those who remained on board to make sail for Tahiti, and leave their companions to their fate'.[10]

The Europeans took the ship into the only feasible landing place, a small, rock-bound bay above which rose cliffs high enough to conceal a settlement behind. (They named this landing place Bounty Bay.) After unloading all the items valuable for their purposes, they ran the ship ashore and burnt it. Pitcairn did offer good food resources for a small colony, for earlier Polynesian settlers had established coconut, plantain, banana, sugar cane, ginger, yam and taro. To these, the newcomers added other kinds of breadfruit, yam, citrus, plantain, sweet potato, watermelon, pumpkin, pigs, goats and poultry.[11] The world was all before them; but it soon became clear that they might not make their lives anew.

* * *

The Bountys divided the arable land on Pitcairn equally among themselves but did not allocate any plots to the Polynesian men, whom they rather set to work. Some of these men possessed status in their own societies and had befriended the Europeans; now, they became servants, not to say slaves. Moreover, the sexual division that the Europeans established meant that, while each of them had a woman, one Raiatian man had his own wife and the other five islander men shared two women. These were circumstances ripe for disaster.

There are at least twenty-five accounts, offered at intervals over eighty years, of what happened on Pitcairn Island between 1790 and 1801. I have termed these accounts Pitcairn Island narratives (PN), and have numbered and in some cases paginated them. They are listed separately in the Bibliography.

Basing their analysis mainly on four of these accounts, historians have constructed a core narrative, which comprises the arrival at Pitcairn Island at the turn of 1790; the unloading and then burning of *Bounty* in January 1790; the contention between the Europeans and the Polynesian men, which culminated in Fletcher Christian's death

---

10   PN 20, vol. 1, p. 46.
11   See PN 16, p. [29]; PN 18, p. 161.

and general mayhem in September 1793; and John Adams's uniting the surviving Polynesian women and mixed race children into a harmonious little society.

The four principal sources for this core narrative are excerpts from a contemporary journal; the accounts of two interviews with Te'ehuteatuaonoa ('Jenny'), the first about 1819, the second about 1821; and the *Pitcairn Island Register*. On the face of things, this appears a good choice of sources. Accounts from a midshipman whose training involved keeping a detailed log or journal, those from the companion of two of the mutineers (John Adams and Isaac Martin), and the island's official record book of births, deaths, marriages and memorable events. Together, these sources would seem likely to possess more authenticity than others written at a remove in time from the central protagonists and events, and subject to the blurring of oral transmission. However, as I shall show, many details in these four sources are problematic, as is who compiled them, when and with what aims; and what the authors or transcribers included and excluded. In particular, they do not clarify the precise circumstances of Fletcher Christian's death, and where and when this occurred.

There are major problems with each of these accounts. The first question is: who wrote the journal? In 1814, Pipon noted that Adams had kept:

> a journal, but it chiefly contained the manner & work they were employed about, as well as what was due from one to the other of Provisions, for it appears they had a regular established allowance, & they frequently exchanged together Salt for fresh Provisions. Again when their Ship's Stock was expended, they mutually assisted each other with Meat & repaid punctually the first good opportunity; all this was carefully noted down in the Journal.[12]

Now, Pipon does not say which years the journal that he saw covered; neither does he place such entries in any context or sequence. On the other hand, Beechey, who also saw a journal when he visited

---

12   PN 9, pp. [6–7].

the island in 1825, mentioned that it contained details of exchange and accounting for the period 1796 and 1798:

> There was also a mutual accommodation amongst them in regard to provisions, of which a regular account was taken. If one person was successful in hunting, he lent the others as much meat as they required, to be repaid at leisure; and the same occurred with yams, taros, etc, so that they lived in a very domestic and tranquil state.[13]

The journal that Beechey saw was shown to him by Adams, who identified it as Young's. Beechey said that this commenced in December 1793 and ended about 1798. A comparison of some details in Pipon's account and some entries copied or summarised by Beechey strongly suggests that these journals were one and the same, at least for the 1790s. For example:

> **Pipon:** Another ship appeared off the Island on the 27 Decr 1795 but did not approach the Island very near, neither could they make out by their Colours what Nation she belonged to.
> **Beechey:** On 27th of December [1795], they were greatly alarmed by the appearance of a ship close in with the island. Fortunately for them there was a tremendous surf upon the rocks, the weather wore a very threatening aspect, and the ship stood to the S.E., and at noon was out of sight. Young appears to have thought this a providential escape, as the sea for a week after was 'smoother than they had ever recollected it since their arrival on the island.

It is also clear that this journal provided the substance of some of the early entries in the *Pitcairn Island Register*.[14]

Who, then, was in fact the author of this journal? Pitcairn islander tradition has it that, towards the end of the first decade, as his health failed, Young taught Adams to read and write; and that after Young's death in 1800, Adams used his newly acquired skills to educate the young islanders and direct their religious observance. However, we may

---

13   PN 13, vol. 1, pp. 88, 91–2.
14   PN 9, p.[9]; PN 13, vol. 1, p. 91; PN 22 and 23.

doubt how advanced these skills were. According to John Buffett, who came to know the islanders well after his arrival in 1823:

> It is generally thought that Mr Adams brought them up in this manner from childhood, but it was many years after the Massacre before he taught any to read, and McCoy's son has told me, that they could not believe for some time that Adams understood what he read, but they thought (to use his own words) 'he spoke out of his own head'.[15]

The merchant captain who delivered books to Adams from the Calcutta Committee of the Society for Promoting Christian Knowledge in January 1819 also brought a letter from his brother and said, 'I read this letter to him'; and when Adams subsequently composed a biographical note, he wrote, 'I was born at Stamford Hill in the parrish of St John, Hackney, Middlesex of poor Bot Honast parrents My farther was drowned in the Theames therefore he left Me and three More poore orfing Bot one Was Married and ot of All Harmes'.[16] In 1821, Jenny told her second interviewers that Adams 'prays extempore, but does not read'. One of the young Pitcairners told Captain Thomas Raine, who called at the island in April 1821:

> We wish very much that person would arrive that is to teach us to read and write and to do what is good towards God, because we don't know enough – John Adams is very good man but he can't teach us any more now, and he don't know enough either.

This suggests that Adams had not been able to make the first generation born on Pitcairn literate, a supposition supported by Frederick Bennett's observation made during a visit twelve years later, when two old Tahitian women were the only survivors of the original party: 'The elder members of the Pitcairn Island family are but indifferently educated: scarcely any of them being able to write their own name, though most can read.'[17] Taken together,

---

15 PN 21, p. 28.
16 See Scott 1982, pp. 35, 36.
17 PN 3a; quoted in Nicholson 1965, p. 72; PN 20, vol. 1, p. 37.

these circumstances suggest that Adams was not literate in the mid-1790s, and that what literacy he subsequently developed was rudimentary. Therefore, it is most likely that Young was the author of the journal the navigators saw.

This conclusion leads to some more puzzles, though. Young was a midshipman, for whom the keeping of a daily record was mandatory. Two of his fellow midshipmen on *Bounty*, George Stewart and Peter Heywood, continued to do so after the mutiny, even though they were not enthusiastic about the course of events. Why then did Young commence his Pitcairn journal *only at the end of 1793*? Or was it rather that he kept it all along, from the time that *Bounty* reached Pitcairn Island, or perhaps even from the time of the mutiny?

Something to give considerable credence to this suggestion is that, in September 1814, visiting Royal Navy captains pointed out that the island's calendar was one day in advance of the true one, because someone had not corrected for the day deducted when, sailing east from the mid-Pacific Ocean, *Bounty* crossed what we know as the International Date Line (see below). The fact that there was a discrepancy of only one day in a period of some twenty-five years (mid-1789 to September 1814) of date-keeping on the island strongly suggests there had been a continuous record. Who had kept it – or, at least, who had begun it? It could scarcely have been John Adams, who – as we have just seen – could neither read nor write before the late 1790s. The best answer seems to be Young; and, if this is right, it follows that he – or someone after his death – destroyed the earlier sections. If so, for what reason? Did the entries for the years 1790 almost to the end of 1793 show the Bountys in an even worse light than does the history we now have? Did these entries gainsay the narrative (whatever its variants) that Adams chose to present when questioned about what had happened?

What we have of Young's journal in Beechey's published narrative is an uncertain mixture of paraphrasing and (seemingly) direct quotation. And then, we simply cannot know, either that Young recorded events fully or scrupulously, or that Beechey attended to all the details contained in what he saw, or recorded them precisely. For example, Beechey observed, 'So little occurred in the year 1796, that one page records the whole of the events.' Yet, as the *Pitcairn Island Register* does not contain any entry for 1796, we can now have no idea which events Young noted for this year.

Then again, while he does not quote directly, Beechey also observed that 'throughout [1797] there are but three incidents worthy of notice'. The first was that the islanders looked for meat to salt; the second was that they sought 'to make syrup from the tee-plant (*Dracæna terminalis*) and sugar-cane'; and the third was 'a serious accident that happened to McCoy, who fell from a cocoa-nut tree and hurt his right thigh, sprained both his ancles and wounded his side'.[18] None of these circumstances is mentioned in the *Pitcairn Island Register*.

Rosalind Young – who was born in 1853, long after the initial events – also evidently drew on her great-grandfather's journal for her *Mutiny of the Bounty and Story of Pitcairn Island, 1790–1894* (1894), but she does not seem to have quoted directly from it. She added details that she obtained from others, and – reflecting the now-prevailing ethos of the islanders and presumably that in particular of her grandfather John Buffett – she also infused her account with Christian moralising, so that it is impossible to distinguish the real nature of original circumstances from her presentation of them. Over decades, rumours have persisted that Young's journal remains extant, and is in the possession of one of the descendants of the mutineers. Without access to it, however, we may only wonder how much, if at all, its entries might elucidate these puzzles.

※ ※ ※

Despite Jenny's narratives exhibiting a strong (though not absolute) consistency, they are also problematic. The first was evidently recorded in 1818 or early 1819, after she had left Pitcairn on an American ship and eventually reached Tahiti via Chile and the Marquesas Islands. It was published in the *Sydney Gazette* on 17 July 1819. There is no indication of the identity of the person who stated in the opening sentence of this report, 'The following account I have just received from a Taheitan woman'; nor do we know exactly how they communicated.[19] This is an important point, for it is uncertain just how well Jenny spoke

---

18   PN 13, vol. 1, pp. 91–2; and see PN 23, p. 31.
19   PN 2. The use of the forms 'Taheiti' and 'Taheitan' perhaps indicates that the interviewer was a missionary (see below).

English, or how much of her native language she may have lost in the thirty-odd years she had been away from Tahiti. Observing that English was the islanders' common language, Pipon said, 'even the old Otaheitan women have picked up a good deal of [it]'. On the other hand, some later visitors to Pitcairn said that while the children spoke both English and an English-Polynesian *patois*, the Tahitian women had learnt either not much English or none at all. The first person to record Jenny's story said that she could speak 'neither English nor Taheitan, but a jumble of both'.[20] Inevitably, then, this interviewer would have had to translate and interpret what she said – for example, it is impossible that Jenny should have said that Adams prays '*extempore*'.

This problem is perhaps not so great where Jenny's second interview is concerned. It was conducted in September 1821 by Henry Nott, who had been sent by the London Missionary Society to Tahiti in 1797, and Captain Peter Dillon, the adventurer who discovered that Lapérouse's ships had been wrecked on the reef at Vanikoro. By this time, Nott knew Tahitian well (in the 1830s, he would translate the Bible into it), and it is said that Dillon also spoke the language 'fluently'. However, the English account of what Jenny told them seems to be the work of Nott alone. There are two printed versions of this interview, with many editorial differences.[21]

There are other problems. As oral historians know only too well, memory can easily falsify; and by 1819/1821 Jenny was recalling events that had occurred twenty to thirty years earlier, events whose traumatic nature may also have influenced how she remembered them. Moreover, we do not know the extent to which those who interviewed her 'adjusted' what they thought she said, in particular by structuring her accounts according to European notions of narrative, or by adding details given by later visitors to Pitcairn Island, or by glossing her accounts according to their own assumptions and their readers' supposed social and religious expectations.

The *Pitcairn Island Register* exists in two manuscript versions. One is identified as compiled by the carpenter become schoolmaster John Buffett. It was formerly in the collection of the Society for Promoting

---

20   PN 9, p. [5]; PN 16, p. [6]; PN 2.
21   PN 3a and 3b.

3 Somewhere Between Sea and Sky

Christian Knowledge and is now in the National Maritime Museum, Greenwich.[22] When Buffet commenced his chronicle is uncertain; however, it could not have been before December 1823, when he settled on the island. According to an annotation in it by George Hunn Nobbs, who arrived in 1828, Buffett composed the entries until 24 March 1839, when he (Nobbs) took over. However, there are indications that Buffett may have written some of the later entries, and W.H. Holman wrote others during Nobbs's nine months' absence from the island in 1852–53. As Sir Charles Lucas observed, 'it is obvious ... that various writers in addition to Buffett and Nobbs had a hand in the Register, there being great variety of hand-writing as well as of expression'.[23]

This record of the 'Births, Deaths, Marriages & Remarkable Family Events' begins with an entry for 23 January 1790, when *Bounty* burnt, and ends with a lengthy one for 14 February 1854, dealing with Frederick Young's developing tetanus from a wound in his foot. It also contains a one-page account of the cost of island produce, seemingly dated 17 February 1834, and an extensive list of shipping arrivals from December 1823 to 13 October 1853. These last dates correlate with Buffett's arrival in December 1823 and Nobbs's July 1854 annotation that as the original volume had become 'so dilapidated from getting wet with salt water', he had copied its contents into another and sent the damaged one to the Rev. T.B. Murray in England. In 1929, Lucas edited this damaged 'Buffett' text for publication by the Society. He said that he reproduced the work 'page by page and word for word, exactly as it stands, with all the varied spellings and mis-spellings'. As a comparison of entries in the manuscript and printed text dealing with the 1790s confirms this is essentially true, in what follows I have quoted from the printed Buffett text (*PIRB*).[24]

The manuscript version of the *Register* identified as by Nobbs is in the Dixson Library, State Library of New South Wales.[25] This too begins with entries for the 1790s, and concludes with one for 23 September 1857. It therefore covers the first fifteen months of the Pitcairners' life

---

22 PN 23.
23 PN 23, p. 22.
24 PN 23, pp. 1, 94.
25 PN 22.

on Norfolk Island, whence they were removed in June 1856, when their numbers had outgrown their original island's resources. The Shipping List covers the period 13 December 1854 to 10 April 1856 – i.e. it ends just before the Pitcairners left for Norfolk Island.

These manuscript versions of the *Register* stand in uncertain relationship to each other, for while there are only minor differences in the essential information the entries in each convey, there are significant variations in the use of the first or third person, in syntax and length, and in details given. For example:

25 April 1831
Nobbs: Lucy Ann Quintall died aged 1 month
Buffett: Lucy Ann Quintal died

29 April 1831
Nobbs: Prudence one of the women brought in the *Bounty* died
Buffett: Prudence a native of Tahiti died

16 May 1831
Nobbs: Polly wife of Edward Young died, aged 17 Years
Buffett: Polly Christian died

14 November 1838
Nobbs: Maria Elizabeth daughter of John & Maria Quintall born
Buffett: Maria Quintal born

24 November 1838
Nobbs: John Quintall died of lock jaw in consequence of the wound in his heel. Aet. 27 Years. The deceased have left a wife and four children (one of whom is the infant born on the 14) with a large circle of friends to mourn their loss.
Buffett: John Quintal died aged 27 years of a locked jaw in consequence of a wound in the foot

14 February 1854
Nobbs: Sent for to attend on Frederick Young, who was suffering much from pain in his right foot caused by a cut of a chisel just above his small toe; this accident had happened ten or twelve

days previous but not paining him any he had paid no attention to it … I saw that no time was to be lost as there was stiffness of the neck, darting pains along the spine and at intervals involuntary contraction of the muscles. In short there was Tetanus in an incipient state. Administered ten grains of calomel combined with two of opium probed the wound very gently … Went to school and remained there untill 1 o'clock. After school returned to the house of the patient, found him with a flushed & anxious countenance complaining of increased pain along the whole spine and the stiffness of the neck had increased … I stopped there all night, as did many others who divided themselves into watches ready for any emergency.

Buffett: This morning the Rev. Mr Nobbs was sent for to attend on Frederick Young, who was suffering much from pain in his right foot caused by a cut from chisel just about his small toe: this accident had happened 10 or 12 days previous but not paining him any he had paid no attention to it … No time was therefore to be lost as there was stiffness of the neck, darting pains along the spine and at intervals involuntary contraction of muscles. In short there was tetanus in an incipient state. Ten grs of calomel combined with two of opium was immediately administered …

The differences in the details given and the variations in voice and person suggest that the Nobbs version may in fact more accurately indicate the entries that Buffett originally wrote, with the more impersonal and less detailed ones in the Buffett version now extant resulting from a process of editing for public presentation. I have numbered them accordingly in the list of Pitcairn narratives.

And if this is not perplexing enough, the entries for the first four years are as follows:[26]

Nobbs: Births Marriages Deaths etc etc Dates
Buffett: Date Parties Names etc

---

26   PN 22; PN 23, pp. 36, 38.

1790
Nobbs: January 23 H.M.S. Bounty burned at Pitcairns Island
Buffett: January 23 H.M. Ship *Bounty* burned at Pitcairn Island
Nobbs:--------- Fasto Wife of John Williams died
Buffett: Same year died Fasto wife of John Williams
Nobbs: October Thursday October Christian born
Buffett: October Thursday October Christian born

1791 & 1792
Nobbs: Matthew Quintall, Daniel McCoy, Elizabeth Mills and Charles Christian born
Buffett: This year Matthew Quintal. Daniel McCoy. & Elizabeth Mills born & Charles Christian

1793
Nobbs: Massacre of part of the mutineers by the Tahitians. The Tahiti Men all killed part by jealousies among themselves, the others by the remaining Englishmen. Mary Christian born
Buffett: Massacre of part of the mutineers by the Tahitians. The Tahiti men all killed, part by jealousies among themselves, the others by the remaining Englishmen. Mary Christian born

There are two striking anachronisms in these entries. The first is the name of Fletcher Christian's son. Jenny gave this as *Friday*, in her published interviews and when she spoke to the explorer Otto von Kotzebue in March 1824. According to Lieutenant John Shillibeer, when he came out to greet the *Briton* and *Tagus* in September 1814, his friends identified him as Friday Fletcher October Christian, which is also how his portrait in Shillibeer's account is titled. Into the 1970s, the Pitcairners knew the path from the island's centre up to Nellie Fall on the north-west coast as 'Friday's Road'.[27]

How may we explain this discrepancy? In discussing how he and Staines landed on Saturday 17 September 1814, which Adams thought was Sunday 18 September, Pipon pointed to the need to correct a day. Seemingly as a consequence of this correction, Pitcairn Island's

---

27   PN 2 and PN3a; PN 11, vol. 1, p. 240; PN 10, p. 82; see Figure 4.

Sunday became Saturday, and its Friday Thursday. Both Pipon and Staines identified the young man as Thursday October Christian.[28] The opening entry in both versions of the *Register*, then, could scarcely have been composed before September 1814.

The second anachronism concerns the use of the spellings 'Tahiti' and 'Tahitians' in the entry for 1793, which forms are used throughout both versions – for example, 'Tahitian woman' occurs in an entry for 1817, and 'Tahiti' appears in seven entries dealing with the temporary removal of the Pitcairners to this island in 1831.[29] 'Tahiti' and 'Tahitian' are modern forms, which did not gain currency over the eighteenth-century ones 'Otaheite' and 'Otaheitan' until the mid-nineteenth century.[30] In the *Narrative* he published in 1831, Beechey used 'Otaheite' and 'Otaheitans', including when he paraphrased or quoted from Young's journal. In summarising this account in 1832, the Royal Geographical Society's reviewer used 'Otaheite'. So too did John Barrow in his history of the mutiny published in 1831; as did Captain Waldergrave in his account of his visit to Pitcairn Island in 1830, which Barrow communicated to the Royal Geographical Society in 1833. Captain Sanderlands used the term 'Otaheite' in his account of how he carried the Pitcairners there in 1831, as did Captain Fremantle in describing his visit to Pitcairn in 1833. Moerenhout continued to use the French form 'O-taïti' into the 1830s.

However, the transition to the modern forms was even then under way. Early in his narrative, Beechey observed of his use of the form 'Otaheite': 'This word has since been spelled *Tahiti*, but as I have a veneration for the name as it is written in the celebrated Voyages of Captain Cook ... I shall adhere to his orthography.' The first interviewer of Jenny used the forms 'Taheite' and 'Taheitan' (though, curiously, the second ones did not). In 1825, Belcher wrote variously 'Otaheite' and 'Taheite', 'Tahiti', 'Tahitan'. In the account of his voyage published in

---

28 PN 8; PN 9, p. 2.
29 PN 23, pp. 31, 35–6.
30 There is a simple explanation for these now-archaic forms. 'O' is a prefix – that is, when the first European visitors asked the inhabitants for the name of their legendary island, they were told 'Otaheite' – 'It is Tahiti'; or when they asked for a personal name they were told (for example) 'Omai' – 'It is / I am Mai'.

English in 1830, Von Kotzebue (or his editor), having noted that the Tahitians 'themselves called it Tahaiti, or with the article, O Tahaiti', used both 'O Tahaiti/O Tahaitians' and 'Tahaiti and Tahaitians' in the running heads and the text. At the beginning of 1832, the *United Service Journal* published a letter, dated 'Tahiti, May 15th, 1831', describing the arrival of the Pitcairners, which was also very critical of the missionaries, and this style was repeated in the text. The *Evangelical Magazine and Missionary Chronicle* for January 1832 used 'Tahiti', as it did in its refutation of the anonymous critic's claims in its March issue. By 1837, the Royal Geographical Society had adopted the modern style, as did Frederick Bennett in his account of his 1834 visit to Pitcairn, which was published in 1840.[31]

Given that by the 1830s they had been active in the Tahitian (Society) Islands for more than thirty years and therefore knew the language much better than the early European explorers had, it is not surprising that missionary writers should have taken up the modern forms earlier than others. However, we may still ask how it was that both the isolated chroniclers of the Pitcairn settlement were using the modern spellings before these had been widely adopted in England.

What the change in the younger Christian's name and the use of the modern spellings together indicate, I think, is that both versions of the *Register* were not compiled contemporaneously with the events recorded but at a later date, probably in the 1840s and 1850s.

If this is right, then it is also likely that George Nobbs was principally responsible for them. This is not to say that he may not have drawn heavily on notes or on an *ur*-version kept by John Buffett, which are now lost. However the case was, though, there is the further question of what information Buffett and Nobbs based the entries for the first dozen years on. Of the mutineers, only John Adams was alive when the chroniclers reached the island, and, given that Nobbs arrived

---

31 PN 13, vol. 1, p. 69; PN 2, 3a; PN 16, pp. [6, 8, 11, 12, 13, 21, 35]; PN 11, vol. 1, p. 122 and pp. 227–50 passim; *United Service Journal and Naval and Military Magazine*, Part 1 (1832), pp. 98–101; *Evangelical Magazine and Missionary Chronicle*, NS, vol. 10 (1832), pp. 30, 118–19; e.g., 'New Group of Islands in the Pacific', *Journal of the RGS*, vol. 7 (1837), pp. 454–5; PN 20, vol. 1, pp. 25–58 passim.

only four months before Adams died, he had much less time than Buffett to talk to the old man. In the second half of the 1820s, several of the Tahitian women were still alive, and the mixed-race children would also have had stories to tell of the first years, but, as we shall see, there are problems in accepting as accurate what these persons said.

This difficulty would diminish if we knew that Buffett and Nobbs had access to Edward Young's journal. This may have been so, but it is not certain, for Beechey's summary of and quotations from that journal contain more information than the *Register*'s entries do. Of course, this may reflect deliberate omission on the part of the chroniclers. On the other hand, the *Register* contains details for the first four years that could not have come from a journal begun only in December 1793. Beechey gives some of this additional information, but then, where did he get it from? The obvious answer is from Young's journal; but this answer returns us to the questions about this journal I raised above.

✳ ✳ ✳

And then there are the questions concerning when *Bounty* reached Pitcairn Island, and when the crew unloaded and burnt it. Various writers have offered the following times for *Bounty*'s sighting of Pitcairn: 'about the end of October or the beginning of November [1789]'; 'January 1790'; 'in the middle of January 1790'; and 'on 15 January 1790, in the evening'.[32] As there are no European records extant of the ship's course after Christian took it out from Tahiti for the last time on 22 September 1789, there is no contemporary source for this precise date. Maude based his timings on 'statements made by Jenny and Adams', of which the more informative was Jenny's telling her second interviewer that 'at length Pitcairn's Island was discovered in the evening. It was then blowing hard, they could not attempt to land till the third day'; that a party then landed, returning two days later, to report that the island was fertile and uninhabited; and that the Bountys then worked the ship inshore and unloaded it.[33] So, working backwards from 23 January 1790 – the date

---

32 Mackaness 1951, p. 210; Rutter 1936b, p. 160; Danielsson 1963, p. 209; Maude 1968, p. 33.
33 PN 3a.

the ship reportedly burnt – Maude calculated that it would have taken two days to unload most of its equipment and stores (21 and 22 January), two days reconnoitring the island (19 and 20 January), and three days before the boat's party could land (16, 17 and 18 January) – which means that the ship sighted Pitcairn Island in the evening of 15 January 1790. This conjecture has been readily accepted by modern writers, who have repeated it without question.[34] It may be a good one; however, it is contingent on 23 January 1790 being the day that the Bountys burnt their ship and confined themselves to the island.

But did *Bounty* in fact burn on 23 January 1790? True, this is the date in both versions of the *Register*. However, as I have just shown, its first entries cannot have been written contemporaneously with the events they record, but were most likely made decades later. Given this, it is much more likely than less that the chroniclers took this date from something other than an island record – that is, from a source published before they had codified the various pieces of information they were aware of. For example, in 1846, Buffett published 'A Narrative of 20 Years Residence on Pitcairn Island' in a Hawaiian church newspaper. In the first instalment, he remarked, 'As an account of the massacre has been published by Captain Beechey, in his narrative of a voyage of discovery, I shall not be minute in my account of [it]'.[35]

Now, it is curious – to say the least – that in this account Buffett does not include dates for *Bounty*'s leaving Tahiti, for its sighting Pitcairn and for its destruction. All he says is, 'they sailed for, and in a few weeks arrived at Pitcairn's Island'. It is pertinent to point out that if *Bounty* left Tahiti in the night of 22 September 1789 and sighted Pitcairn Island in mid-January 1790, its passage was a good deal longer than 'a few weeks' – could it be that Buffett did not in fact know the relevant dates? It is also pertinent to notice that in describing the ship's destruction, Buffett amalgamated two statements from Jenny's published interviews:

---

34   E.g., Nicholson 1965, p. 34; Christian 1982, p. 155; Wahlroos 1989, p. 91; Dening 1988, p. 81; Dening 1992, p. 314; Alexander 2003, p. 369.
35   PN 21, pp. 2–3.

Jenny (1819): They ran the ship ashore. Fletcher Christian wanted to preserve the ship, but Matt [Quintall] said, 'No, we shall be discovered': so they burnt her.

Jenny (1821): Christian now got the ship up under a rocky point and anchored her. They then began to discharge the ship by means of the boat and a raft made out of the hatches ... When all they wanted was landed, they began to consider what they should do with the vessel. Christian wished to save her for a while. The others insisted on destroying her and one of them went off and set fire to her in the fore part: shortly after two others went on board and set fire to her in different places. During the night all were in tears seeing her burn. Some regretted exceedingly that they had not confined Capt. Bligh, and returned to their native country.

Buffett (1846): Christian ... brought the ship to the north side where they came to an anchor, and got 'stern fasts' on shore. Having moored her they commenced landing provisions, and other useful articles; but before they had finished unloading, Quintal went into the store room and set the ship on fire. The other mutineers were very angry with him for so doing. When asked why he did so, he replied, 'I am afraid we shall be discovered'. Seated on shore they watched the progress of the devouring element with tearful eyes.[36]

So the puzzle remains: did *Bounty* burn on 23 January 1790? So far as I can ascertain, Beechey was the first to offer this specific date, in his *Narrative* published in 1831.[37] Presumably, he obtained it at Pitcairn Island in December 1825. But what was his source? This is unlikely – impossible? – to have been Adams, who told Folger that they 'ran the Ship *Bounty* onshore and Broke her up[,] which took place as near as he could recollect in 1790'; and in 1814 Pipon noted, 'By all the accounts we could collect from old John Adams, they have been upon the Island about twenty-five years, but it was impossible to ascertain with certainty the date of their arrival.' That is, in the first decades of the nineteenth century, the only surviving *Bounty* mutineer

---

36   PN 2 and PN 3a; PN 21, pp. 2–3.
37   PN 13, vol. 1, p. 81.

could not remember precisely when they had arrived at Pitcairn Island. It therefore follows that he could not have given the precise date of *Bounty*'s burning.[38]

Nor can this date have come from Jenny. Though she was certainly able to recall sequences of events, given her cultural learning she could have had only a rudimentary sense, if any at all, of the European calendar – e.g. the Tahitians followed a lunar calendar; and neither a date for *Bounty*'s arrival at the island nor for its burning is given in either of her published interviews. Nor did Kotzebue, who heard her story in March 1824, record dates for these events.

Then again, the date could not have come from Young's journal, if the entries there commenced only in December 1793. Additionally, we may assume that, given his interest in the question, Pipon would have mentioned it if the journal he saw had contained this date. Another indication of there not being precise dates available in September 1814 is Staines's saying that Thursday October Christian 'was the first born on the Island, now about 25 years of Age'. This was a good approximation but if Staines had seen a record that said Thursday was born in October 1790, then he would not have needed to estimate his age.[39] Nor are dates given in Beechey's manuscript record of his first interview with Adams on 5 December 1825.[40] It is therefore possible that, just as Maude did for *Bounty*'s sighting Pitcairn, Beechey conjectured the date of 23 January 1790 for the ship's being burnt. Here, it is curious that none of the subordinate officers who recorded his expedition's visit offered this date – not Peard nor Belcher nor Bechervaise.

Nonetheless, as this is a precise date rather than an approximate one (e.g. 'towards the end of January …'), I doubt that Beechey offered it without some historical warrant. I suspect that he took it from a written record, one that is now lost to – or concealed from – history. It

---

38 Entry, 6 February 1808, PN 4; PN 9, p. [6]. Adams was also vague about time when he told his story to later visitors. For example, while he told Jacques Moerenhout in 1829 that they had reached Pitcairn in January 1790 (without giving a precise date), he also said that they had arrived at Tahiti from Tubuai in 'October or November 1789', whereas it was actually in September; PN 17, vol. 2, pp. 291–2.
39 PN 8, p. [2].
40 PN 4, 6 February 1808; PN 9, p. [6]; PN 12, pp. [3–4].

is an intriguing possibility that this lost record may have been Fletcher Christian's own journal. It is an even more intriguing possibility that Beechey may have seen – or learnt of – this record after returning to England rather than at Pitcairn Island!

✷ ✷ ✷

Despite these problems with the sources, which most have not attended to nearly carefully enough, historians have built a core story of what happened on Pitcairn Island from 1790 to c.1800.[41] This is that, after about twelve months, John Williams's wife Fasto (Fa'ahotu) fell to her death while gathering birds' eggs from a cliff, and he demanded another woman. When the other Bountys at first refused, he threatened to leave the island in the one *Bounty*'s boat remaining. Needing his blacksmith's skills, his colleagues then gave him Nancy (To'ofaiti), the wife of Tararo, the high-born Raiatian. Together with their menial status and the ill-treatment that went with it, this enraged the Polynesian men. Tararo took his wife back, and they and the younger Oha took to the bush. Threatened by the whites, the other Polynesian men then killed the two runaways, and Nancy returned to Williams.

Quintal and McCoy's mistreatment of the remaining Polynesian men increased, with beatings and floggings. Taking weapons, Teimua and Niau absconded into the bush. On 20 September 1793, the islander men rose against their oppressors. After Tetahiti obtained a musket from Adams on the pretext of shooting pigs, he and Manari'i were joined by the others. They shot or bludgeoned to death Christian, Williams, Mills, Martin and Brown. Adams was wounded but then had his life spared. Quintal and McCoy hid in the bush. The women sheltered Young.

Within days, violence flared again. The remaining Polynesian men argued over the women, who seem to have had a strong preference for the Europeans. The young man Manari'i shot Teimua and attacked Tetahiti. Manari'i then fled to the bush, where he joined Quintal and McCoy. Adams, Young and the women told Quintal and McCoy they would be welcomed back if they killed Manari'i, which they did.

---

41 I have followed Anne Salmond's transliterations of Polynesian names.

However, these then said they would not return until the remaining two islander men were dead. Accordingly, on 3 October one of the women killed Tetahiti with an axe, and Young shot Niau. After the survivors sent the hands of the dead men as proof to Quintal and McCoy, they returned to the settlement.

The new peace was always uneasy. Several times, the women evidently plotted to murder the remaining Bountys, but their schemes were discovered and they were forgiven. In March 1794, Young found that they had kept the skulls of the dead white men. Greg Dening has suggested that this reflected their belief that 'the active souls of their murdered husbands ... would occupy their own skulls' and thus protect the living family. Young insisted that the skulls should be buried.[42] In mid-1794, responding to the women's pleas to leave the island, the European men built them a boat, but this was swamped when launched in August.

About 1798, McCoy, who had once been employed in a Scottish distillery, began producing a potent alcoholic brew. Crazed by it, he threw himself into the sea. In 1799, Quintal's wife died; and when he threatened murder if he were not given McCoy's woman, Adams and Young killed him. Having now taught Adams to read and write a little, Young died of 'a chest complaint' in 1800. This left Adams the only remaining Bounty and adult man on the island, which he shared with six or seven women and some nineteen mixed-race children. (As an aside, it is curious that there seem to have been no purely Polynesian children born on the island in these years. The women were clearly fertile, and we cannot suppose that the Polynesian men were uniformly infertile. It raises the question that the three women who cohabited with the islander men may either have terminated pregnancies or killed babies at birth. If so, we may conjecture that this reflected a preference for European husbands, something of a puzzle given the violent natures of the white men.)

Adams now extended the policy of prayer and social decorum that Young and he had begun. It was this regimen that so impressed visitors to Pitcairn in the next decades, bringing to mind as it did Biblical archetypes of the good shepherd and his precious little flock.

---

42   PN 13, vol. 1, p. 89; Dening 1988, p. 87.

3 Somewhere Between Sea and Sky

✳ ✳ ✳

Well, on the face of things, this seems a likely scenario. However, when we examine the various Pitcairn narratives critically, it quickly becomes apparent that this core story is deeply problematic, with the narratives differing in many details. For example, in her second recorded interview, Jenny says that one of the mutineers was 'mortally wounded with a spear' at Tubuai. This is contradicted by other sources. Morrison says that Thomas Burkett was wounded in the ribcage, but that the spear 'wanted force to break it and in a short time it got heald'. Burkett was one of the mutineers later arrested by Edward Edwards at Tahiti and executed in England.[43]

Again, in both her narratives Jenny says that, rather than from a fall, Williams's wife died of a 'scrofulous disease' in her neck; and in the second, she says that Quintal died before McCoy. She also says that it was Young, rather than McCoy, who distilled alcohol from the roots of the ti plant. More suspiciously, she says that 'some years' elapsed before the first spate of killings and the second; and that Young died on a Christmas Day, which offers a coincidence probably more reflective of the Christian redemption narrative than of history.[44] We might write these contradictions off as an illiterate person's imprecise memories of events thirty years in the past, or as mistakes arising from slips in translation. In fact, though, they are threads in the pattern of contradiction that permeates the entire series of Pitcairn narratives.

Similar confusion surrounds the question of where and how Fletcher Christian died. Mayhew Folger, the master of the American sealing vessel *Topaz*, was the first navigator to discover the Pitcairn colony after its foundation, when he sighted the island in February 1808, while on a sealing voyage. Three of the islanders came out in a boat and, in English, asked him to land so as to meet their patriarch Aleck [Smith – i.e. John Adams]. When Folger landed, Adams told him that the eight mutineers who stayed with Christian, six islander men and wives of both groups had reached Pitcairn 'as near as he could

---

43 PN 3a; Morrison 1935, p. 63.
44 PN 2 and PN 3a.

recollect, in 1790', and that, after unloading the *Bounty*, they had 'run [her] on shore, and Broke her up'. Then:

> soon after which one of their number ran mad and drowned himself; another died with a fever, and after they had remained about four years on the Island their men Servants rose upon & killed Six of them, Leaving only [Adams] alive & he desperately wounded with a pistol Ball in the neck, however, he and the widows of the deceased arose and put all the Servants to death, which left him the only surviving man on the island, with eight or nine women and several small children.[45]

When Folger retold this story to the Admiralty some years later, he made two significant changes, saying that the massacre of the mutineers occurred 'about six years after they landed', and that 'the same night the Otaheitan Widows arose & murdered all their countrymen'.[46]

Note the discrepancies between these details and those of the core story. According to Folger, the *Bounty* was broken up, not burnt. One of the mutineers drowned himself and another died of a fever *before* the massacres. From c.1794 – or was it from 1796? – Adams was the only European alive on the island, whereas the core narrative has it that Adams, Young, Quintal and McCoy remained alive after the islander men had been extirpated. And why the compounding of the mayhem into a single day, when in other accounts it is presented as a drawn-out business?

The matter gets stranger, though. When Lieutenant William Fitzmaurice made a precis of Folger's log at Valparaíso in September 1808, he added that the second mate of the *Topaz* 'asserts that Christian, the Ringleader, became Insane shortly after their arrival on the Island, and threw himself off the Rocks into the Sea'.[47]

Sir John Barrow published Fitzmaurice's letter in the *Quarterly Review* in 1810. Later, he also published the accounts by Captain Sir

---

45 Entry, 6–7 February 1808, PN 4.
46 Folger to Admiralty, 1 March 1813 (PN 6).
47 Fitzmaurice, Précis of Topaz Log, 29 September 1808, and Smith to Admiralty, 14 March 1809, PN 5.

Thomas Staines of the *Briton* and Captain Philip Pipon of the *Tagus*, who called at Pitcairn in September 1814, each of whom stated that Christian had been shot by an islander while working in his garden.[48]

In 1816, Captain Amasa Delano, who had also sailed the Pacific Ocean and earlier discussed the *Bounty* mutiny and the Pitcairn colony with Folger, contacted him again, asking for further information. Now having read the accounts published by Barrow, Folger reasserted that Adams had told him clearly that the Pitcairn settlers had 'lived under Christian's government several years after they landed; that during the whole period they enjoyed tolerable harmony; that Christian became sick and died a *natural death*; and that it was after this when the Otaheitan men joined in a conspiracy and killed the English husbands of the Otaheitan women, and were by the widows killed in turn on the following night'; and that, therefore, neither the *Topaz*'s second mate's story of Christian's having gone insane and flung himself into the sea nor Staines's and Pipon's version that he was killed in his garden was true.[49]

And then, what of this? Staines and Pipon were competent naval officers, trained in the business of observing carefully and keeping accurate records. They called at Pitcairn together, and they were evidently the only officers to go ashore and question John Adams directly.[50] And yet they came away with divergent accounts of what had happened there in the first ten years. According to Staines, Christian 'fell a sacrifice to the jealousy of an Otaheitan Man within 3 or 4 years after their arrival on the Island', and the islander men 'were all swept away by desperate contentions between them & the Englishmen, & five of the latter died at different periods'. According to Pipon, it was Christian's wife who died, after which he 'forcibly seized on one belonging to one of the Otaheitan men'. This 'exasperated them to a degree of madness', and one murdered Christian 'about eleven months after they were settled in the Island, but the exact dates I could not

---

48 Barrow, review of d'Entrecasteaux's *Voyage à la Recherche de la Pérouse*, *Quarterly Review*, vol. 3, no. 5 (1810), p. 24; and review of Porter's *Journal of a Cruize* (1815), *Quarterly Review*, vol. 13, no. 26 (April 1815), pp. 377-83.
49 Folger in PN 7, vol. l, pp. 140-4.
50 PN 10, p. 90.

learn'. He added, 'We could not learn precisely the exact number of Blacks or Whites who were killed whilst this kind of warfare continued, certainly however, many must have perished by the hands of each other.'[51]

To muddy the waters further, John Shillibeer, the lieutenant in charge of the marines on the *Briton*, was among those who questioned the young men who came out to meet the ships. He recorded these as saying that Christian's wife 'died soon after [his] son was born, and I have heard that Christian took forcibly the wife of one of the black fellows to supply her place, and which was the chief cause of his being shot'; and that this happened 'about two years after his arrival at the Island'. After this, 'the black fellows rose, shot two Englishmen, and wounded John Adams'; and 'the same night, the women enraged at the murder of the English, to whom they were more partial than their countrymen, rose and put every Otaheitean to death in their sleep'.[52]

So this is what we have from these three accounts. After his wife died, Christian seized the wife of one of the islander men, and was then murdered. The core narrative has it that it was Williams who lost his wife. The *Pitcairn Island Register* records Christian and Isabella (Mauatua, 'Mainmast') as having had three children. Jenny said that Mauatua was still alive when she (Jenny) left the island about 1818. Frederick Bennett said that he met Mauatua during his visit to the island in March 1834, noting that her hair was 'very white, and she bears, generally, an appearance of extreme age'. The *Pitcairn Island Register* records her as dying on 19 September 1841. Both stories can't be right.[53]

Again, according variously to Staines, Pipon and Shillibeer, Christian was murdered eleven months, or two years or three years or four years after their arrival. (The core narrative says three and three-quarter years.) The islander men killed three of the Europeans (i.e. Christian plus two more), or four, while the Europeans killed all of the islanders progressively, or the women killed them all at once – or the precise numbers of either party killed could not be established.

---

51   PN 8, p. [2]; PN 9, pp. [8–9].
52   PN 10, pp. 82–5.
53   PN 2; PN 20, vol. 1, p. 32; and PN 23, pp. 31, 46.

3 Somewhere Between Sea and Sky

(The core narrative says that five of the Europeans were killed on 20 September 1793, with three of those remaining dying towards the turn of the decade; while two of the islanders were killed by one of their fellows before 20 September 1793, after which an islander killed one of his fellows and was in turn killed by two of the Europeans; and that the women killed the final two islander men on 3 October.)

Such contradiction marks all of John Adams's recitals of what happened on Pitcairn. Over a period of twenty years, this extraordinary character told the story at least thirteen times to visiting Royal Navy officers and the masters of merchant ships. From these versions, we learn, variously, that the mutineers and their Polynesian companions lived peacefully for 'several years'; that terrible discord broke out after 'six or eight months', or 'eleven months', or 'about four years', or about 'six years'. We learn that the mayhem began when Williams demanded another woman after his wife's death; and that this was one year or two years after their arrival. We also learn that it was rather Christian's wife who died, and Christian himself who seized another woman. Again, we learn that it was Quintal who lost his wife.

We learn that Christian died a natural death after 'several years'; that he became insane and jumped into the sea; that he was killed by the islanders after six or eight months, or eleven months, or four years, or six years. We learn that he was 'always cheerful', and that he was 'always sullen and morose'; that he was a person who indulged his sexuality liberally, and that he was the very reverse of a sensual man; that he cared for the welfare of his party and 'was universally esteemed & beloved by the Officers and Ships Company by his very kind and conciliatory behaviour'; and that he oppressed his companions with 'many acts of cruelty & inhumanity, which soon was the cause of his incurring [their] hatred & detestation'.[54]

The same confusion appears in the reasons Adams gave for the mutiny. He evidently told the master of an American vessel who called at Pitcairn in the early 1820s that the mutiny was caused by 'the remorseless severity with which [Bligh] treated those under his command, the insults he offered them, having subjected even his mate Fletcher Christian to corporal chastisement, combined with the recollection of the pleasant

---

54   PN 12, p. [8]; PN 9, p. [7].

time spent in Tahaiti'.[55] He told Beechey and his officers in December 1825 that the 'principal cause' of the mutiny:

> arose from Captn Bligh, who was also purser of the ship, stinting the people, and not giving them a proper allowance of provisions. He had even served Pumpkins out to them in lieu of bread, and threatened to flog the first man who complained; and at Otaheite they were dissatisfied at having the bones, from which the pork had been cut for salting, given them instead of meat.[56]

He told Moerenhout in 1829 that the mutiny was due to Bligh's having reduced the fresh food ration at Tahiti and to his having 'inflicted rigorous corporal punishment on all who dared to make the slightest complaint'.[57]

Adams offered yet another version of what happened on Pitcairn. According to Buffett, this is effectively that Young had overseen the massacres, for when the rampaging Tahitians called Adams back after wounding him, they said they had forgotten that 'Young told them not to hurt [him]'.[58] Odd as it may seem, this story perhaps receives some correlation from another odd one. In the supposedly fictional *The Mutineers* (1898), Louis Becke has it that after Young had sex with Christian's wife, the Polynesian men and women wanted to kill him, but Christian, 'horror-stricken at the bloodshed that had already taken place, carefully protected the man who seduced his wife'. Immediately, this seems like artistic licence; but Becke insisted it was true, claiming, 'I know the descendants of the *Bounty* Mutineers and the *native* story of Christian and his life better than any man living.'[59] Here, it may or may not be relevant that, as its editor remarked, 'it is difficult to understand [the *Pitcairn Island Register*'s] list of births from 1794 to 1799 inclusive ... and especially difficult to account for the fact of seven out of the total

---

55 PN 11, vol. 1, p. 229.
56 PN 14, p. 80.
57 PN 17, vol. 2, p. 286.
58 PN 21, p. 3.
59 PN 25, pp. 241, 250–7; Becke to Mew(?), 17 June 1898, quoted in Christian 1999, pp. 340–1.

number of children [fourteen] bearing the name of Young' – though the difficulty would diminish if Young had had more than one wife in these years.[60]

Becke added another version of the story. This is that a morose Christian retreated to the cave high on the mountain, and that he afterwards died 'by gunshot accidentally received from John Adams/Alexander Smith whilst endeavouring to prevent Christian from putting to sea in the *Bounty*'s boat'.[61] If Becke did indeed obtain these details from the islanders, he did not do so until the second half of the nineteenth century, long after the events. Nonetheless, it is not impossible that there is some truth to this particular story.

※※※

From this welter of claim and counter-claim, the only thing we may safely conclude is that we simply can't know accurately what happened on Pitcairn Island in the ten years after the mutineers' arrival.

Why Adams should have told such widely divergent stories is again puzzling; and there is no ready answer. The dementia of old age may have been a factor, but none of the visitors to the island observed that he exhibited this affliction. There is a more likely possibility. As most children find out at a young age and as many murderers learn to their cost, it is much easier to be consistent when repeating a true story than when trying to maintain a false one. So what might Adams have had to lie about?

There are three plausible sets of circumstances. The first concerns Adams's role in the mutiny. He repeatedly downplayed or denied involvement in this momentous event. He said on one occasion that he was not 'in the smallest degree concerned in the Mutiny, he being at the time it happened, sick in bed'. On another, he said that he was asleep when the commotion began; that when he went up on deck he 'found every thing in great confusion; but not then liking to take any part in the transaction, he returned to his hammock'; and that he finally joined the mutineers only because he did not wish to be 'on the weaker side'.

---

60   PN 23, p. 32; Lucas, Introduction, PN 23, p. 9.
61   PN 25, pp. 296–7.

On a third occasion, he is reported to have said that he had taken 'no part' in the mutiny, and that he 'abhorred' the mutineers' treatment of Bligh and those men who followed him into the boat.[62]

Other sources directly contradict these claims. Bligh said that Adams was one of the rebels who came down armed to his cabin. He was not one of the four crew members whom Fryer identified as having been kept on the ship against their will. Cole included him among the mutineers under arms on deck. Purcell said that on his asking Adams what the mutineers meant to do, he answered, 'to put Captain Bligh, Hayward, Hallet, and Samuel into [the cutter], to put Captain Bligh on shore'. Since this was the initial intention of those who initiated the mutiny, Adams's saying so indicates he was complicit in it from the beginning. And he was one of those who reportedly told Christian as he prepared to sail from Tahiti for the last time, 'We shall never leave you, Mr Christian, go where you will.'[63]

The second set of circumstances concerns the possibility that the mutineers slaughtered each other. As we have seen, there were factions and dissension among them from the time of the mutiny. So perhaps there was a deal of truth in what Pipon reported from his interview with Adams – i.e. that the mutineers divided into warring parties on Pitcairn, and hunted each other. This scenario gains force from Buffett's story that Adams told him that Young had directed the mayhem; and perhaps also from Becke's story of Adams having shot Christian. If there is substance to all this, it is understandable that Adams would not have wished it to be known that he had played a central role in murder, for if Young was the *éminence grise*, then his friend Adams must also have been implicated in the business – that is, it may not be a matter of chance that Young and Adams were the two Europeans to survive the bloodshed.

The third set of circumstances is the most intriguing. The core story has it that Christian died in the slaughter of September/October 1793. But what if he did not? What if Becke's story, even if in a confused way, conveys the central point that Christian did get away

---

62 PN 9, p. [2]; PN 13, vol. 1, p. 73; PN 11, vol. 1, p. 246.
63 Enclosure in Bligh to Banks, 13 October 1789, Bligh 1989, p. 33; *Bounty Court-Martial (Minutes)*, pp. 10, 12, 14, 30; Christian [1794] 1952, p. 73.

from Pitcairn Island? If this happened, then Adams, isolated as he was on the island, could not possibly have known whether Christian had survived a perilous voyage in an open boat and, if so, where he had fetched up; and whether he had then been apprehended or was living *incognito*. This was a dilemma that Adams could scarcely resolve by asking visiting Royal Navy officers, 'What news of Mr Christian?' In these circumstances, inevitably, he would have struggled to maintain a consistent story.

✳ ✳ ✳

So we now come to two central issues. First, what evidence is there that Christian did die on Pitcairn Island?

Among the entries that Beechey copied from Young's journal was this for 12 March 1794:

> I saw Jenny having a skull in her hand: I asked her whose it was? and was told it was Jack Williams's. I desired it might be buried: the women who were with Jenny gave me for answer, it should not. I said it should; and demanded it accordingly. I was asked the reason why I, in particular, should insist on such a thing, when the rest of the white men did not? I said, if they gave them leave to keep the skulls above ground, I did not. Accordingly when I saw McCoy, [Adams] and Mat. Quintal, I acquainted them with it, and said, I thought that if the girls did not agree to give up the heads of the five white men in a peaceable manner, they should be taken by force, and buried.

According to Beechey, 'on 16 August [1794], they dug a grave, and buried the bones of the murdered people'.[64]

In view of Young's insistence that it must be done, the lapse of five months between the discovery that the women had kept the skulls and their interment is in itself strange. However, let us leave this aside now and ask instead: what are we to conclude from these entries? They seem at least to indicate that the bodies of those killed in the September/

---

64   PN 13, vol. 1, pp. 89–90.

October 1793 mayhem were not buried immediately. Why not? Because the surviving Bountys could not be bothered? Because they did not think it safe to venture into the fields to recover them? Or because *there soon were no bodies to bury*? And are we dealing with skeletons or skulls only? Answering these last two questions involves an appreciation of the rapid disintegration of a body in the moisture and heat of a tropical island, a process aided by worms, birds – and, if there are any, pigs.

Yes, pigs! According to Beechey, summarising an entry for December 1793 in Young's journal, the Pitcairners had turned to 'constructing pits for the purpose of entrapping hogs, which had become very numerous and wild, as well as injurious to the yam-crops'.[65] Remember that the core narrative has it that Tetahiti had borrowed a musket on the pretext of shooting pigs, but used it for shooting the Bountys instead? Once, I travelled to northern New South Wales to discuss the business of pigs with Craig O'Regan, who raises rare breeds in open range conditions near Narrabri. Craig told me that if an animal dies in the summer and he does not immediately find the carcass, after a week there is no point in his looking for it. This is because the flesh decays very quickly in the heat, a process aided by the ravages of birds and worms. But according to Craig, the greatest agents of obliteration are other pigs, which have no problem with cannibalism.

Pigs are ferocious animals, capable of wrecking pens made of concrete and iron. They are similarly determined foragers. The only part of the body of a dead animal they cannot consume is the skull, since they cannot open their jaws wide enough to crunch it. (In 2006, English newspapers reported that a gunman who shot a woman was in turn killed by other members of his gang, and his body, minus the head and hands, fed to pigs so as to remove the evidence of his death.)[66]

In these circumstances, then, it seems likely that the surviving Bountys never buried the bodies of their fallen companions, since after a short time these no longer existed. This would also explain why the Tahitian women had skulls only. If so, two more questions arise. First, how might a skull have been identified surely unless it bore distinctive scars? Jenny said that the islanders crushed the skulls of some of the

---

65   PN 13, vol. 1, p. 88.
66   *Sunday Times*, 1 October 2006, p. 10.

3 Somewhere Between Sea and Sky

Europeans with an axe and a hammer. John Adams also said this.[67] Yet Young seems to have made no mention of crushed skulls.

On the other hand, if the Bountys did bury their dead, where did they do so? John Adams was evidently vague when asked where Christian had been buried. Indeed, one historian says that when Beechey asked him 'to point out Christian's grave, he could not do it'. Immediately, this seems a distortion, for Beechey did in fact say that Adams had indicated a site to him. However, there may be a way to reconcile the two statements. Before publication, Beechey sent a draft of his chapter on Pitcairn Island to Heywood for comment. Heywood's stepdaughter Lady Belcher said in 1870 that up to the time of Beechey's visit in December 1825:

> Adams had invariably evaded all inquiries as to the burial place of Fletcher Christian, alleging his utter ignorance of the spot ... However, the question being put direct by Captain Beechey, he answered that 'Christian had been buried in his own garden.'

Even so, we may wonder whether Adams identified a location where he knew Christian to have been buried to Beechey; and whether he indicated one simply to satisfy an overly inquisitive visitor. And then, what is the significance of Beechey's having written, 'was *first* buried'? Did he mean that at some later date Christian's bones were exhumed and re-interred elsewhere? No one else seems to have said this.[68] In any case, by the 1830s the grave of only one of the Bountys could be located: that of John Adams. Some time in the mid-nineteenth-century, Nobbs wrote of the 'infatuated band' who settled Pitcairn:

> What need I tell their hapless leader's fate;
> (Slain by the hand of one he deem'd his slave)
> Save to the rash I would this fact relate,
> Nor e'en a hillock marks his dubious grave.

---

67 PN 2 and PN 3a; PN 13, vol. 1, p. 85.
68 McKee 1962, p. 202; PN 13, vol. 1, p. 108; Barrow 1830, p. 98; Belcher 1870, p. 51; Belcher 1870, pp. 185–6; PN 13, vol. 1, p. 84.

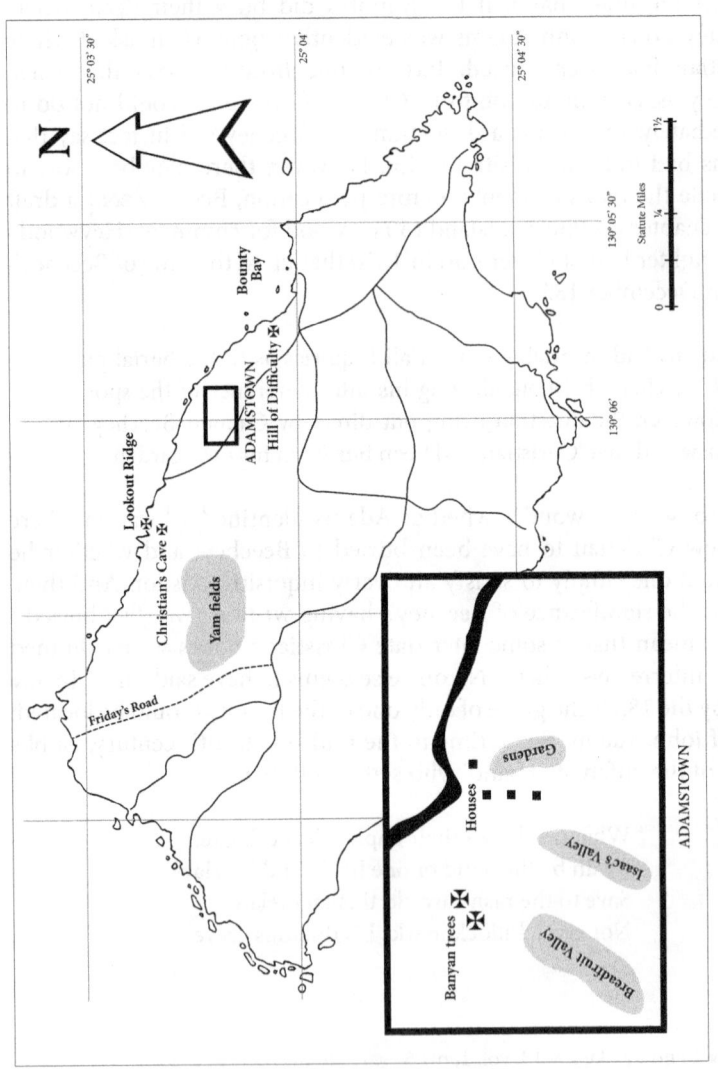

Figure 4 The Pitcairn settlement in the 1790s. This sketch map is highly conjectural, as no maps of the island or sketches of Adamstown exist before 1825, and as sites of settlement and agriculture have changed significantly in the course of 230 years. It is intended only to indicate the likely *relative* relationships of features and sites mentioned in the text. I am grateful to Dr Nigel Erskine for his help.

Rosalind Young stated in 1894 that while the areas 'once owned and cultivated' by the mutineers were still known by their names, 'every trace of their burial places is lost, the grave of John Adams alone excepted'.[69]

* * *

When we sift the records for indications of the location of Christian's grave, we face the possibility of a very significant confusion, one arising from how the Bountys went about feeding themselves on Pitcairn Island. As I said earlier, on arrival they found it to offer coconut, breadfruit, plantain, banana, sugar cane, yam, taro, ti plant, sweet potato, ginger, turmeric and gourds. However, it soon becoming apparent that harvesting these indigenous resources would not alone provide adequate supplies, so they commenced deliberate cultivation as well. There are no descriptions extant of the Bountys' houses and fields in the first years. Moreover, the island's topography has changed significantly since their settlement, as a consequence of, variously, the introduction of foreign species and foraging animals, clearing for cultivation, the loss of early buildings and the selection of other sites for newer ones, and (more recently) the construction of roads.

It is therefore very difficult to identify accurately the first locations of the Bountys' houses and agricultural fields.[70] However, from descriptions in the 1820s and 1830s it seems that they pursued two kinds of cultivation. In the fertile and generally adequately watered soil about their houses, which they built on ridges in the tableland above Bounty Bay so as to avoid floods, they made gardens in which they grew watermelons, sweet potatoes, pumpkins, squash, chillies, ginger and perhaps some citrus. Here, they also kept domestic animals, such as chickens, pigs and goats, in pens. On the 'exposed and sunny declivities' of the poorer-soiled hills to the west and south of the village, they cultivated taro and yam, the latter a variety they had brought with them that was superior to the indigenous one.[71]

---

69 Quoted in Nicholson 1965, p. 99; PN 24, p. 53.
70 See Irskine 2004, particularly Ch. 3.
71 PN 15, p. 78; PN 16, p. [29]; PN 20, vol. 1, pp. 42–3; PN 18, pp. 161–2.

So when the core Pitcairn narrative has it that Christian was killed while working in his 'field' and buried near where he fell, which was the field in question? Was it his garden beside his house, or his yam plot at a distance to the west? According to her second interviewers, Jenny said that Christian was 'clearing some ground for a garden and while in the act of carrying some roots away [the islanders] went behind him and shot him between the shoulders'. Shillibeer, who heard Staines question the young Pitcairners who came out to greet the *Briton*, said that 'Christian was shot in the back while at work in his yam plantation'. Pipon, who went ashore with Staines to question Adams, said, 'from what we could learn he was shot by a black man whilst digging in his field'. Beechey, who questioned Adams first, said that Christian was killed while 'working at his yam-plot'. Peard, who was one of the junior officers who questioned Adams after Beechey had done so, said that after killing Williams the islanders 'proceeded to where Christian was working in his plantation at the bottom of the Valley'. Belcher, another junior officer who heard Adams, said the same thing.[72] Clearly, the burden of these observations is that Christian was killed while at work in his yam plot.

Concerning the location of Christian's grave, Beechey said this was near the yam fields ('plantations') on the hillside. Bennett said that this was 'situated a short distance up a mountain, and in the vicinity of a pond'. Waldergrave made two important distinctions: Christian's and Adams's graves were 'at some distance from each other, – the grave of the former near the spot where he fell, murdered, about one-third from the summit of the island; the latter is buried by the side of his Otaheitan wife, at the end of his cottage-garden'.[73] Together, these statements seem to point to a location to the west of the village, on the southern slope below Lookout Ridge, where the Bountys' yam plots were located.

It was Adams who pointed out a site to Beechey. This last remaining Bounty died in 1829, so the visitors of the 1830s could not obtain direct advice on this point (whatever it may have been worth). (They do not seem to have interviewed the remaining women.) How

---

72 PN 3a; PN 10, p. 83; PN 9, p. [8]; PN 13, vol. 1, p. 84; PN 14, p. 87; PN 16, p. [19].
73 PN 13, vol. 1, p. 108; PN 20, p. 48; PN 18, pp. 156–7.

do we know that the younger Pitcairners who pointed out the site of Christian's grave to Waldegrave and Bennett knew that it was indeed such, particularly if there wasn't any indication of a grave's ever having been there?

※※※

In 1980, continuing his quest for reliable information about his forebear, Glynn Christian sailed to Pitcairn Island. He went in search of Fletcher Christian's grave, at first on the declivity below Lookout Ridge. And he found a pool, in the area now known as Mummas, which the islanders agreed most likely had been named after Christian's wife, whose stature led the other Bountys also to nickname her 'Mainmast'.[74]

However, Glynn Christian quickly came to doubt that this was in fact the place where Fletcher Christian was killed and buried, partly because it did not correlate with the details of two sub-stories that some writers have attached to the main one of his death. The first of these sub-stories is that when Christian was shot, he gave out a loud groan, which McCoy and Mills, who were working in adjacent plots, heard but dismissed as simply Mauatua's calling her children to eat.[75] The second is that Mauatua was calling to tell Christian that her labour had begun, for legend also has it that their third child, Mary, was born on the very day that Christian was shot (whatever day that was).

According to Glynn Christian, the yam fields behind Lookout Ridge were too far from Fletcher's house in the village for the sound (whatever it was) to carry to them:

> There was no reason in those days for the men to garden in the hills. There was plenty of ground close to home for so few to cultivate, and any 'gardens' they did have in other parts of the island were simply divisions of naturally occurring fruit trees. In any case the suspect site is amid especially steep and rugged terrain and it would have been tiresome to walk over to another plot simply to discuss an unexpected sound. The type of territory

---

74 Christian 1982, pp. 236–40.
75 See PN 14, p. 87, PN 16, p. [19].

also makes it unlikely they could have shouted to one another, and for Isabella's voice to have been heard as far away as this, she must have been possessed of something rather more stentorian even than modern electronics can manufacture.[76]

With the help of knowledgeable islanders, Glynn Christian examined old descriptions, drawings and land titles to establish that Fletcher's house had likely been located on the western side of the village, to the north of Adams's across the central lawn, with its garden a little further west. And, citing Jenny as his source, who remembered 'something both intimate to Fletcher and Isabella and important to a Polynesian woman', Glynn Christian says that on the day he was killed Fletcher 'worked close to his home, at the request of his wife, who did not go with the other women [to collect eggs] as she expected the birth of their next child at any time, an exact three years after the arrival of the first'.[77]

So, assuming that on the day of the massacre Fletcher was working in his garden adjacent to his house rather than in his yam plot much further to the west, with some other Bountys in the vicinity, all close enough to have heard Mauatua's call, Glynn Christian went looking for another pond. And yes, he found one:

> As plain a dried-up pool as one could imagine, once one knew. It was right in the middle of Fletcher Christian's original plot, within shouting distance of the original village, close to gardens still being used by Christians, and it was 'a short distance up a mountain', Lookout Point. Not only did the pool fit Bennet's [sic] description, it neatly tied a knot with the threads of my theory and Jenny's accounts.

Christian conceded that 'identifying the pool did not, in itself, prove Fletcher Christian was buried nearby'. However, 'discounting one possible murder site and establishing another was a major step forward

---

76 Christian 1982, p. 241.
77 Christian 1982, p. 241, and 1999, p. 329.

in my research'. He left Pitcairn Island convinced that he had found where Christian had died.[78]

But really, what was Glynn Christian's basis for rejecting the area of the first pond in preference for that of the second as the place of his forebear's death and burial? As I've stated in the Introduction to this book, the detail of Mauatua's having asked him to work close to home on this fateful day does not appear in any of the published interviews with Jenny, so where does it come from? Consider, too, that if Mauatua did indeed give birth to Mary on the same day that Christian was killed, it is unlikely – though not impossible – that she was also out calling her children to eat.

And then, if she was giving birth, it is also unlikely that she was alone. This last point raises a number of issues that are now difficult to resolve with any certainty. According to Douglas Oliver, the best authority on Tahitian cultural practices before European contact, the only accounts of traditional Tahitian birthing practices are European ones. However, by comparing various accounts, and making allowance for possible differences according to social class, he has offered a matrix for birth and its immediate aftermaths. As Oliver enunciated that for a royal birth, I have adjusted his matrix to reflect the less elaborate procedures of lower social classes:

1. Pre-birth imposition of restrictions, and prayers for a safe birth.
2. Delivery, including first cutting of the umbilical cord, at the *fare-rua-maire* ('fern house'). (That is, delivery took place outside the main house, in a purpose-built shelter or on a designated platform (e.g. of stone).)
3. A ceremony of ritual purification and the offering of the newborn to the appropriate god at the family marae.
4. The purification (ritual as well as practical) of the mother, usually with the assistance of her husband, in the sea.
5. The keeping of mother and child apart from others until the birth restrictions have been lifted. (Often, some six to eight weeks, but longer – sometimes much longer with high-status persons.)

---

78   Christian 1982, pp. 243–44.

Concerning the specifics of birth, the baby was delivered downwards. 'Queen' 'Itia's demonstration of the business to Bligh involved her squatting on her heels between the legs of an attendant seated behind, his arms underneath hers so as to be able to assist the contractions by pressing on her upper abdomen. There is a similar account from a later date, with the additional details that two women held the feet of the one delivering to steady her when contractions came, while other persons poured cold water on her to keep her cool. As this birth was protracted, a number of women and some male family members took turns in assisting. There is also an early European account of a woman giving birth without physical assistance, though with others present to impose the requisite rituals.[79]

Now, it is barely possible that the Tahitian women became entirely de-cultured in their first years on Pitcairn Island. However, not only is this unlikely in itself but there are also indications, such as their eating apart from the men and their retaining the skulls of their murdered European husbands, that this was not so. Discarding this possibility, then, we have to conclude that it was very unlikely that Mauatua should have given birth without others being present. Furthermore, given that, so far as we know, all the children born in those years were fathered by European rather than islander men, it was the islander women who would have had the responsibility of imposing the required rituals to the extent that their odd circumstances on Pitcairn allowed. These conclusions cast considerable doubt on Glynn Christian's assertion that Fletcher Christian and Mauatua's daughter Mary was born on the day of her father's death, a day on which Mauatua had asked him to stay close to home, so that she would not give birth alone.[80] This sub-story has the hallmark of later romantic bathos rather than of historical veracity. I suspect that it derives from unreliable family lore.

※ ※ ※

---

79   See Oliver 1974, vol. 1, pp. 413–24.
80   Christian 1982, pp. 198, 241.

3 Somewhere Between Sea and Sky

Figure 5 Mary Christian's headstone on Norfolk Island.

This second sub-story is suspect for another reason. What evidence is there that Mary Christian was indeed born in October 1793? True, the *Pitcairn Island Register* records it as October, though without giving a precise date. As we have seen, however, considerable doubt attaches to the veracity of its entries for the first ten years.

On the other hand, there is the headstone on Mary Christian's grave on Norfolk Island (Figure 5), which states that she dies on 2 January 1866, aged sixty-nine. If we subtract sixty-nine from 1866 (or better, perhaps, from 1865, as the date of death is 2 January 1866), we get 1796, not 1793. There are of course a number of possible ways of explaining this discrepancy. The entry in the *Pitcairn Island Register* may be wrong. Or, the age given on Mary's headstone may be wrong. Or, her father may have been someone other than Fletcher Christian. Or, Fletcher Christian was her father, but he did not die in September/October 1793 – that is, she was conceived later, in 1795 or early 1796. At the very least this is another puzzle in the Pitcairn Island story that needs resolution.

***

At the beginning of *Fragile Paradise*, Glynn Christian claimed a special affinity with tropical places, their sunshine, fruits and flowers, because his 'great-great-great-great grandmother was Tahitian', and because 'the family had lived on Pacific islands for generations'. Similarly, he trusted his 'instincts' in his identification of the second pool site as that of Fletcher's death.[81] But frissons are not good warrants of historical certainty. As with many other parts of the Pitcairn story, where Fletcher Christian's death is concerned we have conflicting possibilities but no authentic information. There are no reliable eyewitness reports of his death. There is no physical evidence, such as a clearly identifiable grave. There is no forensic evidence, such as bones that might bear distinguishing scars or provide us with a DNA match. At the very best, the evidence that Christian died on Pitcairn Island is equivocal; at the worst, it is dubious. To put it bluntly: what proof do we have that Fletcher Christian did in fact die and was buried there?

Conversely, what evidence is there that Fletcher Christian might have escaped Pitcairn – specifically, that he might have returned to England? In 1831, Sir John Barrow published *The Mutiny of the Bounty*. Barrow was well placed to write on this topic. As Second Secretary of the Admiralty, he took a lively interest in voyages of exploration, and he had access to commanders' logs and letters. He knew Peter Heywood well (Heywood had been returned to England on 19 June 1792, along with the other mutineers captured by the *Pandora* on Tahiti). He also knew some of the officers who had visited Pitcairn Island, in particular Beechey and Belcher. And, being from Cumbria, he was familiar with Fletcher Christian's background and country.

After recounting the events of the mutiny (which included details obtained directly from Heywood), and of what happened on Pitcairn, Barrow said in a footnote:

> About the years 1808 and 1809, a very general opinion was prevalent in the neighbourhood of the lakes of Cumberland and Westmoreland, that Christian was in that part of the country,

---

81 Christian 1982, pp. 11, 242–4.

and made frequent private visits to an aunt who was living there. Being the near relative of Mr Christian Curwen, long member of Parliament for Carlisle, and himself a native, he was well-known in the neighbourhood.

Barrow said that this might be dismissed as mere gossip was there not a very strange story to support it, 'for the truth of which the Editor does not hesitate to avouch':

> In Fore Street, Plymouth Dock, Captain Heywood found himself one day walking behind a man, whose shape had so much the appearance of Christian's, that he involuntarily quickened his pace. Both were walking very fast, and the rapid steps behind him having roused the stranger's attention, he suddenly turned his face, looked at Heywood, and immediately ran off. But the face was as much like Christian's as the back, and Heywood, exceedingly excited, ran also. Both ran as fast as they were able, but the stranger had the advantage, and, after making several short turns, disappeared.[82]

In 1870, Lady Belcher, Heywood's stepdaughter, repeated this story, adding the details that the stranger was 'of unusual stature, very much muffled, and with his hat drawn close over his eyes'; and that he did not flee until Heywood, who had come up behind him, 'said in a tone of voice only loud enough to be heard by him, "Fletcher Christian!"' Lady Belcher passed this story off, saying that Heywood 'attached no importance to it, simply considering it a singular coincidence'. However, this is in direct contradiction to what Barrow said, which was, 'That Christian should be in England, Heywood considered as highly improbable, though not out of the scope of possibility'; and that 'the circumstance was frequently called to [Heywood's] memory for the remainder of his life.'[83]

There is another such story. In 1809, Robert Southey, now long-established in Cumbria, reviewed an account of the activities of

---

82   Barrow [1831] 1989, p. 327.
83   Belcher 1870, p. 185; Barrow 1830, pp. 327–8.

Christian missionaries in the South Sea, in which he termed Bligh 'notorious'.[84] When a friend queried this characterisation, Southey replied, 'It was an act of much self-controul not to accompany the sentence with a bitter sarcasm, saying the Missionaries had a lucky escape, for his unendurable tyranny might have driven more Christians to desperation.' He explained, 'I know a great deal of that affair of the *Bounty* from James Losh, who with Professor Christian (poor Fletcher C.'s brother) went to the mutineers that were brought home, and collected their testimony concerning all the circumstances which led to it.' He added, 'I know too, or rather have every reason to believe[,] that Fletcher C. was within these few years in England at his father's house – an interesting circumstance in such a history, and one which I hardly ought to mention – so do not you let it get abroad.'[85]

Southey made a neat distinction here. No, he has himself not seen Christian; but he has been told on good authority that Christian is back in England. Most likely, his informant was James Losh, who was then practising as a solicitor in Newcastle, and with whom Southey had maintained contact. (He stayed with Losh during a short visit in June 1809, for example.)[86]

When his friend, his curiosity aroused, asked for more information, Southey replied:

> [Fletcher Christian] is a native of this country. One of our country gentlemen (a very remarkable and strong headed man) who was his schoolfellow and knows his person as well as you know mine told me, that about five or six years ago, as he was walking near his own house with his daughter, he saw two Gentlemen riding towards him, and recognized one of them time enough to say to his daughter – look at this man – it is F.C. – and also to consider that it would be better not to speak to him – which he was on the point of doing. There was a dog with the horsemen, and presently afterwards some boys came along who had picked up a collar,

---

84 *Quarterly Review*, vol. 2 (1809), p. 25.
85 Southey to Bedford, 23 October 1809, Southey 1965, vol. 1, p. 519.
86 Entries, 12 and 13 June 1809, Losh; and see Southey to Danvers, 15 June 1809, Southey 1965, vol. 1, p. 511.

3 Somewhere Between Sea and Sky

bearing the name of F.C.'s father. My friend had no doubt before of his identity, and this was a confirmation of the fact.[87]

So there are two eyewitness accounts, albeit each at one remove, of Fletcher Christian's having been seen in England. These reports are from persons who, having known him personally, could scarcely have mistaken his distinctive swarthy appearance and bow-legs. Also, these persons had no connection with each other, and their sightings were separated in time and place, which makes them the more difficult to explain away as aberrations, as Glynn Christian and Caroline Alexander try to do.[88]

※ ※ ※

How and when might Fletcher Christian have left Pitcairn Island and returned to England?

The 'how' brings us to another Pitcairn puzzle. The *Bounty* carried three boats: the 16-feet long jolly boat; the 20-feet long cutter; and the 23-feet long launch (respectively, around 5, 6 and 7 metres). The mutineers' first plan was to put Bligh and a few companions into the cutter, but when some pointed out that it was unseaworthy ('her bottom was almost worn out'), they agreed to the loyalists going off in the launch. The Bountys used two boats to land and to repulse attacks at Tubuai, and again in June–July 1789, when they returned after their visit to Tahiti. Some of those who had not supported the mutiny then conspired to repair the cutter and make for Tahiti, but, suspecting a plot, Christian ordered that the boats should be repaired only onshore in his presence. Knowing that while the passage might take only '5 or 6 days', if they encountered 'bad weather our Crazey boat would certainly have made us a Coffin', the plotters held off.

When the mutineers returned to Tahiti for the final time, they had only one usable boat ('only one Boat that would Swim') with which to land those who had decided to stay, along with their belongings and equipment. It seems that this was also the situation when they reached

---

87 Southey to Bedford, 30 October 1809, Southey 1965, vol. 1, pp. 521–2.
88 Christian 1999, pp. 411–17; Alexander 2003, pp. 404–6.

Pitcairn, where they 'discharge[d] the ship by means of the boat and a raft made out of the hatches', with most of the goods being taken ashore 'on the raft by means of a rope fastened to the rocks'.[89]

Let us now return to Beechey's summary of Young's journal. This states that, at about the end of 1792, thoroughly dissatisfied with his single life, John Williams threatened to leave Pitcairn in the boat. Yet Beechey also records that, in 1794, having become tired of life there, the women wished to leave the island, so the remaining Bountys built a boat, which was swamped on launching; and that, in May 1795, the settlers built two canoes, which they used for fishing.[90] What, then, happened to the *Bounty*'s last boat? There is no mention of its decay or destruction in Young's extracted journal, nor in the *Pitcairn Island Register*. Buffett said that the mutineers destroyed it – perhaps they did, but when?[91]

With this in mind, the story of Christian's escape from Pitcairn might go something like this. After being wounded in the mayhem of late 1793, he retreated to the cave high in the mountain, where he recuperated. Then, taking the *Bounty*'s boat, he went out to a passing whaling or sealing ship, staying aboard until it returned to its home port (probably a New England one), whence to England. Or, the ship may have crossed the Pacific Ocean to Macau, where he took a passage home on a European ship. Or, he may have sailed the boat to the west coast of South America. (If this seems improbable, remember Bligh's open-boat navigation. Also, the preacher George Hunn Nobbs sailed from Callao to Pitcairn in six weeks in a small boat in 1828.) From South America, Christian worked his way up to Mexico, crossed to the east coast and took a ship either to Cádiz or to a port in the British West Indies, thence to Bristol.

In any of these variants, this progress may have taken as much as two years, giving 1796 as a postulated year of arrival. On his return, he surreptitiously contacted his family, who directed him to James Losh, then living in Bath. Such a progress would explain how Wordsworth

---

89 See Fryer's evidence, *Bounty Court-Martial (Minutes)*, p. 7; Morrison 1935, pp. 48, 50, 55, 60, 75; PN 3a.
90 PN 13, vol. 1, pp. 89, 91.
91 PN 21, p. 2.

became interested in Christian's story in 1796–97. (To pay for it, Christian may have worked his passages; or he may have used the ducats given to Bligh to buy items in the east on his way to the West Indies. These one hundred ducats have never been accounted for.)

There are perhaps some other indications of such a return. As many writers have pointed out, there are parallels between Coleridge's *The Rime of the Ancient Mariner* and the story of Fletcher Christian and the *Bounty*. Written in October 1797, Coleridge's poem tells the story of a voyage into the Pacific Ocean and the covert return of a single mariner. The route of the Mariner's ship imitates *Bounty*'s, and there is a good deal of imagery common to both voyages. (Particularly intriguing, in view of Christian's evidently having tied a lead weight about his neck so as to drown himself if his mutiny failed, is Coleridge's having the albatross drop off the Mariner's neck and 'sink like lead into the sea'.) However, while I can envisage Wordsworth's encouraging Coleridge in the composition with such questions as 'How might someone like Fletcher Christian return secretly?', I very much doubt that Coleridge knew of an actual return. Here, I agree with Alexander that if he had known this, he would not have been able to keep it a secret.[92]

Then there is this. In 1953, C.S. Wilkinson published *The Wake of the Bounty*, in which he hypothesised that Fletcher Christian returned. He took up this topic, he says, because he found an old scrapbook that had come from the last member of the Losh family, which contained a business letter written from the western Scottish sea town of Portnessock in 1812, signed 'F. Christian'(Plate 3).[93] Wilkinson says that he was unable to locate a genuine signature by Christian so as to verify this one. Sadly, now that we have several examples of Christian's signature, the letter that Wilkinson saw is lost.

※ ※ ※

An abiding mystery attaches to the story of Fletcher Christian's fate then. Until it is resolved, either version exists as a possibility: death on Pitcairn Island, or return to England – somewhere between sea and

---

92   Alexander 2003, p. 447.
93   Wilkinson 1953, pp. 1–2.

sky. In view of the bewildering variations in Adams's stories and those of others, and of the lack of any physical evidence of Christian's death on the island, I think that the eyewitness accounts of his being seen in England turn the balance of probability in favour of this circumstance.

We are disposed to find conspiracies more interesting than those mundane circumstances that more often than not provide a more reliable historical explanation. Did Lee Harvey Oswald act alone when he shot John F. Kennedy in Dallas? Is Lord Lucan still alive? Was Pope John Paul I murdered? So perhaps in my inclination I am merely reflecting the predilections of my age.

Perhaps ... But then, it was after a visit to James Losh in Bristol in March 1797 that Wordsworth became interested in Fletcher Christian's story and incorporated it into his play; and who was the 'Mr *' who called on Losh there in May 1797?[94]

---

94 Entry, 4 May 1797, Losh.

Plate 1 *The Bread Fruit of Otahytey* by George Tobin, from Tobin's sketches on the HMS *Providence*, 1791–93. Tobin later recalled Captain Bligh's 'violent tornados of temper' during the voyage. (State Library of New South Wales.)

Plate 2 William Wordsworth, aged twenty-eight, by William Shuter, 1798. (Rare Books and Manuscripts, Cornell University)

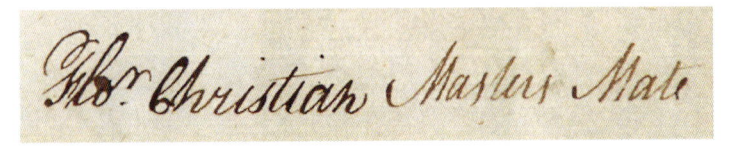

Plate 3 Fletcher Christian's signature.

Plate 4 William Hodges, *The Resolution and Adventure among Icebergs*. (State Library of New South Wales).

Plate 5 George III posthumously awarded James Cook with a coat of arms in September 1785, six years after Cook's death. The latin mottos mean 'Around the world' and 'He left nothing unattempted'. (State Library of New South Wales)

Plate 6 The frontispiece of Thomas Bankes's *System of Geography* (1787) shows Cook ascending to glory. Fame heralds his arrival and Neptune urges Clio to record his story. William Bligh aspired to similar acclamation. (Rare Books and Special Collections, the University of Sydney Library)

Plate 7 The author's daughters, Melissa and Clea, beneath a breadfruit tree, Tahiti, 1976.

Part II
The Making of *Bounty*'s Story

4

Discovering Nature: The Rise of British Scientific Exploration, 1660-1800

As I said in the Introduction, close textual analysis and more rigorous argument are needed if we are the better to understand aspects of *Bounty*'s voyage and its various aftermaths.

However, better understandings of these things do not of themselves provide a sound explanation of the public's enduring interest in the voyage. To have this we need to view the nature of scientific exploration as it developed in the Age of Enlightenment; and how the results of the many scientific expeditions, rboth at sea and on land, were presented to the public, a process which resulted in the emergence of a distinctive literary genre. And then, we need to see that this developed genre also contained elements of structure and presentation that derived from much older modes of discourse that were anything but scientific.

As it was given to the public in the 1790s, the story of *Bounty*'s voyage exhibits both the modern scientific outlook and the tropes of archaic myth. It is the quintessential example of the exploration narrative. William Bligh's *A Voyage to the South Sea* (1792) may be regarded as the 'official' narrative of *Bounty*'s voyage, and as such it is the quintessential example of the fully developed exploration narrative. However, in being so it at once conceals as much as it reveals; and this dual nature – or rather, the failure to understand what is concealed and the manner in which the so-called facts are presented – has been the root cause of much bad history about Bligh and the voyage. My Chapters 4 and 5 may initially seem to be strange digressions from

Bligh's and *Bounty*'s histories. However, it is only when we understand the beginnings of the systematic recording of scientific explorations and refinements to published accounts in the course of the eighteenth century, and how other, unscientific, narratives came to infuse them, that we may develop a clearer understanding of the whole story of *Bounty*'s voyage. This process began with Bligh's earliest reports of the progress of the voyage and the mutiny, and even perhaps – to draw a longer bow – with his intense desire to be seen as someone who has emulated James Cook.

※ ※ ※

Though curious about the world, the ancients were also credulous, with authors bequeathing a number of fantastic stories to posterity. While Herodotus and Pliny, for example, tried diligently to present coherent history, they also included accounts of the cannibalistic Anthropophagi, who wore the scalps of their victims, hair still attached, on their chests, and the Blemmyes, whose eyes, nose and mouth were in their chest.

In the Middle Ages, when extensive travel from the West was usually to the Holy Land, when learning was restricted to the few who were literate, and when the bulk of the population was fervent for miracles, medieval writers offered an undifferentiated mixture of fact, speculation and fantasy, a combination that entertained if it did not always reliably instruct. In the unknown fourth, torrid continent were the Sciapodes, a race of one-legged beings who hopped with astonishing speed, and 'in the heat they lie on their backs in the shade of their own enormous foot'.[1]

In his narrative, versions of which circulated in manuscript c.1357–71, 'Sir John Mandeville' told how he had gone in search of the mysterious Prester John, the leader of a Christian country in darkest Africa. Mandeville's narrative probably reflects some obscure knowledge of Ethiopia, but many, if not most, of his details are fabulous – for example, he also describes the gruesome Blemmyes.

---

1   Quoted in Perry 1982, p. 12.

Even that most famous of accounts of marvellous lands, *The Travels of Marco Polo*, which gave the West its first substantial sense of the Far East, may not be what it seems, for there is some doubt that Polo actually did, as he claimed, spend twenty-four years in China, mostly in attendance at the court of the great conqueror Kublai Khan. He did not mention the Chinese habits of binding women's feet, using chopsticks or drinking tea, for example; and he gives Persian versions of Mongol place names. He also confuses some of the historical events he claims to have witnessed, and mistakes details that a direct observer would not have done, such as describing Kublai Khan's warships as having five rather than three masts. What seems probable is that Polo took at least some of his details from his uncles, who had travelled through Central Asia, and/or from Persian merchants he dealt with on the shores of the Black Sea, and perhaps also from Persian guidebooks, and worked them up into an entertaining narrative.[2]

The veracity of accounts of exotic lands improved with the discovery of the New World, and the invention of the printed book. Though inevitably limited by religious and cultural assumptions, and not without some impulse to fabulise, the accounts by Spanish, Portuguese and French explorers and clerics of the West Indies, Mexico and Brazil are recognisably modern in their authors' desire to record historical circumstances accurately and to present insights into societies very different from European ones. Notable examples are Fernández de Oviedo's *Historia general y natural de las Indias* (1535), Bernal Díaz's *Historia verdadera de la conquista de la Nueva España* (written c.1550–68, published 1632), and Jean de Léry's *Histoire d'un voyage fait en la terre de Brésil* (1578). Influencing this development were changes in the theory and practice of geography (as exemplified in such works as Martin Fernández de Enciso's *Suma de Geographia* (1518), Roger Barlow's *A Brief Summe of Geographie* (1541) and John Dee's *General and Rare Memorials pertayning to the Perfect Arte of Navigation* (1577)); and growing accuracy in cartography, in particular in the work of Abraham Ortelius and Gerhard and Rumold Mercator.

---

2   See Wood 1995 and Nick Squires, 'Marco Polo's Exploration May Have Pulled Up Short', *Age* (Melbourne), 11 August 2011, http://bit.ly/2le85Cj.

It was also reinforced by reflective works based on the explorers' and conquerors' narratives, such as Michel de Montaigne's essays.

As Europeans extended their exploration of the outer world, authors began presenting first-hand accounts of the new geographical and cultural wonders. Among the earliest were those in Petrus Martyr ab Angleria's *De orbe novo decades*. Often based on interviews with the explorers, Martyr wrote his accounts in Latin between 1493 and 1525. The *Decades* were published together in 1530, and were subsequently widely translated (e.g. into English in 1555 and German in 1582). They became the model for editors and authors eager to offer accounts in vernacular languages to a reading public interested in the new discoveries. Foremost among these collections were Giovanni Ramusio's *Delle navigationi et viaggi* (3 vols, 1550–59), João de Barros's *Décadas da Ásia* (4 vols, 1552–1615), Richard Hakluyt's *The Principall Navigations, Voiages and Discoveries of the English Nation* (1589, 1598–1600), Jan Huygen van Linschoten's *Itinerario, voyage ofte schipvaert, van Jan Huygen van Linschoten naer Oost ofte Portugaels Indien* (1596), and Samuel Purchas's *Hakluytus Posthumus, or Purchas his Pilgrimes, contayning a History of the World in Sea Voyages and Lande Travells, by Englishmen and others* (4 vols, 1625).

However, while these authors generally sought to present reliable eyewitness accounts, they were not entirely able to escape the medieval past. Ramusio and Purchas, for example, offered versions of Polo's narrative; Hakluyt and Purchas included old travellers' tales of uncertain accuracy; and Purchas repeated the nonsense, put out by Antonio Pigafetta, who had sailed with Magellan, that the Patagonian men were ten feet (three metres) tall.

Nonetheless, these works and the individual explorers' accounts they were based on represent the beginnings of a new kind of travel literature, the development of which was then furthered by a new approach to knowledge. To illustrate the fundamental nature of the change with a cliché: whereas the ancients would have cited the necessary symmetry of creation to prove that a badger's legs are of equal length, Francis Bacon would go out and measure the animal's legs. Bacon enunciated his empirical approach, first in *The Advancement of Learning* (1605) and then in the *Novum Organum: or, True Directions concerning the Interpretation of Nature* (1620). These quickly became

4 Discovering Nature

keystones of the emerging modern scientific outlook, one neatly exemplified by Bacon's central premise that 'Man, the servant and interpreter of nature, does and understands only as much as he has observed, by fact or mental activity, concerning the order of nature; beyond that he has neither knowledge nor power'.[3] Moreover, the production of reliable scientific information required the strict adherence to certain methods of thought and expression:

> In the first place then, no more of antiquities, citations and differing opinions of authorities, or of squabbles and controversies, and, in short, everything philological [i.e. a commentary on an earlier text rather than an empirical investigation of the physical reality being described]. No author should be cited save in matters of doubt; and no controversies be introduced save in matters of great moment; and as for everything to do with oratorical embellishment, similitudes, the treasure house of words, and such like emptinesses, get rid of it entirely. Also make sure that everything which is adopted is set down briefly and concisely, so that they are not exceeded by the words that report them.[4]

Bacon also recognised that exploration was producing important new information about the world:

> Nor should this fact count for nothing: that by prolonged voyages and journeys (which have become prevalent in our times) many things in nature have been disclosed and found out which could shed new light on philosophy. And surely it would be a disgrace to mankind if, while the expanses of the material globe, i.e. of lands, seas, and stars, have in our times been opened up and illuminated, the limits of the intellectual globe were not pushed beyond the narrow confines of the ancients' discoveries.[5]

---

3 Aphorism 1, Bacon [1620] 2004, p. 65.
4 'Parasceve: A Preparative to a Natural and Experimental History', Bacon [1620] 2004, p. 457.
5 Aphorism 84, Bacon [1620] 2004, p. 133.

From the middle of the seventeenth century, the new scientific outlook began to influence strongly the nature of explorers' accounts. Soon after its inception in 1660, the Royal Society of London issued 'Directions for Sea-men, Bound for far Voyages'.[6] Among other things, it urged explorers to:

- record latitude and longitude and compass declination
- record details of tides, winds and currents at different times of the day and year, and ocean depths
- take soundings, and determine the nature of the seabed
- 'observe and record all Extraordinary *Meteors*, Lightnings, Thunders, *Ignes fatui*, Comets, etc'.

Shortly afterwards, Robert Boyle expanded this advice to include information to be gathered on land. Travellers should note the natural features and products of each country they visited, including:

> Its dimensions, scituation, East, West, North, and South: its Figure, its Plains, and Valleys, and their Extents[;] its Hills and Mountains, and the height of the tallest ... What Promontories, fiery or smoking Hills, etc the Country has, or hath not: Whether the Country be coherent, or much broken into Ilands ... What the Nature of the Soyle is, whether Clays, Sandy, etc or good Mould; and what Grains, Fruits, and other Vegetables, do the most naturally agree with it: As also, by what particular Arts and Industries the Inhabitants improve the Advantages, and remedy the Inconveniences of their Soyl: What hidden qualities the Soyl may have (as that of *Ireland*, against Venomous Beasts, etc).

Relevant here, too, were the geological features of the earth and minerals within it. Travellers were also to note:

> What Grasses, Grains, Herbs, (Garden and Wild) Flowers, Fruit-trees, Timber-trees (especially any Trees, whose wood is considerable)[,] Coppices, Groves, Woods, Forrests, *etc* the Country has or wants:

---

6   'Directions for Sea-men, Bound for Far Voyages', *Philosophical Transactions*, vol. 1 (1665–6), pp. 140–3.

What peculiarities are observable in any of them: What Soyles they most like or dislike; and with what Culture they thrive best. What *Animals* the Country has or wants, both as to wild Beasts, Hawks, and other Birds of Prey; and as to Poultrey, and Cattle of all sorts, and particularly, whether it have any *Animals*, that are not common, or any thing, that is peculiar in those, that are so.

In addition, travellers should give a 'careful account':

of the *Inhabitants* themselves, both *Natives* and *Strangers*, that have been long settled there: And in particular, their Stature, Shape, Colour, Features, Strength, Agility, Beauty (or the want of it), Complexions, Hair, Dyet, Inclinations and Customs that seem not due to Education.[7]

Furthermore, the Royal Society advised voyagers and travellers to keep 'an exact *Diary*', precisely describing what they saw in plain language, so as 'to separate the knowledge of *Nature*, from the colours of *Rhetorick*, the devices of *Fancy*, or the delightful deceit of *Fables*', which only obscured reality. What was required, urged Royal Society Fellow Thomas Sprat, was 'a close, naked, natural way of speaking; positive expressions; clear senses; a native easiness; bringing all things as near the Mathematical plainness, as they can: and preferring the language of Artizans, Countrymen, and Merchants, before that, of Wits, or Scholars'. It was only such plain language that would give rise to 'faithful *Records* of all the Works of *Nature*, or *Art*', so that:

the present Age, and posterity, may be able to put a Mark on the Errors, which have been strengthened by long prescription: to restore the Truths, that have lain neglected: to push on those, which are already known, to more various uses; and to make the way more passable, to what remains unreveal'd.[8]

---

7   'Directions for Sea-men, Bound for Far Voyages', pp. 141; Boyle 1665–6, pp. 186–9.
8   Sprat [1667] 1958, pp. 61–2, 113.

That is, the Royal Society hoped that those who ranged far through the world would return with data to assist it to realise its fundamental purpose, which was 'to study *Nature* rather than *Books*, and from the Observations, made of the *Phaenomena* and Effects she presents, to compose such a History of Her, as may hereafter serve to build a Solid and Useful Philosophy upon'.[9]

✻ ✻ ✻

It was not long before enterprising men were responding to the Royal Society's call. In 1669, Charles II sent John Narborough on a voyage into the southern Atlantic and eastern Pacific oceans. His tasks were, first, to explore the coast of South America south of the River Plate and, after he had passed through the Strait of Magellan, north to Valdivia; and second, if possible, 'to lay the foundation of a [Trade]' in this large region. As part of this mission, he was instructed to observe the features of the coasts and their plants and animals, and to 'remarque the temper and inclination of the inhabitants'.[10]

As he sailed, Narborough recorded details of wind and weather, took soundings, constructed charts and sketched coastal profiles and harbours, and drew up careful sailing directions for others. His chart of the Strait of Magellan, published in 1673, is particularly noteworthy, as are his directions for those entering it from the west, where there was the danger in foggy weather of mistaking one of the fjords to the north for its entrance and thereby driving onto shoals. Throughout, he calculated latitudes and longitudes and puzzled about magnetic variation.

Narborough also attended to his other instructions. At one point, he recorded how he 'digged in several places but saw nothing but gravelly Sand and Rocks; no sort of Metals or Minerals; I looked also among the broken Rocks for Metals, but saw no sign of any'. The guanacos were:

---

9   'Directions for Sea-men, Bound for Far Voyages', pp. 140–1.
10   'Instructions for Captain John Narborough', 29 August 1669, BL Add. MS 88980.

very like Deer, but larger, and had longer Necks, but no Horns; reddish coloured on the Back and aloft, whitish under their Bellies and up their Flanks; when we had got within a Furlong of them they fell a neighing like Horses, one answered another, and then all run away.

There were several kinds of porpoise, 'unlike ours in *Europe*: some pied white and black, and some grey and large ones'.[11]

Repeatedly, though not always successfully, he tried to make contact with native peoples. He briskly put paid to the nonsense that the Patagonians were giants:

> These People are of a middle stature, both Men and Women, and well-limbed, and roundish Faced, and well shaped, and low Foreheaded; their Noses of a mean size, their Eyes of the mean and black ... [Both men and women] are full Breasted, they are tawny Olive-coloured, and redded all over their Bodies with red Earth and Grease ... The Men have a harsh Language, and speak rattling in the Throat, and gross; the Women sh[r]iller and lower.[12]

Not all of Narborough's observations found their way into the account of his voyage published in 1694; however, enough did for the Royal Society to praise it for its 'many uncommon and useful Things upon most of the Heads of Natural and Mathematical Sciences, as well as Trade and other Profitable Knowledge, which contribute to the enlarging of the Mind and Empire of Man'.[13]

In 1673, Sir George Wheler commenced a journey through southern Europe that would take him to Greece and the Levant. In Italy, he sought instruction about ancient history; and as he travelled further east he was careful to make 'a considerable Collection of useful Observations', which included compass declinations, latitudes and conjectured longitudes. He also took pride in describing antiquities and

---

11   Narborough 1694, pp. 29, 113.
12   Narborough 1694, pp. 64–5.
13   Review of '*An Account of the Several Late Voyages and Discoveries* ... ', *Philosophical Transactions*, vol. 18 (1694), p. 167.

gathering inscriptions, artefacts, coins and rare plants. He said of the Parthenon, for example, that it was 'absolutely, both for Matter and Art, the most beautiful piece of Antiquity remaining in the World'. He described it and its statues, gave its measurements, and provided a drawing. But Wheler attended to the nondescript as well as to the sublime. When he went 'a simpling' (i.e. in search of 'simples', or plants with medicinal properties) on one Mediterranean island, he found what he identified as *Scorpoides Limoniis foliis*, 'a small Plant, that hath Leaves much resembling *Limonium*, among which are yellow Flowers, set on the top of a Stalk, like those of wild *Lotus*; after which succeed little Cods with Seed, in shape much resembling Caterpillars, turned round together, when touch'd'. When he presented the results of his travelling to the public in *A Journey into Greece* (1682), he acknowledged that some might consider it to contain only 'insipid descriptions of Weeds', and a record of his 'hobbl[ing] ... over broken stones, decayed buildings, and old rubbish'. However, as Narborough did, in his descriptions Wheler conformed to the principles enunciated by the Royal Society.[14]

So too did the buccaneer William Dampier, who was the most notable English sea explorer in the last decades of the seventeenth century. Dampier is a very curious figure. He was born in 1651 and as a young man began to travel widely, being in the East Indies in 1671, fighting against the Dutch in 1673, and sailing to the West Indies in 1674. Between 1675 and 1678, he cut logwood in the Bay of Campeachy, and joined the buccaneers briefly before returning to London in 1678. In 1679, he sailed to the West Indies again, ostensibly to trade, but in 1680 he once more joined the buccaneers.

Among other actions, he took part in the attack on Portobelo, in Panama, in 1680, various unprofitable cruises, and then the abortive campaign against Panama in 1685. In 1686, he was in the *Cygnet*, which Charles Swan took across the Pacific Ocean to the Philippines in the hope of capturing the galleon bringing silver from Mexico. This venture also failing, Dampier continued in the ship, now under the command of John Read, who had led a mutiny against Swan. They spent most of 1687 cruising among the East Indian islands. In January

---

14   Wheler 1682, Preface and pp. 3, 360.

4 Discovering Nature

1688, they careened the ship in the Buccaneer Archipelago off the north-west Australian coast. Dampier then left it in the Nicobar Islands, eventually reaching England again in September 1691.

In January 1699, having persuaded the Admiralty to give him a ship, Dampier set off on a voyage of discovery to New Holland and New Guinea, which took him as far as New Britain. As he was returning home, his decrepit *Roebuck* sank at Ascension Island, in the Atlantic Ocean. This voyage was marked by mismanagement and dissension between the officers; and a subsequent court martial fined Dampier the whole of his salary and declared him unfit to hold another command in the Royal Navy.

In 1703, Dampier made another buccaneering voyage round Cape Horn into the Pacific Ocean, returning to England in 1707. He sailed as pilot on Woodes Rogers's privateering voyage in August 1708, during which they sacked Guayaquil, in Ecuador, and in December 1709 captured the Manila galleon. Dampier returned to England again in 1711, and died in March 1715.

Dampier was what modern crime reporters would term a 'colourful' character; but, rather than notoriety, it is how he followed the guidelines of the Royal Society that has given him a permanent place in history. As he sailed and fought, Dampier maintained careful records of what he saw, which at one point he kept safe from the elements in a bamboo cylinder sealed with wax. He announced in the title page of the narrative of his first circumnavigation that he had gathered information about the 'Soil, Rivers, Harbours, Plants, Fruits, Animals, and Inhabitants' of the countries he had seen, and about people's 'Customs, Religion, Government [and] Trade'. And this he did in plain language, with appropriate illustrations.

For example, he said of the Condore Islands near Manila that their soil was 'for the biggest Part ... blackish, and pretty deep, only the Hills are somewhat stony'. There was one sort of tree that he had not seen elsewhere, which was 'about three or four Foot Diameter in the Body, from whence is drawn a sort of clammy Juice, which being boiled a little becomes perfect Tar; and if you boil it much it will become hard as Pitch'. The mango trees were as big as English apple trees. The wild nutmeg tree grew as tall as an English walnut, 'but it does not spread so much'. There were many sorts of birds, such as:

Parrots, Parakites, Doves and Pigeons. Here are also a sort of wild Cocks and Hens: They are much like our tame Fowl of that kind; but a great deal less, for they are about the bigness of a Crow. The Cocks do crow like ours, but much more small and shrill; and by their crowing we do first find them out in the Woods where we shoot them. Their flesh is very white and sweet.[15]

And he presented a coastal profile of one island and a chart of its harbour.

Then there was his famous description of the people of New Holland:

The Inhabitants of this Country are the miserablest People in the World. The *Hodmadods* of *Monomatapa*, though a nasty People, yet for Wealth are Gentlemen to these; who have no Houses, and skin Garments, Sheep, Poultry, and Fruits of the Earth, Ostrich Eggs, etc, as the *Hodmadods* have: And setting aside their Humane Shape, they differ but little from Brutes.[16]

Culturally limited as this description is, it was a genuine attempt to describe a people who differed markedly from Europeans; and, as Glyn Williams has put it, it was 'to live long in the European memory'.[17]

Dampier continued his habits of careful observation during later voyages. The six weeks that he spent careening the *Roebuck* at Shark Bay in 1699 was then the longest stay by a European on the Australian coast. He described other aspects of Aboriginal culture, and collected specimens of birds and plants, illustrations of which he published in his narrative.[18] Nor was this all. In an addendum to *A New Voyage round the World*, Dampier presented a 'Discourse of the Trade-Winds, Breezes, Storms, Seasons of the Year, Tides and Currents of the *Torrid Zone* throughout the World'.

---

15 Dampier [1697/1729] 1927, title page and pp. 265–7.
16 Dampier [1697/1729] 1927, p. 312.
17 Williams and Frost 1988, p. 122.
18 Dampier [1703/1729] 1939, pp. 95–[112].

This constituted the first substantial attempt at a comprehensive description of oceanic systems, and paved the way for later ones.[19]

* * *

Many people contributed to the spread of the new scientific outlook in the decades about the turn of the eighteenth century. Prominent among them was Sir Hans Sloane. Born in Ireland in 1660, Sloane trained in London, Paris and Montpellier as a physician. However, from an early age he was also fascinated by animals, plants and 'curiosities'. Instructed by John Ray, Robert Boyle and a number of distinguished French scientists, he became proficient in botany and chemistry as well as in medicine.

Sloane was elected a Fellow of the Royal Society in January 1685, and of the Royal College of Physicians two years later. In 1687–9, appointed personal physician to the Duke of Albemarle, he went to the West Indies, where he collected assiduously:

> After I had gather'd and describ'd the Plants, I dried as fair Samples of them as I could, to bring over with me. When I met with Fruits that could not be dried or kept, I employ'd the Reverend Mr Moore, one of the best Designers I could meet with there, to take the Figures of them, as also of the Fishes, Birds, Insects, etc in Crayons, and carried him with me into several places of the Country, that he might take them on the place.[20]

He returned to England with some 800 specimens of plants, most of them new to science, together with precise descriptions of them.

In the following decades, even as he built an extensive medical practice and took on many professional tasks (including the presidency of the Royal Society), Sloane published scientific catalogues and travel accounts written in a plain style. And he constantly added to his collections. Always, he was mindful that 'there is noe thing constantly

---

19   Dampier [1699/1729] 1927, pp. 227–96.
20   Sloane 1707–25, vol. 1, Preface.

observable in nature, which will not always bring some light with it, and lead us farther into the knowledge of her ways of workeing'.[21]

Towards the end of Sloane's life, visitors to his house saw hundreds of rare books and manuscripts; 'drawers fitted with all sorts of precious stones in their natural beds'; jewels 'polish'd and set after the modern fashion'; tables 'spread with *gold* and *silver ores*'; a myriad butterflies; large animals 'preserved in the skin'; hundreds of volumes of dried plants; and 'curious and venerable antiquities of *Egypt, Greece, Hetruria, Rome, Britain,* and even *America*'.[22] After his death in 1753, his collections formed the basis of the new British Museum.

∗ ∗ ∗

A series of wars abroad and distractions at home resulted in a long hiatus in British exploration of the outer world in the first half of the eighteenth century. The most notable maritime expedition was a military rather than a scientific one, but it needs to be mentioned because of its longer term consequences. This was George Anson's circumnavigation of 1740–4, during which he captured the galleon carrying bullion to Manila. In 1748–9, he proposed that Britain should send a large exploring expedition to the Pacific Ocean, but this did not proceed when the Spanish objected.[23]

Nonetheless, there were developments in these decades that were to enhance exploration further when it resumed. Two of the central features of the Scientific Revolution were the refinement and extension of mathematical knowledge, and its application to discovering the geophysical mechanics of the world. Driving these developments were calculations, observations and experiments by innovators such as Copernicus, Galileo, Cassini, Descartes, Pascal, Huygens, Hooke, Boyle, Flamsteed and Newton.

One of the fundamental problems facing cartographers and navigators in this age was the accurate calculation of longitude. This was made difficult by the lack of precise knowledge of the circumference of

---

21 Quoted in MacGregor 1994, p. 16.
22 Quoted in MacGregor 1994, p. 35.
23 See Frost and Williams 1997.

4 Discovering Nature

the earth at the equator, and therefore of the extent of a full degree of longitude.

As stars were mapped and as knowledge of the solar system, of the earth's rotation and oscillation, and of the operation of its magnetic poles grew, so too did mathematics offer the possibility of calculating longitude more accurately. It was in pursuit of these goals that Edmond Halley sailed to Saint Helena in 1676, and later undertook two voyages in the Atlantic Ocean to study the variation of the compass and terrestrial magnetism (1698–9, 1699–1700). In 1701, Halley published his 'General Chart of the Variation of the Compass'.

Accumulating information led to the development of 'lunar tables', which gave the time taken by the moon to move from one star to another at a base location throughout the year. When the equivalent time at another location was compared, then its longitude could be determined. In the 1760s, Nevil Maskelyne, the British Astronomer Royal, refined this method significantly, publishing a series of elaborate tables of lunar distances for captains to take to sea.

The lunar tables method did allow navigators to determine longitude much more accurately than they had previously been able to. However, it required specialist astronomical instruments; calculations were very complex, requiring many hours a day; and unfavourable weather conditions might make it impossible to obtain the necessary observations. Clearly, a simpler method would be preferable; and one emerged as a consequence of a stunning technological breakthrough.

In 1714, stirred by the disastrous loss seven years earlier of 2000 men when four warships ran aground on the Scilly Isles, the British Parliament established a Board of Longitude, and offered the very large prize of £20,000 (around £2.6 million in today's values) for a 'practicable and useful' method of determining longitude.

The new method involved the accurate determination of the difference in time between a base point and at a second location at sea. However, conventional pendulum clocks did not permit the determination of 'elapsed time', as the pitching of the ship disrupted their rhythm and therefore rendered them useless. In the early 1760s, after decades of effort, the self-taught John Harrison succeeded in producing a chronometer small enough to be portable that gave very accurate results during a trial voyage to Barbados. While lunar tables were not immediately superseded, the use of the new 'timekeeper' spread very rapidly. Captain James Cook, for example, used Maskelyne's lunar tables on his first circumnavigation (1768–71) but took chronometers with him on the second (1772–5). By the 1780s, the Admiralty was routinely issuing chronometers to those whom it sent on discoveries, and advising the East India Company to supply them to its captains. And by this time, foreign navigators were also sending to London for them.

A second significant development was in scientific classification. In the seventeenth century, a number of different systems of identifying and classifying plants were used, including one by Sloane's mentor John Ray; but these were piecemeal, and not always compatible. In the 1730s and 1740s, the Swedish botanist Carolus Linnaeus formulated his binominal system, based on the analysis and comparison of the sexual organs of plants. Linnaeus's 'artificial' system was eventually supplanted by Antoine Laurent de Jussieu's 'natural' one; but for much of the eighteenth century it provided a clear, formal means of identifying and classifying botanical species.

✳ ✳ ✳

European interest in further exploration of the Pacific Ocean revived in the middle of the eighteenth century, with a series of influential publications in which authors speculated on the extent, products and people of *Terra Australis*, the immense continent supposed to extend from south of the East Indies eastwards to Cape Horn (and, in some maps, also into the southern Atlantic Ocean). In 1744–8, John Campbell published the massive *Navigantium atque Itinerantium Bibliotheca*. In 1756, Charles de Brosses published his *Historie des Navigations aux Terres Australes*, of which John Callander offered an English version in 1766–8. Then, in 1767–9, Alexander Dalrymple produced *An Account of the Discoveries made in the South Pacifick Ocean, Previous to 1764*.

When comprehensive victories over the French and Spanish at sea and in the colonies in the Seven Years' War (1756–63) had given the British unchallenged naval mastery, they turned their attention to the Pacific Ocean again, with the dual purposes of increasing knowledge of the world and of developing new sources of trade. Between 1764 and

4 Discovering Nature

1780, they mounted a series of expeditions: those of John Byron (1764–6); Samuel Wallis and Philip Carteret (1766–8/9); and James Cook (1768–71, 1772–5, 1776–80). These expeditions were generally marked by their increasingly scientific character. All of the commanders were instructed to keep detailed records of weather and wind and latitude and longitude and compass variations; and, on finding land:

> to Observe the Nature of the Soil and Various kinds of Trees, Fruits Grains etc: that it produceth, the Beasts and Fowles that Inhabit or frequent [it], and the Fishes that are to be found in the Rivers, Harbours, or the Coasts thereof, and in what Quantaties, that you may be enabled, upon your return to give us full information of the same: and in case you shall find any Mines, Minerals, or Valuable Stones, you are to bring home with you Specimens of each, and transmit them to our Secretary in Order that we may cause them to be properly Examined.

They were also to:

> get the best information you can of the Genius, Temper and Inclinations of the Inhabitants of such Islands or Lands as you may Discover, that have not been visited by any European Power, and endeavor by all proper means to cultivate a friendship and Alliance with them.[24]

In order to assist in the gathering of such information, specialist personnel sailed on the voyages. Wallis, for example, took with him the purser Mr Harrison, who, 'having a very Mathematical Turn', was skilled in using Maskelyne's lunar tables. On his return, he presented Harrison's observations to the Admiralty, together with 'Plans, Views & Charts of the whole Voyage', and the 'Abundance of Seeds of different Kinds' that he had collected.[25]

---

24 Admiralty, Secret Instructions to Wallis, 16 August 1766, in Carteret 1965, vol. 2, pp. 302–6.
25 Wallis to Egmont, 19 May 1768, Clements, Shelburne vol. 75, pp. 435–45.

This scientific voyaging reached a peak of development with Cook's first and second expeditions. As an adolescent, Cook had studied mathematics, and he learnt the principles of astronomical observation while serving in the Royal Navy in Newfoundland and Lower Canada in the Seven Years' War. There, he observed a lunar eclipse, and charted coastlines and the Saint Lawrence River. When the Royal Society and the Admiralty decided to send personnel to Tahiti, the island in the central Pacific Ocean that Wallis had discovered, to observe the transit of Venus that was to occur in June 1769, they chose Cook to command the vessel, and sent the professional astronomer Charles Green out with him.

Cook was instructed, first, to observe the transit, and then to sail through the Southern Ocean in search of the supposed *Terra Australis*, and, if found, to claim it and any other unknown lands for Britain. As his predecessors had been, he was also told to observe and record what he saw diligently.[26] The young botanist Joseph Banks went on the voyage, taking with him at his own huge expense a scientific party composed of Daniel Solander and Herman Spöring, botanical disciples of Linnaeus, the artist Sydney Parkinson and the draftsman Alexander Buchan. Banks's party also sailed with an extensive array of scientific equipment.

During the voyage, Cook and Green used Maskelyne's lunar tables to determine the longitudes of the coastlines they charted, which included the only partially known ones of the major islands of New Zealand, and the entirely unknown eastern one of New Holland. Banks and Solander collected some 3400 specimens, which included 'about 1,000 Species of Plants that have not been at all describ'd by any Botanical author; 500 fish, as many Birds, and insects Sea and Land innumerable'.[27] In informing Linnaeus of these results, the English merchant and naturalist John Ellis remarked that Banks and Solander had returned 'laden with the greatest treasure of Natural History that ever was brought into any country at one time by two persons'.[28]

---

26   Admiralty, Instructions to Cook, 30 July 1768, Cook 1955–67, vol. 1, pp. cclxxix–cclxxxiv.
27   Banks to Lauraguais, December 1771, in Banks 1962, vol. 2, p. 328.
28   Ellis to Linnaeus, 10 May and 16 July 1771, Linnaeus 1821, vol. I, pp. 259–60, 263–4.

4 Discovering Nature

Banks and Cook wrote very detailed ethnographic descriptions, of which the most notable perhaps was Cook's of the Australian Aboriginal people. Reprising Dampier's account, and showing just how much he had made himself capable of seeing outside the confines of his own culture, Cook summed this up with:

> They may appear to some to be the most wretched people upon Earth, but in reality they are far more happier than we Europeans; being wholy unacquainted not only with the superfluous but the necessary Conveniencies so much sought after in Europe, they are happy in not knowing the use of them. They live in a Tranquillity which is not disturb'd by the Inequality of Condition: The Earth and sea of their own accord furnishes them with all things necessary for life, they covet not Magnificent Houses, Houshold-stuff etc, they live in a warm and fine Climate and enjoy a very wholsome Air, so that they have very little need of Clothing and this they seem to be fully sencible of, for many to whome we gave Cloth etc to, left it carelessly upon the Sea beach and in the woods as a thing they had no manner of use for.[29]

※ ※ ※

Cook did not find the fabled southern continent on the *Endeavour*'s voyage. However, there was one area of the southern Pacific Ocean that he did not traverse, where there might still be a substantial landmass. He returned to England with a comprehensive scheme to settle this question that had 'ingrossed the attention of some of the Maritime Powers for near two Centuries past and the Geographers of all ages'.[30] As he told the Admiralty:

> Now I am upon the subject of discoveries I hope it will not be taken a Miss if I give it as my opinion that the most feasable Method of making further discoveries in the South Sea is to enter it by the way of New Zeland, first touching and refreshing at the

---

29 Entry, 23 August 1770, Cook 1955–67, vol. 1, p. 399.
30 Entry, 21 February 1775, Cook 1955–67, vol. 2, p. 643.

Cape of Good Hope, from thence proceed to the Southward of New Holland for Queen Charlottes Sound where again refresh Wood and Water, takeing care to be ready to leave that place by the latter end of September or beginning of October at farthest, when you would have the whole summer before you and after geting through the Straight might, with the prevailing Westerly winds, run to the Eastward in as high a Latitude as you please and, if you met with no lands, would have time enough to get round Cape Horne before the summer was too far spent, but if after meeting with no Continent & you had other Objects in View, then haul to the northward and after visiting some of the Islands already discover'd, after which proceed with the trade wind back to the Westward in search of those before Mintioned [i.e. those indicated by the Polynesian navigator/priest Tupaia], thus the discoveries in the South Sea would be compleat.[31]

The Admiralty accepted this proposal for another voyage, provided two ships and gave Cook the command. The astronomers William Wales and William Bayly went on it, as did the German scientists Johann and George Forster. Cook sailed from England in July 1772 and proceeded down the Atlantic Ocean. He left the Cape of Good Hope in November and crossed the southern Indian Ocean to New Zealand, which he reached in March 1773. He then made a great sweep into the Antarctic Ocean, before turning north, to reach Juan Fernández and Easter islands, then looping back to the Marquesas Islands and Tahiti. From Tahiti, he continued west to the Samoan and Fijian islands, then to the New Hebrides, New Caledonia and Norfolk Island on the way back to New Zealand. From New Zealand, he sailed east to Cape Horn, through the southern Atlantic Ocean to the Cape of Good Hope, and thence up the Atlantic Ocean to England.

Cook's second voyage was remarkable on a number of counts. As he himself commented, he made 'the circuit of the Southern Ocean in a high Latitude and traversed it in such a manner as to leave not the least room for the Possibility of there being a continent, unless near the Pole and out of the reach of Navigation'. 'By twice visiting the Pacific Tropical Sea,' he

---

31   [Postscript], Cook 1955–67, vol. 1, p. 479.

continued, 'I had not only settled the situation of some old discoveries but made there many new ones and left, I conceive, very little more to be done even in that part.' During this voyage, Cook sailed 70,000 miles (around 112,000 kilometres) further, and 10,000 miles (around 16,000 kilometres) further out of sight of land, than anyone before him. He became the first navigator to cross the Antarctic Circle, which he did three times. Using a chronometer, he recorded longitude and charted coastlines with unprecedented accuracy. When he returned to England, he found that his error in longitude was only 7'45", a tiny amount for such a long voyage.[32] Losing only four of his crew, three of them to accident, he showed how scurvy might be contained on long voyages (though it is only right to point out that he did not understand properly what caused this scourge of seamen and therefore what cured it).

The scientists who went with Cook collected much meteorological information, and hundreds of new biological and botanical specimens. The gifted artist William Hodges created many striking depictions of phenomena, icebergs, islands and people (Plate 4). Cook himself returned with a wealth of ethnographic information. Indeed, so determined had his habits of observation become that he even watched a Maori consume human flesh, so as to be certain of the fact of cannibalism:

> The sight of the head and the relation of the circumstances just mentioned [Maori bringing on board body parts] struck me with horor and filled my mind with indignation against these Canibals, but when I considered that any resentment I could shew would avail but little and being desireous of being an eye wittness to a fact which many people had their doubts about, I concealed my indignation and ordered a piece of the flesh to be broiled and brought on the quarter deck where one of these Canibals eat it with a seeming good relish before the whole ships Company which had such effect on some of them as to cause them to vomit.

He commented, 'That the New Zealanders are Canibals can now no longer be doubted.'[33]

---

32 Entries, 21 February and 29 July 1775, Cook 1955–67, vol. 2, pp. 643, 678.
33 Entry, 23 November 1773, Cook 1955–67, vol. 2, pp. 293–4.

Cook then explained his interest in confirming this gruesome fact:

> The account I gave of it in my former Voyage was partly founded on circumstances and was, as I afterwards found, discredited by many people. I have often been asked, after relateing all the circumstance, if I had actualy seen them eat human flesh my self, such a question was sufficient to convence me that they either disbelieved all I had said or formed a very different opinion from it, few considers what a savage man is in his original state and even after he is in some degree civilized.[34]

In its realisation of its stated purpose, in its length and the accuracy of its records, in the wealth of information that it produced, Cook's first *Resolution* voyage was the most nearly perfect of all the great voyages of scientific exploration.

On this return to England, James Cook was again feted. He dined with members of the Royal Society; and he began preparing an account of his voyage for publication. When it appeared in 1777, it contained an apologetic preface, in which he asked readers to excuse his 'inaccuracies of style', for he was a person 'who has not had the advantage of much school education, but who has been constantly at sea from his youth'. The reading public must therefore not expect 'the elegance of a fine writer, or the plausibility of a professed book-maker' from him. Rather, he was 'a plain man, zealously exerting himself in the service of his Country, and determined to give the best account he is able of his proceedings'.[35] And, as befitted works of serious scientific and educational purpose, his account included tables of coordinates, charts, coastal profiles, engravings of animals, plants and people, and vocabularies of native languages.

Recognising that he had done more than could reasonably be asked of any navigator, at his request the Admiralty offered Cook the sinecure of Fourth Captain of the Seamen's Hospital at Greenwich; and he prepared for a much less arduous life on land. But he was soon restless, writing to his old master John Walker:

---

34 Entry, 23 November 1773, Cook 1955–67, vol. 2, p. 294.
35 Cook 1777, vol. 1, p. xxxvi.

4 Discovering Nature

my fate drives me from one extream to a nother[,] a fews Months ago the whole Southern hemisphere was hardly big enough for me and now I am going to be confined within the limits of Greenwich Hospital, which are far too small for an active mind like mine, I must however confess it is a fine retreat and a pretty income, but whether I can bring my self to like ease and retirement, time will shew.[36]

When the Admiralty planned another voyage, this time to explore the northern Pacific Ocean, with the particular goal of finding the entrance of the strait supposed to link this ocean with the Atlantic, Cook volunteered to lead it.

Cook sailed in the *Resolution* on 12 July 1776, reaching Table Bay three months later, where he was joined by Charles Clerke in the *Discovery*. They sailed again on 1 December, sighting Prince Edward, Crozet and Kerguelen islands on their way to Van Diemen's Land, where Cook took on wood and grass for the cattle from 26–30 January. From there, he took the expedition across to New Zealand and refreshed at Queen Charlotte Sound. He sailed around the Cook Islands in March and April, and spent May, June and July among the Tongan Islands. He reached Tahiti again on 12 July. Leaving on 29 September, he sailed among the Society Islands until 11 December, when he turned north for the north-west American coast. He discovered the Hawaiian Islands on 18 January 1778, then sighted 'the long looked for coast of new Albion [i.e. northern California]' on 6 March.[37]

As he followed the coast north, Cook looked unsuccessfully for the strait. After spending a month in Nootka Sound, on Vancouver Island, repairing the ships and refreshing, he resumed the search for a north-west passage. He sailed along the Alaskan coast, examining its inlets, islands and passages. On 9 August, he entered Bering Strait off Cape Prince of Wales, 'the Western extremity of all America hitherto known'.[38] For the next ten days, he sailed north into the Arctic Ocean. Then, faced with impassable ice, he turned south-west, until he reached

---

36 Cook to Walker, 19 August 1776, Cook 1955–67, vol. 2, p. 960.
37 Entry, 6 March 1778, Cook 1955–67, vol. 3, p. 289.
38 Entry, 9 August 1778, Cook 1955–67, vol. 3, p. 409.

the coast of Asia. On 2 September, having re-entered Bering Strait, he took the ship past Cape Dezhneva, the easternmost point of Asia. Cook had found no passage, and as winter was coming on he decided to return to the Hawaiian Islands, and then continue the search the following summer. He reached Hawaii again at the end of November.

After Cook's death in a conflict with the islanders on 14 February 1779, Clerke took the *Resolution* and *Discovery* across to Kamchatka, Russia, which he reached in late April. He then explored the Asian coast northwards in the summer months. After Clerke's death in August, captains John Gore and James King decided to terminate the expedition. They went through the Kurile Islands down past Japan to Macau, then through the Indian Ocean to the Cape of Good Hope. They reached England again in early October, having been away more than four years.

In some ways, the third voyage was the equal of the earlier ones. The explorations were as extensive, the charting as thorough as before; and once more a large geographical misconception was cast into doubt. The expedition again gathered wide-ranging natural history collections, and obtained a wealth of new ethnographic information. At Tonga, Cook stripped to the waist and loosened his hair so that he might witness the *'inasi*. His account of this harvest festival remains the best we have. At Tahiti, he witnessed a human sacrifice and, despite his personal repugnance, recorded the details with his usual objectivity. On the north-west coast, he and his officers and surgeons and the artist John Webber recorded details of native cultures previously unknown to Europeans.

However, there were points where this third voyage did not – could not – match the earlier ones. The fact that there was no Strait of Anián meant that Cook could not succeed in realising his major objective; and his death cast a comprehensive pall over the voyage, which precluded another triumphant return of the great explorer. However, William Bligh did return, and was later aggrieved, when the credit for charts which he claimed to have drawn was given to his deputy. He wrote of the charts and plans published in *A Voyage to the Pacific Ocean* (1784):

> None of the Maps and Charts in this publication are from the original drawings of Lieut. Henry Roberts, he did no more than

copy the original ones from Captain Cook who besides myself was the only person that surveyed & laid the Coast down ... Every Plan & Chart from C. Cook's death are exact Copies of my Works.[39]

※ ※ ※

There was one further major British maritime expedition before the end of the eighteenth century: that of George Vancouver (1791–5), which had a much more overt political purpose than had Cook's. After some of Cook's sailors sold the sea-otter pelts they had obtained at Nootka Sound at Macau for extravagant prices, adventurers from England, India, China, Russia and the United States swarmed to the north-west coast. In April 1789, asserting his nation's claim to possession, a Spanish naval officer seized two British ships and sent the crews to prison in Mexico, where some died. In late 1790, after a display of overwhelming naval might, Britain forced Spain to relinquish this claim.

Vancouver's immediate task, then, was to accept restitution of land and buildings at Nootka Sound. His larger purpose was to continue the search for the north-west passage and, if found, to claim possession of it on the basis of first discovery – a task made urgent by Spain's having despatched a lavish scientific expedition under the command of Alejandro Malaspina to the Pacific Ocean in July 1789. If Malaspina discovered the strait first, then Spain would gain control of it by establishing a settlement at its entrance. The British government was anxious:

> that an Establishment should be formed ... with a view to the opening a Commercial intercourse with the Natives, as also for establishing a line of communication across the Continent of America, and thereby to prevent any future intrusion, by securing to this Country the possession of those parts which lye at the back of Canada and Hudson's Bay, as well as the Navigation by such Lakes as are already known or may hereafter be discovered.

---

39 Gould 1928, p. 371.

More generally still, the expedition was to assert the right of British subjects to hunt whales and seals 'in any Part of the American Seas, or of the Pacific Ocean', and to trade freely about it. As Henry Dundas observed when he announced the terms of the Nootka Convention to parliament, he and his colleagues had been contending not 'for a few miles, but a large world'.[40]

Nonetheless, there was an intensely scientific core to Vancouver's voyage. He sailed with two ships in April 1791, pausing at Cape Town and touching at the south-west tip of Western Australia on his way to New Zealand. He reached Tahiti at the end of December, and went north to the Hawaiian Islands. He arrived on the American coast at Cape Cabrillo, at 39°N latitude, in April 1792. For the next three summers, often in difficult conditions, he traced that tortuous coastline and examined its indentations for some 10,000 miles (16,000 kilometres), from the Strait of Juan de Fuca to Alaska, in a fruitless search for the north-west passage. The expedition returned to England in September 1795. Vancouver's charting was a model of scientific exactitude; and he and his officers also returned with more botanical and ethnographic information.

※ ※ ※

There were also significant inland explorations in the second half of the eighteenth century. Like his seagoing counterpart, the land explorer ventured into regions that were at best unfamiliar to Europeans, and sometimes quite unknown to them. Now, he too was dedicated to the causes of science and careful observation. He too recorded atmospheric conditions, and latitudes and longitudes, where these had not been taken before. He noticed the features of the earth, its geological formations and minerals, its plants and animals, its peoples and their customs. As did the voyager, the traveller saw himself generating useful

---

40 [Nepean], Draft Instructions for Vancouver, c. December 1790, NA, HO 28/7, fos 392-9; Leeds to Fitzherbert, 16 May 1790, NA, FO 185/7, [n.p.]; Dundas' speech, 14 December 1790, *Parliamentary History*, vol. 28 (1789-91), col. 979.

4 Discovering Nature

and reliable knowledge; and he (or his editor) illustrated his account with engravings: charts, maps, views, plants, animals, people.

Prominent among British and American land explorers were James Bruce, William Bartram, Samuel Hearne and Mungo Park. Bruce undertook his quest for the source of the Nile River between 1768 and 1773. The location of the great river's 'fountains' had been speculated about from Antiquity, but never properly identified. Bruce's extensive preparations included becoming proficient in mathematics, astronomy and drawing; learning languages (French, Spanish, Portuguese, Italian, Greek, Arabic and other North African ones) and some medicine; and seeking relevant historical and geographical information from old books and manuscripts.

Bruce's party included an artist, persons trained in architecture, linguists, guards and servants. Starting along the coast of North Africa, he crossed to the Levant and went down the Red Sea. Making many excursions to inspect and sketch ruins, he gathered much information about the ancient history of the countries he travelled through, and about their contemporary governments and societies. Given that we now have a radically different understanding of historical linguistics, and that archaeological excavations and the deciphering of ancient inscriptions and manuscripts have given us very different chronologies of the ancient Near East, many of Bruce's details and arguments are now superseded. However, in terms of what was then known, he does present himself throughout as an earnest scientific traveller.

From Arabia, Bruce crossed to East Africa. As he progressed to Abyssinia, he observed the face of the country, and its minerals and agricultural productions. He noted its plants and animals, and obtained specimens. At the end of the third volume of his account of his travels, he gave an extensive record of the region's rainfall in 1770 and 1771; and he devoted his final volume to the natural history of the various countries he saw. Using his chronometer, telescope and quadrant, he determined many latitudes and longitudes. Indeed, there is something comical – but also something admirable – in his accounts of how he and his servants and animals struggled to get his weighty instruments up mountains and over rivers. (The quadrant was so heavy that it required four men to carry it.)

In order to realise his quest, Bruce had to overcome many difficulties: illness; extreme geographical and weather conditions; untrustworthy guides; bandits; rapacious petty rulers; fierce tribes not under the authority of the major rulers. He also had to contend with the inability of people to understand what motivated him – how could anyone in their right mind travel to find the source of a river?

After a number of lengthy interruptions, Bruce began the final leg of his quest on 4 April 1770. He reached the Nile at Lake Tana, but news that two warlords had rebelled against the king, who was with his army in the field against his enemies, caused him to abandon the attempt. After the wet season, he tried again, leaving the royal city of Gondar on 27 October 1770, to reach at last the place where the great river springs from under the Geesh mountains. 'It is easier to guess than to describe the situation of my mind at that moment,' he wrote, 'standing in that spot which had baffled the genius, industry, and enquiry of both ancients and moderns, for the course of near three thousand years.'[41] In the next days, by repeated observations, he established that the fountains lay at 10°59'25"N latitude and 36°55'30"E longitude.

After his return to Britain, Bruce spent much of the next sixteen years studying the books and manuscripts he had gathered and earlier travellers' accounts before writing his own narrative. In it, he stressed that he relied in the first place on direct observation: 'to see distinctly and accurately, to describe plainly, dispassionately and truly, is all that ought to be expected from one in my situation.'[42] At moments, his personal experience was akin to Cook's observing Maori cannibalism directly – for example, some North African Arabs did indeed eat lion; Abyssinians did cut steaks from the rumps of living animals that they then drove on; and only personal inspection of the pyramids might give an accurate sense of them. And when he discussed the narratives and theories of former authors, he was careful to point out where he thought their details might be suspect.

※※

---

41 Bruce 1790, vol. 3, p. 597.
42 Bruce 1790, vol. 1, p. lxvi.

4 Discovering Nature

William Bartram was a trained botanist, and the primary motive for his expedition through the south-eastern quarter of North America in the mid-1770s was 'the discovery of rare and useful productions of nature, chiefly in the vegetable kingdom'. Accordingly, descriptions of flora bulk large in his account. Indeed, most modern readers will probably consider these tedious in their length and detail. However, he was also concerned to describe other things. As its title page stated, his *Travels* included, 'An Account of the Soil and Natural Productions of those Regions, Together with Observations on the Manners of the Indians'; and it was 'Embellished with Copper-Plates'. In the introduction, he said:

> The attention of a traveller should be particularly turned, in the first place, to the various works of Nature, to mark the distinctions of the climates he may explore, and to offer such useful observations on the different productions as may occur. Men and manners undoubtedly hold the first rank – whatever may contribute to our existence is also of equal importance, whether it be found in the animal or vegetable kingdom; neither are the various articles which tend to promote the happiness and convenience of mankind, to be disregarded.[43]

※ ※ ※

Samuel Hearne's twin purposes were to see whether there was a navigable passage from Hudson Bay west to the Pacific Ocean, and to locate rumoured rich copper mines on the Arctic coast. He undertook three expeditions between 1769 and 1772. For various reasons, he did not succeed with his first and second. On the third, though, which lasted nineteen months, he established there was no passage as supposed; and he reached the copper district, only to discover that Indian informants had greatly exaggerated the worth of its deposits. As he travelled through regions never before seen by Europeans, Hearne calculated latitudes and longitudes, noted geographical details, the distributions of animal and bird populations, and customs of the native peoples.

---

43 Bartram [1791], pp. 15, 29.

Like Bruce, Hearne was careful to correct mistaken geographical assumptions and faulty descriptions of animals and peoples. For example, against what the Indians had reported, it was not true that European ships would be able to navigate up the Coppermine River from the Arctic Ocean. The northern lights were indeed accompanied by sound – 'a rustling and crackling noise, like the waving of a large flag in a fresh gale of wind'. Previous accounts of beavers were greatly flawed. Sagacious these animals may be, and skilful at building. However, they did not 'drive stakes as thick as a man's leg into the ground three or four feet deep'; nor did they weave structures of wattle between these stakes and plaster them using their broad tails. They did not have two 'doors' to their 'houses' – to have had a landward entrance would have allowed wolverines to attack them. They did not divide these houses into rooms, including one for excretion. Rather, they voided their bowels outside their houses. They were not in the habit of 'assembling in great bodies, and jointly erecting large towns, cities, and commonwealths'. Contrary to previous report, white beavers were exceedingly rare. The females did not give birth to ten to fifteen young, the usual number being from two to five. There were no 'slave' beavers.[44]

Both in the main body of the work, and in his final chapter, Hearne wrote of the presence of birds and animals in different areas and seasons, of the taste of their flesh and of the utility of their hides. Bison and moose, for example, were to be found in the south-west, but not in the tundra. Black bears were uncommon in northern regions, while brown ones were never found there. Swans and a variety of geese migrated north in the spring. The southern species of deer was much larger than that found north of the Churchill River. Either might be plentiful or scarce, depending on preceding seasonal conditions. Deer skins were at their best in September, when the hair on them was full. The flesh of old musk-oxen was rank, as was that of male deer in the rutting season.

Hearne was just as concerned to provide accounts of the lives and customs of the Indians, interpolating his accounts of his journeys with descriptions, and giving his second last chapter over to a more detailed

---

44   Hearne 1795, pp. 224–46.

consideration of these subjects. Having no habits of moderation, Indians ate to excess when game was abundant, making themselves sick. However, they had an extraordinary ability to remain cheerful when hunger griped their stomachs; but when food was scarce, the men had what there was before the women. A woman was expected to be able to move on with the group immediately after giving birth. Wife-beating, wife-stealing, rape and murder were common. Medicine men ('conjurers') had some very strange practices, such as blowing into the anus of a sick person. The tribes abandoned the old, infirm and terminally ill.

Throughout, Hearne stressed the veracity and usefulness of his accounts. In refuting the common assertion that male deer shed their penises at the end of the rutting season, he drew a sharp contrast between purported facts from armchair experts at home who did not bother to ascertain them at first hand and those that people 'who are necessitated to be travellers are able or willing to give them'. Tongue-in-cheek, he apologised for being one of the latter, at the same time assuring readers that he would not, 'in the course of this Journal, advance any thing that will not stand the test of experiment, and the skill of the most competent judges'.[45]

Time and again, Hearne repeated this assurance of veracity. While the flesh of the large southern deer is good eating, that of the small northern one 'is by far more delicious, and the finest I have ever eaten, either in this country or any other'. This he could 'affirm from my own experience'. He knew about beaver. He had studied them in the wild and kept them as pets. Previous accounts of this animal had emanated from French Canada. However, 'those accounts differ so much from the real state and economy of all the beaver to the North of that place, as to leave great room to suspect the truth of them altogether'. Bison could easily outrun even the swiftest Indian hunters through heavy snow. 'To this I have been an eye-witness many times,' he said, 'and once had the vanity to think that I could have kept pace with them; but though I was at that time celebrated for being particularly fleet of foot in snow-shoes, I soon found that I was no match for the buffaloes, notwithstanding they were then plunging through such deep snow, that their bellies made a

---

45   Hearne 1795, pp. 200–1.

trench in it as large as if many heavy sacks had been hauled through it.'[46] He provided his extensive details about Indian life as a consequence of his 'long residence in the country'; and while he did not use 'technical terms' to identify the animals and birds of Canada's arctic region, he drew on the highly regarded Thomas Pennant's *Arctic Zoology* (1784–5) to do so accurately.[47]

✳✳✳

Mungo Park also explored in order to elucidate geographical puzzles and to obtain useful information about people and products. Park was a Scot who had trained in botany and medicine. In the mid-1790s, the Association for Promoting the Discovery of the Interior Parts of Africa, in the founding of which Sir Joseph Banks played a leading part, sent him to West Africa with the main aims of tracing the course of the Niger River and locating the legendary cities of Hausa and Timbuktu.[48]

As he himself put it, Park had 'a passionate desire to examine into the productions of a country so little known; and to become experimentally acquainted with the modes of life, and character of the natives'.[49] For two years, in the face of considerable difficulties, he stuck to his tasks, observing the nature of the country he traversed, its animals and plants, and the habits of its peoples, recording latitudes and longitudes and compass bearings as he went. Park's vision was influenced by cultural assumptions that we now find limiting. For example, he instinctively believed in the four stages of civilisation (hunter/gatherer, pastoral, agricultural, commercial), and he had no doubt about the superiority of the Christian religion. Nonetheless, he travelled through areas that only one other European had ever seen before, who had not survived to report on them; and Park returned with much new information about the western interior of the 'dark' continent and its peoples.

---

46 Hearne 1795, pp. 225, 242, 253.
47 Hearne 1795, p. ix.
48 Park 1799, p. 3
49 Park 1799, p. 2.

4 Discovering Nature

In publishing the narrative of his travels, Park announced bluntly that, as a 'composition', it had 'nothing to recommend it, but *truth*. It is a plain, unvarnished tale; without pretensions of any kind, except that it claims to enlarge, in some degree, the circle of African geography.'[50] In addition to details of his arduous journey, he offered readers accounts of the peoples, with particular attention to the Mandingoes, whose language he had learnt, and the 'Moors' of the interior; of the practice of slavery; and of the products and trade of this vast and varied region. The Appendix composed by Major James Rennell added significantly to the scientific character of Park's account. Rennell was one of the most competent surveyors and cartographers of the day. He carefully compared Park's data with those of other explorers, so as to produce an integrated account of the geography of North and West Africa, which included charts of magnetic variation. Particularly noteworthy was his map of North Africa showing the results not only of Park's journey but also of James Bruce's.

※ ※ ※

A new optimism is discernible in British thinking from the middle of the eighteenth century. Comprehensive victories over France and Spain in the Seven Years' War had given the nation mastery of the oceans. Enlightenment values were spreading. Scientific knowledge was increasing rapidly, with theoretical and practical advances that would quickly lead to the mechanisation of the cloth industry. New scientific disciplines, such as geology, chemistry and mineralogy, were developing. The expeditions of scientific exploration were adding very rapidly to navigational, geographical, botanical and ethnographic knowledge. The potential for expanding commerce grew.

The public well understood that Enlightenment values, the new scientific outlook, geographical exploration and commercial expansion were intimately connected. In introducing his compilation of Byron's, Wallis's, Carteret's, Cook's and Banks's journals, John Hawkesworth praised George III for sponsoring discovery, 'not with a view to the

---

50   Park 1799, p. [vii].

acquisition of treasure, or the extent of dominion, but the improvement of commerce and the increase and diffusion of knowledge'.[51]

In the public mind, two iconic figures represented the fields of theoretical and practical science: Isaac Newton and James Cook. William Wordsworth linked these two fields when he wrote of Newton's statue at Cambridge 'with his prism and silent face, / The marble index of a mind for ever / Voyaging through strange seas of Thought, alone'.[52] Newton was the great mathematician who invented calculus, who deployed his mathematical knowledge to elaborate the laws of motion, gravity and optics. Cook was the navigator who used scientific advances (lunar tables, chronometers) to practical effect, the explorer who charted more extensively than anyone had ever done previously, and who followed the dictates of the Royal Society in recording precisely what he saw.

In 1787, George Forster, who had accompanied Cook on the second voyage, wrote:

> his mind, which was never idle, was always trying to conceive of ways to ease the hardships of his countrymen, in the process extending the duration of his voyages, making his discoveries more widely known, and enriching our knowledge about the realm of truth with his observations of the nature of men and animals, plants, and even inanimate objects.

Calling attention to 'those careful studies which, for as long as the printer's art immortalizes thought, will be read as sources of useful, reliable and pleasant instruction, with interest and admiration', Forster asserted, 'Nobody knew the value of the fleeting moment better than Cook, and nobody used it as conscientiously. Nor has anybody, in a similar period of time, extended the boundaries of our knowledge in the same measure.' And in the summary of of relevant exploration with which he introduced his account of his own voyage, George Vancouver wrote of Cook, 'the labours of that distinguished character will remain a monument of his pre-eminent abilities, and

---

51   Hawkesworth 1773, dedication, vol. 1.
52   Wordsworth, *Prelude* (1850), Book III, ll. 61–3.

4 Discovering Nature

dispassionate investigation of the truth, as long as science shall be respected in the civilized world'.[53]

* * *

Some of the luminaries of intellectual England were less than impressed by exploration narratives. The indefatigable letter writer Horace Walpole dismissed Hawkesworth's account of South Sea voyages as 'at best ... but an account of the fishermen on the coasts of forty islands'. Crabbed old Samuel Johnson also found the information the explorers brought back to be of little worth. He characterised the volumes describing Cook's third voyage as being so uninteresting that 'they will be eaten by rats and mice, before they are read through'.[54]

However, these views were not shared by the British reading public, who embraced the explorers' accounts avidly. *Voyages* and *Travels* were among the most popular works of the second half of the eighteenth century. For example, in the period 1773–84, Hawkesworth's account was borrowed 201 times from the Bristol Library (with the next most popular work being Patrick Brydone's *Tour through Sicily and Malta* (1773), which was borrowed 192 times). Cook's *A Voyage towards the South Pole and round the World* (1777) sold out on the day it appeared and went into a second edition immediately, with a third in 1779 and a fourth in 1784. It was borrowed 113 times from the Bristol Library up to 1784. Georg Forster's account, *A Voyage round the World* (1777), was borrowed 65 times.[55] James Cook and James King's account of the third circumnavigation, *A Voyage to the Pacific Ocean*, published in 1784 in three volumes, which included twenty-four charts and plates, sold out in three days, despite its hefty price of £4.14.6, and was soon being resold for £9. Bruce's *Travels* sold out in two days.

There were also a myriad redactions of these primary narratives, including shorter accounts by others who went on the voyages; extracts in periodicals such as the *Gentleman's Magazine* and the *Annual*

---

53 Forster 1787, pp. 172–3; Vancouver [1798] 1986, p. 275.
54 Walpole to Mason, 5 July 1773, Walpole 1937–83, vol. 28, p. 96; Boswell [1791] 1934–64, vol. 4, pp. 308–9.
55 See Kaufman 1960.

Register; abridged versions; distillations into geography books, which ranged in size from folio volumes running to hundreds of pages, to more manageable quarto and octavo versions, down to elementary texts for young children; and poems utilising the explorers' information, such as Anna Seward's 'Elegy on Captain Cook' (1780), Erasmus Darwin's 'Zoonomia' (1794–£6) and 'The Temple of Nature' (1803), and William Lisle Bowles's 'The Spirit of Discovery by Sea' (1804).

Perhaps the generic *System of Geography* offers the best indication of the popularity of the new knowledge. Running to hundreds of pages, these behemoths were published at regular intervals and in large numbers from the 1770s into the nineteenth century. Let Thomas Bankes's stand for them all.

Understanding that 'an enterprising spirit still prevails amongst us with unabating ardour, and the latest discoveries, from their nature and importance, appear to engross conversation from the politest circles, and throughout every class in the kingdom', Bankes published *A New Royal Authentic and Complete System of Universal Geography, Antient and Modern* in ninety weekly parts, with the first issue appearing in January 1787. This massive work ran to 990 folio pages, and comprehended not only the recent discoveries but also the 'respective Situations' of all countries in the world, with their 'Extent, Latitude, Longitude, Boundaries, Climates, Soil, natural and artificial Curiosities, Mines, Metals, Minerals, Trees, Shrubs, the various Kinds of Fruits, Flowers, Herbs and vegetable Productions'; together with accounts of 'the Religion, Laws, Customs, Manners, Genius, Tempers, Habits, Amusements, and singular Ceremonies of the respective Inhabitants: their Arts, Sciences, Manufactures, Learning, Trade, Commerce, Governments, etc'; and 'the various Kinds of Beasts, Birds, Fishes, amphibious Creatures, Reptiles, Insects, etc peculiar to each Country; including every Thing curious, as related by the most eminent Travellers and Navigators, from the earliest Accounts to the present Time'. And the whole was 'enriched' with 'upwards of One Hundred and Fifty beautiful Engravings', consisting of 'Views, Whole-sheet Maps, Plans, Charts, Antiquities, Quadrupeds, Birds, Fishes, Reptiles, Vegetables, Men, Manners, Customs, Ceremonies, etc[,] the Whole executed in a superior Stile, by the first Artists in the Kingdom'. For good measure, Bankes also included 'a Complete Guide to

Geography, Astronomy, the Use of the Globes, Maps, etc', and gave an account of the 'Rise, Progress, and present State of Navigation throughout the Known World'.[56]

This was knowledge fit for citizens of an enlightened age.

※ ※ ※

It was also knowledge that the small group of young men might utilise in the new mode of poetry they were developing. With Samuel Coleridge's encouragement, William Wordsworth contemplated incorporating the new knowledge in an epic poem, writing in March 1798:

> I have written 1300 lines of a poem in which I contrive to convey most of the knowledge of which I am possessed. My object is to give pictures of Nature, Man, and Society. Indeed I know not any thing which will not come within the scope of my plan ... If you could collect for me any books of travels you would render me an essential service, as without much of such reading my present labours cannot be brought to a conclusion.[57]

Robert Southey had the same sense of the importance of understanding 'the manners of other nations, and the condition of men in states and stages of society different to our own'.[58]

Repeatedly, the new generation of poets reflected this theoretical stance in their work. Wordsworth took the narrative of 'The Complaint of a forsaken Indian Woman' from Hearne, and the imagery of the Aurora Borealis making 'a rustling and crackling noise'. From Bartram, he took the images of the white-flowered magnolia grandiflora, cyprus and scarlet-flowered hibiscus that he presented in 'Ruth'. Coleridge took the route of the Ancient Mariner's ship from Cook's second voyage and from *Bounty*'s voyage. His imagery of Antarctic ice and its sounds came from Cook. He took the shooting of the albatross from George

---

56   Bankes [1787–8], title page and p. [5].
57   Wordsworth to Tobin, 6 March 1798, Wordsworth 1967, vol. 1, p. 212.
58   Southey 1829, vol. 2, p. 365.

Shelvocke's *Voyage*. He took the extreme thirst fortuitously relieved by rain from Shelvocke's *Voyage*, and by blood from Anson's *Voyage*. Various of the narratives in that massive compilation *Purchas his Pilgrimes* provided him with the ship's passage from the dangerous frozen ocean into the peaceful sea (Schouten); the becalmed ship (Knivet and Noort); the shrunken deck (Hawkins); the dead and dying men with their blackened skin (Knivet); the water snakes (Hawkins); and the earthquake whose resultant tidal wave sunk the ship (Schouten).

Southey took details from Watkin Tench's narratives of the convict colony at Port Jackson (Sydney) for his 'Botany Bay Eclogues', including the one that would later give rise to considerable amusement: that in the uncultivated land, instead of 'the music of the bleating flocks, / Alone is heard the Kangaroo's sad note / Deepening in distance'.

The *Voyages*, *Travels* and *Systems of Geography* that these young poets took into their studies sent them out into the great world, and they returned from their armchair explorations with rich freights of images and stories.

Bounty's story contributed to this store. In the early 1790s, Coleridge and Southey became caught up in an impossible dream of a simple, classless society of married couples who would share in communal work, with the men also giving themselves over to philosophical enquiry and literary endeavour. This dream was founded in a very flawed understanding of life in Tahiti. Southey wrote:

> Why is there not some corner of the world where wealth is useless! Or rather why was not I like Emilius taught a trade! Is humanity so very vicious that society cannot exist without so many artificial distinctions linked together as we are in the great chain. Why should the extremity of that chain be neglected? At this moment I could form the most delightful theory of an island peopled by men who should be Xtians not Philosophers and where Vice only should be contemptible. Virtue only honourable where all should be convenient without luxury all satisfied without profusion – but at the moment when Imagination is almost wrought up to delirium, the ticking of the clock or the howling of the wind reminds me what I am and I sigh to part with so enchanting

a delusion. If the *Bounty* mutineers had not behaved so cruelly to their officers I should have been the last to condemn them. Otaheitia independent of its women had many inducements not only for the sailor but the philosopher. He might cultivate his own ground and trust himself and friends for his defence – he might be truly happy in himself and his happiness would be increased by communicating it to others. He might introduce the advantages and yet avoid the vices of cultivated society. I am again getting into my dreams.[59]

Just as Bligh claimed that it had led the *Bounty* mutineers astray, so too did the mirage of Tahiti's easeful life lead the young Romantic poets and contemporary readers to dream of a better one than they had. However, as events on Pitcairn Island were even then showing, it was an impossible dream.

---

59   Southey to G.C. Bedford, 8 February 1793, in Southey 1965, vol. 1, p. 19.

5

Information and Entertainment, Image and Archetype: The Cardinal Points of the Exploration Narrative

The British explorers who ranged over oceans and through continents, and their editors and publishers, developed a distinctive literary genre with which to present the results of the expeditions to the public. With its observations of natural phenomena, its records of latitudes and longitudes, weather conditions and temperatures, its descriptions of places, soils and minerals, animals, plants and peoples, the exploration narrative potentially encompassed all of nature. As J.R. Forster, one of the German scientists who sailed on Cook's second voyage, put it, his 'object was nature in its greatest extent; the Earth, the Sea, the Air, the Organic and Animated Creation, and more particularly that class of Beings to which we ourselves belong'.[1] In the later decades of the eighteenth century, the exploration narrative was a work to satisfy the curiosity of a new, improving age.

Well, it was – and it wasn't! It is important to understand that the exploration narrative was never entirely as it seemed, for there was always a divergence, at times considerable, between what the explorers actually saw and recorded in their journals, and what the public read. In the first instance, this divergence arose from the inevitable tension between, on the one hand, presenting a mass of data that, no matter how useful to the savants of the Royal Society and future explorers, was not in itself of compelling interest to general readers; and, on the other, arousing and holding these readers' curiosity – that is, entertaining them. This tension

---

[1] Forster 1778, p. 9.

usually meant that editors and publishers truncated the original accounts and 'cherry-picked' among their myriad details.

In addition, the explorers might represent themselves in ways not in accordance with the facts – for example, as diligent in their scientific endeavours and compassionate in their dealings with native peoples. Nor were editors averse to adding philosophical and moral observations where these were absent from the original. As the literary historian Philip Edwards has observed:

> all voyage-narratives are self-serving, and ... to watch (as we so often can) the development of a narrative is to see the record being adjusted, massaged and manipulated ... The writing [of voyage-literature], in all its deviousness, is a continuing involvement with and a continuing attempt to dominate the reality it is claiming to record.[2]

Discrepancies between original records and published texts mark the exploration narrative from the very beginning of the period we are considering. As mentioned in the previous chapter, by no means all of Narborough's observations were published; but it is William Dampier's *A New Voyage round the World* (1697) that offers the most striking example of the 'adjustment' of the original record with the needs of the general audience in mind. The British Library holds a manuscript version of this narrative, which shows that Dampier revised it carefully, making extensive changes and additions.[3] Yet even this heavily revised text was not the final one. Omitted from the printed version were Dampier's sketch maps of coasts and harbours. Added to it were many new details of places and peoples, in order 'to gratify [the Reader's] curiosity; as one who rambles about a Country can give usually a better account of it, than a Carrier who jogs on to his Inn, without ever going out of his Road'.[4]

These changes made for a curious work. As Edwards points out:

---

2 Edwards 1994, p. 10.
3 BL, Sloane MS 3236.
4 Dampier [1697/1729] 1927, p. 4.

5 Information and Entertainment, Image and Archetype

the version of [A New Voyage] which was eventually published bears little resemblance to this amplified manuscript version. The printed book is very much longer. Almost every incident has been reworked and enlarged, and a huge amount of new material on natural history and geography, and on the appearance and customs of the inhabitants of different countries, has been added. Bits of the amplified manuscript version turn up in all sorts of different places in the printed version. Sometimes the weaving-in of new material is quite crude: a 1,200 word account of the Moskito Indians is simply inserted in the middle of one of the original sentences.[5]

Moreover, Dampier's manuscript criticisms of those with whom he sailed are consistently toned down in the printed work. Another series of changes concerns his role as a buccaneer. In the manuscript, he was casual about the violence and illegality of this marauding life: 'If it is objected that the point of right was not so well studied in these aduentures as it ought to haue been I can only say that the Pollitical rights, Alliances and Engagements between Empires and states are too high for me to discuss.'[6] In the printed work, however, he glossed over his activities and his part in decisions. In describing how he accompanied Captain Edmund Cook from Virginia via the Cape Verde Islands to the Pacific Ocean in 1683, for example, he omits any mention of their seizing a Danish ship off the African coast and using it in their campaign.

Dampier also downplayed his interest in enriching himself by plunder, asserting rather that his major concern had been 'a hearty Zeal for the promoting of useful knowledge, and of any thing that may never so remotely tend to my Countries advantage'. And he stressed that, in order to do so, he wrote in a plain style, for 'it cannot be expected, that a Seaman should affect Politeness'.[7] Mind you, this did not prevent him – or his editor – adding moralistic comments from time to time.

The situation was similar with John Hawkesworth's amalgamation of Byron's, Wallis's, Carteret's, Cook's and Banks's journals. Along with

---

5   Edwards 1994, p. 20.
6   Quoted in Edwards 1994, p. 23.
7   Dampier [1697/1729] 1927, pp. 1, 4.

other authors and editors, Hawkesworth recognised the inherent tension between offering a mass of practical information and holding the reader's interest. In his general introduction, he apologised to those who might find tedious his frequent details of nautical events, such as the ship's position and progress, and his many descriptions of 'bays, headlands, and other irregularities of the coast; the appearance of the country, its hills, vallies, mountains, and woods, with the depth of water, and every other particular that might enable future navigators easily to find, and safely to visit every part of it'. He hoped 'that those who read merely for entertainment will be compensated by the description of countries which no European had before visited, and manners which in many instances exhibit a new picture of human life'.[8]

One of the strategies that Hawkesworth pursued as he adjusted the original journals was to give one voice (effectively, Cook's) to the explorers, because 'it was readily acknowledged on all hands, that a narrative in the first person would, by bringing the Adventurer and the Reader nearer together, without the intervention of a stranger, more strongly excite an interest, and consequently afford more entertainment'.[9] Another was to improve the voyager's character, so as to make him a heroic exemplum of admirable national virtue and of European civilisation. He also added such 'sentiments and observations as my subject should suggest'. His personal interventions were 'not indeed numerous', he explained, 'and when they occur, are always cursory and short; for nothing would have been more absurd than to interrupt an interesting narrative, or new descriptions, by hypothesis and dissertation'. He also declined to ascribe any of his protagonist's escapes from extreme danger to 'particular interposition of Providence', which led to the work becoming notorious in the minds of religious readers.[10]

Hawkesworth's treatment of Cook's and Banks's journals indicates his general practice.[11] First, he combined these into a continuous narrative, truncating as he did so. For example, Cook wrote that the Tahitians were

---

8   Hawkesworth 1773, vol. 1, pp. vi-vii.
9   Hawkesworth 1773, vol. 1, p. iv.
10 Hawkesworth 1773, vol. 1, pp. v, xix.
11 For an extended account of Hawkesworth's changes, see Pearson 1972, from whom I have taken some examples.

5 Information and Entertainment, Image and Archetype

'open affable and courtius and from all I could see free from threachery'. Banks said similarly that they were 'so free from deceit that I trusted myself among them as freely as I could do in my own countrey'. Hawkesworth turned these comments into the Tahitians being 'brave, open, and candid, without either suspicion or treachery, cruelty or revenge; so that we placed the same confidence in them as in our best friends'.[12]

Hawkesworth also shifted the explorers' observations around. For example, he applied Cook's famous remarks about the 'happy' condition of the Australian Aboriginal people to the Tierra del Fuegians, a very strange alteration in view of the miserable climate these fringe-dwellers had to endure. And in identifying the 'artless' Tahitians, who were unburdened by common European concerns, also as 'happier than we', he added some trite moralising:

> Yet if we admit that they are upon the whole happier than we, we must admit that the child is happier than the man, and that we are the losers by the perfection of our nature, the increase of our knowledge, and the enlargement of our views.[13]

Such portentousness also marked Hawkesworth's embellishment of the explorers' prose. As they left Tahiti, Cook wrote:

> [We] took our final leave of this people after a stay of just Three Month, the most part of which time we have been upon good terms with them: some few differences have now and than happen'd, owing partly to the want of rightly understanding one another and partly to their natural thievish disposission which we could not at all times, neither bear with or guard against, but these have been attended with no ill concequences to either side except the first in which one of them was kill'd, and this I was very sorry for.

---

12 'Description of King Georges Island', July 1769, Cook 1955–67, vol. 1, p. 124; 'Manners & customs of S. Sea Islands', August 1769, Banks 1962, vol. 1, pp. 333–4; Hawkesworth 1773, vol. 2, p. 188.
13 [Description of New South Wales], August 1770, Cook 1955–67, vol. 1, p. 399; Hawkesworth 1773, vol. 2, pp. 59, 104–5.

Hawkesworth turned this to:

> Thus we took leave of Otaheite, and its inhabitants, after a stay of just three months; for the greater part of the time we lived together in the most cordial friendship, and a perpetual reciprocation of good offices. The accidental differences which now and then happened, could not be more sincerely regretted on their part than they were on ours: the principal causes were such as necessarily resulted from our situation and circumstances, in conjunction with the infirmities of human nature, from our not being able perfectly to understand each other, and from the disposition of the inhabitants to theft, which we could not at all times bear with or prevent. They had not, however, except in one instance been attended with any fatal consequence; and to that accident were owing the measures that I took to prevent others of the same kind.[14]

When Cook read the published work on his return from his second voyage, he complained that Hawkesworth had diminished the precision of his account and ascribed to him opinions he did not hold; that he 'made in his book a general conclusion from a particular fact, and would take as a fact what they had only heard'. These criticisms led James Boswell to comment, 'Why, Sir, Hawkesworth has used your narrative as a London tavern keeper does wine. He has *brewed* it.'[15]

The published accounts of Cook's second and third voyages also had an editor, Dr John Douglas. I shall analyse his 'brewings' in the next chapter.

✳ ✳ ✳

At the same time as it was to provide readers with accurate and useful knowledge about the world, the exploration narrative was also intended to 'amuse' them, where amusement might range from

---

14 Entry, 13 July 1769, Cook 1955–67, vol. 1, p. 117; Hawkesworth 1773, vol. 2, p. 182.
15 Boswell 1963, pp. 308–9. Here, 'brewed' means other substances mixed in.

5 Information and Entertainment, Image and Archetype

frissons of danger – exciting because experienced only at a remove – to providing materials for mature reflection.

William Bartram's *Travels* is replete with vivid descriptions of physical danger. Once when he was proceeding by canoe across a coastal lagoon, several alligators launched a concerted action:

> My situation now became precarious to the last degree: two very large ones attacked me closely, at the same instant, rushing up with their heads and part of their bodies above the water, roaring terribly and belching floods of water over me. They struck their jaws together so close to my ears, as almost to stun me, and I expected every moment to be dragged out of the boat and instantly devoured.

When he beached his canoe, another 'old daring one, about twelve feet [about 3.5 metres] in length', lurked at his feet. When he killed this one, another sought to stun him with a sweep of its tail. As he settled down to supper, he had to scare off two bears.[16]

In his turn, Mungo Park dwelt on the risks to life that travellers in Africa faced. At one point, he needed to proceed at night:

> As soon as the people of the village were gone to sleep (the moon shining bright) we set out. The stillness of the air, the howling of the wild beasts, and the deep solitude of the forest, made the scene solemn and impressive. Not a word was uttered by any of us, but in a whisper; all were attentive, and every one anxious to shew his sagacity, by pointing out to me the wolves and hyaenas as they glided, like shadows, from one thicket to another.

On another occasion, as he was crossing a plain during the day, his guide suddenly exclaimed, '*Soubah an allahi* (God Preserve us!), and to my great surprise, I then perceived a large red lion, at a short distance from the bush, with his head couched between his fore paws. I expected he would instantly spring upon me.'

---

16   Bartram [1791], pp. 116–19.

It seems, however, that the lion wasn't hungry. And when in the desert 'the disconsolate wanderer, wherever he turns, sees nothing around him but a vast interminable expanse of sand and sky; a gloomy and barren void, where the eye finds no particular object to rest upon, and the mind is filled with painful apprehensions of perishing with thirst'.[17] There was the ever-present threat of being robbed by bandits.

Then, there were extreme weather conditions. Park told of how on one occasion:

> about four o'clock in the afternoon, a whirlwind passed through the camp, with such violence that it overturned three tents, and blew down one side of my hut ... I have seen five or six of them at one time. They carry up quantities of sand to an amazing height, which resemble, at a distance, so many moving pillars of smoke.

Bartram wrote of another event:

> Now the earth trembles under the peals of incessant distant thunder, the hurricane comes on roaring, and I am shocked again to life: I raise my head and rub open my eyes, pained with gleams and flashes of lightning; when just attempting to wake my afflicted brethren and companions, almost overwhelmed with floods of rain, the dark cloud opens over my head, developing a vast river of the ethereal fire; I am instantly struck dumb, inactive and benumbed; at length the pulse of life begins to vibrate, the animal spirits begin to exert their powers, and I am by degrees revived.[18]

As we shall see, Cook's account of his passages through polar seas and Bligh's of his attempt to round Cape Horn also conveyed the threat of imminent annihilation.

What Hawkesworth termed the 'new pictures of human life' provided materials for a more philosophical reflection. Sometimes, these turned on the inability of native peoples to understand the unfamiliar. Mai, the Polynesian who visited England, for example, had

---

17   Park 1799, pp. 57, 157, 208.
18   Park 1799, p. 135; Bartram [1791], p. 311.

5 Information and Entertainment, Image and Archetype

no terms for a horse and cow except 'a great Hog that carries people' and 'a great Hog that gives milk'.[19] Then there were attitudes of less civilised and sophisticated people, who in their naivety could not understand the motives that drove European explorers. The Queen of Abyssinia told James Bruce in puzzlement:

> Every day of our life punishes us with proofs of the perverseness and contradiction of human nature; you are come from Jerusalem, through vile Turkish governments, and hot, unwholesome climates, to see a river and a bog, no part of which you can carry away were it ever so valuable, and of which you have in your own country a thousand larger, better, and cleaner, and you take it ill when I discourage you from the pursuit of this fancy, in which you are likely to perish, without your friends at home ever hearing when or where the accident happened.[20]

There were barbarous customs, such as the Northern Indians' habit of abandoning the aged and ill; or the Maori's of cannibalism; or the Tahitians' of human sacrifice. These were things to turn the stomachs of civilised people, even those for whom public executions were a commonplace.

Inevitably, it was the strange sexual proclivities of exotic peoples that most interested those who read for entertainment; and here the Tahitians held centre stage. Hawkesworth described how some nubile young women honoured Banks with 'some very singular ceremonies', which involved shedding their clothes in front of him and presenting themselves to him. There was the tall young man who:

> performed the rites of Venus with a little girl about eleven or twelve years of age, before several of our people, and a great number of the natives, without the least sense of its being indecent or improper, but as appeared, in perfect conformity to the custom of the place. Among the spectators were several women of superior rank, particularly Oberea, who may properly be said to

---

19 *St James's Chronicle*, 16 January 1787.
20 Bruce 1790, vol. 3, pp. 377–9.

have assisted at the ceremony; for they gave instructions to the girl how to perform her part, which, young as she was, she did not seem much to stand in need of.[21]

And there was the Tahitian *arioi* society, whose members, the explorers gathered, gave themselves over to untrammelled licentiousness, killing the children of their unions at birth so as to be able to continue their promiscuous life. The *arioi* were strolling players, who entertained at festivals. Some of their more conspicuous performances involved the men performing grotesqueries with their genitals. At one *heiva* Bligh attended, two young girls suddenly 'dropped all their dress'; and the men 'danced' in a way 'more indecent than any I had before seen, but was not the less applauded on that account by the natives, who seemed much delighted'.[22]

Nor were the primary narratives the only works to which the reading public went for this kind of entertainment. Banks's enthusiasm for Tahiti's pleasures spawned a series of salacious poems that inflamed the imagination further: *An Epistle (Moral and Philosophical) from an Officer at Otaheite* (1774); *An Epistle from Oberea, Queen of Otaheite, to Joseph Banks, Esq.* (1774); *An Epistle from Mr Banks, Voyager, Monster-hunter, and Amoroso, to Oberea, Queen of Otaheite* (1774); *Mimosa: or, The Sensitive Plant* (1779).

The accounts of Cook's voyages and these derivative, salacious poems formed a context in which contemporary readers might readily accept Bligh's claims that 'I can only conjecture that the mutineers had assured themselves of a more happy life among the Otaheiteans, than they could possible have in England; which, joined to some female connections, have most probably been the principal cause of the whole transaction.'[23] In doing so, they took Bligh far too much at his word.

※ ※ ※

---

21   Hawkesworth 1773, vol. 2 pp. 124–5, 128.
22   Bligh 1792, pp. 77–9, 126–7.
23   Bligh 1790b, p. 9.

5 Information and Entertainment, Image and Archetype

Whatever the editorial truncations, flourishes, interventions and stress on entertaining episodes, the exploration narrative retained a notable scientific character, but it had other dimensions too. Just as the set of surface waves can conceal the direction of powerful counter-currents, in the course of the eighteenth century this genre developed features that owed very little to scientific endeavour or immediate stimulation, but that also contributed powerfully to its attraction.

That is, the exploration narrative came to be inscribed with two powerful motifs that gave it an archetypal structure. The first of these was the heroic protagonist who overcame all the perils that implacable nature and malevolent men might put in his way. To a considerable extent, of course, this motif only reflected the reality of those who explored far-flung regions. In the standard printed will that it asked men to sign before they went to sea the Admiralty warned of 'the Perrills & Dangers of the Seas & other Uncertainties of this Transitory life';[24] and the voyager's way was indeed fraught with danger, whether from treacherous seas, accident, illness, enemy attack, hostile savages, or emotional conflict spurred by the close confines of a ship and the privations of life at sea.

Of these perils and dangers, the exploration narrative conveyed a myriad. In May 1688, together with three Europeans and four Malays, William Dampier left the *Cygnet* at the Nicobar Islands. They then set out in a canoe for Achin (now Aceh) On 18 May, when far out to sea, they ran into a fierce tropical storm:

> The Sea was already roaring in a white Foam about us; a dark Night coming on, and no Land in sight to shelter us, and our little Ark in danger to be swallowed by every Wave; and, what was worst of all, none of us thought our selves prepared for another World. The Reader may better guess than I can express, the Confusion that we were all in. I had been in many imminent Dangers before now, some of which I have already related, but the worst of them all was but a Play-game in comparison with this. I must confess that I was in great Conflicts of Mind at this time. Other Dangers came not upon me with such a leisurely and dreadful Solemnity. A sudden

---

24 There are examples of this will in, e.g., NA, PROB 6/108 and PROB 11/653.

Skirmish or Engagement, or so, was nothing when one's Blood was up, and pushed forwards with eager Expectations. But here I had a lingring View of approaching Death, and little or no hopes of escaping it; and I must confess that my Courage, which I had hitherto kept up, failed me here; and I made very sad Reflections on my former Life, and looked back with Horrour and Detestation on Actions which before I disliked, but now I trembled at the remembrance of. I had long before this repented me of that roving Course of Life, but never with such Concern as now. I did also call to mind the many miraculous Acts of God's Providence towards me in the whole Course of my Life, of which kind I believe few Men have met with the like. For all these I returned Thanks in a peculiar Manner, and this once more desired God's Assistance, and composed my Mind as well as I could in the Hopes of it, and as the Event shew'd, I was not disappointed of my Hopes.[25]

Somehow, they kept the canoe upright.

In April 1742, as he waited off the west coast of Mexico in the hope of capturing the Manila galleon, George Anson sent a cutter to watch for its leaving Acapulco. The cutter was supposed to be out for twenty-four days, and when it did not return after this time, the British feared that the Spanish had captured it. When it did reappear after six weeks, 'the wan and meager countenances of the crew, the length of their beards, and the feeble and hollow tone of their voices, convinced us that they had suffered much greater hardships than could be expected from even the severities of a *Spanish* prison'. At one point, after high surf for some days had prevented them from landing for water, they had drunk the blood of a turtle to quench their thirst.[26] This episode exemplifies the circumstances in general of the voyage. Anson had left England in September 1740 with eight ships and 1955 seamen. When he returned four years later, he had one ship and only 145 of his original

---

25   Dampier [1697/1729] 1927, pp. 332–3. The religious moralising here is another instance of editorial embellishment, for it is not present in the manuscript version – see Edwards 1994, p. 29.
26   Anson [1748] 1974, pp. 251–2.

5 Information and Entertainment, Image and Archetype

crews. Almost 1300 men had died of illness during the expedition, approximately 1000 of them from scurvy.

Then there was James Cook's experience along the Queensland coast in 1770. As he took the *Endeavour* up inside the Great Barrier Reef, he had a linesman sounding twenty-four hours a day, and watchmen constantly aloft. Nonetheless, the ship ran upon a coral shoal, and Cook was able to free it and beach it for repairs only with great difficulty. Hawkesworth adjusted the explorers' descriptions of this event to add to its dramatic effect and provide a mythic dimension, observing that as the crew struggled to free the ship, 'no passionate exclamations, or frantic gestures, were to be heard or seen'. This was based on a comment by Banks rather than by Cook; and to it Hawkesworth added the reflections that 'every one appeared to have the most perfect possession of his mind, and every one exerted himself to the uttermost, with a quiet and patient perseverance, equally distant from the tumultuous violence of terror, and the gloomy inactivity of despair'.[27] Facing death at the end of the world, coarse sailors became preternaturally silent, and worked together for the common good.

When he set out again, seeking a safer passage, Cook went through a narrow entrance of the Barrier Reef into the Coral Sea, only to find himself in the dreadful situation of being just one roll of the massive surf away from being swept back against the reef, with no bottom at 120 fathoms (220 metres) and the land 30 miles (around 50 kilometres) to the west. Mercifully, a small land breeze sprang up. Using it, and with the boats towing, Cook was able to move the ship out, before finding another gap in the reef, through which he reached calm water.

These were potent intimations of mortality, and Cook knew it. In evoking the second one, he deployed language radically different from his usual objective style, which Hawkesworth followed closely:

> Rocks and shoals are always dangerous to the mariner, even where their situation has been ascertained; they are more dangerous in seas that have never before been navigated, and in this part of the globe they are more dangerous than in any other; for here they are reefs of coral rock, rising like a wall almost perpendicularly out

---

27 Hawkesworth 1773, vol. 3, p. 552. Cf. Entry, 11 June 1770, Banks 1962, vol. 2, p. 78.

of the unfathomable deep, always overflowed at high-water, and at low-water dry in many places; and here the enormous waves of the vast Southern Ocean, meeting with so abrupt a resistance, break, with inconceivable violence, in a surf which no rocks or storms in the northern hemisphere can produce.[28]

On his second circumnavigation, Cook's repeated probes into the reaches of the southern oceans in search of the elusive continent took him and his ships into an alien and immensely hostile world, in which disaster was only an iceberg away. In December 1773, as he crossed the Antarctic Circle for the second time, he met with numerous 'ice islands', and then an 'immense' field of pack ice. This he worked his way around, as he did not 'think it safe to venture through, as the wind would not permit us to return the same way that we must go in'. Then, some days later, as he took a westerly direction, they encountered:

> a strong gale at North, attended with snow and sleet, which froze to the rigging as it fell, making ropes like wires, and the sails like boards or plates of metal. The sheaves also were frozen so fast in the blocks, that it required our utmost efforts to get a top-sail down and up; the cold so intense as hardly to be endured; the whole sea, in a manner, covered with ice; a hard gale, and a thick fog.[29]

Cook retreated north. Then, in an extraordinarily audacious gesture, which had much less to do with scientific curiosity than with his now well-developed sense of his explorer's destiny, he swung the ships' bows south again. This time, more than the southern continent, he was attempting to reach the South Pole. Early in the morning of 30 January 1774, when in 71°10'S latitude, with the sky lit by 'an unusual snow-white brightness', he encountered a huge field of ice, which 'extended East and West, far beyond the reach of our sight', and which contained ninety-seven 'hills', 'besides those on the outside; many of them very large, and looking like a ridge of mountains, rising one above

---

28 Hawkesworth 1773, vol. 3, pp, 606–7; cf. Entry, 16 August 1771, Cook 1955–67, vol. 1, p. 378.
29 Cook 1777, vol. 1, pp. 253, 257.

5 Information and Entertainment, Image and Archetype

another till they were lost in the clouds'. 'Such Mountains of ice as these', he asserted, 'were never seen in the Greenland Seas', and presented a new challenge to navigation. He decided to turn back: 'I will not say it was impossible any where to get farther to the South; but the attempting it would have been a dangerous and rash enterprise, and what, I believe, no man in my situation would have thought of.'[30]

* * *

Land travellers could also expect to encounter extreme difficulties and dangers. James Bruce found the going particularly arduous in Abyssinia, and not only because of its rugged terrain and his being ill repeatedly. A bloody civil war raged there during his time, with many acts of unspeakable cruelty. Ras Michael (Mikael), for example, the governor of Tigré (Tigray) Province and the head of the royal council ('Ras' = Duke), was given to blinding minor enemies, and to flaying major ones alive. Rulers, great and lesser, were demanding, capricious and vindictive. There was constant palace intrigue as princes, generals, courtiers and noblewomen strove for political ascendency for themselves, children and favourites; and the local priests persisted in identifying Bruce as a 'Frank', and therefore an adherent to the detested Romish religion. As well as on crocodile-infested rivers and in districts where lions roamed and along the goat paths of Abyssinia's mountains, Bruce had to make a very wary way among the society's morasses of intrigue and extortion.

Bruce was assisted in this by his physical strength and horsemanship, his knowledge of languages, and the presents he gave. His medical knowledge was also very useful, as he had some success in treating nobles for smallpox and other ailments that were impervious to traditional cures. His habit of taking astronomical readings helped too, as people supposed that his studying the stars gave him the ability to foretell the future.

But even these attributes could not give him final control of events. When changed political circumstances suddenly led to an uneasy alliance between the king and his old enemy Fasil, in whose territory the springs of the Nile lay, Bruce thought that he had obtained the

---

30   Cook 1777, vol. 1, pp. 267–8; cf. Entry, 30 January 1774, Cook 1955–67, vol. 2, pp. 320–2.

warlord's agreement to proceed to them, only for him to change his mind suddenly. Calling him a Frank, Fasil told Bruce, 'you white people are all effeminate; you are like so many women; you are not fit for going into a province where all is war, and inhabited by men, warriors from their cradle'. Bruce angrily replied that he had:

> passed through many of the most barbarous nations in the world; all of them, excepting this clan of yours, have some great men among them above using a defenceless stranger ill. But the worst and lowest individual among the most uncivilized people never treated me as you have done today under your own roof, where I have come so far for protection.

Bruce added that a good British officer 'would not think it an action in his life to vaunt of, that with 500 men he had trampled all yon naked savages into dust', and that he himself would be more than a match for Fasil's best two horsemen.

It was a moment of great danger, for Roman Catholics might be summarily stoned to death, and in any case Fasil was not one to brook such defiance. Bruce feared that success had now become impossible, that:

> my hopes of arriving at the source of the Nile were forever ended; all my trouble, all my expences, all my time, and all my sufferings for so many years were thrown away, from no greater obstacle than the whimsies of one barbarian, whose good inclinations, I thought, I had long before sufficiently secured; and, what was worse, I was now got within less than forty miles [65 kilometres] of the place I so much wished to see; and my hopes were shipwrecked upon the last, as well as the most unexpected, difficulty I had to encounter.[31]

Then Fasil changed his mind again and told Bruce he might proceed.

Like Bruce, Samuel Hearne endured much hardship during his journeys. There were the difficulties of moving by foot in the harsh

---

31 Bruce 1790, vol. 3, pp. 512–15.

5 Information and Entertainment, Image and Archetype

Arctic winters and over sodden ground in the springs. He travelled in company with Indians who had had some contact with the Europeans at the Hudson Bay Company's outposts. He needed their guidance and skills at finding food, and the protection they provided from attack by other Indians, or by wild animals. However, their priorities were not always his, so that his progress was often impeded by their lack of cooperation, as it was also by fatigue, hunger and illness.

Mungo Park likewise had a hard time of it. He suffered much from West Africa's notorious 'fevers'. At different times, he encountered monsoonal floods and the heat and thirst of the desert. When his horse was exhausted, he was forced to walk. He depended on other travellers to show him the way from one place to the next, but these were often uncooperative, either because they were afraid of being attacked or because his itinerary did not suit them. There were wild animals: crocodiles in the rivers; lions in the woods and on the plains. Each time he passed from one territory or state to another, he was forced to pay taxes, and to give rulers and headmen presents. He was robbed repeatedly; and when he no longer had money or goods to exchange for food, he could not always find succour in the towns and villages. The Moors whom he encountered on the fringe of the desert distrusted him because he was a Christian, and enslaved his companions – a fate he himself only narrowly avoided. And everywhere, men in authority, whether Negro or Moor, disbelieved his explanation of his presence, that he travelled to find a river. One ruler told him that it was impossible 'that any man in his senses would undertake so dangerous a journey, merely to look at the country, and its inhabitants'. Another asked him 'if there were no rivers in my own country, and whether one river was not like another?'[32] Clearly, he must be travelling with a secret purpose; and death was the common fate of spies.

By the end of the eighteenth century, then, the motif of the heroic explorer had become central to the exploration narrative. Repeatedly, the explorer's determined pursuit of his mission brought him to the brink of death, only for him to triumph over dangers and to return with much new geographical, biological, botanical and ethnographic

---

32   Park 1799, pp. 54, 200.

information. In his skills, his dedication and his courage, he richly deserved the admiration of his audience.

✳ ✳ ✳

The other powerful motif also derived in the first instance from the explorers' common experience, but its resonances were much wider. James Cook's repeated ventures into the high southern latitudes of the Indian, Pacific and Atlantic oceans, and his relieved retreats from them, set up a great oscillation in his account of the second voyage. On the one hand, there are the weird reaches of ocean, with their cold, their comparative lack of animal life, their fogs and their threatening icebergs that make strange sounds as they crunch and crumble. On the other, there are the places of respite from the rigours of this inhospitable and dangerous world, which also provide food and company: Cape Town, Dusky and Charlotte sounds in the southern island of New Zealand, and the lush islands of the central Pacific Ocean.

The various narratives of Cook's second circumnavigation eloquently present this motif. George Forster, for example, wrote of the 'dull hours, days and months' they spent at the end of 1772:

> We were almost perpetually wrapt in thick fogs, beaten with showers of rain, sleet, hail, and snow, the temperature of the air being constantly about the point of congelation in the height of summer; surrounded by innumerable islands of ice against which we daily ran the risk of being shipwrecked, and forced to live upon salt provisions, which concurred with the cold and wet to infect the mass of our blood.

And he wrote of their reaching Tahiti in August 1773:

> It was one of those beautiful mornings which the poets of all nations have attempted to describe, when we saw the isle of O-Taheitee, within two miles [3 kilometres] before us. The east-wind which had carried us so far, was entirely vanished, and a faint breeze only wafted a delicious perfume from the land, and curled the surface of the sea. The mountains, clothed with forests, rose

5 Information and Entertainment, Image and Archetype

majestic in various spiry forms, on which we already perceived the light of the rising sun: nearer to the eye a lower range of hills, easier of ascent, appeared, wooded like the former, and coloured with several pleasing hues of green, soberly mixed with autumnal browns. At their foot lay the plain, crowned with its fertile breadfruit trees, over which rose innumerable palms, the princes of the grove. Here every thing seemed as yet asleep, the morning scarce dawned, and a peaceful shade still rested on the landscape.[33]

It is easy enough to understand how the nature of sea exploration gave this motif its force. However, it is also present in varying degrees in the land travel narratives discussed here. As he passed through Tigré, Bruce and his party had to guard against crocodiles, hippopotamus, lions, boars and hyenas. At the same time, though, they found the Tacazzé to be:

one of the pleasantest rivers in the world, shaded with fine lofty trees, its banks covered with bushes inferior in fragrance to no garden in the universe; its stream is the most limpid, its water excellent, and full of good fish of great variety, as its coverts are of all sorts of game.[34]

When on his second journey his Indian companions decided to wait for the onset of spring before proceeding, Hearne commented that the situation they chose was 'truly pleasant'. It was:

on a small elevated point, which commanded an extensive prospect over a large lake, the shores of which abounded with wood of different kinds, such as pine, larch, birch, and poplar; and in many places was beautifully contrasted with a variety of high hills, that shewed their snowy summits above the tallest woods.

It also offered a constant supply of food.[35]

---

33 Forster [1777] 2000, vol. 1, pp. 70, 143.
34 Bruce 1790, vol. 3, pp. 152–67.
35 Hearne 1795, p. 20.

Mungo Park too interspersed his descriptions of his difficulties with bandits, wild animals, floods, fevers, sandstorms and lack of charity to a poor traveller with accounts of prosperous villages in the midst of productive fields, such as those to the south of Soolo (perhaps Ségou, a village on the banks of the Niger river), which 'surpassed every thing I had yet seen in Africa', and fertile tracts, such as those in Senegal, where he crossed 'beautiful country, interspersed with a pleasing variety of hill and dale, and abounding with partridges, guinea-fowls and deer'.[36] Repeatedly, he also drew attention to the unexpected kindness of strangers.

※※※

During his progress through a hostile world, the heroic explorer experienced moments that encapsulated what Aristotle termed the pity and terror of the human condition. When James Cook reached Tahiti again on his second voyage, an old woman sought him out. She was the mother of Tuaha, who had befriended Cook and Banks in 1769. 'She seized me by both hands,' Cook related, 'and burst into a flood of tears, saying, *Toutaha Tiyo no Toutee matty Toutaha* – (Toutaha, your friend, or the friend of Cook, is dead). I was so much affected with her behavior, that it would have been impossible for me to have refrained mingling my tears with hers, had not Otoo come and taken me from her.'[37]

After they had won a notable victory over Fasil, Ras Michael's commanders pursued the routed warriors, killing them mercilessly. Having interrogated Woosheka, one of the enemy warlords, Michael asked his men if anyone knew how to make a 'leather bottle'. Bruce relates:

> The soldiers understood the command, though the miserable victim did not, and he was brought to the king, who would not suffer him to speak, but waved with his hand to remove him; and they accordingly carried him to the river side, where they

---

36   Park 1799, pp. 88, 330.
37   Cook 1777, vol. 1, p. 155. Cf. Entry, 27 August 1773, Cook 1955–67, vol. 2, p. 207.

5 Information and Entertainment, Image and Archetype

flayed him alive, and brought his skin stuffed with straw to Ras Michael.[38]

Soon after they reached the Coppermine River, Hearne's Indian companions determined on slaughtering a band of Inuit camped beside it. 'The poor unhappy victims were surprised in the midst of their sleep,' Hearne relates, 'and had neither time nor power to make any resistance; men, women, and children, in all upward of twenty, ran out of their tents stark naked, and endeavoured to make their escape; but … they all fell a sacrifice to Indian barbarity! The shrieks and groans of the poor expiring wretches were truly dreadful.'

In this mayhem:

a young girl, seemingly about eighteen years of age, [was] killed so near me, that when the first spear was stuck into her side she fell down at my feet, and twisted round my legs, so that it was with difficulty that I could disengage myself from her dying grasps. As two Indian men pursued this unfortunate victim, I solicited very hard for her life; but the murderers made no reply till they had stuck both their spears through her body, and transfixed her to the ground. They then looked me sternly in the face, and began to ridicule me, by asking if I wanted an Esquimaux wife; and paid not the smallest regard to the shrieks and agony of the poor wretch, who was twining round their spears like an eel!

Hearne said that he persuaded the men to end the girl's agony.

The Indians then crossed to the other side of the river, where there was a second Inuit camp. With the same brutality, they repeatedly speared an old man, so that 'his whole body was like a cullender', and they killed a poor, blind old woman 'in the most savage manner'. Hearne remarked of these events:

My situation and the terror of my mind at beholding this butchery, cannot easily be conceived, much less described; though I summed up all the fortitude I was master of on the occasion,

---

38 Bruce 1790, vol. 2, pp. 715–7.

it was with difficulty that I could refrain from tears; ... even at this hour I cannot reflect on the transactions of that horrid day without shedding tears.[39]

This centrepiece of Hearne's narrative provides the clearest example of how, by the end of the century, the exploration narrative had become as much an artefact of literary creation as it was a record of scientific endeavour. Hearne's account of the slaughter at what came to be known as Bloody Fall exists in three forms: in field notes that he evidently made at the time (17 July 1771) or soon afterwards; in a journal fragment transcribed by the fur trader Andrew Graham at some time between 1773 and 1792; and in the published text of 1795. As I.S. MacLaren has shown, there are such differences between, particularly, the field notes and the later accounts as strongly to suggest that either Hearne or his publisher's editor grossly embellished the account to achieve the mandatory dramatic effect. It is possible that Hearne was not, as he claimed, an eyewitness to the event; more, it is even possible that it never occurred at all.[40]

In the field notes, after describing their stealthy approach to the first Inuit camp, on the west side of the river, Hearne says that the Indians:

> crept under some of the rocks within 100 yards [90 metres] of the tents where they lay some time to watch the motions of the Esquimaux but finding all asleep as they supposed by seeing nobody stir without they ran on the tent[s] on a sudden & killed every soul before they had power to rise[,] in the whole 21 persons.

He says that he refused to join in directly, as he was 'at peace with all nations', and that when the attackers approached the tents, 'I accompanied them[,] at least followed them close at their backs[,] where I stood neuter & saw the cruel massacre which was soon accomplished.' He also says that in the attack on the second camp, on

---

39 Hearne 1795, pp. 153–9.
40 See MacLaren 1991, and Driscoll 2002.

5 Information and Entertainment, Image and Archetype

the east side of the river, they killed 'only one man'. That is, there is no mention in these notes either of the old man whose pierced body resembled a colander or of the slaughter of the blind old woman.

Especially, there is no mention of the girl who, in her death throes, entwined herself around Hearne's legs. She does appear in the fragmentary transcription of the journal, where she is described as 'twining and twisting round the spears like an eel'. As this is a transcription, though, we cannot be certain whether this is Hearne's own addition, or when it was made. In any case, it is only in the published work that a 'full' description of the incident appears. And while it is true that in the field notes Hearne uses the expressions 'cruel massacre' and 'cruel murder', he does not express there those heightened emotions that he says in the published narrative he felt at the time and continued to feel long afterwards.

As MacLaren observes, in preparing an exploration narrative for publication, it was possible – indeed, as a number of the comments quoted above suggest, probably necessary from the point of view of public appeal – to change the emphasis from the conveying of factual details of sea, land and weather, natural productions and impediments to progress, to the amplification and dramatisation of events and reflections upon them, so as the better to delineate 'the figure of the explorer' and therefore to mingle 'entertainment' with instruction.[41]

※ ※ ※

If they conveyed the terror of existence, though, again in line with Aristotelian theory, the exploration narratives also offered catharsis. When Cook decided to turn away from the Antarctic ice fields, he wrote with a curious mixture of hubris and understatement, 'I, who had ambition not only to go farther than any one had been before, but as far as it was possible for man to go, was not sorry at meeting with this interruption.'[42]

One night, though he was not far away from the Nile's springs, Bruce was overwhelmed with a sense of failure:

---

41   MacLaren 1991, p. 30–4.
42   Cook 1777, vol. 1, p. 268.

> The rashness and imprudence with which I had engaged myself in so many dangers without any necessity for so doing; the little prospect of my being ever able to extricate myself out of them, or, even if I lost my life, of the account being conveyed to my friends at home; the great and unreasonable presumption which had led me to think that, after every one that had attempted this voyage had miscarried in it, I was the only person that was to succeed; all these reflections upon my mind, when relaxed, dozing, and half oppressed with sleep, filled my imagination with what I have heard other people call the *horrors*.

We would term it a massive anxiety attack. He arose and went to the door of the tent, 'when the outward air perfectly awakened me, and restored my strength and courage.'[43]

After he was once more robbed, Park's courage ebbed. 'Which ever way I turned,' he remembered, 'nothing appeared but danger and difficulty.' He went on:

> I saw myself in the midst of a vast wilderness, in the depth of the rainy season; naked and alone; surrounded by savage animals, and men still more savage. I was five hundred miles [around 800 kilometres] from the nearest European settlement. All these circumstances crowded at once on my recollection; and I confess that my spirits began to fail me. I considered my fate as certain, and that I had no alternative, but to lie down and perish.

Then he was struck by 'the extraordinary beauty of a small moss, in fructification' growing near him; and from this tiny plant's existence he drew comfort:

> Though the whole plant was not larger than the top of one of my fingers, I could not contemplate the delicate conformation of its roots, leaves, and capsula, without admiration. Can that Being (thought I), who planted, watered, and brought to perfection, in this obscure part of the world, a thing which appears of so

---

43 Bruce 1790, vol. 3, pp. 436–7.

5 Information and Entertainment, Image and Archetype

small importance, look with unconcern upon the situation and sufferings of creatures formed after his own image? Surely not!

Park found the strength to resume his journey.[44]

* * *

What these motifs of the indomitable hero and his arduous journey together present, then, is the archetypal myth of the hero's descent into the underworld (Hell), where malign forces seek to destroy him, his triumph over them, and his return to the world ordered by comfort and companionship (which in this trope is the analogue of Heaven). Mircea Eliade termed this the myth of the eternal return. In Greek myth, its strongest manifestation is Orpheus's journeying into Hades in an attempt to rescue Eurydice. In Christian religious outlook, its central manifestations are the stories of John the Baptist's spending forty days in the wilderness, then, knowing that the revelation of the Messiah was imminent, emerging to 'make straight the way of the Lord'; and of the crucifixion and resurrection of Christ himself. In literature, its most powerful and enduring manifestation comes in Homer's *Odyssey*, but there are countless variants – for example, Shakespeare's late plays *Pericles*, *The Winter's Tale* and *The Tempest*.

In *On the Origin of Stories*, Brian Boyd has argued that, since imaginative grasp and problem-solving are central elements in them, stories gave humans a distinct evolutionary advantage: as we increased our ability to tell and to interpret stories, so too did our intelligence increase, leading to our developing superior survival skills:

> We humans owe our competitive success, among ourselves and against other species, to intelligence. The appeal of the cognitive play in art makes art as compulsive for us as play, enticing us to forgo mental rest for mental stimulation that helps us to learn and overlearn key cognitive skills, especially our capacity to produce and process information *patterns*. Art entices us to engage our *attention* and activate our minds in ways that we find most

---

44   Park 1799, pp. 242–4.

pleasing, and allows the most gifted individuals to earn *status* by their power to command the attention of others.[45]

Utilising a vast range of information about human nature or culture from anthropology, biology, economics, history, psychology, sociology, literature and art, *On the Origin of Stories* is a work of great complexity. Those competent in the various disciplines will no doubt dispute some of Boyd's assertions. Nonetheless, it is not necessary that he be exactly right in all his points for his general argument to be persuasive; or better, for his analysis to offer us a means of understanding the centrality of the archetypes of the hero and his journey into the underworld to our perception of our human condition. For what greater challenge for our ingenuity can there be than that of overcoming death?

I think that not only are these two archetypes the usual means by which Europeans have dealt (even if unconsciously) with this ultimate challenge since they began to tell stories, but also that the very essence of our perception of our reality inheres in the central story they form. In common with all living nature, we humans are bound by time: there is no release from a 100 per cent mortality rate, except in the stories we can tell. The most powerful and intriguing stories are those that allow us, if only ever so briefly, to transcend time.

Neither is it necessary for the archetypes to be fully realised for us to feel their potent imaginative force. The hero's failure to accomplish his quest and return from the underworld can, just as much as his success in doing so, summon forth pity and terror, and thereby lead to catharsis. At the end of *Moby-Dick*, Melville describes how, taking revenge on its tormentors, the stricken whale stove in Captain Ahab's ship:

> A sky-hawk that tauntingly had followed the main-truck downwards from its natural home among the stars, pecking at the flag, and incommoding Tashtego there; this bird now chanced to intercept its broad fluttering wing between the hammer and the wood; and simultaneously feeling that ethereal thrill, the submerged savage beneath, in his death-grasp, kept his hammer frozen there; and so

---

45 Boyd 2009, pp. 381–2.

5 Information and Entertainment, Image and Archetype

the bird of heaven, with archangelic shrieks, and his imperial beak thrust upwards, and his whole captive form folded in the flag of Ahab, went down with his ship, which, like Satan, would not sink to hell till she had dragged a living part of heaven along with her, and helmeted herself with it.

Now small fowls flew screaming over the yet yawning gulf; a sullen white surf beat against its steep sides; then all collapsed, and the great shroud of the sea rolled on as it rolled five thousand years ago.[46]

✷ ✷ ✷

In one of the essays in *The Classical Tradition in Poetry*, Gilbert Murray wrote:

In plays like *Hamlet* or the *Agamemnon* or the *Electra* we have certainly fine and flexible character-study, a varied and well-wrought story, a full command of the technical instruments of the poet and the dramatist; but we have also, I suspect, a strange, unanalyzed vibration below the surface, an undercurrent of desires and fears and passions, long slumbering yet eternally familiar, which have for thousands of years lain near the root of our most intimate emotions and been wrought into the fabric of our most magical dreams. How far into past ages this stream may reach back, I dare not even surmise; but it seems as if the power of stirring it or moving with it were one of the last secrets of genius.[47]

As we shall see in the next chapter, so was it too with Cook's death at Hawaii, with Bligh's open-boat voyage and with Fletcher Christian's passage into oblivion. *Bounty*'s story resonates with these emotions and dreams.

---

46 Melville [1851] 1967, p. 469.
47 Murray [1927] 1968, pp. 239–40.

6

Men Who Strove with Gods: James Cook, William Bligh, Fletcher Christian

> My mariners,
> Souls that have toiled, and wrought, and thought with me –
> That ever with a frolic welcome took
> The thunder and the sunshine, and opposed
> Free hearts, free foreheads – you and I are old;
> Old age hath yet his honour and his toil;
> Death closes all: but something ere the end,
> Some work of noble note, may yet be done,
> Not unbecoming men that strove with Gods.
> The lights begin to twinkle from the rocks:
> The long day wanes: the slow moon climbs: the deep
> Moans round with many voices. Come, my friends,
> 'Tis not too late to seek a newer world.
> Push off, and sitting well in order smite
> The sounding furrows; for my purpose holds
> To sail beyond the sunset, and the baths
> Of all the western stars, until I die.
> It may be that the gulfs will wash us down:
> It may be we shall touch the Happy Isles,
> And see the great Achilles, whom we knew.
> Though much is taken, much abides; and though
> We are not now that strength which in old days

> Moved earth and heaven; that which we are, we are;
> One equal temper of heroic hearts,
> Made weak by time and fate, but strong in will
> To strive, to seek, to find, and not to yield.
> Alfred Tennyson, 'Ulysses'

✳ ✳ ✳

As we've seen, in the last three decades of the eighteenth century the exploration narrative emerged as a distinctive literary genre, with the accounts of James Cook's three circumnavigations providing the generic model for others, of which the most notable are those of James Bruce (1790), William Bartram (1791), William Bligh (1792), Samuel Hearne (1795), Mungo Park (1799) and George Vancouver (1799).

Each of these narratives exhibits a tripartite structure. The first involves the explorer's leaving the known world with its nurturing community. The second presents his venturing into unknown and hostile realms. The third consists of one or other alternative: either the 'Ulysses' one of return to the known world and community, or the 'Ahab' one of failure and death. As I pointed out in the previous chapter, in the first instance this structure derived from the actual, historical experiences of the explorers. However, it also drew on another reality, disembodied but powerful, for once we recognise the archetypes behind the immediate images, we may see that, pared back to its essentials, the exploration narrative tells the story of departure from Heaven, enduring Hell, and *either* return to Heaven *or* annihilation. Understanding – whether consciously or unconsciously – that readers were more engaged by heroic actions than scientific detail, towards the end of the eighteenth century authors and editors took to defining the narrative's central structure more clearly and embellishing its details, so as to bring out its mythic import.

In this chapter, I trace the processes by which history was transmuted into mythic story, so that James Cook, William Bligh and Fletcher Christian became archetypal heroes. In understanding this, we may the better understand the abiding intrigue of the story of *Bounty*'s voyage.

6 Men Who Strove with Gods: James Cook, William Bligh, Fletcher Christian

* * *

James Cook may have apologised for his lack of formal education, but, having charted the Saint Lawrence gulf and river up to Quebec and the coast of Newfoundland and observed an eclipse, by the time he began the *Endeavour* voyage he was skilled in mathematics, astronomical observation and the drawing of charts. During the course of *Endeavour's* voyage (1768–71), he added to these skills extensive experience in oceanic navigation and the management of a ship during a very long voyage in often perilous conditions. He also developed a very strong sense of what it meant to be an explorer. After *Endeavour* had only narrowly escaped destruction a second time in north Queensland waters, he wrote:

> Was it not for the pleasure which naturly results to a Man from being the first discoverer, even was it nothing more than sands and Shoals, this service would be insuportable especialy in far distant parts, like this, short of Provisions and almost every other necessary.[1]

During the course of his first circumnavigation, Cook and Banks discussed intensely what they observed, and Cook learnt much from seeing how Banks wrote his journal up. By the time he arrived home, he understood the differences between a sailor's daily observations and a coherent account of a voyage of discovery that would interest curious readers. Accordingly, he kept two accounts of his second circumnavigation: the usual ship's log and a more extensive and reflective narrative of events.

Even so, the published version of this second account was not exactly as Cook wrote it, for it was edited by Canon John Douglas. Douglas summarised or removed much technical detail; he regularised spelling and punctuation; and he made changes to the prose style so as to add to the literary character of the work. He remarked:

> I did a great deal to the Capt's Journal to correct its Stile; to new point [i.e. re-punctuate] it; and to divide it into Sentences, & Paragraphs, &

---

1   Entry, 17 August 1770, Cook 1955–67, vol. 1, p. 380.

Chapters & Books. Tho little appears to be done by me, the Journal if printed as the Captain put it into my Hands, would have been thought too incorrect, & have disgusted the Reader.[2]

However, while Douglas did truncate Cook's original text, he did not significantly alter the narrative's basic shape. He did not need to. As he compiled his record, Cook himself was well aware of the voyage's import. He wrote to his old master John Walker in 1772, as he was leaving Cape Town for the southern reaches of the Indian and Pacific oceans:

> Having nothing new to communicate I should hardly have troubled you with a letter was it not customary for Men to take leave of their friends before they go out of the World, for I can hardly think my self in it so long as I am deprived from having any Connections with the civilized part of it, and this will soon be my case for two years at least. When I think of the Inhospitable parts I am going to, I think the Voyage dangerous, I however enter upon it with great cheerfullness, providence has been very kind to me on many occasions, and I trust in the continuation of the divine protection; I have two good Ships well provided and well Man'd.[3]

Departure from what was familiar and comfortable; the venturing into a watery underworld; return: this was the fundamental dynamic of Cook's second circumnavigation. There was the outward passage down the Atlantic Ocean to the Cape of Good Hope, one that thousands of voyages had made familiar to European navigators. Then there were the probes into the weird and inhospitable reaches of the southern oceans and the retreats to the warm, lush tropical islands of the central Pacific, during which there were grave dangers to overcome: icebergs, shoals, lee shores, tempests, poisonous fish, threatening islanders. And finally there was the return to England three years later.

※ ※ ※

---

2 Quoted by Beaglehole in his introduction to Cook 1955–67, vol. 2, p. cxliv.
3 Cook to Walker, 20 November 1772, Cook 1955–67, vol. 2, p. 689.

6 Men Who Strove with Gods: James Cook, William Bligh, Fletcher Christian

As I said, Douglas did not need to alter Cook's narrative to evoke this powerful dynamic; and, equally wisely, he chose to retain much of Cook's own voice, for the explorer was now more than capable of adequately describing the nature of his experiences. Interestingly, though, Cook thought there were some moments whose essence could not be conveyed in words alone. This was especially so of the cold oceans where the icebergs took on phantasmagoric shapes and refracted light in myriad ways, together with the weird sounds made by lapping water and crumbling ice.

The astronomer William Wales wrote of 24 February 1773:

> About 22h we passed by one of the most curious Islands of Ice I ever saw: Its form was that of an old square Castle, one End of which had fallen into Ruins, and it had a Hole quite through it whose roof so exactly resembled the Gothic arch of an old Postern Gateway that I believe it would have puzzled an Architect to have built it truer.[4]

Cook himself observed that, while the icebergs constituted ever-present dangers:

> they are now become so very familiar to us that the apprehensions they cause are never of long duration and are in some measure compencated by the very curious and romantick Views many of these Islands exhibit and which are greatly heightned by the foaming and dashing of the waves against them and into the several holes and caverns which are formed in most of them, in short the whole exhibits a View which can only be discribed by the pencle of an able painter and at once fills the mind with admiration and horror, the first is occasioned by the beautifullniss of the Picture and the latter by the danger attending it, for was a ship to fall aboard one of these large pieces of ice she would be dashed to pieces in a moment.[5]

---

4   Wales, entry, 24 February 1773, Cook 1955–67, vol. 2, p. 99.
5   Entry, 24 February 1773, Cook 1955–67, vol. 2, pp. 98–9; Joppien and Smith, 1985–7, vol. 2, p. 16.

This invocation of an able artist and his pencils seems a curious rhetorical flourish from a seaman very conscious of his lack of formal education. However, there is a precise explanation. Cook wrote in a marginal note to his journal entry, 'See Views 1 and 2.' This was a reference to sketches produced by the gifted William Hodges, who during the course of the voyage became more and more interested in how to convey the ever-changing character of masses of water and air. Hodges's practice was to make pencil sketches at the moment, which he then developed into more elaborate depictions in water colours and oils. The sketches that Cook referred to seem no longer to exist. However, Hodges's 'The *Resolution* & *Adventure* 4 Jan 1773 Taking in Ice for Water. Lat 61°S' and '[The *Resolution* and *Adventure* among Icebergs]' (Plate 4) suggest what they would have conveyed, albeit probably with a more turbulent sea and more imminent danger.[6]

In the published narrative, Douglas conveyed this entry as:

> These dangers were, however, now become so familiar to us, that the apprehensions they caused were never of long duration; and were, in some measure, compensated both by the seasonable supplies of fresh water these ice islands afforded us, (without which we must have been greatly distressed) and also, by their very romantic appearance, greatly heightened by the foaming and dashing of the waves into the curious holes and caverns which are formed in many of them; the whole exhibiting a view, which at once filled the mind with admiration and horror, and can only be described by the hand of an able painter.[7]

Truncated as this description was, it nonetheless retained the allusion to the ability of an artist to convey these particular circumstances more vividly than a writer could. This was an insight that another voyager would keep well in mind.

※ ※ ※

---

6   See Joppien and Smith, 1985–7, vol. 2, Plates 14 and 15 (pp. 17, 18).
7   Cook 1777, vol. 1, p. 57.

6 Men Who Strove with Gods: James Cook, William Bligh, Fletcher Christian

So readers of *A Voyage towards the South Pole* (1777) sailed with Cook through the desolate southern oceans with their ice fields and ice 'islands'. They marvelled at the shapes of the icebergs they passed and the odd refractions of light. They heard the strange sounds of waves slapping against the ice and of the ice grinding and crumbling. Samuel Coleridge condensed Cook's descriptions into twelve evocative lines:

> Listen, Stranger! Mist and Snow,
>   And it grew wond'rous cauld:
> And Ice mast-high came floating by
>   As green as Emerauld.
>
> And thro' the drifts the snowy clifts
>   Did send a dismal sheen;
> Ne shapes of men ne beasts we ken –
>   The Ice was all between.
>
> The Ice was here, the Ice was there,
>   The Ice was all around:
> It crack'd and growl'd, and roar'd and howl'd –
>   Like noises of a Swound.

And, repeatedly, vicarious voyagers wondered at the sailors' diligence and their commander's dedication in such extreme conditions. Against the passage in which Cook described how 'the ropes [became] like wires, and the sails like boards or plates of metal. The sheaves also were frozen so fast in the blocks, that it required our utmost efforts to get a top-sail down and up; the cold so intense as hardly to be endured; the whole sea, in a manner, covered with ice; a hard gale, and a thick fog', one reader exclaimed, 'What Resolution!'[8]

And if they needed any further persuasion of the fact of Cook's greatness, readers also found it in *A Voyage towards the South Pole*, for Sir John Pringle's address to the Royal Society on the occasion of

---

8   Coleridge, *Ancient Mariner*, ll. 49–60; annotation on vol. 1, p. 257 of the Rush Rees Library's copy of *A Voyage towards the South Pole* (University of Rochester, NY).

its presentation *in absentia* of the Copley medal to the again-voyaging Cook was printed as an Appendix. In this, Pringle pointed out ringingly:

> how meritorious ... that person must appear, who hath not only made the most extensive, but the most instructive voyages; who hath not only discovered, but surveyed, vast tracts of new coasts; who hath dispelled the illusion of a *terra australis incognita*, and fixed the bounds of the habitable earth, as well as those of the navigable ocean, in the southern hemisphere.[9]

✽ ✽ ✽

The design for Cook's third voyage involved a pattern similar to that of the second, with the qualification that the focus of exploration would now be the northern Pacific Ocean. From the Cape of Good Hope, he would sail through the southern Indian Ocean to New Zealand and up to the central island clusters. He would then cross the equator for the north-west American coast, where he was to look in high latitudes for the entrance of the strait supposed to run across to the Atlantic Ocean. If he located it, he would follow it through, charting it as he went. If not, he would return via one or other of the generic routes from the Pacific to Europe.

As he sailed, with publication distinctly in mind, Cook composed an account of the voyage that differed markedly in character from the ship's log, which he kept as usual. As Dr Douglas put it, Cook knew 'that it was expected from him to *relate*, as well as to *execute*, [the expedition's] operations', so he prepared 'such a journal as might be made use of for publication'. Following Cook's death, the task of editing this narrative again fell to Douglas, who asserted that in doing so he 'faithfully adhered' to it, though he added that he had also 'enriched' it with 'considerable communications from Mr Anderson, Surgeon of the *Resolution*'.[10] This was rather disingenuous, not only because in his version Douglas made extensive use of James King's account of the

---

9   Pringle's address, in Cook 1777, vol. 2, pp. 369–70.
10 Douglas, Introduction, in Cook and King 1784, vol. 1, pp. lxxvii-lxxviii.

voyage too, but also because he adjusted all the primary accounts. As he stated privately:

> the Public never knew, how much they owe to me in this work. The Capt's M.S.S. was indeed attended to accurately; but I took more Liberties than I had done with his Acct of the second Voyage; and while I faithfully represented the facts, I was less scrupulous in cloathing them with better Stile than fell to the usual Share of the Capt.[11]

Douglas's additions and alterations significantly altered Cook's record.[12]

It is with the continuing mythologising of Cook in the published account that I am here concerned. To a greater or lesser degree, this myth-making process appears throughout. As we saw with Bligh's narrative, in part it involves the same kind of 'tidying up' and suppression of unpalatable details, such as Cook's rages and brutal treatment of islanders; however, I shall examine in detail only Douglas's presentation of Cook's death at Kealakekua Bay, Hawaii, on 14 February 1779.

In a complex conjunction of sacred and profane time, Cook's presence in the Hawaiian Islands in the months of December 1778 and January 1779 coincided with the *makahiki*, the annual festival in honour of Lono, the god of peace and fertility. Spread over several lunar months, this festival involved a land procession of priests and icons clockwise about the island and myriad ceremonies, including the ritual offering of pigs. It reached its peak during the five or so weeks that the Pleiades were visible after sunset. In 1778–79, the Pleiades appeared around 19 November, a week before the arrival of Cook's ships; and *Welehu*, the main lunar month, was from 14 December

---

11 Quoted by Beaglehole, Introduction, Cook 1955–67, vol. 3, p. cxcix.
12 As Glyn Williams has pointed out, 'Beaglehole's edition of the Journal of Cook's third voyage should always be consulted in preference to the official contemporary account [James Cook and James King, *A Voyage to the Pacific Ocean*], for although the first two volumes were Cook's in name, they were Dr John Douglas' in style'; and that 'until Professor Beaglehole's labours scholars could only guess at how much of the published account was Cook's and how much his meddlesome editor's.' See Williams 1979, p. 167.

1778 to 3 January 1779. During the most intense period of worship, 31 December to 4 January, the sea was *tabu* and men did not fish. Hence, while the Europeans were able to trade for fish on arrival, they did not do so from 27 November 1778 to 5 January 1779.[13]

To Cook, the putting in to Kealakekua Bay may have reflected only his need to repair his ships, rest his crews and take on food and water. To the Hawaiians, though, his appearance was potent with cosmic purpose. Lono was expected to arrive by sea. Cook's ships, with their masts, spars and sails, reflected Lono's iconography; and the explorer's clockwise progress around the coast mirrored Lono's during his visitation. Lono's principal temple was at Kealakekua Bay, where his cult predominated. Here, the priests and people welcomed Cook as an incarnation of the god, setting him on a throne, draping him with sacred cloths, making offerings of food to him.

Then the winter solstice ended, and the Pleiades sank below the horizon. The celebration of the harvest concluded, and men turned to fishing for bonito. Lono's opposite, Kū, the god of war and human sacrifice, became ascendant. At the beginning of February, the priests asked anxiously when Lono would leave. Cook did, but when a storm cracked his foremast, he put back in to Kealakekua Bay on 11 February. This arrival now out of joint with ritual time, and their presence again putting much strain on food resources, the Europeans were no longer welcome. Relations between them and the Hawaiians quickly deteriorated; and Cook was killed in a violent confrontation.

If he wrote one, Cook's account of how the Hawaiians received him no longer exists. However, James King made a detailed record of their 'remarkable homage', which 'on the first visit of Captn Cook to their houses seemd to approach to Adoration'.[14] While he truncated it heavily, Douglas stayed quite close in sense to King's account. Where he did embellish, though, was in the assessment of Cook's character and achievements that followed the relation of his death.

In describing how the ships sailed away from Hawaii, King contented himself with:

---

13 See Sahlins 1995, pp. 17–84.
14 King, [Observations], January 1779, in Cook 1955–67, vol. 3, pp. 509–10.

> Thus left we Karacacooa bay, a place become too remarkably famous, for the very unfortunate, & Tragical death of one of the greatest Navigators our Nation or any Nation ever had; how uncertain is our existence, of all kind of death's no one would have supposd Captain Cook liable to die in the way he did, he who had so particularly a happiness, often by a well timed boldness & apparent Confidence, of gaining the friendship of Indians, in the most distant parts of the World, of the most contrary dispositions; or of soon fathoming their Views & avoiding their Machinations.[15]

Douglas offered a much more wide-ranging assessment, beginning with, 'Thus fell our great and excellent Commander! After a life of so much distinguished and successful enterprize, his death, as far as regards himself, cannot be reckoned premature; since he lived to finish the great work for which he seems to have been designed.' He continued with details of Cook's childhood; his self-education for a naval career; his service in North America; his constitution and character. He followed his assertion that 'perhaps no science ever received greater additions from the labours of a single man, than geography has done from those of Captain Cook' with details of his discoveries on his three circumnavigations. Then he offered high praise of Cook's skills in navigation, and of his method 'of preserving the health of seamen, [which] forms a new era in navigation, and will transmit his name to future ages, amongst the friends and benefactors of mankind'.[16]

Clearly, Douglas was determined that readers should be left in no doubt that Cook was one of the great men of history. Moreover, as I.S. MacLaren has shown,[17] this was only one aspect of Douglas's pervasive portrayal of Cook's expedition as an imperial and civilising mission, enveloped by a Christian carapace.

The representation of James Cook as a mythic hero culminated in a series of awards and depictions of his accomplishments and fate. On 3 September 1785, King George III posthumously awarded him a coat of arms, which showed the azure Pacific Ocean between golden pole stars,

---

15 Entry, 23 February 1779, Cook 1955–67, vol. 3, pp. 567–8.
16 Cook and King 1784, vol. 3, pp. 46–52.
17 MacLaren 1992.

with his routes marked in red (Plate 5). The crest is 'an arm embowed, vested in the uniform of a captain of the Royal Navy. In the hand is the Union Jack on a staff proper. The arm is encircled by a wreath of palm and laurel.' Unusually, there are two mottos: *Circa orbem* ('Around the world'); *Nil intentatum reliquit* ('He left nothing unattempted') (Plate 5).

Johann Ramberg's engraving, published as the frontispiece to Thomas Bankes's *System of Geography* (1787), shows Cook ascending to glory, with him standing on a rock as Fame heralds his arrival and Neptune urges Clio to record his story. Below, Britannia receives gifts from young women representing the four continents (Plate 6).[18]

※ ※ ※

William Bligh aspired to being a navigator and discoverer like James Cook, with whom he sailed to the Pacific Ocean as master of the *Resolution* in 1776. He was incensed when the charts included in *A Voyage to the Pacific Ocean* (1784) were credited to Henry Roberts, his mate:

> None of the Maps and Charts in this publication are from the original drawings of Lieut. Henry Roberts, he did no more than copy the original ones from Captain Cook who besides myself was the only person that surveyed & laid the Coast down … Every Plan & Chart from [the time of] C. Cook's death are exact Copies of my Works.[19]

As he took *Bounty* east from the Cape of Good Hope, Bligh wrote that, after calling at Van Diemen's Land and Dusky Sound in New Zealand, he would 'endeavour to pursue a New Track by which means it will be of use to future Navigators, and the Voyage may very properly so far be said to be on discoveries. On such a piece of service all Voyages have been considered as matter of Publick concern.'[20]

---

18   For more details, see Smith 1979, pp. 174–77, on which my description is based.
19   Bligh, annotations to the copy of *A Voyage to the Pacific Ocean* in the Hydrographic Office – see Gould 1928, p. 371.
20   Entry [c. 1 July 1788], Bligh Log 1, vol. 1, p. 235.

That is, Bligh wished to be seen as the equal of Cook; and with more benign opportunity he might have been, at least where charting was concerned. The accuracy with which he fixed the locations and took profiles of the Fijian Islands and the shoals and islets of the Great Barrier Reef in the very adverse circumstances of the open boat, poor weather and lack of equipment is a tribute to his determination and skill in this regard.[21] Writing to Banks from the Cape of Good Hope, he emphasised these things in the hope that they might mitigate despair at his failure to accomplish the voyage's main purpose:

> Altho I have failed in the completion of my undertaking, I had accomplished most assuredly the most difficult part of it. My sufferings have been very great, but through the whole, that no dishonor could be reflected on your recommendation I have endeavor'd to make the remaining part of my Voyage of some avail. Even in my distressed situation, I went in search of Fidgee Islds & discovered them, or a number of others through which I sailed, and have made decent survey of them with respect to their situation. I have also done the same on the Coast of New Holland from the latd. 13° South, & passed to the north[erd] of Capt. Cook through the Prince of Wales's Islands in latd. about 10°30'S. I was fearful having no Arms to go near to New Guinea, otherwise I would have determined how far Endeavor Streights was an elligible pass for Shiping.[22]

And his extraordinary 3618-nautical-mile (4164 mile, 6700-kilometre) boat passage from the western Pacific Ocean to Timor is compelling testimony to his ability as a navigator.

For William Bligh, though, it was not enough that he should have the private satisfaction of believing that his sailor's skills were the equal of Cook's; it was also necessary that naval authorities and the public should recognise this, by promotion, accolades and financial reward. And this is what happened. After Bligh arrived back in London on 14 March 1790, the Admiralty and the Home Office mounted a campaign

---

21   See David 1977.
22   Bligh to Banks, 18 December 1789, Banks Online, 46.28.

of what we would term 'political spin' designed to show the public that Bligh was not in any way responsible for the mutiny, the loss of the ship and the failure of the expedition. A series of favourable notices appeared in the newspapers. At the end of the month, one commented that the fact that 'the secret of the conspiracy should be so well kept by *twenty-seven* men (most of them very young) as not to give the least suspicion to the rest of the crew' was a circumstance 'unparalleled in the annals of mutiny'.[23] In an open letter to the Admiralty, 'A Captain in the Navy' praised those men who had stayed loyal to Bligh and suggested special rewards for their 'meritorious' behaviour.[24]

As we've seen in the Introduction, when Bligh's *Narrative* of the mutiny and the open-boat voyage appeared, it was 'By Authority of the Lords Commissioners of the Admiralty'. Bligh was, in turn, exonerated by his court martial, promoted to the rank of master and commander, promoted again to post captain, and paid 500 guineas (£550) by the Jamaica House of Assembly 'to compensate him for his troubles and losses.'

Significant as these gestures were, though, they were by no means weighty enough to assuage the unease caused by the irruption of ungovernable chaos. To achieve this desirable end, something more was required. It was necessary that William Bligh be located in the pantheon of the nation's naval heroes, that he should join the company of Drake and Anson, who had returned from harrowing voyages with holds full of treasure; of Cook, who had voyaged more extensively than any before him, charting thousands of miles of previously unexplored coastlines; of Hawke, Keppel and Rodney, who with their stirring victories had humbled the nation's enemies.

Here, Bligh and the authorities could not simply memorialise *Bounty*'s voyage, for even if it had succeeded in carrying its cargo of plants from Tahiti to the West Indies, it still would not have possessed an intrinsic grandeur. The bringing of eighteen men in a small craft, its gunnels lapped by the waves, with very scanty provisions, through 3600 nautical miles of barely known sea in seven weeks was certainly an extraordinary achievement, one almost without parallel. Even so, it scarcely bore on the nation's fate or enhanced its glory.

---

23   *General Evening Post*, 23–25 March 1790.
24   E.g. *St James's Chronicle*, 1–3 April 1790.

6 Men Who Strove with Gods: James Cook, William Bligh, Fletcher Christian

What was required for Bligh to be placed among the immortals was that *Bounty*'s voyage be located within a mythic context that showed how the resolute commander, through no fault of his own, had been sucked into the vortex of the underworld and emerged triumphant from it. What was needed was a narrative such as to accompany Robert Dodd's evocative engraving (reproduced on the cover of this book) showing Bligh in the launch with his eighteen companions at the moment of their being cast away, the men in various aspects of alarm and despair, and Bligh, bare-headed, standing, reaching out a white-sleeved arm, imploring succour from the tormentors, who throw out a few miserable cutlasses. Published on 2 October 1790, Dodd's depiction took its power partly from the fact that by this time the public knew how William Bligh had overcome this heartless abandonment.

As we saw in Chapters 4 and 5, the developed *Voyage* or *Travel* narrative differed markedly from the explorer's original record, as authors or editors condensed and rearranged materials to present a coherent account. This was only to be expected, for writers and publishers were not wrong to think that the public's attention would not long be held by interminable details of waves, winds and weather, which were as tedious to read about as they were to experience. What was needed was a story that presented interesting or stirring details at the same time as it conformed to the established narrative structure; and this is how Bligh, James Burney and Joseph Banks constructed the story of *Bounty*'s voyage that they presented to the public.

The source materials allow us to follow almost all stages of the process, though some are more nearly completely represented than others. These materials comprise:

1. Rough notes or short accounts written at the time of or soon after the events they relate. These include Bligh's notebook from the open-boat voyage, in the National Library of Australia. As Bligh wrote, 'This account was kept in my bosom as a common memorandum of our time & transposed into my fair Journal every day when the Weather would admit with every material circumstance which passed.'[25]

---

25 Bligh 1987, p. 43.

2. Bligh's ship's log, which records daily positions and 'Remarks' about occurrences. There are two copies of this log. The earlier version is in the State Library of New South Wales; the later one is in the Admiralty collection in the National Archives, Kew, Richmond, Surrey. However, it is certain that, in either version, some of the remarks were not contemporary with the entries they stand against, for their content indicates that Bligh either wrote or revised them at a later – perhaps a much later – date.[26]
3. Short accounts of events written at a somewhat later date, but still during the course of the voyage, which contain considered reflections. Prominent among these are the letters and narratives that Bligh sent home from Coupang and Batavia.
4. The revised versions of certain remarks in the logs, though it is now difficult to specify the time(s) of revision. My supposition is that these were made at or about the same time as Bligh prepared his first extended narrative of the voyage (see 1 below).
5. Accounts by others who were on the voyage, which describe events that Bligh did not mention, or show some that he did mention in a different light. The most important of these are John Fryer's narrative and letters; James Morrison's journal; and the minutes of the court martial of the mutineers. The minutes exist in two forms: the official version in ADM 1/5330 and printed as *The Court-Martial of the Bounty Mutineers* (1931); and Stephen Barney's version printed at the request of Edward Christian (1794).

Then there are the accounts of the voyage prepared by Bligh and his editors for publication:

1. Bligh's 'Original Narrative from Otaheite towards England, with an account of the loss of … Bounty … coppied out of his common Log of daily occurrences, written by himself at Timor, and Batavia, in

---

[26] See, e.g., Bligh's 'Remarks concerning Matavia and Oparré, [April 1789]': 'The loss of my Ship has rendered my description of these places very imperfect, for having only had time to complete up my General Observation Book on my passage to the Friendly Islands my remarks were of course not copied into this'. Bligh Log 2, vol. 2, p. 75.

order to convey to his Friends and the Public a knowledge of the Event' (This was not published in this form).
2. The *Narrative of the Mutiny on board H.M. Ship Bounty*, which deals with the passage west from Tahiti that began on 4 April 1789; the mutiny; the open-boat voyage to Timor; and (very briefly) the subsequent stages of Bligh's return to England. This work was published on 1 June 1790.
3. The extended account, *A Voyage to the South Sea*, based on Bligh's earlier narratives, but with some significant variations. This was published on 21 February 1792.

These materials allow us to follow the construction of *Bounty*'s story quite closely. Let me begin with a short survey of how details were selected; how there was some rearrangement of events and descriptions; and how some additional information was incorporated.

Bligh began the process with the Original Narrative, from which he omitted much technical detail, and in which he presented a developed story. He seems to have begun work on this version at Coupang and continued with it at Batavia, with perhaps some adjustments on the next leg of the homewards voyage. He had evidently completed it by the time he left Cape Town on 2 January 1790, this being the date of the fair copy in the Mitchell Library.[27]

Bligh arrived back in London on Sunday, 14 March 1790. Within two weeks, Banks had proposed to the Admiralty that the narrative be published and received its approval, with the *Whitehall Evening Post* announcing this at the beginning of April.[28] In preparing it for publication, Bligh had the help of James Burney, who had also sailed on Cook's third voyage and was to become a distinguished historian of Pacific exploration. The members of the Burney family were prominent in literary and musical circles, and well connected socially. We may suppose that Banks commissioned Burney to undertake the work on behalf of the Admiralty.

---

27 Bligh 1790a, p. 160.
28 Stephens to Banks, 27 March 1790, Banks Online, 48.03; *Whitehall Evening Post*, 30 March–1 April 1790.

Burney was soon at work. His sister Fanny recorded on 20 April that she and he had 'read a good deal of Captain Bligh's interesting narrative'; and that in preparing it for publication he was taking 'every word as much to heart as if it were his own production'. Then, on 11 May, the pair met Burney's good friend William Windham, a prominent politician also with literary connections, and the conversation turned to Bligh. 'They talked the narrative over,' Fanny Burney wrote, 'as far as Mr Windham had in manuscript seen its sketch; but as I had not read it, I could not enter into its detail.' (I take it that she was this time referring to her brother's adaptation of Bligh's text.) The *Narrative* was published on 1 June.[29]

Burney and Banks were even more involved in preparing the full account of the voyage for publication. Bligh may have begun to do so before he left on the second breadfruit voyage in early August 1791; but, if he had, partly because it was to include the now customary charts and plates, the task was far from complete. In the weeks before he sailed, Bligh made arrangements for others to finish the work. Burney would prepare the text in conjunction with Banks; Alexander Dalrymple would assist with the engraving of the charts and views; and Banks would see the work through the press. On 17 July, Bligh informed Banks that, before he left London to join his ship at Portsmouth, he had given Dalrymple his chart of Pare harbour at Tahiti, and 'a Copy of my log from Timor to Batavia which describes the places I touched at on the North side of Java, & will complete the account of my Voyage whenever you may be at leisure to give directions to Capt. Burney about it'. Soon after, he wrote to Burney to advise 'of my Log being left with Mr Dalrymple which you will be able to get the moment you want it'.[30]

Banks replied on 21 July, noting what Bligh said about Dalrymple and advising that 'Burney & myself are Forward in your Voyage'. As we have seen in the introduction to this book, Banks went on to assure Bligh, 'We shall Abridge considerably what you wrote in order as far as

---

29 D'Arblay 1904–5, vol. 4, pp. 365, 376–8.
30 Bligh to Banks, 17 July 1791, Banks Online 50.05; Bligh to Burney, 26 July 1791, quoted in Du Rietz [2003] 2009, pp. 16–17.

we are able to Satisfy the Public & place you in such a Point of view as they Shall approve.'[31]

And so it was. Early in September, Burney told Banks that he had divided the work into:

Chapter I: As in Proof.
Chapter II: Departure from England. Arrival at Teneriffe. Sail from thence. Arrive off Cape Horn – Severity of the weather. Obliged to bear away for the Cape of Good Hope.
Chapter III: Passage towards the Cape of Good Hope, and search after Tristan da Cunha. Arrival at False Bay. Occurrences there. Reports concerning the *Grosvenor*'s people. Departure from the Cape.
Chapter IV: Goes as far as to leaving Van diemen's Land, but I have not the copy with me at present and cannot recollect the exact title.
Chapter V: Arrives at Otaheite.

He added, 'There are other particulars which I wished to mention, but as they are in a more advanced part of the voyage they can be deferred till I have an opportunity of waiting upon you in Town.'[32]

In mid-October, Burney told Banks breezily that 'we have left Van demens land and are on our passage to Otaheite which makes 7 sheets: but I cannot proceed much farther without being favoured with your advice'; and he sent some reflections concerning the *arioi* society for Banks to approve of and suggested including the idea of encouraging migration from Tahiti to New Holland. In a letter now missing, Banks agreed to both additions and suggested further topics for extended treatment, for Burney to reply, 'The ideas in your letter would be so great an addition, and are so much wanted, that I hope you will give permission for their being inserted.'[33]

So Burney and Banks set about their work with a will, omitting much mundane material, merging incidents and sometimes altering the

---

[31] Banks to Bligh, 21 July 1791, Banks 2008–13, vol. 3, no. 178, p. 242.
[32] Burney to Banks, 5 September 1791, Banks 2008–13, vol. 3, no. 197, pp. 280–1.
[33] Burney to Banks, 13 and 22 October 1791, Banks 2008–13, vol. 3, nos 200, 203 (pp. 284, 290).

chronology of events. For example, Bligh reached Matavai Bay on 26 October 1788. On 28 October, the paramount chief Tu (called Otou by Bligh, and in the *Voyage* Tinah) and his wife, 'Itia (Iddeeah), his father, Teu (Otow), two of his brothers and some lesser chiefs and their wives visited the ship. Bligh gave them many presents. As he had done with Cook, Tu insisted on exchanging names, so that the pair became *taio* (bonded friends), which required, among other things, that Tu offer Bligh his wife. In his log, Bligh related that, as Tu wished to eat with him, he had a large meal prepared, and that his royal guest 'fed most voraciously, and was fed by a Towtow [servant] who held the Meat to his Mouth and who at times took a bite with him. The Women eat none.'[34] These practices reflected Tu's royal status, and the Tahitians' cultural prohibition on women eating with men.

In Burney and Banks's version, this became:

Tinah (i.e. Tu) is a very large man, much above the common stature, being not less than six feet four inches [nearly 2 metres] in height, and proportionably stout: his age about thirty-five. His wife (Iddeah) I judged to be about twenty-four years of age: she is likewise much above the common size of the women at Otaheite, and has a very animated and intelligent countenance. Whydooah [Vaetua], the younger brother of Tinah, was highly spoken of as a warrior, but had the character of being the greatest drunkard in the country; and indeed, to judge from the withered appearance of his skin, he must have used the pernicious drink called Ava ['*ava*, kava], to great excess.[35]

Here, the editors have provided more details of the royal personages, and taken Bligh's account of his meeting Tu's father Teu on 2 November in a drunken state, and applied it to Vaetua, who was evidently equally addicted to kava.[36] This is a typical example of their routine editorial work. They also augmented Bligh's accounts of places, things and people, and added new material, in order to give the

---

34   Entry, 28 October 1788, Bligh Log 2, vol. 1, pp. 373–4.
35   Bligh *Voyage* 1992, p. 66.
36   Entry, 2 November 1788, Bligh Log 2, vol. 1, p. 382.

Voyage more intellectual or entertaining content. These latter changes included a description of the breadfruit, together with a drawing of it and the plan of the *Bounty* showing the arrangement of the pots to accommodate the young plants;[37] the paragraphs on the *arioi* society ('described in the accounts of the former voyages'); and the suggested possibility of migration.[38]

That is, adding details from other sources and some curious information, Burney and Banks organised the narrative of Bligh's *Voyage* so as to make a more readable account. To be sure, the routes Bligh took and his log entries provided the basis of the final narrative; however, the editors divided Bligh's work into manageable sections and greatly reduced the amount of technical detail. They also shifted materials around and amalgamated some descriptions. They added some rhetorical flourishes. Given the form that the exploration narrative had developed, all this is only what we should expect – after all, these editors had some powerful precedents, for Hawkesworth and Douglas had done the same with Cook's accounts of his previous voyages.

※※※

However, other processes – variously of alteration, enhancement and transformation – were present in Bligh, Burney and Banks's construction of *Bounty*'s story. As I have already examined the deliberate misrepresentation of Bligh as a good and caring commander in the Introduction, I shall not deal with this again here. The evidence makes it abundantly clear, and Bligh and his editors perpetrated this fraud – to speak plainly – to save his hide. However, there is another feature commonly found in autobiographical writing that also distorts history. This is the presentation of earlier events within a frame of later insights and emotions, which imbues them with a significance they simply didn't have at the time.

Here is one example. As I said earlier, William Wordsworth's long autobiographical poem *The Prelude* is one of the most extraordinary works in English literature, as he makes epic the growth of his

---

37   Bligh *Voyage*, facing pp. [1] and 10, and pp. 9–13.
38   Bligh *Voyage* 1992, pp. 77, 79–81.

imagination, his becoming aware of his destiny to be a poet, and the loss and then recovery of his powers. His 'spots of time' insight is central to the whole work; but he also offers extended accounts of some moments (above others) when his being merged with the one that he believed informed all of nature. In the course of their long European walking tour, Wordsworth and Robert Jones crossed the Alps from Switzerland into Italy via the Simplon Pass on 17 August 1790. Wordsworth's letters home and various later reminiscences make clear that at the time he was greatly struck by the grandeur of the scenery, but the actual crossing was a muddle. The young men lost contact with the party of muleteers they had attached themselves to, took a wrong path, and did not know that they had crossed the Alps until a peasant told them so. When he wrote up the experience fourteen years later, though, Wordsworth gave it a cosmic significance that he had not been conscious of at the time:

> ... The immeasurable height
> Of woods decaying, never to be decayed,
> The stationary blasts of waterfalls,
> And everywhere along the hollow rent
> Winds thwarting winds, bewildered and forlorn,
> The torrents shooting from the clear blue sky,
> The rocks that muttered close upon our ears,
> Black drizzling crags that spoke by the wayside
> As if a voice were in them – the sick sight
> And giddy prospect of the raving stream,
> The unfettered clouds and region of the heavens,
> Tumult and peace, the darkness and the light –
> Were all like workings of one mind, the features
> Of the same face, blossoms upon one tree,
> Characters of the great apocalypse,
> The types and symbols of eternity,
> Of first, and last, and midst, and without end.[39]

---

39 Wordsworth [1805] 1979, Book VI, ll. 556–72.

Yes, this example is a highly wrought literary one, but such retrospective embellishment is also present in *Bounty*'s published story. To begin with, Bligh's public image as a good and caring commander might be enhanced by demonstrating, first, the ingratitude and then the remorse of the villains who overthrew him. In the letters he sent home from Coupang and Batavia, Bligh expanded his early account of the mutiny, adding such observations as the 'great Villains', 'these very young Men I placed every confidence in … joined with the most able Men in the Ship[,] got possession of the Arms and took the *Bounty* from me'. These unpalatable facts gave rise to the bitter reflections, 'I have now reason to curse the day I ever knew a Christian or a Heywood or indeed a Manks man', and, 'I have been run down by my own Dogs.'[40]

Again and again, Bligh professed himself mystified at how completely the mutineers had concealed their intentions. In his first letter, he told Philip Stephens, 'The secrecy of this mutiny was beyond all conception, so that I cannot discover that any who were with me had the least knowledge of it'; and he repeated this claim in his letters to his wife, Campbell and Banks. He slept 'always with my cabbin door open for the officer of the watch to have access to me on all occasions, for the possibility of such a catastrophe was ever the farthest from my thoughts', he explained further to Philip Stephens. In the shorter of his letters to Banks from Cape Town, he asserted:

> as an Officer and a Navigator I have ever looked with horror on Neglect and Indolence, and I have never yet crossed the Seas without that foresight which is necessary to the Welldoing of the Voyage; but in the present instance I must have been more than a human Being to have foreseen what has happened.[41]

He began to enlarge this contention in his second letter to Stephens:

---

40   Bligh to Elizabeth Bligh, 19 August 1789, Bligh 1989, pp. 23–4.
41   Bligh to Stephens, 18 August and 15 October 1789, *HRNSW*, vol. 1, pt 2, pp. 692, 697; to Mrs Bligh, 19 August, to Campbell, 12 October 1789, Bligh 1989, pp. 24, 29; Bligh to Banks, [undated], Bligh 1790.

> The secrecy of this mutiny was beyond all conception, and surprising it is that out of thirteen of the party who came with me, and lived always forward near the people and among them, no one could discover some symptoms of their bad intentions;

He continued to do so in the Log and the Original Narrative:

> The Secresy of this Mutiny is beyond all conception, and surprising it is that out of thirteen of the party who were sent with me and lived always forward among the People, and the Messmates of Christian, Stewart, Haywood, & Young, no one could discover some symptoms of bad intentions among them. With such deep laid plans of Villany, and my mind free of any suspicions, it is not to be wondered at that I have been got the better of.

With some smoothing of the prose, this paragraph was repeated in the *Narrative*.[42]

In none of the early accounts, though, did Bligh offer any comment about Christian's state of mind at the time of the mutiny. Neither does either copy of the log contain any such comment. Bligh's first mention of Christian's having been psychologically disturbed comes in the Original Narrative:

> When they were forcing me out of the Ship I asked Christian if this treatment was a proper return for the many instances he had received of my friendship. He replied with emotion, That Capt. Bligh – that is the thing, *I am in Hell I am in Hell*.[43]

However, this passage was evidently added to the fair copy of the Original Narrative at a later date, for it is not written within the pencil-ruled borders of the page, and the words that I have put in

---

42 Bligh to Stephens, 15 October 1789, *HRNSW*, vol. 1, pt 2, p. 697; entry, 28 April 1789, Bligh Log 2, vol. 2, p. 123; Bligh 1790, p. 20; Bligh 1790b, p. 10.
43 Bligh 1790, p. 21.

6 Men Who Strove with Gods: James Cook, William Bligh, Fletcher Christian

italics have been cropped in binding and then added in pencil in another hand.[44]

Additional notes have been added to this paragraph in the *Narrative*:

> Notwithstanding the roughness with which I was treated, the remembrance of past kindnesses produced some signs of remorse in Christian. When they were forcing me out of the ship, I asked him, if this treatment was a proper return for the many instances he had received of my friendship? he appeared disturbed by my question, and answered, with much emotion, 'That, – captain Bligh, – that is the thing; – I am in hell – I am in hell.'[45]

What seems most likely is that Burney suggested that the portrayal of Christian as distracted and remorseful would both heighten the dramatic effect of the description of the mutiny and show more powerfully the wrong done to Bligh, a solicitous officer and good friend. Presented in this way, Christian's rebellion against Bligh was a profound violation of what Coleridge in his rendering of the story termed the 'laws of hospitality' – he might equally have said 'of friendship'.[46] And just behind these surfaces lie the analogues of Cain killing Abel, Brutus stabbing Caesar, Judas betraying Christ.

Next, despite the manifest evidence to the contrary, Bligh repeatedly claimed that he had all but succeeded in his mission. He said in the Log:

> What Mans situations could be so peculiarly flattering as mine twelve hours before? I had a Ship in the most perfect order and well Stored with every necessary both for Service and health; by early attention to those particulars I had acted against the power of Chance in case I could not get through Endeavor Straights as

---

44 I am grateful to Paul Brunton for this information. There is one other instance of something being written outside the margin. This is the note on p. 110 concerning Robert Lamb.
45 Bligh 1790b, p. 8.
46 'Argument', Coleridge, *Ancient Mariner* (1800).

well as against any Accident that might befall me in them, and to add to this I had very successfully got my Plants in the most flourishing and fine order, so that upon the whole the Voyage was two thirds completed and the remaining part no way doubtfull. Every person in the most perfect health, to establish which I had taken the greatest pains and bore a most anxious care the whole course of the Voyage.[47]

He repeated these statements in his letters to his wife, Stephens, Campbell and Banks. In his shorter letter to Banks from Cape Town, he wrote that he had undertaken the mission 'zealously and I trust you will find I have executed [it] faithfully, securing every object but my return with the wonderfull success I had acquired'; while in the longer one he said, 'altho I have failed in the completion of my undertaking, I had accomplished most assuredly, the most difficult part of it'.[48] In the *Narrative*, these sentiments appeared as:

> A few hours before, my situation had been peculiarly flattering. I had a ship in the most perfect order, and well stored with every necessary both for service and health: by early attention to those particulars I had, as much as lay in my power, provided against any accident, in case I could not get through Endeavour Straits, as well as against what might befall me in them; add to this, the plants had been successfully preserved in the most flourishing state; so that, upon the whole, the voyage was two thirds completed, and the remaining part in a very promising way; every person on board being in perfect health, to establish which was ever amongst the principal objects of my attention.[49]

Equally, it was necessary both to maintain his *amour propre* and to obtain Banks's, the Admiralty's and the public's approval that Bligh should present himself as always in control, as always resolute in the

---

47 Entry, 28 April 1789, Bligh Log 2, vol. 2, pp. 122–3.
48 Bligh to Banks [undated], in Bligh 1790, and 18 December 1789, Banks Online, 46.28.
49 Bligh 1790b, p. 9.

6 Men Who Strove with Gods: James Cook, William Bligh, Fletcher Christian

face of every adversity. After describing his woes, he told his wife from Coupang, 'I however have every expectation to get the better of everything.' He told Banks from Cape Town that he hoped his Original Narrative would show 'that to the last I never lost that presence of mind, or professional skill, which you have been pleased to allow was the first cause of my being honored with your notice'.[50]

In an astonishing statement in his Log and Original Narrative, which reappeared in his published accounts, Bligh asserted that after he had had been forced from the ship, he:

> had scarce got a furlong on my way when I began to reflect on the vicissitude of human affairs; but in the midst of all I felt an inward happyness which prevented any depression of my Spirits, conscious of my own integrity and anxious solicitude for the good of the service I was on. I found my mind most wonderfully supported, and began to conceive hopes notwithstanding so heavy a Calamity, to be able to account to my King & Country for my misfortune.[51]

There is a reference to Cook here, for Bligh's description is reminiscent of that by Hawkesworth of how the *Endeavour's* crew had worked silently, without swearing or profanity, to free it from the coral reef.[52] However, we may also legitimately ask how Bligh could possibly have been so calm when only 220 yards (200 metres) away from his lost ship and his enemies, and with the magnitude of his failure to deliver the cargo of plants so plain?

The short answer is that he couldn't have been – or, if he was, then he certainly was 'more than a human Being'. However, time and again in the Original Narrative, Bligh represented himself as calm and in control. It is Christian, not Bligh, who is in emotional turmoil. When

---

50 Bligh to Mrs Bligh, 19 August 1789, Bligh 1989, p. 24; Bligh to Banks [undated], with Bligh 1790.
51 Bligh 1790, pp. 16–17. Cf. Bligh Log 1, vol. 2, pp. 63–4; Bligh Log 2, vol. 2, p. 122; Bligh 1790b, pp. 8–9; Bligh 1792, p. 161.
52 Hawkesworth, vol. 3, p. 552. Hawkesworth adjusted the account given in entry, 11 June 1770, Banks 1962, vol. 2, p. 78.

Robert Lamb slunk away so as not to share the birds he caught with his companions, Bligh gave him 'a good beating'. After weeks on their meagre diet, he felt 'no extreme hunger or thirst. My allowance satisfies me[,] knowing I can have no more'. Even when most of his companions were overcome by hunger, lassitude, pains in their muscles, bones and bowels, depression and mental dissolution, Bligh remained resolute: 'Even in our present situation we are reduced Beings horrible to be beheld, yet while my fortitude and Spirit remain we drag on.' When the boatswain told him he looked worse than anyone else, Bligh 'had good humour enough to return him a better compliment'.[53]

But Bligh himself repeatedly gave the lie to this assertion of an unnatural calmness during the passage in the launch. When the Tongans threatened to overwhelm them, he became anxious that 'I should not be able to return to my King & Country to give an account of the transaction'. When the launch ran before a violent storm:

> the Sea flew over us with great force & kept us bailing with horror and anxiety. At Dawn of day I found every one in a most distressed condition, and I now began to fear that another such Night would produce the end of several who were no longer able to bear it.

When he argued with Purcell on Sunday Island, not seeing 'where this [i.e. discontent] was to end', he took a cutlass and 'determined to strike a final blow at it, and either to preserve my command or die in the attempt'. Thereafter, he always kept a cutlass close at hand. Becoming afraid that if Aboriginal people on the mainland had seen their fires on Bird Island they would be massacred, he wrote, 'the relief I expected from a little sleep was totally lost, and I anxiously looked for the flowing of the Tide to proceed to Sea'.[54]

Bligh's habit of extolling his virtues and denying them in others pervades the Original Narrative. Repeatedly, he castigated Fryer, Purcell and others for being querulous, argumentative, mutinous, careless. On the other hand, he, William Bligh, never behaved badly

---

53   Bligh 1790a, pp. 21, 110, 121, 128–9.
54   Bligh 1790a, pp. 39–40, 67a, 96, 98, 108–9.

6 Men Who Strove with Gods: James Cook, William Bligh, Fletcher Christian

and was always solicitous of his companions' welfare. He took pride in how resolutely he had husbanded their meagre rations in the launch, even in the face of his companions' pleas for more:

> This I so sacredly stuck to that I brought eleven days of allowance [of bread] in with me, it is therefore evident that the least degree of inattention or want of Care in the distribution of this article would have put an end to our existence; but from a strict adherence to the agreement we set out with, it is equally certain if I had missed Timor, I could have pursued my Voyage to Java; where ... I knew I could get everything I wanted.

But then, Purcell said that he had repeatedly seen Bligh give himself more food than he allowed to the others, which might explain Bligh's somewhat greater strength. Which man was lying? And how was it that, when they reached Coupang, the compassionate commander ordered Fryer to stay in the launch so as to work it into the harbour when the tide turned, while he himself and the others landed to be succoured. In his weakened state, Fryer required the assistance of sailors from another ship to accomplish this task – as he remarked bitterly, 'all this time I might have gone to the Devil for my good friend Captain Bligh'.[55]

※ ※ ※

As he worked up his various accounts, William Bligh proved unable to rest content with simple statements of fact. He wrote and rewrote so as to represent himself as a superior navigator and a good and caring commander. However, there was more to Bligh's presentation of circumstances in the Log, the letters from the East Indies and the Original Narrative than the exaggeration of his own merits. There was also some striking rhetorical embellishment, which when analysed shows just how much he yearned to be ranked among the immortals.

Given the length of the voyage in the open boat, and the privations they had suffered during it, it is only to be expected that Bligh and his

---

55   Bligh 1790a, p. 157; Fryer 1934, pp. 76, 78.

men were in terrible physical and mental condition when they reached Coupang in Timor on 14 June 1789. Bligh wrote first of their arrival:

> I now ordered everyone to come on shore which was as much as some of them could[,] being so weak as to be scarce able to walk. – Among these were the Surgeon Mr Ledward, who was reduced to meer skin & bones and Lawrence Lebogue a Seaman equally as bad – those would certainly have died in a few days – Some others were getting ill through a want of resolution and spirits, and all in a very weak condition & scarce able to walk & support themselves. I ranked Among the few of the heartyest ones & was certainly the strongest on my Legs but reduced like the others very much.[56]

He told his wife, simply, that 'perhaps a more miserable set of Beings were never seen', a statement that he repeated to Stephens, Campbell and Banks.[57]

However, as Bligh reported to the Admiralty, the deputy-governor's 'zeal to render services to His Majesty's subjects has been unremitting', and 'the surgeon of the fort, a Mr Max, has also been ever attentive to my sick people, and has daily and hourly attended them with great care'.[58] With the benefit of food and medical attention, most of *Bounty*'s party recovered. The exception was David Nelson, who died on 20 July. It is unclear whether the three men who later died at Batavia did so primarily as a result of their previous privations, or as a consequence of contracting one or another of that noxious city's fevers.

Bligh began the rhetorical embellishment of this part of his story at Coupang, with the intention of heightening the reader's sense of the pity and terror of life *in extremis*, so as the better to convey his heroic achievement in having accomplished 'a voyage of the most extraordinary nature that ever happen'd in the world, let it be taken either in its extent, duration, or so much want of the necessaries of

---

56 Entry, 14 June 1789, Bligh 1987, pp. 175–7.
57 Entry, 14 June 1789, Bligh 1987, pp. 175–7; Bligh to Stephens, 18 August 1789, *HRNSW*, vol. 1, pt 2, p. 691; to Mrs Bligh, 19 August, to Campbell, 12 October, to Banks, 13 October 1789, Bligh 1989, pp. 24, 28, 38.
58 Bligh to Stephen, 18 August 1789, *HRNSW*, vol. 1, pt 2, pp. 692–3.

life'.[59] Bligh was familiar with Cook's *A Voyage towards the South Pole*. Aware of how the great explorer had invoked the superior power of artistic depiction, Bligh wrote the trope of the skilled artist into a striking paragraph that appears (with inconsequential variations) in both copies of the Log and in the Original Narrative:

> The abilities of the most eminent Artist perhaps could never have more brilliantly shone than in a delineation of two Groups of Figures that at this time presented themselves, and at which one might be so much at a loss to know the one most to admire; whether the Eyes of Famine sparkling at immediate relief, or their Preservers horror struck at the Spectors of Men. For any one to conceive the picture of such poor miserable Beings; let him fancy that in his House he is in the moment of giving relief to eighteen Men whose ghastly countenances, but from the known cause, would be equally liable to affright as demand pity; let him view their limbs full of sores, and their Bodies nothing but skin & Bones habited in Rags; and at last let him conceive he sees the Tears of Joy and Gratitude flowing over their cheeks at their benefactors. With the mixture of horror[,] surprise & pity that his mind will be then agitated, were the people of Timor on giving us relief.[60]

Bligh included a shortened version of this description in his second letter to Stephens. It appeared in the *Narrative* as:

> The abilities of a painter, perhaps, could never have been displayed to more advantage than in the delineation of the two groups of figures, which at this time presented themselves. An indifferent spectator would have been a loss which most to admire; the eyes of famine sparkling at immediate relief, or the horror of their preservers at the sight of so many spectres, whose ghastly countenances, if the cause had been unknown, would rather have excited terror than pity. Our bodies were nothing but

---

59   Bligh to Stephen, 18 August 1789, *HRNSW*, vol. 1, pt 2, p. 691.
60   Bligh 1790, pp. 144–5. Cf. Entry, 14 June 1789, Bligh Log 1, vol. 2, pp. 166–7, and Bligh Log 2, vol. 2, p. 227.

skin and bones, our limbs were full of sores, and we were cloathed in rags; in this condition, with the tears of joy and gratitude flowing down our cheeks, the people of Timor beheld us with a mixture of horror, surprise, and pity.

It was republished without essential change in *A Voyage to the South Sea*.[61]

In the course of twenty months, then, Bligh's description of the arrival at Timor changed from a direct, simple conveyance of fact to an elaborate presentation embellished with the tropes of the skilful artist, the concerned host and the living ghosts. He wrote the artist into his description for the same reason as Cook had done so, the better to convey the imaginative intensity of the moment. Just as Cook's was, so too did Bligh intend his to be a story for the ages, one to show how he too had shown supreme skill, courage and perseverance in the face of extreme adversity – how, in short, he had braved the underworld and emerged triumphant from it.

※ ※ ※

In their turn, the editors of *A Voyage to the South Sea* also made strenuous efforts to depict Bligh as the dauntless hero. Given that he did not start *Bounty*'s voyage until 23 December, he lost the favourable season for entering the Pacific Ocean by rounding Cape Horn. For five weeks from 20 March, he tried to do so, but strong opposing winds and currents beat him back, which together with the exceptionally cold weather strained the ship and brought the men to the limits of endurance. In his log, Bligh recorded of 14 April, for example:

> The repeated Gales seem now to become more Violent. The Squalls so excessively severe that I dare scarce show any Canvas to it. The motion of the Ship is so very quick and falls so deep between the Seas that it is impossible to stand without man ropes across the Decks.[62]

---

61 Bligh to Stephens, 15 October 1789, *HRNSW*, vol. 1, pt 2, p. 701; Bligh *Narrative*, pp. 79–80; Bligh *Voyage*, p. 234.
62 Entry, 14 April 1788, Bligh Log 2, vol. 1, p. 161.

6 Men Who Strove with Gods: James Cook, William Bligh, Fletcher Christian

By 22 April, Bligh had decided that unless he took the eastern route (i.e. through the southern Indian Ocean and past New Holland and New Zealand) to Tahiti, he would not be able to accomplish his mission. He wrote, 'It was with much concern I saw it improper and even unjustifiable in me to persist any longer in a passage this Way to the Society Islands' – that is, round Cape Horn. Among his considerations were that the weather conditions would not improve; his men were exhausted; the condition of the ship was deteriorating; and if he changed his route, he might still reach the Society Islands in time for the growing season of young breadfruit plants. He wrote further:

> on 9 April at Noon I was in Longitude 76°58' West, or counting my Longitude from Cape St John by Time Keeper which most likely is not a half degree wrong, too far to the West, I was nearly 13°39' West of the Cape and had every hopes of accomplishing the Passage round; but from this time we had no intermissions from hard Gales and very severe Weather, scarce ever leaving it in my power to do much better than lye too. The Sails & Ropes were worked with much difficulty, and the few Men who were obliged to be aloft felt the Snow Squalls so severe as to render them almost incapable of getting below, and some of them sometimes for a While lost their Speech; but I took care to Nurse them when off duty with every comfort in my power.

Accordingly, he 'ordered the Helm to be put a Weather to the universal joy of all hands at 5 O'Clock, and as the Gale continued it was an additional satisfaction to think we had lost no time'.[63]

Now, if Bligh's own account was not eloquent enough about the extreme difficulties he and his crew faced, Burney and Banks decided to intensify it. In his log, Bligh did refer to Lord Anson's description of conditions in the ocean about Cape Horn as the best he knew of, but he did not quote it.[64] Taking this hint, the editors rendered Bligh's account of his decision to abandon the attempt to pass Cape Horn in this way:

---

63 Entry, 22 April 1788, Bligh Log 2, vol. 1, pp. 177–8.
64 Entry, 13 April 1788, Bligh Log 2, vol. 1, p. 159.

It was with much concern I saw how hopeless, and even unjustifiable it was, to persist any longer in attempting a passage this way to the Society Islands. We had been thirty days in this tempestuous ocean. At one time we had advanced so far to the westward as to have a fair prospect of making our passage round; but from that period hard gales of westerly wind had continued without intermission, a few hours excepted, which, to borrow an expression in Lord Anson's voyage, were 'like the elements drawing breath to return upon us with redoubled violence'. The season was now too far advanced for us to expect more favourable winds or weather, and we had sufficiently experienced the impossibility of beating round against the wind, or of advancing at all without the help of a fair wind, for which there was little reason to hope. Another consideration, which had great weight with me, was, that if I persisted in my attempt this way, and should, after all, fail to get round, it would occasion such a loss of time, that our arrival at Otaheite, soon enough to return in the proper season by the East Indies, would be rendered precarious.[65]

While this passage is largely faithful to Bligh's original, the inclusion of Anson's description makes it portentous in a way in which the original isn't – like one of Britain's greatest naval heroes, Bligh has done battle with a hostile cosmos; he may not have won, but neither has he been overwhelmed.

This sense might only be reinforced by the account of Bligh's extraordinary open-boat voyage from near Tofua to Timor. That in the *Voyage* is a shortened version of that published in the *Narrative*. However, the editors have preserved the embellished description of the emaciated party's arrival at Coupang in full. And while in the earlier account Bligh did reflect on how providence had repeatedly saved their lives during the passage, the editors enhanced this perception, so as to leave readers in no doubt that Bligh was a genuine hero who had bested the underworld: 'Thus, through the assistance of Divine Providence, we surmounted the difficulties and distresses of a most perilous voyage,

---

65   Bligh 1792, p. 33.

and arrived safe in an hospitable port, where every necessary and comfort were administered to us with a most liberal hand.'[66]

Altogether, the way in which Burney and Banks portrayed Bligh in the *Voyage* was intended to evoke just such awed praise as we saw in the introduction from William Windham: 'This Captain Bligh – what feats, what wonders he has performed! What difficulties got through! What dangers defied! And with such cool, manly skill!'[67]

※ ※ ※

As Bligh, Burney and Banks presented them, then, the accounts of Bligh's contending with the elements at Cape Horn and of his extraordinary open-boat voyage would have been enough to command the interest of readers. Here was someone who had braved the dangers of the oceans; who had overcome the machinations of evil-hearted men; who had survived the privations and perils of a long passage in a small boat through scarcely known seas; who had brought all but one of the men who stayed with him safely to land; who had then reached home again to tell his story.

However, what makes *Bounty*'s story the more compelling is that it embodies a second narrative, much more shadowy yet also more potent. Without Bligh's and Christian's having developed a symbiotic relationship involving authority and disobedience, pride and humiliation, there would not have been a mutiny; and, at least equally with Bligh's, Fletcher Christian's story contributes to the mythic import of the whole affair.

The way in which Christian was represented to the public by his relatives and friends parallels how Bligh was represented, though of course the materials available to them were much less extensive. Though we cannot trace the process in the same detail, no doubt Edward Christian, in pleading the case for understanding and compassion, also presented the best aspects of his brother's character and actions, and suppressed the worst. As we saw in Chapter 2, he said that Fletcher:

---

[66] Bligh 1792, p. 238.
[67] D'Arblay 1904–5, vol. 4, p. 378.

having staid at school longer than young men generally do who enter into the navy, and being allowed by all who knew him to possess extraordinary abilities, is an excellent scholar, and every one acquainted with him from a boy, till he went on board the *Bounty*, can testify, that no young man was ever more ambitious of all that is esteemed right and honourable among men, or more anxious to acquire distinction and advancement by his good conduct in his profession.

Edward Christian added to this brief introduction a summary of the Bountys' opinions of his brother:

- He was a gentleman, and a brave man; and every officer and seaman on board the ship would have gone through fire and water to have served him.
- He was a good and worthy gentleman, and was dear to all who ever knew him; and before the fatal day, his conduct was in every respect such as became an officer, a gentleman, and a man of honour.
- He was adorned with every virtue, and beloved by all.
- As much as I have lost and suffered by him, if he could be restored to his country, I should be the first to go without wages in search of him.[68]

Then there was the report of Christian's address to the disaffected Bountys who wished to return to Tahiti from Tubuai:

Gentleman, I will carry you, and land you wherever you please; I desire no one to stay with me, but I have one favour to request, they you will grant me the ship, tie the foresail, and give me a few gallons of water, and leave me to run before the wind, and I shall land upon the first island the ship drives to. I have done such an act that I cannot stay at Otaheite. I will never live where I may be carried home to be a disgrace to my family.[69]

---

68   Christian [1794] 1952, pp. 76–7.
69   Christian [1794] 1952, p. 73.

6 Men Who Strove with Gods: James Cook, William Bligh, Fletcher Christian

With its stoic acceptance of responsibility and awareness of impending doom, it anticipates by fifty years the sentiment Tennyson gave to the ageing Ulysses: 'my purpose holds / to sail beyond the sunset, and the baths / of all the western stars, until I die'.

So Fletcher Christian was the young hero destroyed by a vindictive commander and malign fates. In the end, though, it is what we do not know about Christian's story that most gives it its elemental power. As I observed earlier, absences inform his story: we do not know when he first went to sea; there is no portrait of him; if he made a will, it has not survived; no grave is known; there are no letters between him and his family and friends. He disappears halfway through Bligh's story of *Bounty*'s voyage; and we have only information from others about his life thereafter.

Especially, we have no account from him of his reasons for rising against Bligh. What exactly drove Fletcher Christian to mutiny? Was it, as Bligh conjectured, that he was one of those who 'flattered themselves with the hopes of a more happy life among the Otaheiteans, than they could possibly enjoy in England; and this, joined to some female connections, most probably occasioned the whole transaction'?[70] With its elements of pleasant climate, absence from labour, abundant food and carefree sex, this explanation resonates with the fantasies of men accustomed to the rigours of northern European life. On the other hand, based on what he learnt from interviewing many of those who sailed on the *Bounty*, Edward Christian claimed that Bligh's humiliations had driven his brother mad. Which view should we accept as the more accurate? As I discussed in Chapter 2, to be able to answer this question satisfactorily, we should need to know much more about Fletcher Christian than we do.

There is something we may know with certainty, though. This is that, by his mutiny, by his seizure of the ship and his abandonment of Bligh and the men loyal to him, Christian placed himself beyond the possibility of redemption, human or divine; and he knew it. As we've seen, he told Bligh some days before the mutiny, 'I have been [in] hell for weeks with you.' And he told John Fryer during it, 'I've been in hell for weeks past.'[71]

---

70 Bligh 1792, p. 162.
71 Fryer 1934, p. 53; Fryer, testimony, *Bounty Court-Martial (Minutes)*, p. 7.

There would be no release for Christian from this hell. From the time of the mutiny, death was all about him. Early on, he and the other mutineers argued so bitterly that he had to carry loaded pistols. They slaughtered the Tubuaians. On Pitcairn, they mistreated the islanders, and fought with them and each other. As we have seen, some accounts have Christian being killed in the mayhem of September/October 1793; but even if – as I think – he did not in fact die then and there but returned to England, this was scarcely something to bring him much comfort. As an outlaw, he might only live secretly, roaming a rugged country like a wild animal, afraid of exposure, arrest and execution.

Either way, then, Christian's was a miserable fate. For him, there might be no real regaining the comforts of country and hearth. With its ineluctable mysteries, Christian's story engages our interest. Though we do not know nearly as much about him as we should like to, we understand that, like Coleridge's Ancient Mariner, after the mutiny he was:

> Alone, alone, all all alone
> Alone on the wide wide Sea;
> And Christ would take no pity on
> My soul in agony.[72]

Even more than Bligh's, Fletcher Christian's story bespeaks the pity and terror of life lived at the margins of the world and of the self, and therefore embodies the essential human condition.

Appropriately, it is another weathered voyager who has best perceived this. Amasa Delano (1763–1823) was the captain of a New England sealing vessel. He undertook a series of very extensive voyages, accounts of which he published under the title *A Narrative of Voyages and Travels in the Northern and Southern Hemispheres*, in 1817. In the course of his sailing, he read Edwards's journal of the *Pandora*'s voyage and wreck, which he found at Coupang, and became close friends with Mayhew Folger, with whom he discussed the business of

---

72   Coleridge, *Ancient Mariner* (1798). ll. 224–7

6 Men Who Strove with Gods: James Cook, William Bligh, Fletcher Christian

Bounty's voyage in considerable detail before Folger found the Pitcairn settlement. Delano afterwards remembered:

> We were both much interested to know what ultimately became of Christian, his ship, and his party. It is not easy for landsmen, who have never had personal experience of the sufferings of sailors at sea, and on savage coasts or desolate islands, to enter into their feelings with any thing like an adequate sympathy. We had both suffered many varieties of hardship and privation, and our feelings were perfectly alive to the anxieties and distresses of a mind under the circumstances of Christian, going from all he had known and loved, and seeking as his last refuge a spot unknown and uninhabited. The spirit of crime is only temporary in the human soul, but the spirit of sympathy is eternal. Repentance and virtue succeed to passion and misconduct, and while the public may continue to censure and frown, our hearts in secret plead for the returning and unhappy transgressor. It was with such a state of mind that Folger and myself used to speak of the prospects before the mutineers of the *Bounty*, when she was last seen steering to the northwest from Otaheite on the open ocean, not to seek friends and home, but a solitary region, where no human face, besides the few now associated in exile, should ever meet their eyes.[73]

---

73   Delano 1817, p. 138 [PN7].

Conclusion: The Enduring Intrigue of *Bounty*'s Voyage

As I said at the outset, if it had succeeded, *Bounty*'s voyage would most likely have soon faded into a scarcely remembered past. The idea of bringing breadfruit to the West India islands so as to provide a cheap food for slaves had been mooted for decades; and in 1787, wishing to see the planters increasing the production of cotton so as to provide Britain's rapidly expanding capacity to manufacture cloths with raw materials, imperial planners decided to implement it.

However, even as the expedition proceeded, this scheme was being superseded by a much grander one. For, having in mind how India had been the home of cotton production since time immemorial, the cheapness of Indian labour when compared with that of slaves, and the potentially vast markets of Asia for cloths and other manufactures, Joseph Banks, Lord Hawkesbury and Henry Dundas were acting to transform the subcontinent into a gigantic plantation for the production of raw materials: cotton, dyes, hemp, naval timbers, tea. From 1787 into the nineteenth century, the Pitt administration worked to achieve this grand goal, but it had only limited success. In any case, by the beginning of the new century the southern United States and the islands off the coast of Georgia had supplanted the West India islands as the major source of cotton for British manufacturers. As one scholar has put it, 'in 1803 only about half as much cotton left the West Indies as in 1790, and its market share in Britain was now reduced to 10 per cent'.[1] It seems a fitting epitaph that, after the second breadfruit

---

1   Beckert 2015, p. 96.

voyage succeeded and the trees were widely propagated in the West India islands, the slaves did not readily develop a taste for their fruit.

Yet, as the public's enduring interest attests, the mutiny on this small ship in an obscure part of the western Pacific Ocean has become the most famous one in all the history of the sea. There is seemingly no end to the stream of books telling the story anew. Indeed, scarcely a year goes by without another study or fictional presentation of *Bounty*'s voyage and the mutiny, or such attendant circumstances as the pursuit and trial of the mutineers, the second breadfruit voyage, events on Pitcairn Island, or Bligh's life more generally. In the past eighteen or so years, for example, there have appeared: a second edition of Glynn Christian, *Fragile Paradise* (1999); a facsimile of George Hamilton, *A Voyage Round the World in His Majesty's Frigate Pandora* (2000); Fiona Mountain, *Isabella* (2000); a reprint of Rosalind Young, *Mutiny of the Bounty and Story of Pitcairn Island, 1790–1894* (2003); Caroline Alexander, *The Bounty* (2003); Peter Corris, *The Journal of Fletcher Christian* (2005); Val McDermid, *The Grave Tattoo* (2006); Roy Schreiber, ed., *Captain Bligh's Second Chance* (2007); John Boyne, *Mutiny on the Bounty* (2008); Donald A. Maxton, ed., *After the Bounty* (2010); Rob Mundle, *Bligh: Master Mariner* (2010); Jennifer Gall, ed., *In Bligh's Hand* (2010); Anne Salmond, *William Bligh in the South Seas* (2011); Vanessa Smith and Nicholas Thomas's edition of James Morrison's journal, *Mutiny and Aftermath* (2013); Donald Maxton and Rolf Du Rietz's edition of the letters of Peter and Nessie Heywood, *Innocent on the Bounty* (2013); and Diana Preston's *Paradise in Chains* (2017).

Why this fascination with the *Bounty*'s voyage? Again as I said earlier, it was not that it resulted in any really notable new geographical information. Bligh's surveys of some of the Fijian islands and the cays of the Great Barrier Reef, skilful as they were, only faintly resonate with Cook's accomplishments; and while he did obtain additional information about Polynesian society, this was also slight in comparison to that which Cook gathered. Neither did *Bounty* carry home extensive collections of plants and animals, as Banks and his colleagues did on the *Endeavour*, or the Forsters on Cook's second voyage. Unlike Charles Darwin's voyage on the *Beagle* and Alfred Russel Wallace's travels in the East Indies, Bligh's *Bounty* voyage did not give rise to any startling new theory, such as the evolution of species. The attempt to transport plants between

Conclusion: The Enduring Intrigue of *Bounty*'s Voyage

hemispheres is interesting in itself, and also as part of a larger imperial endeavour, but not necessarily compellingly so (and, in any case, the imperial dimension was not highlighted in the first published narratives and has not been much studied since).

And in the grand scheme of mutinies, in itself the *Bounty* one was decidedly mundane. Though there was tumult, it involved no mayhem; and as I have shown, it did not arise from widespread grievance or political agitation, as did those in the massive squadrons of the Royal Navy at Spithead and the Nore in 1797. Certainly, Bligh's open-boat voyage from the western Pacific Ocean to Timor was singular, but its outcome did not bear on the welfare of the nation.

※ ※ ※

So the answer to the question 'Why this continuing fascination?' is not as obvious as it may seem. Rather than to its scientific accomplishments or its intellectual or social ramifications, we must look elsewhere for the explanation of the public's abiding interest in *Bounty*'s voyage. Various other explanations have been advanced over the past 227 years. The first was admiration for heroic achievement wrought in the face of terrible adversity – witness Windham's and Matra's gushing praise. The title of the second novel in Charles Nordhoff and James Hall's immensely popular *Bounty* trilogy, *Men against the Sea* (1934), serves to indicate how this attraction continued into the twentieth century.

As Bligh's reputation as a good and honourable man declined and the image of him as a cruel tyrant firmed, a second focus of attention quickly developed: the sufferings of poor, oppressed Fletcher Christian. What made this particular story so poignant was that it showed a young and promising life ruined by (in his brother's words) a 'sudden unpremeditated act of desperation and phrenzy'. This was a story to demonstrate 'the uncertainty of human prospects', for here was:

> a young man ... condemned to perpetual infamy, who, if he had served on board any other ship, or had perhaps been absent from the *Bounty* a single day, or one ill-fated hour, might still have been an honour to his country, and a glory and comfort to his friends.

This focus also continued strongly into the twentieth century, with Owen Rutter, for example, commenting in 1936 that Christian 'was not the stuff of which mutineers are made, and that is why his story is remembered'.[2]

Then, in the mid-nineteenth century, nourished by the age's passion for missionary activity, the miracle of the Pitcairn Island colony's emergent spiritual life became a strong focus of the whole story. In the much less God-fearing twentieth century, some writers offered a secular version of this trope, when they pointed out how the Pitcairn colony's life resonated with the Romantic ideal of living in intimate and continuous contact with nature. More recently, Glynn Christian interwove both versions: 'Pitcairn's way of life showed me that the message of basic Christianity can work.' 'What Rousseau dreamed, Christian did.'[3]

Each of these explanations now appears tired and inadequate. In this book, I have offered two additional ones, which function on different levels. The first concerns not only what can be known about the protagonists and the mutiny but also, equally importantly, what now can't be known. So while the intricacy of the details invites analysis, which serves to make the story more interesting, so too do the silences increase its intrigue.

The second explanation concerns the broader nature of the story. And here, while previous writers have naturally sought to explain its appeal, they have arrived at no consensus.

Glynn Christian thought that the reason for the public's abiding interest in his forebear is that he 'struck a seminal chord in universal yearnings for adventure and freedom, goals few achieve in reality'. Gavin Kennedy reasoned that the *Bounty* story fascinates 'because it encompasses the drama of an almost inexplicable conflict between two men: one ambitious, determined and talented, and the other less experienced, less ambitious, less determined, though every bit as talented'. Sven Wahlroos saw that Fletcher Christian's 'name has become a symbol of adventure, of revolt against pettiness, and of the romance of the sea'.[4]

Greg Dening considered that in the *Ancient Mariner*,

---

2   Christian [1794] 1952, p. 79; Rutter 1936a, p. 85.
3   Smith 1960, p. 248; Christian 1982, p. 244 and 1991, p. 42.
4   Christian 1982, p. 249; Kennedy 1989, [p. ix]; Wahlroos 1989, p. 246.

Conclusion: The Enduring Intrigue of *Bounty*'s Voyage

Coleridge took Christian out of history and transformed his story into a mystery play about how a heinous act perpetrated against society but done in ignorance might be redeemed. For that, Christian need not be a hero, or be right or wrong, nor need we be the judge of either. Trivial persecution *can* make a man desperate; unthinking acts *can* change the world. However, he was, by his act, an object of universal sympathy. That the inconsequential should be so consequential is an albatross around all our necks.[5]

To Caroline Alexander, Christian's 'fantastic tale of escape to paradise at the far end of the world had the allure of something epic', especially to a nation wracked by 'revolution and the travails of war'. In her view, what with his personal anguish, 'his long hair loose, his shirt collar open, he with his gentlemanly pedigree and almost mythic name', Fletcher Christian was the forerunner of the 'full-blown Romantic hero' whom Byron would epitomise in his poems a generation later.[6]

There are no doubt elements of truth in each of these explanations. However, none is complete in itself, as neither do all of them together offer a fundamental explanation. Their common weakness is that each is time- and circumstance-bound, and limited by the concepts of psychology available to the writers, while, at least for Western audiences, the appeal of the story is not so confined. K.A. Reimann came closer to the essential explanation when she said, 'it is not the incident itself, but the way in which the *Bounty* mutiny was originally written into the public consciousness that has generated the continuing interest'; and specifically that Bligh's published texts 'do not tell the audience the story that they want to know. The elements in the mutiny that have subsequently come to be regarded as of interest were remote from Bligh's agenda in writing [his] publications.'[7]

Reimann is right to think that the permanent intrigue of *Bounty*'s story arises from the way(s) in which it has been presented to the public, but she has not properly understood that what holds the public's interest *is* in fact written into Bligh's narratives and into the shadowy

---

5 Dening 1992, p. 310.
6 Alexander 2003, pp. 343–5.
7 Reimann 1996, pp. 198–9.

history we have of the Pitcairn Island settlement. That is, in addition to recognising its various aspects as a narrative of scientific endeavour, a tale of bullying and betrayal, of a clash of wills, of mental aberration and mutiny, of heroism, of wasted promise and of a good life simply lived, we need to understand that *Bounty*'s story encapsulates an archaic myth of great imaginative power.

It does so because, by the end of the eighteenth century, writers had come to present the results of scientific explorations in the form of a distinctive literary genre, the dynamics of which were quite other than scientific. By this time, the Enlightenment explorer had been transformed into a mythic hero whose task it was to venture into the underworld. Whether or not he survived its dangers and emerged from its darkness, his endeavour was such as befitted a man who aspired to emulate the gods. In the last decades of the eighteenth century, James Cook was the model *par excellence* of this dauntless explorer; and the narratives of his voyages provided the template for the genre. William Bligh and his editors consciously shaped his story to show how he had shadowed the great Captain Cook, with whom he had sailed.

Moreover, as details (certain or uncertain) of Fletcher Christian's life after the mutiny slowly emerged, so too did his story contribute to the character of the whole. *Bounty*'s story possesses a binary mythic structure. On the one hand, there is the first protagonist's heroic return from the underworld; on the other, there is the second protagonist's tragic demise. For the most part, the story derives from historical circumstance, though its presentation involved a considerable amount of falsification and literary artifice. In the form in which it has come down to us, *Bounty*'s story is one that resonates with what Gilbert Murray termed the 'undercurrent of desires and fears and passions' that shape our emotions and suffuse our dreams.[8] It is primarily for this reason that it has commanded our attention for more than 200 years.

---

8   Murray [1927] 1968, pp. 239–40.

Acknowledgements

In the course of a long scholarly life, one accumulates many debts of various kinds.

My largest is to Glyn Williams. We first met at the extraordinary Captain James Cook and His Times conference held at Simon Fraser University, British Columbia in 1978. Since then, we have continued to share information, discuss puzzling points and read each other's work. Glyn has read all the chapters in this book more than once, and offered many good suggestions. Sarah Palmer and Glyn Williams also provided wonderful moments of friendship and hospitality during my many visits to England.

Peter Barber, Roger Knight, Sarah Palmer, and Nicholas Rodger clarified points and provided additional information. Michelle Novacco helped with archival research.

In Australia, my greatest debt is, first, to the State Library of New South Wales and its officers. At the core of the Library's matchless holdings on William Bligh and the *Bounty* voyage are the personal collections of those remarkable bibliophiles David Scott Mitchell and William Dixson. Here I must particularly acknowledge the very generous way that Paul Brunton, formerly Senior Curator of the Mitchell Library, shared his deep knowledge of the Library's Bligh materials with me; and the help from Nigel Erskine in establishing in broad terms the original topography of Pitcairn Island.

Materials in Crown Copyright in the british National Archives and the National Museum of the Royal Navy have been used in accordance with the terms of the Open Government License.

The following institutions have also given permission to cite or quote from materials in their collections: the British Library; Royal Museums Greenwich; Nantucket Historical Association Research Library; William L. Clements Library, University of Michigan, Ann Arbor; the State Library of New South Wales, Sydney; the National Library of Australia, Canberra; the Alexander Turnbull Library, National Library of New Zealand, Wellington.

Where other copyrights are not acknowledged, this is either because I have private permission, or because I have been unable to trace the present copyright holders.

Richard Neville, the Mitchell Librarian, has generously agreed to the State Library of New South Wales providing many illustrations, and Maggie Patton arranged their conveyance. The William Schuter portrait of William Wordsworth is from the Rare and Manuscript Collections, Cornell University Library.

At Sydney University Press, Denise O'Dea and Kevin O'Brien made many suggestions for structural and editorial improvements, and Agata Mrva-Montoya oversaw the work's production.

References

Abbreviations

BL: British Library
    Add. MSS: Additional Manuscripts
    Egerton MSS: Egerton Manuscripts
    Sloane MSS: Sloane Manuscripts
Clements: William L. Clements Library, University of Michigan (Ann Arbor)
    Shelburne: Shelburne Papers
NA: National Archives (Kew, Surrey)
    ADM: Admiralty
    FO: Foreign Office
    HO: Home Office
    PROB: Prerogative Court of Canterbury
NLA: National Library of Australia (Canberra)
NLNZ: National Library of New Zealand: Te Puna Mātauranga o Aotearoa (Wellington)
NMM: National Maritime Museum (Greenwich)
    ADM/A, B, BP, C: Navy Board Papers
    Caird MSS
NMRN: National Museum of the Royal Navy (Portsmouth)
    ADM: Admiralty MSS
PN: Pitcairn Narratives
SLNSW: State Library of New South Wales (Sydney)
    Dixson: Dixson Library
    Mitchell: Mitchell Library

Manuscript, Electronic and Printed Sources

Anson [Richard Walter and Benjamin Robins]. [1748] 1974. *A Voyage round the World ... by George Anson*, ed. Glyndwr Williams. London: Oxford University Press.
Bacon, Francis. [1620] 2004. *The Instauratio Magna, Part II: Novum Organum and Associated Texts*, ed. Graham Rees, with Maria Wakely (The Oxford Francis Bacon, vol XI). Oxford: Clarendon Press.
Bankes, Thomas. 1787-8. *A New, Royal, Authentic and Complete System of Universal Geography, Antient and Modern*. London.
Banks Online: SLNSW, Banks Papers Online.
Banks, Joseph. 1958. *The Banks Letters: A Calendar of the Manuscript Correspondence of Sir Joseph Banks*, ed. Warren R. Dawson. London: British Museum, London.
Banks, Joseph. 1962. *The Endeavour Journal of Joseph Banks, 1768-1771*, ed. J. C. Beaglehole, 2 vols. Sydney: Angus and Robertson.
Banks, Joseph. 2007. *Scientific Correspondence of Sir Joseph Banks, 1765-1820*, ed. Neil Chambers, 6 vols. London: Pickering and Chatto.
Banks, Joseph. 2008-13. *The India and Pacific Correspondence of Sir Joseph Banks, 1768-1820*, ed. Neil Chambers, 6 vols. London: Pickering and Chatto.
Bartram, William. [1791] n.d. *Travels through North & South Carolina, Georgia, East & West Florida*, ed. Mark Van Doren. New York: Dover.
Belcher, Lady Diana. 1870. *The Mutineers of the Bounty and their Descendants in Pitcairn and Norfolk Islands*. London.
Bligh Index: Index (23 October 1788-5 April 1787) to the version of Bligh's Log in the SLNSW Mitchell MS Safe 1/46a.
Bligh Log 1: Log of the Proceedings of His Majesty's Ship *Bounty* in a Voyage to the South Seas (to take the Breadfruit plant from the Society Islands to the West Indies, under the Command of Lieutenant William Bligh (1 December 1787-22 October 1788) and Log of the Proceedings of His Majesty's Ship *Bounty* Lieut. Wm Bligh Commander from Otaheite towards Jamaica (5 April 1789-13 March 1790), SLNSW, Mitchell MSS, Safe 1/46, 47.
Bligh Log 2: Log of the *Bounty* voyage, NA, ADM 55/151. This has been published as *The Log of the Bounty*, ed. Owen Rutter, 2 vols (Golden Cockerel Press, London, 1936-37), from which I quote.
Bligh Miscellaneous: William Bligh, Legal Papers and Notes (1789-94), SLNSW, Mitchell MS Safe 1/43.
Bligh, William. 1790a. 'Original Narrative from Otaheite towards England, with an account of the loss of ... Bounty ... coppied out of his common Log of daily occurrences, written by himself at Timor, and Batavia, in order to convey to his Friends and the Public a knowledge of the Event', 2 January. This fair copy

References

is in the SLNSW, Mitchell MS Safe 1/37. Although Bligh clearly composed with publication in mind, in the event it did not appear in this form.

Bligh, William. 1790b. *A Narrative of the Mutiny on board His Majesty's Ship Bounty*. London.

Bligh, William. 1792. *A Voyage to the South Sea*. London.

Bligh, William. [1794] 1952. *An Answer to Certain Assertions Contained in the Appendix to a Pamphlet*. Melbourne: Georgian House.

Bligh, William. 1934. *The Voyage of the Bounty's Launch, as Related in William Bligh's Despatch to the Admiralty and the Journal of John Fryer*, ed. Owen Rutter. London: Golden Cockerel Press.

Bligh, William. 1937. *Bligh's Voyage in the Resource: from Coupang to Batavia: Together with the Log of His Subsequent Passage to England in the Dutch Packet Vlydt, and His Remarks on Morrison's Journal*, ed. Owen Rutter. London: Golden Cockerel Press.

Bligh, William. 1987. *The Bligh Notebook*, ed. John Bach. Sydney: Allen and Unwin.

Bligh, William. 1988. *Return to Tahiti: Bligh's Second Breadfruit Voyage*, ed. Douglas Oliver. Melbourne: Miegunyah Press.

Bligh, William. 1989. *Awake, Bold Bligh!: William Bligh's Letters Describing the Mutiny on HMS Bounty*, ed. Paul Brunton. Honolulu: University of Hawaii Press.

Bond, Francis Godolphin. [1949] 1976. *Some Correspondence of Captain William Bligh, R.N., with John and Francis Godolphin Bond*, ed. George Mackaness. Dubbo, NSW: Review Publications.

Bond, Francis Godolphin. [1953] 1976. *Fresh Light on Bligh, Being Some Unpublished Correspondence of Captain William Bligh, R.N., and Lieutenant Francis Godolphin Bond, R. N.*, ed. George Mackaness. Dubbo, NSW: Review Publications.

Bond, Francis Godolphin. 1961. 'Extracts from a Log-Book of HMS *Providence*, kept by Lieut. Francis Godolphin Bond, RN, on Bligh's Second Breadfruit Voyage, 1791–3', ed. George Mackaness, *JRAHS*, vol. 46, pp. 24–66.

Boswell, James. [1791] 1934–64. *The Life of Samuel Johnson*, ed. G.B.. Hill, revised L. Powell, 6 vols. Oxford: Oxford University Press.

Boswell, James. 1963. *Boswell: The Ominous Years, 1774–1776*, ed. Charles Ryskamp and Frederick A. Pottle. London: Heinemann.

Bounty Court-Martial: The Court-Martial of the Bounty Mutineers, ed. Owen Rutter. Toronto: Canada Law Book Company, 1931.

Bounty Court-Martial (Minutes): Minutes of the Court-Martial. Melbourne: Georgian House, 1952.

Boyle, Robert. 1665–6. 'General Heads for a *Natural History of a Countrey*, Great or Small', *Philosophical Transactions*, vol. 1, pp. 186–9.

Bruce, James. 1790. *Travels to Discover the Source of the Nile, in the Years 1768, 1769, 1770, 1771, 1772, and 1773*, 5 vols. Edinburgh.
Burney, James, ed. 1805-17. *A Chronological History of the Discoveries in the South Sea or Pacific Ocean*, 5 vols. London.
Byron, John. 1964. *Byron's Journal of His Circumnavigation, 1764-66*, ed. Robert E. Gallagher. Cambridge: Hakluyt Society.
Callander, John. 1766-8. *Terra Australis Cognita*, 3 vols. Edinburgh.
Campbell, John, comp. 1744-8. *Navigantium atque Itinerantium Bibliotheca*, 2 vols. London.
Carteret, Philip. 1965. *Carteret's Voyage Round the World, 1766-1769*, ed. Helen Wallis, 2 vols. Cambridge: Hakluyt Society.
Churchill, John. 1704. *A Collection of Voyages and Travels*, 4 vols. London.
Christian, Edward [1794] 1952: *The Appendix to the Minutes of the [Bounty] Court-Martial*. Melbourne: Georgian House.
Cobbett, William. 1806-20. *Parliamentary History of England, from the Norman Conquest in 1066, to the Year 1803*, 36 vols. London.
Coleridge, Samuel Taylor. *The Rime of the Ancient Mariner*: S.T. Coleridge's famous poem has had variant titles in successive printings, including 'The Rime of the Ancyent Marinere' (1798) and 'The Ancient Mariner: A Poet's Reverie' (1800), when the text has also varied. I have adopted the generic title *Ancient Mariner* and indicated which text I am quoting from by its date.
Coleridge, Samuel Taylor. 1956-71. *Collected Letters of Samuel Taylor Coleridge*, ed. E. L. Griggs, 6 vols. Oxford: Clarendon Press.
Cook, James. 1777. *A Voyage towards the South Pole, and Round the World*, 2 vols. London.
Cook, James. 1955-67. *The Journals of Captain James Cook on His Voyages of Discovery*, ed. J.C. Beaglehole, 3 vols. Cambridge: Hakluyt Society.
Cook, James and James King. 1784. *A Voyage to the Pacific Ocean*, 3 vols. London.
D'Arblay, Mrs [Fanny Burney]. 1904-5. *The Diary and Letters of Madame d'Arblay*, ed. Charlotte Barrett, 6 vols. London: Macmillan.
Dalrymple, Alexander. [1767] 1769. *An Account of the Discoveries Made in the South Pacifick Ocean, Previous to 1764*. London.
Dampier, William. [1697/1729] 1927. *A New Voyage round the World*, ed. Sir Albert Gray. London: Argonaut Press.
Dampier, William. [1699/1729] 1931. *Voyages and Descriptions*. Republished as *Voyages and Discoveries*, ed. Clennell Wilkinson. London: Argonaut Press.
Dampier, William. [1703/1729] 1939. *A Voyage to New Holland*, ed. James Williamson. London: Argonaut Press.
de Brosses, Charles. 1756. *Histoire des Navigations aux Terres Australes*, 2 vols. Paris.

References

Delano, Amasa. 1817. *A Narrative of Voyages and Travels in the Northern and Southern Hemispheres: Comprising Three Voyages round the World; together with a Voyage of Survey and Discovery, in the Pacific Ocean and Oriental Islands*. Boston.

Forster, George. [1777] 2000. *A Voyage round the World*, ed. Nicholas Thomas and Oliver Berghof, 2 vols. Honolulu: University of Hawai'i Press.

Forster, George. [1787] 2007. *Cook, the Discoverer*, trans. G. K. Sydney: Horden House.

Forster, Johann Reinhold. [1778] 1996. *Observations Made During a Voyage Round the World*, ed. N. Thomas, H. Guest and M. Dettelbach. Honolulu: University of Hawai'i Press.

Fryer Naval Service 1. 'Statement of service of John Fryer, recorded by one of his children', NLA MS 6592.

Fryer Naval Service 2, 'The Naval Service of John Fryer, Master in His Majesty's Navy 1781–1817', compiled by Owen Rutter, SLNSW, Mitchell Safe 1/38.

Fryer, John. 1934. *The Voyage of the Bounty's Launch, as Related in William Bligh's Despatch to the Admiralty and the Journal of John Fryer*, ed. Owen Rutter. London: Golden Cockerel Press. A facsimile of a second (and later) version of this narrative was published in 1979: *The Voyage of the Bounty Launch: John Fryer's Narrative*, with an introduction by Stephen Walters. London: Genesis, 1979.

Hakluyt, William, ed. [1582] 1850. *Divers Voyages touching the Discouery of America and the Islands Adjacent vnto the same*. London: Hakluyt Society.

Hakluyt, William, ed. [1589] 1903–5. *The Principal Navigations Voyages Traffiques & Discoveries of the English Nation*, 12 vols. Glasgow: James MacLehose.

Hakluyt, William. [1584] 1935. 'Discourse of Western Planting', in *The Original Writings and Correspondence of the Two Richard Hakluyts*, ed. E.G.R. Taylor, vol. 2, pp. [211]–326. London: Hakluyt Society.

Hawkesworth, John. 1773. *An Account of the Voyages … for making Discoveries in the Southern Hemisphere*, 3 vols. London.

Hearne, Samuel. 1795. *A Journey from Prince of Wales's Fort in Hudson's Bay, to the Northern Ocean … in the Years 1769, 1770, 1771, & 1772*. London.

Heywood Journal: Captain Edward Edwards's summary of Peter Heywood's journal, NMRN, ADM MS 180.

HRNSW (*Historical Records of New South Wales*). 1892–1901. Ed. A. Britton and F. M. Bladen, 7 vols. Sydney: Government Printer.

Kippis, Andrew. 1788. *The Life of Captain James Cook*. London.

Linnaeus, Carl. 1821. *A Selection of the Correspondence of Linnaeus, and Other Naturalists*, ed. Sir J.E. Smith, 2 vol. London.

Losh, James. Diaries, 33 vols. Carlisle Library.

Mackaness, George, ed. [1938] 1981. *A Book of the Bounty*. London: Dent.
Maxton, Donald A. and Rolf E. Du Rietz, eds. 2013. *Innocent on the Bounty: The Court-Martial and Pardon of Midshipman Peter Heywood, in Letters*. Jefferson, NC: McFarland & Company, 2013.
Morrison Memorandum: 'Memorandum and Particulars respecting the Bounty and her Crew', SLNSW, Mitchell Z Safe 1/33.
Morrison, James. 1935. 'Journal on HMS Bounty and at Tahiti, 9 September 1787–1791, written in 1792', SLNSW, Mitchell MS Safe 1/42. This journal was published as: *The Journal of James Morrison, Boatswain's Mate of the Bounty*, ed. Owen Rutter (London: The Golden Cockerel Press, 1935). It has now been republished as: *Mutiny and Aftermath: James Morrison's Account of the Mutiny on the Bounty and the Island of Tahiti*, ed. Vanessa Smith and Nicholas Thomas (Honolulu: University of Hawai'i Press, 2013). As this more recent edition was not available when I wrote these chapters, I have quoted from that by Rutter.
Nagle, Jacob. 1988. *The Nagle Journal: A Diary of the Life of Jacob Nagle, Sailor, from the year 1775 to 1841*, ed. John C. Dann. New York: Weidenfeld & Nicolson.
Narborough, Sir John. 1694. *An Account of the Several Late Voyages and Discoveries to the South and North*. London.
Park, Mungo. 1799. *Travels in the Interior Districts of Africa ... in the Years 1795, 1796 and 1797*. London.
Pitt, William. 1817. *The Speeches of William Pitt*, 3rd ed., 3 vols. London.
PT: *Philosophical Transactions (of the Royal Society of London)* (London, 1665–).
Purchas, Samuel. 1905–7. *Hakluytus Posthumus, or Purchas His Pilgrimes*, 20 vols. Glasgow: James MacLehose.
Raynal, Abbé. 1770. *Histoire Philosophique et Politique, des établissements and du commerce des Européens dans les deux Indes*, 2 vols. Amsterdam.
Raynal, Abbé. 1776. *A Philosophical and Political History of the Settlements and Trade of the Europeans in the East and West Indies*, trans. J. Justamond, 2 vols. London.
Robertson, George. 1948. *The Discovery of Tahiti: A Journal of the Second Voyage of HMS Dolphin round the World by George Robertson, 1766–1768*, ed. Hugh Carrington. London: Hakluyt Society.
Royal Navy. 1787. *Regulations and Instructions Relating to His Majesty's Service at Sea*, 12th ed. London.
Sloane, Sir Hans. 1696. *Catalogus plantarum*. London, 1696.
Sloane, Sir Hans. 1707–25. *A Voyage to the Islands Madera, Barbados, Nieves, St Christophers and Jamaica, with the Natural History of the ... Last of Those Islands*, 2 vols. London.

References

Southey, Robert. 1829. *Sir Thomas More: or, Colloquies on the Progress and Prospects of Society*, 2 vols. London.

Southey, Robert. 1965. *New Letters of Robert Southey*, ed. Kenneth Curry, 2 vols. New York: Columbia University Press.

Sprat, Thomas. [1667] 1958. *History of the Royal Society*, ed. Jackson I. Cope and Harold Whitmore Jones. St Louis, MO: Washington University Press.

Stewart Journal: Captain Edward Edwards's summary of George Stewart's journal, NMRN, ADM MS 180.

Vancouver, George. [1798] 1986. *A Voyage of Discovery to the North Pacific Ocean and Round the World, 1791–1795*, ed. W. Kaye Lamb, 4 vols. London: Hakluyt Society.

Walpole, Horace. 1937–83. *The Yale Edition of Horace Walpole's Correspondence*, ed. W.S. Lewis et al., 48 vols. New Haven, Conn.: Yale University Press.

Wheler, Sir George. 1682. *A Journey into Greece*. London.

Wordsworth, William. *Prelude*. The dates in the footnotes indicate which edition is being used: *The Prelude, 1798–1799*, ed. Stephen Parrish. Ithaca, NY: Cornell University Press, 1977); Wordsworth, *The Thirteen-Book Prelude*, ed. Mark L. Reed, 2 vols. Ithaca, NY: Cornell University Press, 1991; *The Prelude, or Growth of a Poet's Mind*, ed. Ernest de Selincourt, 2nd ed., rev. Helen Darbishire. Oxford: Clarendon Press, 1959; *The Prelude, 1799, 1805, 1850*, ed. Jonathan Wordsworth, M.H. Abrams, and Stephen Gill. New York: Norton, 1979.

Wordsworth, William. 1967. *The Letters of William and Dorothy Wordsworth: The Early Years, 1787–1805*, ed. E. De Selincourt, rev. Chester L. Shaver. Oxford: Oxford University Press.

Wordsworth, William. 1974. *The Prose Works of William Wordsworth*, ed. W.J.B. Owen and J.W. Smysert, 3 vols. Oxford: Clarendon Press.

Wordsworth, William. 1982. *The Borderers*, ed. Robert Osborn. Ithaca, NY: Cornell University Press, 1982.

Wordsworth, William. 1993. *The Fenwick Notes of William Wordsworth*, ed. Jared Curtis. London: Bristol Classical Press.

Wordsworth, William and S. T. Coleridge. [1798] 1991. *Lyrical Ballads*, ed. R. L. Brett and A. R. Jones, 2nd ed. London: Routledge.

Pitcairn Island narratives (PN)

There are at least twenty-five accounts of what happened on Pitcairn Island between 1790 and 1801. In the footnotes I have referred to them using the numbers below. See Chapter 3 for a discussion of their origins and reliability.

Various accounts, 1794–1826

1794–c. 1821

1. Edward Young, Journal (as extracted and published by Captain Beechey – see Beechey (2), PN 13)).

1819

2. Jenny (1819) 'Account of the Mutineers of the Ship *Bounty*, and their Descendants at Pitcairn's Island', *Sydney Gazette*, 17 July 1819. Jenny's Tahitian name was Te'ehuteatuaonoa. However, these essays were published under her given English name.

1821

3a. Jenny (1821a), ['Narrative, taken from the lips of an Otaheitan woman, widow of one of the mutineers from the *Bounty* in Captain Dillon's presence by Mr Nott, a Missionary'], *Bengal Hurkaru*, 26 October 1826
3b. Jenny (1821b), 'Pitcairn's Island – The *Bounty*'s Crew', *United Service Journal and Naval and Military Magazine*, (November 1829), pp. 589-93.
The editor has made many minor changes to the phrasing in 1821a.

John Adams's Accounts

Visit of the Topaz, February 1808

4. Mayhew Folger, Log, Nantucket Historical Association Research Library, MS 220, Ship's Logs no. 105 (Reel 17, no. 206).
5. Lt Fitzmaurice, 'Extract from the Log Book of Captain Folger, the American Ship *Topaz* of Boston', 29 September 1808. A copy, dated 10 October 1808, was forwarded to the Admiralty by Sir Sidney Smith, 14 March 1809. It was published in

References

the body of Sir John Barrow's review of d'Entrecasteaux's *Voyage à la Recherche de la Pérouse,* 2 vols (1808) in the *Quarterly Review,* vol. 3, no. 5 (February 1810), p. 24; and printed by Barrow again in *The Mutiny of the Bounty,* pp. 300-1. It is included in a series of papers relating to the discovery of the Pitcairn colony compiled in 1815, probably by Sir John Barrow, Second Secretary of the Admiralty, for Admiral Keith. There are copies of these papers in the Banks papers in the SLNSW (see Banks Online, 72.01, 71.02).

6. Mayhew Folger to Admiralty, 1 March 1813. A copy was forwarded by Admiral Rodham to the Admiralty on 5 January1815. There is a copy in Banks Online, 71.03. It was published in the body of Barrow's review of Porter's *Journal of a Cruize* (1815) in the *Quarterly Review,* vol. 13 (April 1815), pp. 377-80.

7. Mayhew Folger, conveyed in conversation and writing to Amasa Delano, and published by Delano in *A Narrative of Voyages and Travels* (Boston, 1817), pp. 136-44.

Visit of the Briton and Tagus, 17 September 1814

8. Captain Sir Thomas Staines to Admiralty, 18 October 1814. (This letter was forwarded to the Admiralty by Admiral Dixon, 1 December 1814.) There is a copy in Banks Online, 71.07, which I have paginated individually. It was published in the body of Barrow's review of Porter's *Journal of a Cruize* (1815) in the *Quarterly Review,* vol. 13 (April 1815), pp. 377-8.

9. Captain Philip Pipon, 'Narrative of the late Mutineers of HM Ship *Bounty* settled on Pitcairn's Island in the South Seas, in September 1814'. What appears to be the original is in NMM, REG 14/000215. There is a copy in Banks Online, 71.05, which I have paginated individually. It was paraphrased by Barrow, ibid., pp. 378-83.

10. Lieutenant John Shillibeer, in *A Narrative of the Briton's Voyage to Pitcairn's Island* (London, 1817), pp. 81-97.

Visit of the American, 1821, and interview with Jenny at Tahiti, 1824

11. Otto von Kotzebue, *A New Voyage Round the World, in the years 1823, 24, 25 and 26,* (London, 1830), vol. 1, pp. 227-50.

Visit of the Blossom, December 1825

12. Beechey (1): Account given to Captain Beechey, 5 December 1825, SLNSW, Mitchell MS A 1804.

13. Beechey (2): Captain F. W. Beechey, *Narrative of a Voyage to the Pacific and Beering's Strait* (London, 1831), vol. 1, pp. 66–136.
14. Lieutenant George Peard: *To the Pacific and Arctic with Beechey: The Journal of Lieutenant George Peard of H.M.S. Blossom, 1825–1828*, ed. B. M. Gough. (London: Hakluyt Society, 1973), pp. 75–93.
15. John Bechervaise, *Thirty-six Years of a Seafaring Life* (Portsea, 1839), pp. 168–90.
16. Edward Belcher, Private Journal [and] Remarks etc HMS *Blossom* on Discovery during the years 1825, 6, 7, NLNZ, MS-0158. I have paginated the section dealing with Pitcairn Island individually.

Visit of the Volador, January 1829

17. J.A. Moerenhout, *Voyages aux Îsles du Grand Océan* (Paris, 1837), vol. 2, pp. 283-322.

After John Adams's death in March 1829

Visit of the Seringapatam, March 1830

18. Captain William Waldergrave, 'Recent Accounts of the Pitcairn Islanders', in *Journal of the Royal Geographical Society of London*, vol. 3 (1833), pp. 156–68.

Visit of the Tuscan, March 1834

19. Thomas Stavers, Journal, 1798–1867. Thomas Tyler has placed an edited version of a typescript of this journal (more properly, an autobiography) online at bit.ly/TRStavers. The typescript is in the possession of Mr Bos (Netherlands). The location of the original narrative is unknown.
20. Frederick Debell Bennett, *Narrative of a Whaling Voyage round the Globe, from the year 1833 to 1836* (London, 1840), vol. 1, pp. 25–58.

Buffett's account

21. John Buffett, 'A Narrative of 20 Years Residence on Pitcairn Island', *The Friend*, vol. 4 (1846), pp. 2–3, 20–1, 27–8, 34–5, 50–1, 66–7.

Pitcairn Island Register

22. Nobb's manuscript version (SLNSW, Dixson MS Q7).

23. 'Buffett's' manuscript version (NMM, Caird REC/61). Ed. by Sir Charles Lucas, this version has been published as *The Pitcairn Island Register Book* in 1929 (SPCK, London, 1929).

Two much later Pitcairn/Norfolk Island Versions

24. Rosalind Amelia Young, *Mutiny of the Bounty and Story of Pitcairn Island, 1790–1894* (Oakland, Ca: Pacific Publishing Co., 1894).
25. Louis Becke and Walter Jeffrey, *The Mutineer: A Romance of Pitcairn Island* (London, 1898).

Select Bibliography

Alexander, Caroline. 2003. *The Bounty: The True Story of the Mutiny on the Bounty.* New York: Viking.

[An Officer on the Brunswick]. *Gentleman's Magazine*, vol. 62, pt 2 (December 1792), p.1097. (This letter is undated, but was written after 29 October and before 21 November 1792.)

Barker, Juliet. 2000. *Wordsworth: A Life*. London: Viking.

Barrow, Sir John. [1831] 1989. The Mutiny of the Bounty. Oxford: Oxford University Press.

Batten, Charles. 1978. *Pleasurable Instruction: Form and Convention in Eighteenth-Century Travel Literature*. Berkeley and Los Angeles, University of California Press.

Baugh, Daniel, ed. 1977. *Naval Administration 1715–1750*. London: Navy Records Society.

Beaglehole, J.C. 1967. *Captain Cook and Captain Bligh*. Wellington: Victoria University.

Beaglehole, J.C. 1968. *The Exploration of the Pacific*, 3rd ed. Stanford: Stanford University Press.

Beckert, Sven. 2015. *Empire of Cotton: A Global History*. New York: Knopf.

Boyd, Brian. 2009. *On the Origin of Stories: Evolution, Cognition, and Fiction.* Cambridge, Mass.: Belknap Press.

Bredin, Miles. 2000. *The Pale Abyssinian: A Life of James Bruce, African Explorer and Adventurer*. London: HarperCollins.

Cameron, H.C. 1952. *Sir Joseph Banks*. Sydney: Angus and Robertson.

Campbell, Joseph. 1968. *The Hero with a Thousand Faces*, 2nd ed. Princeton, NJ: Princeton University Press.

Christian, Glynn. [1982] 1999. *Fragile Paradise: The Discovery of Fletcher Christian Bounty Mutineer.* Sydney: Doubleday.

Christian, Glynn. 1989. 'Mutineer Who Made History', in *Mutiny on the Bounty 1787-1989*, pp. 47-56. Greenwich: National Maritime Museum, Greenwich.

Christian, Glynn. 1991. 'Mutineer Who Made History', in *Mutiny on the Bounty*, pp. 25-42. Sydney: State Library of New South Wales.

Coats, Ann and Philip, MacDougall, ed. 2011. *The Naval Mutinies of 1797: Unity and Perseverance.* Woodbridge: Boydell Press.

Cook, Warren L. 1973. *Floodtide of Empire: Spain and the Pacific Northwest, 1543-1819.* New Haven, Conn.: Yale University Press.

Danielsson, Bengt. 1963. *What Happened on the Bounty,* trans. Alan Tapsell. London: George Allen and Unwin.

Darby, Marge. 1965. *Who Caused the Mutiny on the Bounty?* Sydney: Angus and Roberston.

Darby, Marge. 1966. 'The Causes of the Bounty Mutiny: A Short Reply to Mr Rolf du Rietz's Comments', in *Studia Bountyana* 2, Uppsala.

David, A.F.C. 1977. 'The Surveys of William Bligh', *The Mariner's Mirror*, vol. 63, no. 1, pp. 69-70.

De Lacey, Gavin. 1997. 'Plagiarism on the Bounty: a Note on the Composition of Morrison's Journal', *The Mariner's Mirror*, vol. 83, no. 1 (February), pp. 84-90.

Dening, Greg. 1988. *The Bounty: An Ethnographic History.* Parkville, Vic.: History Department, University of Melbourne.

Dening, Greg. 1992. *Mr Bligh's Bad Language: Passion, Power and Theatre on the Bounty.* New York: Cambridge University Press.

Denman, Arthur. 1903. 'Capt. Bligh and the Mutiny of the Bounty', *Notes and Queries*, 9th series, vol. 12, pp. 501-2.

Driscoll, Heather. 2002. The Genesis of a Journey to the Northern Ocean. PhD thesis, University of Alberta.

Du Rietz, Rolf E. 1965. *The Causes of the Bounty Mutiny: Some Comments on a Book by Madge Darby.* Uppsala: Almqvist and Wiksell.

Du Rietz, Rolf E. 1979. *Thoughts on the Present State of Bligh Scholarship.* Uppsala: Dahlia Books.

Du Rietz, Rolf E. 1981. *Fresh Light on John Fryer of the Bounty.* Uppsala: Dahlia Books.

Du Rietz, Rolf E. [2003] 2009. *The Bias of Bligh: An Investigation into the Credibility of William Bligh's Version of the Bounty Mutiny,* 2nd ed. Uppsala: Dahlia Books.

Du Rietz, Rolf E. 2007. 'The Nature of the Bounty Mutiny: An Attempt at Definition', *The Mariner's Mirror*, vol. 93, no. 2, pp. 196-208.

References

Edwards, Philip. 1994. *The Story of the Voyage: Sea-Narratives in Eighteenth-Century England*. Cambridge: Cambridge University Press, Cambridge, 1994.

Eliade, Mircea. [1954, 1965] 1971. *The Myth of the Eternal Return: or, Cosmos and History*, trans. Willard R. Trask. Princeton, NJ: Princeton University Press.

Erskine, Nigel. 2004. The Historical Archaeology of Settlement at Pitcairn Island, 1790–1856. PhD thesis, James Cook University.

Fletcher, William. 1876-7. 'Fletcher Christian and the Mutineers of the Bounty', *Transactions of the Cumberland Association for the Advancement of Literature and Science*, pp. 77–106.

Frost, Alan. 2003. *The Global Reach of Empire: Britain's Maritime Expansion in the Indian and Pacific Oceans, 1764–1815*. Melbourne: Miegunyah Press of Melbourne University Publishing.

Frost, Alan and Glyndwr Williams. 1997. 'The Beginnings of Britain's Exploration of the Pacific Ocean in the Eighteenth Century', *The Mariner's Mirror*, vol. 83, no. 4, pp. 410–18.

Gould, Rupert T. 1928. 'Bligh's Notes on Cook's Last Voyage', *The Mariner's Mirror*, vol. 14, no. 4, pp. 371–85.

Greenfield, Bruce. 1986-7. 'The Idea of Discovery as a Source of Narrative Structure in Samuel Hearne's *Journey to the Northern Ocean*', *Early American literature*, vol. 21, pp. 189–209.

Harlow, V.T. 1952, 1964. *The Founding of the Second British Empire, 1763–1793*, 2 vols. London: Longmans, Green and Co.

Hay, Douglas. 2000. 'Moral economy, political economy and law', in *Moral Economy and Popular Protest: Crowds, Conflicts and Authority*, ed. Adrian Randall and Andrew Charlesworth, pp. 93–122. Basingstoke, UK: Macmillan.

Hough, Richard. [1972] 1979. *Captain Bligh and Mister Christian: The Men and the Mutiny*. 1st ed: London: Hutchinson. 2nd ed: London: Cassell.

Jacobus, Mary. 1976. *Tradition and Experiment in Wordsworth's Lyrical Ballads (1798)*. Oxford: Clarendon Press.

Joppien, Rudiger and Bernard Smith, eds. 1985-7. *The Art of Captain Cook's Voyages*, 3 vols (Oxford University Press, Melbourne).

Kaufman, Paul. 1960. *Borrowings from the Bristol Library, 1773–1784: A Unique Record of Reading Vogues*. Charlottesville: Bibliographical Society of the University of Virginia.

Kaufman, Paul. 1962. 'Wordsworth's *Candid and Enlightened Friend*', *Notes and Queries*, new series, vol. 9, issue 11 (November), pp. 403–8.

Kennedy, Gavin. 1978. *Bligh*. London: Duckworth.

Kennedy, Gavin. 1981. 'Introduction', *A Book of the Bounty*, ed. George Mackaness. London: Dent.

Kennedy, Gavin. 1989. *Captain Bligh: The Man and His Mutinies*. London: Duckworth.
Knight, C. 1936. 'H.M. Armed Vessel *Bounty*', *The Mariner's Mirror*, vol. 22, no. 2, pp. 183–99.
Knight, Roger and Martin Wilcox. 2010. *Sustaining the Fleet, 1793–1815: War, the British Navy and the Contractor State*. Woodbridge, UK: Woodbridge, Boydell Press.
Liebershon, Harry. 2006. *The Travelers' World: Europe to the Pacific*. Cambridge, Mass.: Harvard University Press.
Lloyd, Christopher. [1968] 1970. *The British Seaman, 1200–1860: A Social Survey*. London: Paladin.
Macdonald, Janet. 2006. *Feeding Nelson's Navy: The True Story of Food at Sea in the Georgian Era*. London: Chatham.
MacGregor, Arthur, ed. 1994. *Sir Hans Sloan: Collector, Scientist, Antiquary, Founding Father of the British Museum*. London: British Museum Press.
Mack, James D. 1966. *Matthew Flinders, 1774–1814*. Melbourne: Nelson.
Mackaness, George. 1951. *The Life of Vice-Admiral William Bligh, R.N., F.R.S*, 2nd ed. Sydney: Angus and Robertson.
MacLaren, I.S. 1991. 'Samuel Hearne's Accounts of the Massacre at Bloody Fall, 17 July 1771', *Ariel*, vol. 22, pp. 25–51.
MacLaren, I.S. 1992. 'Exploration/Travel Literature and the Evolution of the Author', *International Journal of Canadian Studies*, vol. 5, pp. 39–68.
MacLulich, T. D. 1979. 'Hearne, Cook, and the Exploration Narrative', *English Studies in Canada*, vol. 5 (1979), pp. 187–201.
Marshall, John. 1825. 'Peter Heywood, Esq.', *Royal Naval Biography*, vol. 2, pp. 747–97. London.
Maude, H. E. 1968. 'In Search of a Home', in *Of Islands and Men: Studies in Pacific History*, pp. 1–34. Melbourne: Oxford University Press.
McKee, Alexander. 1962. *H.M.S. Bounty*. New York: Morrow.
Melville, Herman. [1851] 1967. *Moby-Dick*, ed. H. Hayford and H. Parker. New York: Norton.
Montgomerie, H.S. 1937. *William Bligh of the Bounty in Fact and in Fable*. London: Williams and Norgate.
Morrisby, Edwin. 1987. 'The *Bounty* Mutineers: In the wake of Errol Flynn and Marlon Brando', *Quadrant*, vol. 31, no. 4 (April), pp. 46–50.
Mundle, Rob. 2010. *Bligh, Master Mariner*. Sydney: Hachette.
Murray, Gilbert. [1927] 1968. *The Classical Tradition in Poetry*. New York: Russell and Russell.
Neale, Jonathan. 1990. 'Forecastle and Quarterdeck: Protest, Discipline and Mutiny in the Royal Navy, 1793–1814'. PhD thesis, University of Warwick.

References

Nicolson, Robert B. 1965. *The Pitcairners*. Sydney: Angus and Robertson.

Oliver, Douglas L. 1974. *Ancient Tahitian Society*, 3 vols. Canberra: Australian National University Press.

Onslow, S.M., ed. [1914] 1973. *The Macarthurs of Camden*. Adelaide: Rigby.

Pearson, W.H. 1972. 'Hawkesworth's Alterations', *The Journal of Pacific History*, vol. 7, pp. 45–72.

Preston, Diana. 2017. *Paradise in Chains: The Bounty Mutiny and the Founding of Australia* London: Bloomsbury.

Randall, Adrian and Andrew Charlesworth, ed. 2000. *Moral Economy and Popular Protest: Crowds, Conflict and Authority*. Basingstoke, UK: Macmillan.

Reimann, K.A. 1996. '"Great as he is in his own good opinion": The *Bounty* Mutiny and Lieutenant's Bligh's Construction of Self', in *Tradition in Transition: Women Writers, Marginal Texts, and the Eighteenth-Century Canon*, ed. Alvaro Ribeiro and James G. Basker, pp. 198–218. Oxford: Clarendon Press.

Rodger, N.A.M. 1986. *The Wooden World: An Anatomy of the Georgian Navy*. Annapolis, MD: Naval Institute Press.

Rodger, N.A.M. 2004. *The Command of the Ocean: A Naval History of Britain, Vol. 2: 1649–1815*. London: Allen Lane.

Rutter, Owen. 1936a. *The True Story of the Mutiny in the Bounty*. London: Newnes.

Rutter, Owen. 1936b. *Turbulent Journey: A Life of William Bligh, Vice-Admiral of the Blue*. London: Ivor Nicholson and Watson.

Sahlins, Marshall. 1995. *How 'Natives' Think: About Captain Cook, for Example*. Chicago: University of Chicago Press.

Salmond, Anne. 1993. 'Kidnapped: Tuki and Huru's Involuntary Visit to Norfolk Island in 1793', in *From Maps to Metaphors: The Pacific World of George Vancouver*, ed. Robin Fisher and Hugh Johnson, pp. 191–26. Vancouver: University of British Columbia Press.

Salmond, Anne. 2011. *Bligh: William Bligh in the South Seas*. Auckland: Viking.

Scott, Brian W. 1982. 'The True Identity of John Adams', *The Mariner's Mirror*, vol. 68, no. 1, pp. 31–9.

Scrheiber, Roy. 1991. *The Fortunate Adversities of William Bligh*. New York: Peter Lang.

Shapiro, H.L. 1936. *The Heritage of the Bounty: The Story of Pitcairn through Six Generations*. London: Victor Gollancz.

Sharman, Ivan M. 1981. 'Vitamin requirements of the human body', in *Starving Sailors*, ed. J. Watt et al., pp. 17–26. London: National Maritime Museum.

Smith, Bernard. 1960. *European Vision and the South Pacific, 1768–1850: A Study in the History of Art and Ideas*. Oxford: Clarendon Press.

Smith, Bernard. 1979. 'Cook's Posthumous Reputation', in *Captain James Cook and His Times*, ed. Robin Fisher and Hugh Johnson, pp. 159–85. Canberra: Australian National University Press.

Smith, D. Bonner. 1936. 'Some Remarks about the Mutiny of the *Bounty*', *The Mariner's Mirror*, vol. 22, no. 2, pp. 200–39.

Smith, D. Bonner. 1937. 'More Light on Bligh and the *Bounty*', *The Mariner's Mirror*, vol. 23, no. 2, pp. 210–28.

Smyth, W.H. 1831. 'Sketch of the Career of the Late Capt. Peter Heywood, R.N.', *United Services Journal*, no. 29, pp. 468–81.

Stallybrass, Peter and Allon White. 1986. *The Politics and Poetics of Transgression*. Ithaca, NY: Cornell University Press.

Thompson, E.P. 1971. 'The Moral Economy of the English Crowd in the Eighteenth Century', *Past and Present*, no. 50 (February), pp. 76–136.

Wahlroos, Sven. 1989. *Mutiny and Romance in the South Seas: A Companion to the Bounty Adventure*. Topsfield, Mass.: Salem House.

Watt, Sir James. 1989. 'The Colony's Health', in *Studies from Terra Australis to Australia*, ed. John Hardy and Alan Frost, pp. 137–51, notes pp. 262–6. Canberra: Australian Academy of the Humanities.

Wilkinson, C.S. 1953. *The Wake of the Bounty*. London: Cassell.

Williams, Glyndwr. 1962. *The British Search for the Northwest Passage in the Eighteenth Century*. London: Longmans.

Williams, Glyndwr. 1979. 'Captain James Cook', in *Dictionary of Canadian Biography*, vol. 4, pp. 162–7. Toronto: University of Toronto Press.

Williams, Glyndwr and Alan Frost, eds. 1988. *Terra Australis to Australia*. Melbourne: Oxford University Press.

Wood, Frances. 1995. *Did Marco Polo Go to China?* London: Secker and Warburg.

Index

Adams, John 13–15, 27, 51, 92, 117, 130–136, 144–159, 161–163, 164
Alexander, Caroline xvii, 21, 173, 294, 297
Allen, James 77–78
Anson, George xx, 198, 222, 236, 266, 285

Banks, Sir Joseph 2–4, 31–36, 38, 114, 202, 229, 234, 269–273, 278–279
Barrow, Sir John 11, 14, 31
  The Mutiny of the Bounty 11
Bartram, William 211, 213, 221, 231–232
Beechey, Captain F.W. 117–119, 133, 136, 143–149, 159–164, 174
beer 72, 74, 75
Belcher, Lady Diana 12, 15, 161, 171
  The Mutineers of the Bounty and Their Descendants in Pitcairn and Norfolk Islands 12
Belcher, Sir Edward 143, 161–164, 171
Bligh, William
  A Voyage to the South Sea 32–38, 269, 284
  and Captain Cook 2, 265–266
  as commander 21, 81, 83, 273
  as navigator 19, 264–267, 275, 294
  as purser 81, 83, 156
  his character 7–12, 17, 18–20, 24, 280, 295
  his log 5, 31–33, 38–41, 267, 279, 284
  his manipulation of food rations 62, 84, 86–93
  his relationship with Fletcher Christian 96, 106–120, 122, 276, 289
  his relationship with his crew 4, 22, 26, 42, 62–69
  misconceptions about 27–30
  Narrative of the Mutiny on board His Majesty?s Ship Bounty 4, 31, 266, 269, 276, 278–283
  on reaching Coupang 3, 37, 65, 275, 282, 282; *see also* Timor: Coupang
  on HMS *Providence* 2
Bond, Francis 7–8
Bounty, HMS
  and its cargo 2, 113–114
  dimensions of 1, 173
  the burning of 145
  the mutiny of 2, 11, 17–33, 57–59, 68, 118, 127–131, 266, 275, 289
  the voyage of 2–9, 31–47, 61–68, 80, 113–117, 266, 294–298

317

Bountys, The (crew of the *Bounty*) 3, 80, 86, 92, 112, 123, 131–132, 149, 160–165
Boyd, Brian 249
breadfruit 80, 85, 86, 270, 285, 293
Brown, William (assistant gardener) 68, 111, 149
Bruce, James 211–212, 239–240, 243, 247
Burkett, Thomas (able-bodied seaman) 57, 111, 118, 151
Burney, James (editor) 34, 35, 38, 269–273, 287
Byrne, Michael (able-bodied seaman) 59

Campbell, Duncan 32, 106, 275, 278, 282
Campbell, Joseph xxi
cannibalism 205, 233
Chatham, Lord 2, 6
Chesterfield, HMS 61
Christian, Charles 25
Christian, Edward 6, 7, 31, 40, 92, 99, 105, 107, 110, 113, 117, 123, 268, 287–290
Christian, Fletcher
 and the catalyst for mutiny 12, 21, 31, 289
 and William Wordsworth 123
 his character 18, 21, 107, 108, 276
 his childhood 104
 his relationship with William Bligh 21, 36, 46, 52, 287
 his skills as a seaman 21, 44
 life and death on Pitcairn Island 127, 127–132, 141, 149, 152–159, 161, 165–175, 290
Christian, Glynn 16, 25, 50, 165–170, 296

Christian, Mary 142, 169
Churchill, Charles 35, 57, 68, 112
Cole, William (boatswain) 44–47, 117
Coleridge, Samuel Taylor 101, 123, 175, 221, 259, 290
The Rime of the Ancient Mariner 175, 259, 290
Cook, Captain James 45, 74–75, 116, 200–209, 218–220, 221, 227–230, 237–238, 244, 254–265, 294
Coupang *see* Timor: Coupang
court-martial 3, 6, 9, 11, 59

Dampier, William 194–196, 226–227, 235
Danielsson, Bengt xvii, 18, 27, 38–41, 145
Darby, Marge 19, 27, 38, 52–54
Delano, Captain Amasa 153, 290
Dening, Greg 21–26, 42–43, 54, 69, 296
Diana, HMS 77
Douglas, Canon John 255, 258, 260–263
Du Rietz, Rolf xvii, 23, 30, 38, 42, 50, 54, 294

Edwards, Captain Edward 3, 130
Eliade, Mircea xxi, 249
Ellison, Thomas (able-bodied seaman) 28, 28, 59, 111
Elphinstone, William 67, 114
England 3, 9, 41, 96, 120, 170–176, 195, 204
 Cumbria 96, 105, 109
 London 4, 99, 200, 265, 269
 Portsmouth 30, 77, 270
Eurydice, HMS 43, 106, 108

Falcon, HMS 5

Index

Fasto (Faʻahotu) 142, 149; *see also* Williams, John (able-bodied seaman)
Flinders, Matthew 6
French Revolution 53, 123
Friendly Islands *see* Tonga
Fryer, John (master) 34, 35–37, 41–50, 61, 63–68, 79, 114–116, 118, 268, 280

Godwin, William 120, 123
Great Barrier Reef 45, 47, 116, 237

Hallett, John (midshipman) 33, 57, 67, 111, 118
Hayward, Thomas (midshipman) 35, 57, 67, 118
Hawaii 74, 207, 210, 261–262
Hawkesworth, John 227–230, 232, 237
Hearne, Samuel 211, 213–215, 240, 243, 245–247
Hermione, mutiny on the 61
Heywood, Peter (midshipman) 11, 28, 59, 111, 118, 130, 170
Hough, Richard 19, 27, 41, 52

Kennedy, Gavin 19–21, 38–44, 52, 296
'Knights of Otaheite' 69, 112

Lamb, Robert (butcher) 35, 48, 111, 280
Lamb, Edward 106, 108
Losh, James 123, 124, 172, 174

McCoy, William 29, 111, 118, 137, 149–152, 165
McKee, Alexander xvii, 20, 28–30, 43, 161
Martin, Isaac 28, 34, 111, 149
Matra, James 3

Medea, HMS 5
Melville, Herman
  Moby-Dick 250
Mills, John (gunner's mate) 35, 57, 68, 118, 132, 149, 165
Millward, John 29, 35, 70, 111
Montgomerie, H.S. 25, 27, 41–43
morality 14, 121, 229
Morrison, James (boatswain's mate) 11, 12, 46, 59, 64–65, 68, 81–89, 127, 151, 268
Mundle, Rob 22, 42, 294
Murray, Gilbert 251, 298
Muspratt, William 35, 70, 111
mutiny 60–61, 79, 121, 124; *see also* *Bounty*, HMS: the mutiny of

Nancy (Toʻofaiti) 149; *see also* Tararo
Narborough, John 192–194
Nelson, David (gardener) 2, 92, 111
Nootka Sound 5, 74, 207–209
Norfolk Island 140, 204

Pandora, HMS 3, 5, 290
pardon 3, 11, 59
Peckover, William (gunner) 2, 49, 58, 67, 84, 111
Pipon, Captain Philip 13, 133–138, 142, 147, 153–158, 164
Pitcairn Island 3, 13–17, 131–140, 141–165, 168–170, 173, 290, 296
Providence, HMS *see* Bligh, William: on HMS *Providence*
punishment 17, 34, 112
  flogging 30, 34, 75, 91, 111, 149
  manipulation of rations 17, 80, 90, 91; *see also* rations
Purcell, William (carpenter) 35–37, 41–42, 61–68, 116, 280

Quintal, Matthew 29, 111, 118, 130, 142, 147, 149–152

rations 72–76, 82, 90, 281
Royal Navy 32, 60–61, 109, 195
Royal Society of London 190, 191–197, 202, 206, 218
Rutter, Owen xvii, 16–17, 41–43, 54, 296

Salmond, Anne 22–25, 51, 54, 69, 294
scientific discovery 187–221
Short, Captain Joseph 9
Skinner, Richard 28, 111
Smith, Alexander (able-bodied seaman) *see* Adams, John
Staines, Sir Thomas 13, 143, 148, 153–154, 164
Stewart, George (midshipman) 18, 27–31, 115, 117, 127
Sumner, John 57, 79, 91, 111, 130
Surabaya 38, 40, 67

Tahiti 3, 17–19, 33, 43–47, 52, 69–70, 84–86, 91–93, 110–114, 127–132, 137, 143–151, 167, 173, 228, 233
the lure of 22, 69, 234
Tararo 149; *see also* Nancy (To'ofaiti)
taro 87, 129, 163
Tasmania
Adventure Bay 62–66, 111
Tennyson, Alfred
Ulysses 254

Terra Australis 200, 202
Thompson, Matthew 111, 118
Timor 118
Coupang 3, 37, 66, 281, 286
Tobin, George 8
Tonga 22, 45, 208
Torres Strait 116

Van Diemen's Land *see* Tasmania
Victualling Board 70–72, 76, 78; *see also* rations
voyage literature (as a genre) 185–208, 218–219, 221, 226–231, 235–236, 255–261, 267–273, 286, 290

Wahlroos, Sven 23–25, 146, 296
Williams, John (able-bodied seaman) 35, 81, 111, 118, 142, 149, 149, 154, 164; *see also* Fasto (Fa'ahotu)
Windham, William 270, 287
Wheler, Sir George 193
Wordsworth, Dorothy 97, 100, 103
Wordsworth, William 96–105, 119–125, 174, 218, 221, 273
Borderers, The 120, 124
Lyrical Ballads 102–103
Prelude, The 98–104, 273

Young, Edward (midshipman) 53, 68, 79, 118, 134–137, 149–151, 156–161
Young, Frederick 140
Young, Rosalind 15, 137, 163